Kay-Robinson, Denys.

Devon & Cornwall

Devon & Cornwall

By the same author:
Hardy's Wessex Reappraised (David & Charles)

Devon & Cornwall

Denys Kay-Robinson

ARCO PUBLISHING COMPANY, INC.
New York

Other Titles in this Series:

Cumbria JOHN PARKER
South Wales RUTH THOMAS
The Scottish Highlands JOHN A. LISTER

Published by Arco Publishing Company, Inc.
219 Park Avenue South, New York, N.Y. 10003

Copyright © 1977 by Denys Kay-Robinson

Maps copyright © John Bartholomew & Son Limited

Book and jacket design: Susan Waywell

Printed in Great Britain

Library of Congress Cataloging in Publication Data

Kay-Robinson, Denys.
  Devon & Cornwall.

  (Bartholomew)
  Bibliography: p. x plus 246
  Includes index.
  1. Devon, Eng. – Description and travel – Guide-books.
2. Cornwall, Eng. – Description and travel – Guide-books.
I. Title.
DA670.D5K38   914.23'5'04857   77-23331
ISBN 0-668-04235-4

To the memory of
Gertrude Octavia Milburn
through whom many, many years ago
I first came to know and love the
Far South-West

Regional Map

Showing the Area Covered by this Guide

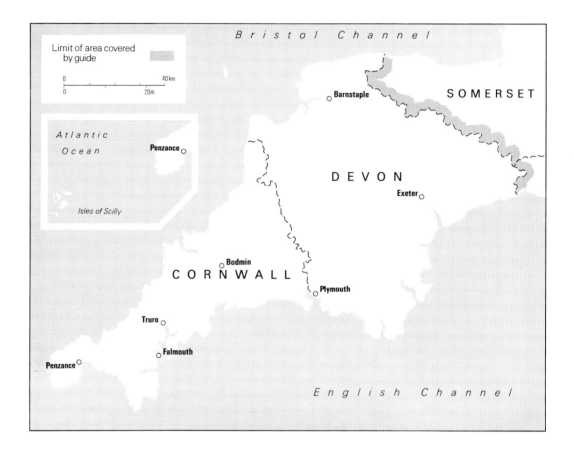

Contents

CONTENTS

* The map section at the end of the book is numbered separately,
in bold type.

Preface

Devon and Cornwall tend to be referred to either as though they were identical twins (the outsider's version), or as though they have nothing remotely in common (the Cornish and Devonian version). A Cornishman faced with writing about Devon usually begins by telling his readers how much, despite his own unavoidable superiority, he admires the shire across the Tamar. A Devon writer about to discourse on Cornwall begins with the same assurance. A very few, of mixed parentage, give the impression of writing on a camp-stool set halfway across Saltash Bridge. The present book has been written by one who has in his veins no drop of blood belonging to either county, and in more than half a century of affectionate familiarity with both has found it less and less easy to choose between them: to choose, but not to distinguish, for there *are* differences between Devon and Cornwall and between their inhabitants, and the better one gets to know them the clearer the differences become.

Not that they are always the differences the Cornish and Devonians imagine. The obsessive idea, for example, that the former are all pure Celts and the latter all pure 'English' does not bear too close an examination. There is pre-Celtic blood and Anglo-Saxon blood in the Cornish, and Celtic blood in many Devonians. The subject is gone into in some detail in the two introductions that follow, but the real point is that it hardly matters. The discrepancies between the two counties spring far more from the facts of geography – small, end-of-the-line Cornwall, dominated and squeezed by her enormous coastline, roomy Devon where one coast seems a continent away from the other and there is land to the west as well as the east – and from historical and, even more, religious evolution.

It is in an attempt to clarify these matters for the general reader that a separate introduction was decided on for each county, although a common gazetteer follows. Whether the aim will succeed, only reactions will disclose: one disadvantage of 'neutrality' is that the writer incurs the wrath of both sets of partisans, not to mention the criticism of every specialist with his own pet axe to grind. Similarly with the gazetteer, the choice of entries will inevitably draw accusations of bias from those whose favourite haunt has been left out, or worse, given short shrift. For the policy here has been individualistic. There are many guides to Devon or Cornwall that attempt to cover every spot, and by consequence can say very little about any; many others that are content to follow the 'milk round', ignoring any place not on the coach-tour list. The selection that follows has been made on the basis that it is of greater advantage to the reader to find a limited (but not too limited) number of places treated in depth, than a larger number treated superficially, and that the places chosen should be included solely for their interest, regardless of their importance or familiarity. Thus several large towns and popular resorts do not appear, while out-of-the-way spots like Werrington and Holy City receive generous treatment. Inevitably this method is highly subjective; equally so is the inclusion in the alphabetical headings of towns, villages, individual houses, and natural features, the only criterion being that of their appeal. Many entries include one or more subsidiary headings, the choice of which to group together having been dictated mainly by geographical convenience for the traveller. For any and all shortcomings I must take full responsibility and offer my apologies.

In preparing my material I have received immense help from the West Country and Cornwall Tourist Boards, numerous local-authority information bureaux, librarians, and museum directors, and an army of private individuals in many walks of life. To all these my sincere thanks. I have also, not surprisingly, been helped by a great many books, magazines, local brochures, church guides, National and Landmark Trust publications, and even newspaper articles. The books will all be found listed in the Further Reading (pp. 205–7). Lastly I must thank the patient lady who valiantly waded through my manuscript to type it, and my patient wife who at the wheel of our car valiantly waded through those notorious Devon and Cornwall lanes to a succession of improbable destinations.

Denys Kay-Robinson
Burbage
Wiltshire   July 1976

Publishers' Note
The publishers of this guide are always pleased to acknowledge any corrections brought to their notice by readers. Correspondence should be addressed to the Guide-book Editor, John Bartholomew & Son Limited, 216 High Street, Bromley BR1 1PW.

Introduction

Devon

Devon is nearly twice the size of Cornwall – 671,080ha. (or 2,610 square miles) against 354,260ha.; until the reorganization of counties in 1974, Devon, in fact, was second in area only to Yorkshire in all England. The changes that then altered the boundaries of so many counties left Devon, like Cornwall, as before; though one should perhaps point out that only eight years earlier Cornwall had been given the large Devon salient beyond the Tamar containing the parishes of North Petherwin and Werrington, north of Launceston. Exactly seventy years before that, in 1896, Devon's eastern boundary had been pushed forward by the acquisition of Chardstock, formerly in Dorset. In population Devon's figure more than doubles Cornwall's – 898,404 to 381,672 – but the origins of the Devon people do not involve anything like the same complexities.

History

Old and Middle Stone Age inhabitants must have been very few and far between, because virtually the only traces of them that have come to light in the whole county are those discovered in three systems of limestone caves, all on the south coast, at Plymouth, Brixham, and Torquay. As in Cornwall, these people were hunters and fishermen, but their prey was very different from that of a modern or even a medieval hunter, for the animal remains found in the caves with the human bones are largely of species now extinct. Moreover, the men had not learnt to use either horse or dog to help them.

By Neolithic times, that is to say the New Stone Age, the immigrants who moved into Devon after crossing to south-east England from France and Belgium had mastered the art of tending livestock and growing simple crops. Whether they exterminated the sparse Middle Stone Age population or gradually absorbed them we do not know. The Neolithic people built stone tombs, long barrows, and 'causewayed camps', concentric rings of earth, their intervening ditches interrupted by causeways or transverse banks serving no apparent purpose, since they did not lead to entrances. These camps were not primarily for defence against human enemies, but served as corrals into which the livestock could be herded to protect them from wild beasts. They may well have been used only in winter. A splendid example occurs in east Devon, Hembury Fort, between Honiton and Sidmouth; this was thought to be an entirely Iron Age construction, until excavation disclosed New Stone Age embankments underneath an Iron Age superstructure. There are a few other Neolithic vestiges in the county, but many have certainly been destroyed in later times by ill-informed treasure-seekers or uninterested farmers, and others no doubt remain hidden below subsequent work. However, from what has been learnt of the Neolithic people in general we know that the occupants of Hembury Fort were of a type that had discovered the uses of both those ancient helpers of Man, the horse and the dog. They lived in circular huts composed of a wattle-and-daub wall about 1m. high, surmounted by a conical roof of thatch-covered poles. Of the four megalithic tombs of the period that survive in Devon, corresponding with Cornwall's quoits, the most impressive is the Spinsters' Rock, north of Chagford. Such tombs were not built by the migrants from the south-east, but by related tribes who sailed direct to Britain from Brittany and further south.

The New Stone Age men, having discovered that underground flints were of superior quality to surface ones, learned to operate genuine mines, the remains of which, in the form of hollows where the shafts were sunk and mounds where the chalk was discarded, are to be seen in many places on Dartmoor and to a lesser extent elsewhere. They also learned the uses of metal, and imported implements of bronze before a fresh wave of invaders ushered in the Early Bronze Age proper. This event is variously estimated as having taken place some time between 1900 and 1600 BC. The newcomers were of two types, who may be briefly characterized as those who settled on Dartmoor and those who did not. The Dartmoor dwellers were those who built the long stone rows, of which there are about fifty on the Moor and, except for a single series on Exmoor, none elsewhere. Because of the affinity of these rows with similar rows in Britanny there is little doubt that the Dartmoor Bronze Age invaders came from there. The rest appear to have come along the coast, like some of their Neolithic predecessors, from south-east England.

In terms of remains, the division between those of the New Stone and Early Bronze

Ages is remarkably clear-cut. The Hembury-type corrals for man and beast were no longer thrown up, nor megalithic tombs, and round barrows replaced long. On the other hand, in addition to the stone rows stone circles appeared, single upright stones, hut circles in village groups with or without a protective enclosing wall, and enclosed fields. The number of all these on Dartmoor is enormous. On Exmoor there are many round barrows and single standing stones, a few rows (though only one series, as already stated, within Devon), but no pounds – walled villages – or hut circles; there is also a feature not found on Dartmoor, several squares or triangles marked out by stones at the corners. In east Devon, too, there are many round barrows, but no hut remains. One tentative theory is that where we have no signs of dwellings the immigrants came from stock that had originated in central Asia and lived in tents made of skins, as many central Asians do today. The stone rows, the standing stones, the changes in burial methods, all indicate a considerable change in religion from Stone Age times: then the great stone quoits must have served in some measure as temples as well as tombs, but now the tombs and the temples were separate structures.

During the Late Bronze Age iron began to replace bronze, but as in Cornwall the Iron Age proper is generally reckoned to have begun with the Celtic invasions of about 450 BC onwards. In Devon, too, the most striking relics of these invaders are their great hill-forts, the defensive nature of which is shown by their prevalence along the Axe Valley line and the northern edge of Dartmoor. The evidently mellow climate that had attracted earlier farmers to the middle and western parts of Dartmoor had by now deteriorated, and their relics show that the last generations of Bronze Age people dwelt only in the north-eastern, eastern, and southern areas. Nor has the climate improved, for notwithstanding modern techniques and the increased pressure to grow food the greater part of Dartmoor is not farmed even today.

Up to this point the histories of Cornwall and Devon have been very similar, except that there was no tin-export trade in Devon, the rich veins there not having been discovered yet, and the prehistoric remains in the two counties bear a marked affinity. The warrior Celts assumed the leadership throughout the peninsula, and the Romans, when they learned of them through trade (and the Devonian Celts *did* trade, extensively, though not in tin), lumped them all together as the Dumnonii. But after the Roman conquest of Britain the Cornish and Devonian paths began to diverge. There is a tradition that when the Roman commander Vespasian first turned his attention to Devon in AD 49 he laid siege to the hill-fort at Exeter, whereupon the King of the Dumnonii met him in battle; neither side won, but Vespasian was allowed to leave a garrison at Exeter in exchange for a cessation of hostilities. At any rate, we know from excavations that the Roman occupation does date from almost exactly that time. We also know, and further work is still enlarging our knowledge, that Isca Dumnoniorum, as the Romans called it, was the only settlement in the Celtic realm that without too great a stretch of the imagination could be called a town. This no doubt was why the Romans chose it for their own frontier city, now the subject of a long and highly informative programme of excavation (*see* gazetteer section, Exeter City).

A long-held illusion that modern research is in the course of dispelling is that because they built no towns west of Exeter that was the limit of the Romans' penetration. But already we have found out that minor Roman roads, if not the celebrated highways, extended from Exeter to a garrison centre near North Tawton and perhaps from Exeter to Teinbridge and on to the Dart; and two signal stations near Countisbury and Martin-hoe respectively show that there were troops on the distant north coast. Further west still, the Iron Age trading-post at Mount Batten, on Plymouth Sound, continued to be active throughout the Roman era, though whether under Roman or Celtic direction we do not know; possibly its abandonment precisely at the time when the Romans left Britain may be taken as a pointer. But however far afield they spread in tiny pockets, it is clear that any admixture of 'Roman'* blood in the make-up of the people of Devon, even in Exeter and points east, is negligible. After the withdrawal of the legions in the decades before 410 the same black fog closes in on the history of the Devonian half of the king-dom of Dumnonia as on the Cornish. However, the point has been made that the very lightness of the Roman influence on most of Devon meant that its cessation would have had a far less disruptive effect than in eastern England. It would perhaps not be too much to say that the Dumnonian kings (who were hereditary) simply took over where the Romans left off. Christian memorial stones continued to be inscribed in Latin, and in the secular or pagan sphere there were the institutions common to the Celtic peoples everywhere. But there is no literature, as in Wales and Ireland, to inform us of actual facts, and apart from the memorial stones meaningful archaeological finds have so far been few. Just one or two events are known to us, and those only because they involved the world outside. The first event – a migration of Britons from Dumnonia to Brittany – occurred a century or more after the Romans had gone. There is no evidence that the Anglo-Saxons, who were already established further east, forcibly drove the Celts out; more likely, a succession of bad harvest years, possibly with the additional impetus of some plague, drove the more enterprising to seek better luck in a new land. It is intriguing to speculate whether they chose Brittany because it was near and the voyage relatively safe from Saxon attacks, because continuing contacts kept them aware that people of their own race, speaking their own tongue, lived in the Breton peninsula, or because there remained a folk-memory that it was from there that many of their forebears had migrated in the opposite direction. Possibly there was an element of all three incentives.

The second event of which we have some knowledge is the irruption of missionaries, the majority later canonized, into Cornwall and Devon from Britanny, Wales, and in particular Ireland. (Those arriving from Brittany are proof of the continuing contacts with that region.) Christianity had reached Devon well before the end of the Roman occupation, but the numerous monastic communities founded in Devon during the interval between Roman and Saxon occupations meant that the earliest form of *organized* Christianity in Devon as well as in Cornwall followed the Celtic pattern.

Certain place-names – Colyton, Sidbury, Otterton, and Kingsteignton are a few – and the fact that the possessors of them are all situated a short distance up estuaries, are our clue that the first Saxon settlers sailed along the south Devon coast and into the river-mouths, probably during the sixth century. They may have met and mastered opposition, but it is much likelier that they found the land abandoned by the emigrants, yet obviously fertile and still showing the evidences of recent cultivation. Soon after the opening of the seventh century, however, the West Saxons who already occupied all the area we now call the South-West, except Devon and Cornwall, decided to move in on eastern Dumnonia in earnest. Their first attack was along the old Roman road from

---

* Roman garrisons could of course be made up of troops from any part of the Empire.

Dorchester to Exeter, represented today by the A35; and they heavily defeated the British force sent to meet them at Bindon, near Axmouth. The effect of this was that the Saxon settlements on the estuaries now became merged in a general Saxon occupation of all south-east Devon as far as the Otter. There was no further advance for nearly half a century, during which the West Saxons were preoccupied with a defensive war on their northern border, but in 658 they again advanced and again defeated the British at Pinhoe, outside the walls of Exeter, which enabled them to take over that city and much else; and in 661 a further victory near Crediton permitted them to advance down the south coast to Torbay and deep into central Devon north of Dartmoor. The occupation of virtually the whole county was achieved in 682 by still another Saxon victory at a place unidentified, but probably in mid Devon, which pushed the British back to the north coast. The final stage, as noted in the introduction to Cornwall, was the penetration of the invaders into the north-east of that county, where there was no Tamar to form an obstacle, driving the British, Celts, or Dumnonians still further westward.

One must beware, however, of imagining every Celt driven headlong from Devon soil. Not only did a great many remain, albeit compelled to live and farm in the least fertile areas while their conquerors took over the fat of the land, but various enclaves continued to carry on deep inside the Saxon territory, including one at Exeter itself, where the dedications of the churches suggest a Celtic northern and Saxon southern division of the city. How much inter-marriage took place we do not know, but it is likely to have been very little before the Norman Conquest subjected both races to a common inferior status. That the British nurtured a very long hatred of their conquerors is proved by the brief alliance of the Cornish Celts with the Danes as late as the ninth century. Nor did Christianity do much to act as a bond, for although the West Saxons had become converted by the time of their first penetration of Devon, their form of faith was that of Rome while that of the British remained unswervingly Celtic.

Eventually – inevitably – the Roman practice prevailed. Under the Saxons the church gained enormous power throughout Britain. Instead of the wandering-missionary type of ecclesiastic favoured by the Celts, England was mapped out into fixed sees, which were subdivided into parishes. The Saxon kings gave huge tracts of land into ecclesiastical ownership. Churches began to be built of stone. Church music, always a potent fascinator of the masses, spread rapidly from Kent. And Devon was not left out of all this. The Abbey of St Mary and St Peter, which preceded the cathedral at Exeter, certainly existed by 670, a mere dozen years after the Saxons had entered the city, and may even have been founded before their arrival (it is hoped that evidence from the current excavations will eventually resolve the uncertainty). In 739 Crediton became the site of a minster that observed the Roman ritual, not the Celtic; and as the years passed the promotion of Crediton to a bishopric (later transferred to Exeter) and the building of other churches, including the Abbey of Tavistock and Exeter Cathedral, quickly spread the Roman ascendancy. Meanwhile the West Saxons, or the people of the Kingdom of Wessex, were having to contend with the second era of Nordic invasions, those of the Danes. Devon had been a shire since about 800, divided into thirty-three hundreds, and in spite of the colonies of British still in its midst it was now an integral part of England. The first Danish raid occurred in 851, in the Torbay area; the Anglo-Saxon Chronicle records a battle at *Wicgeanbeorg*, which would seem to be Weeka-borough, a farm lying between Paignton and Ipplepen.

After this came a lull, but in 876 a body of Danish horsemen, having deceived King Alfred by a piece of shocking bad faith, managed to enter Exeter. They were driven out, but the incident was the prelude to a campaign in which they overwhelmed the whole county, together with nearly all Alfred's kingdom. Alfred, cooped up with a handful of followers in the Somerset marshes, never lost heart but bided his time until he could counter-attack and defeat his foes. But before he did this (in 878) Devon had scored a victory on her own, a Saxon force under the ealdorman of the shire defeating a sizeable Danish force that had landed on the north coast from Wales.

After Alfred had won back his whole kingdom, and more, there were further Danish raids during the ensuing century and a half, notably that in which the raiders entered the Tamar in 997 and got far enough inland to sack Tavistock Abbey, and the raid of 1001 in which they reached Exeter but were unable to enter it, thanks to the strengthening of its walls by King Athelstan three-quarters of a century earlier. Athelstan had also ordered the Celtic community in Exeter to remove themselves to Cornwall. This raises an interesting point that most historians overlook: was Athelstan thinking of the occasions when the Cornish had eagerly helped the Danes against the Saxons, and did he suspect that the Danish penetration of Exeter in 876 was not entirely the fault of the dilapidated walls?

Ironically it was a Frenchman, not a Celt, who eventually betrayed Exeter to the Danes. In 1003 came the final invasion under Sweyn that resulted in Canute becoming King of all England; and Sweyn's Danes opened the proceedings by an attack on Exeter that proved unexpectedly successful because the French Reeve, one Hugh, let them in. They wrought destruction to a degree not to be experienced again by the unfortunate city until 1941. Fortunately for the rest of the county, the terrible attack was not repeated against other towns, and in 1016 Devon became part of Canute's realm without further hostilities. How many Danes, if any, actually settled in Devon we cannot tell, but it is unlikely to have been many: the only Danish-origin name in the whole county is Lundy. The Danes settled down and merged very rapidly with the Saxons, who in the West probably absorbed the few newcomers without trace.

The people of Devon, then, are made up of pre-Celtic races differing only slightly from those who occupied Cornwall, and of Celts and Anglo-Saxons as in Cornwall, but with the proportions reversed. In both counties the Normans made their presence felt administratively, architecturally, and culturally, but not racially; they simply did not colonize in sufficient numbers. After William's siege of Exeter (*see* gazetteer entry) the rest of Devon offered no appreciable resistance, and apart from a curious little 'invasion' by King Harold's two sons near the mouth of the Exe in 1069, which was instantly crushed, there were no counter-attacks. The Domesday survey, like most of its modern counterparts, was a long-winded affair, and unlike its counterparts was abridged to a manageable length before its emergence as the Domesday Book. In Exeter Cathedral Library, however, we have an eleventh-century copy of part of the unabridged original (the Exon Domesday, surveying the five south-western counties), and it is most informative about the Devon of its day. Exeter was the largest of the four towns, with 268 houses; there had been 316, but the remainder had been pulled down, presumably to make a space in which to build the castle. As many as 1,200 other places are described, including many manors. The distribution of crop-growing and cattle-breeding over the county was similar to today's, but there were still large areas of heath and forest to be tamed and brought into use. Under the Normans this was steadily accomplished. Stone walls, hitherto unique to Exeter, were built round Barnstaple and Totnes (though not round the fourth town, Lydford), and a few other Saxon villages were enlarged into towns, beginning with Okehampton and Dartmouth. Tavistock had become a town by virtue of the accretion of persons attached to the great abbey, rather as in much later times towns grew up round important factories.

During the twelfth and thirteenth centuries many more new towns were founded by either the ecclesiastical or the secular land-owners, for a town that could support a market was a lucrative investment, particularly in the south-west now that the great Dartmoor tin deposits had been discovered. Not that these experiments always succeeded; Devon is rich in sites of would-be towns that for one reason or another – generally because they were in the wrong place – failed to make the grade and remained just villages. Under the Normans, too, a great programme of church-building was launched – one has only to think of the number of present-day churches whose earliest fragments are Norman to realize the extent of this. Foremost was the ambitious new cathedral at Exeter (qv in gazetteer section), though what the builders of that would have thought if they could have foreseen how their no doubt very fine work was to be systematically nibbled away to extinction, except for the towers, by the successive builders of the present cathedral, it is hard to say. At least, assuming they could appreciate styles not their own, any of them returning in spirit to contemplate the building that succeeded theirs must have acknowledged its handsomeness, which is more than we can do when we look at most of the replacements of medieval handiwork by the Victorian 'restorers'. Exeter was not unique in this experience, however; over the county as a whole – as indeed over England as a whole – the next great outburst of ecclesiastical reconstruction, in the fifteenth century, destroyed much of the Normans' work, perhaps beyond their artistic deserts, to the extent, in fact, that there is not now one church in the county that has escaped the reformers of both fifteenth and nineteenth centuries and is pure Norman. The most that is left to us is a very few Norman towers, the odd window or doorway, and a sprinkling of fonts.

Apart from all the building of towns and churches and the development of trade in tin and cloth, the most salient happening in medieval Devon was the particular outbreak of bubonic plague known as the Black Death. It reached England at Weymouth, and therefore Devon was one of the first counties to experience it. In recent years one or two learned and deeply intriguing works have been published in which evidence is marshalled to show that the Black Death was not the terrible visitation historians have always supposed, but merely one of a number of factors that caused a sudden heavy mortality throughout the country in the mid fourteenth century. This introduction being no place in which to justify or repudiate the theory, and it being an incontrovertible fact that in 1349 and subsequent years a great many people did die of disease, let us assume for convenience that the cause was bubonic plague. The first outbreak (and it *was* the first – England had never suffered from this ailment before) was the worst; it was followed by numerous recurrences until 1361, after which it almost died out for nearly 200 years. As every schoolboy now knows, bubonic plague is carried by the fleas of black rats, but since no one found that out until relatively modern times, and in the Middle Ages the black rat was at least as common as the brown rat is today – and had a free run of even the best houses – the sudden drying-up of the disease is puzzling. Immunity can hardly have been built up in those who had escaped infection, and those who recovered from it were far too few to constitute a check. The reach of the plague was infinite; the remotest Dartmoor farms experienced it, brought in presumably by one of the household who had gone to market, or even by an itinerant friar. Probably in Devon there was not the incidence of whole villages abandoned, or their populations wiped out, that occurred in other parts of the country, but archaeology and aerial photography between them have brought to light the sites or remnants of a number of farms deserted at about the time of the plague.

The suppression of monasteries in Devon came in three stages. First, Henry V suppressed a few smaller ones on the ground that they were administered from France and therefore, like the Celtic communities in the eyes of the Saxon Athelstan, potential supporters of the King's enemies; then in 1536 Henry VIII dissolved the county's seven smaller monasteries, and finally in 1539 he dissolved the ten larger. Many Devonians had by then accepted the reformed faith, but the Roman Catholic element remained large, and inevitably, as elsewhere in England, was much incensed at what seemed to it acts of sacrilege. But it was the introduction of the English Prayer-Book and other reforms under Edward VI that triggered off the great Catholic Rebellion in Devon and Cornwall in 1549. This is treated more fully in the introduction to Cornwall, and further references will be found under entries in the gazetteer section; suffice it to repeat here that the uprising was put down with great ferocity by Lord Russell, who fell somewhat short of anticipating the well-known pacifism of his twentieth-century descendants. But the rebellion helps to explain the action of Elizabeth only a decade later, at the shaky outset of her reign, in ordering the destruction of all church 'images' and other Roman Catholic symbols first removed, but rarely destroyed, under Edward VI, restored with the maximum propagandist symbolism under Mary, and now a constant incentive, Elizabeth thought, to further trouble. This was the first and most understandable, however keenly we may feel the loss to art, of the three waves of assault against the beauty of our churches. The second was the iconoclasm of the Puritans during the Commonwealth. The third and most sweeping was the campaign of 'restoration' by the Victorians, though Devon was at least spared more than a small fraction of the attentions bestowed on his native Cornwall by the grand master of church vulgarization, J. Piers St Aubyn.

But if the start of Elizabeth I's reign brought selective vandalism to the churches of Devon as to others, the middle and later years coincided with a golden age such as few if any other counties can match at any period of their history. It was the age of the great sea-captains – the explorers, merchants, warriors, pirates, colonizers, ruffians, who made Plymouth, Devon, and England great and safe. The story of Plymouth is outlined under that heading in the gazetteer section. But other parts contributed to Devon's maritime glory, including Dartmouth, which only by chance was not selected instead of Plymouth as the naval base against Spain, and on the north coast Bideford, not only Sir Richard Grenville's town but the harbour from which Stephen and William Burrough sailed to discover the Arctic coast of Russia and to name Europe's most northerly cape. In all this the Cornish, despite their proximity to Plymouth, their many ports and multitude of fisherfolk, had no discernible rôle at all.

During the Civil War the pattern in Devon was broadly that of England as a whole: the nobility and the landowners were for the King, and the merchants (which meant the towns) and farmers were for Parliament. The Roman Catholic Church and its followers were Royalist almost to a man, Protestant clergy and the followers of the various Dissenting groups for Parliament. Farmers were divided, and the peasantry tended to side with their landowner unless he was very unpopular. But there were many exceptions, in all spheres – more than in Cornwall. Towns where there was a strong Catholic element, such as Exeter, were divided accordingly. Some of the great families with seats in half a dozen areas found themselves divided too, with supporters on either side. Some of the most aristocratic names were staunch Cromwellians. One or two smaller towns, usually those overshadowed by a Royalist-held castle, such as Kingswear, were on the King's side. And, last but not least, there were the shrewd neutrals, whether towns, families, or individuals. In general it may be said that Devon was markedly less Royalist than Cornwall; but one of the fascinations for the historian of the period is that despite ample contemporary documentation on the *events* of the Civil War, the motives that prompted many of the great families to side as they did will either remain forever unknown, or are to be found only in private papers not yet made available.

One thing the people of the two counties – and for that matter, of the two sides – shared in common was the ruinous cost of the war in terms of high prices, exorbitant financial levies, and in many cases the expense of repairing buildings. To this can be added the general miseries of billeting troops – often those of one army and then of the other – of having military operations either going on then and there or threatening to, of losing loved ones in battle – as in any war – and of never being certain whether to trust one's neighbour – as only in a civil war. But if Devon was less Royalist than Cornwall, the Royalists at first had it all their own way there. After Sir Ralph Hopton and Sir Bevil Grenville had heavily defeated the Parliament army under the Earl of Stamford at Stratton, the Royalists, who had already secured Cornwall, swept through Devon, forcing obedience from almost the whole shire and capturing Exeter before the autumn of 1642. Only Plymouth, which had been strongly Parliamentary from the outset, refused to surrender. And it never did. Although completely isolated, with (at any rate at first) a national Royalist triumph more than likely, with unknown retribution to follow, the port defied alternate assaults and blockades for three and a half years, until relieved by the war's end in 1646. Its resistance, more than anything else except perhaps the death of the idolized Sir Bevil in the Battle of Lansdown, near Bath, eventually demoralized the South-Western Royalist soldiers and began the wholesale desertions and drift back home.

Brief comments on the Civil War as it affected various Devon towns and mansions are made under the appropriate headings in the gazetteer section. After the war a corner of Devon came briefly on to the political scene again when William of Orange landed at Brixham in 1688 and proceeded through Exeter and Axminster on his way to London. But this time there were no heroics, especially after the awful spectacle of what had happened to the supporters of Monmouth. The people cheered, as mobs will cheer (or abuse) anyone who provides a modicum of distraction from life's routine. But the authorities just did not want to know. They saw to it that William was sumptuously entertained, in case he won, but they themselves all had business elsewhere, in case he lost. The 1640s, let alone 1685, were too close to inspire anything more committal than the utmost caution. The hero-figure of the time was cast in the mould neither of Grenville nor of Fairfax (and still less of poor William) but in that of the Vicar of Bray.

The eighteenth century rolled by with the same prosperity of the rich and poverty of the poor that was seen in other parts. A whole crop of entertaining writers, beginning with the delightful Mrs Celia Fiennes and Daniel Defoe, have left us their impressions of the century and the years immediately preceding and following it. Defoe noted the great trade in cloth manufacture that, with farming, was still, as it had been for centuries, the county's main means of livelihood. Fishing, too, played its part, but it was never as important as it was to Cornwall. Take away the Cornish ports and former mining-areas, and not much scope for production is left; in Devon there are huge productive inland areas, and they were not neglected. The century was one of great road improvement, partly financed by the universally unpopular turnpike trusts. In the old days of horse (and pedestrian) traffic only, the best – because driest – routes had lain over the hill-tops; now that the waggon and the coach were common, the horses could not climb or even safely descend the more precipitous hills, and a number of alternative courses were laid down over flatter land. In many places both routes survive, though perhaps none offering such a dramatic contrast as the old and new roads between Dorchester and Sherborne in the next county. Finally, the eighteenth century was the century of the Wesleys. Samuel Wesley was headmaster of Blundell's School at Tiverton; in 1739 he died, and while his brothers John and Charles were visiting their widowed sister-in-law John was asked to preach at Exeter. This he did, upon securing the necessary clerical invitation, and so began his work in Devon. He never regarded it as of the same importance as his work among the rude Cornish, but he did preach on many occasions in a number of Devon towns and villages, including Sticklepath, near Okehampton (where he had made friends with the colony of Quakers – *see* Sticklepath in gazetteer section), and Plymouth, or more precisely its sister-town on the Hamoaze, Devonport, then still called Dock. Although his method swayed many thousands of his hearers, the effect was less universal than in Cornwall, and he had to endure opposition both from the gentry and orthodox clergy on one side, and from elements of the mob on the other. Wesley continued to preach in Devon until the last year of his long life, but Methodism never established itself there as it did beyond the Tamar. Things might have been better if it had, for there was certainly no spiritual comfort to be had from the Church of England of the time, which was as tumbledown and uninspiring as its churches. And when reform did eventually come, it was as harsh and unsympathetic as the restoration of the buildings.

The pre-Napoleonic and Napoleonic wars with France brought much naval activity to Plymouth, were responsible for the building of Dartmoor prison (*see* Plymouth and Princetown in gazetteer section), and also had the effect of launching a number of the south-coast towns on their careers as holiday resorts several decades before the advent of the railway. The Fleet used to anchor in Torbay as often as in Plymouth Sound, and the officers' families wanted somewhere to live that was both convenient and agreeable. Various developers such as the Palk family saw their opportunity, and not only Torquay but Sidmouth and other spots benefited by the interest of the fashionable new clientele, whose gracious arrival was in savage contrast to the brutalities being simultaneously practised by the press gangs.

Commerce

During the centuries Devon's chief commercial support, sustaining her through all the political fluctuations and the strains imposed by wars (not least the Civil War), had been the wool trade. Wool had been to Devon what fishing had been to Cornwall, and if the symbol of Cornish prosperity should have been a golden pilchard, that of Devon should have been a golden lamb. But early in the nineteenth century the gold for both counties began to turn to dross. The pilchard shoals switched to remoter waters, and although the Devon sheep did not migrate to other counties, the trade did, and as in so many other fields of commerce the reason was steam. As the wool mills of Yorkshire multiplied, with steam-driven looms powered by coal mined almost at their doors, the Devonians found they could not compete. Conservatism was partly to blame, but mainly it was lack of easily-got fuel. Had north Devon possessed a Plymouth or a Dartmouth, coal might have been imported from south Wales at an economic price; but Barnstaple was the only port above the minuscule on the whole of that beautiful but impracticable coast, and as the size and weight of vessels grew (again owing to the use of steam) the treacherous sand-bar across the Taw–Torridge estuary was like a slowly closing gate. The great wool-cloth trade dwindled until, by a curious quirk, it remained important only in the Buckfast-leigh–Ashburton area where the monks had brought it to birth.

For a short time, however, the blow to Devon's economy was offset by the boom in another industry – mining. Dartmoor's many prehistoric remains have proved that tin-working was known in pre-Roman days, but the Romans did not exploit it (they could get cheap tin from Spain), their British successors were too barbaric to know or care, and if the Saxons or the Danes were aware of Dartmoor tin they did nothing about it; even the energetic Normans had reigned over the country for a century before tin-streaming on the Moor is mentioned. But then, in the twelfth century, there was a minor boom; in 1199, for instance, Dartmoor tin contributed £600 in taxes to the Royal exchequer – a goodly sum for those days. The next landmark is seen early in the sixteenth century, when underground mining (as opposed to surface streaming) began and a second boom followed, to be ended by the Civil War.

For a long time there had been four stannary towns for assaying the tin – Chagford, Tavistock, Plympton, and Ashburton – and since 1305 the Devon tinners had been meeting separately from those of Cornwall to discuss their problems and enact regulations in a Stannary Parliament on Crockern Tor, or at least (less romantically but more comfortably) in a building near it. However, although all these trappings of an important industry continued to flourish until well into the eighteenth century in the case of the Stannary Parliament, and until 1837 in the case of the Stannary Laws, the tin trade in Devon was never important after Tudor times: it was copper that brought the mining boom in the nineteenth century – a boom as sudden, extreme, and short-lived as any in British history. The area involved lay between the western foothills of Dartmoor and the Tamar, and the 'capital' of the whole undertaking was Tavistock. The copper rush, to be accurate, anticipated the new century by a few years: the Wheal Friendship Mine was opened in 1796 at the scene of the first strike near Mary Tavy. The peak was reached in 1850, after the opening of the Devon Great Consols Mine (*see* Tavistock). For a few years then, Devon and Cornwall produced more than half the world output of copper, and there were profitable sidelines of which the chief was arsenic, eagerly bought as an insecticide by the cotton-growing interests of the United (and while they existed, Confederate) States of America. By 1885, indeed, the arsenic output had nearly supplanted that of the copper, and was the greatest source of arsenic on earth. But by 1900 the whole fantastic enterprise had fizzled out like some spectacular firework display. The Devon Great Consols, which in less than sixty years had brought the Bedford family more than a quarter of a million pounds in royalties, paid its shareholders more than one million in dividends, and overshadowed the rest of the globe in the output of its two main products, was played out, and the lesser mines with it. In 1901 it was closed down altogether. It is doubtful whether any other commercial venture in Britain, of comparable magnitude in relation to its period, ever blossomed and withered with such spectacular rapidity. Today in the Tavistock area – and that is to say in Devon – there is just one tiny copper-producing unit, and even this represents a revival after decades of no activity at all. Far more important to the economy of the Moor today are the granite quarries, again largely in the Tavistock area, and the china-clay pits north-east of Plymouth.

What saved Devon after the decline of wool and copper was what saved Cornwall after the loss of its tin and pilchard profits – the coming of large-scale tourism in the wake (with a few precocious exceptions) first of the railway and then of the motor-car. (One excepts Plymouth, with its great Naval dockyards employing in 1976 about 12,000 men – though even this did not prevent a 7 per cent unemployment rate.) Nor of course should farming be underestimated, with its transition of emphasis from wool-bearing sheep to milk-producing cows; and there are various industries of local benefit – the Dartmoor granite and china clay as mentioned, ship-building at Appledore, ball-clay production at Teignmouth, fishing at Brixham, textiles at Buckfastleigh, assorted manufacturing activities at most of the larger towns as well as the two cities; but tourism, now that the disruption of the Second World War has been made up for, is the fairy godmother. The First World War affected the county only in terms of economic stringencies and loss of life at the Front, but the Second World War brought the German bombers to Exeter and Plymouth with (literally) devastating impact.

Although individual holiday resorts, be they small like Clovelly or enormous like Torquay–Paignton, become densely packed during the main holiday season, Devon's generous size means that she has never suffered problems of overcrowding to the same claustrophobic degree as Cornwall. As for the resident population, the failure of the Industrial Revolution to make headway in the county meant that growth during the nineteenth century was spectacular for its slowness rather than its speed. During the first half of the period, it is true, the population increase was nearly 230,000, but during the second half it was less than 100,000, owing to large-scale emigration both to more prosperous parts of England and to English-speaking countries overseas. However, there was never, as there was in Cornwall, an actual decline. During the twentieth century the rise has been steady but slight: not since 1831 has the rate of increase per year reached 1 per cent. In 1901 the total was slightly above 662,000. In 1971 it was 898,400, of whom nearly 240,000, or more than a quarter, lived in the administrative area of Plymouth; the three county boroughs, as they then were – Exeter, Plymouth, and Torbay – accounted for not quite half the entire Devon population, leaving very little for the twenty-four other towns and scores of villages. The Exmouth urban mass accounted for nearly 26,000; the largest real town, Barnstaple, had a population of only about 17,000.

Geology

There are two 'empty quarters' where there is virtually no population: central Dartmoor, and much of the Devon share of Exmoor. A glance at the map of Devon and Cornwall shows that Dartmoor is an eastward extension of the obtruded granite masses of which four manifest themselves in Cornwall, extending from West Penwith to Bodmin Moor; and that just as the Cornish masses increase in size from west to east, so Dartmoor is the largest of all. North and west of Dartmoor something like half the county area consists of the sandstones and dark shales, known as the Culm Measures, that are to be found in north-east Cornwall. The Old Red Sandstone that gives much of Devon its celebrated red cliffs and soil accounts for the whole of the Devon area of Exmoor, and in the south most of the terrain enfolding the southern half of Dartmoor, down to the coastline of the South Hams, with the exception of the southernmost part of all between Start Point and Hope Cove where gneisses and schists predominate.

From Torbay up to the Somerset border east of Bampton runs a strip of New Red or Permian Sandstone, a long lateral form that extends west into the Culm Measures through Silverton and Thorverton nearly as far as Hatherleigh. East of this again, that is to say east of a line running approximately north from between Exmouth and Budleigh Salterton, there is a complex mixture of chalk, upper greensand, sandstone, and Keuper Marls. The foregoing is, obviously, a very much simplified picture of the Devonian make-up. Small pockets of other rocks are found in many areas: Devon limestone around Chudleigh, tuffs, lavas, and other igneous rocks in the northern part of the South Hams and near Tavistock, granite in the whole composition of Lundy.

For the traveller who does not specialize in geology, the most interesting formations occur along the two coasts. There are broadly four types of north coast, extending in succession from the Cornish border to Hartland Point, from Hartland to Westward Ho!, from there to Ilfracombe, and from Ilfracombe to Somerset. Along the first stretch the coastline cuts almost at right-angles across the trend of the rocks, leaving ribs of harder rocks projecting out to sea in the form of chains of stacks or huge boulders and innumerable headlands, between which the cliff-faces show a clear cross-section of the fantastically folded and crumpled strata. The colour of the cliffs is dark brown or grey, and the thundering seas whipped up by the frequent gales make it easy to appreciate that here is a shore under constant erosion. One result is that where small rivers have cut ravines for themselves, the encroaching ocean has often bitten into the face of the ravine, leaving a cliff over which the stream falls in a cascade. The second section, from Hartland to Westward Ho!, differs because the shoreline, having turned a right-angle, is now parallel with the strata. The cliffs continue to be high and impressive, but the shore is much less 'untidy'. The best-known – indeed, almost the only – settlement along this span is Clovelly.

From Westward Ho! north to Bull Point lie the quiet, sandy shores of Bideford Bay, Croyde Bay, and Morte Bay, separated by headlands where the harder rock, again lying at right-angles to the shore, has been left when the sea ate its way into the softer formations on either side. Between Ilfracombe and Somerset lies what for many is the finest coast anywhere in the two counties, namely where Exmoor meets the Bristol Channel, falling sometimes almost sheer from heights that average well over 300m. Exmoor is characteristically an area of rough hill pasture, much of it bare and bleak, but with little naked rock showing through the heather and bracken. As on Dartmoor and Bodmin Moor, there are dangerous bogs. Rivers and streams, of which the chief is the Lyn, have carved out valleys, now in the main generously wooded. Certain coastal stretches are wooded even between the valleys, the trees extending down the tremendous escarpments nearly to sea-level. The most beautiful example of this is at Woody Bay, where the woods that cling to the slope (representing a vertical drop of 285m.) are threaded by a stream, the Hanging Water, that plunges in a series of longer and longer leaps to the shore. There is a small hotel halfway down the cliff, two or three houses, and at the bottom a tiny pier – all that is left of an Edwardian plan to turn Woody Bay into a smart resort to which the patrons would be brought by steamer. The scheme collapsed when its promoter was charged with embezzling the funds. On either side the coast is indented in a sequence of bays and headlands where the sea has eaten into the slates and left the sandstone outstanding. In places the slate has been battered into isolated stacks and grotesque crags, and this contrast of form with that of the bolder, smoother sandstone, accentuated by the difference in colour (the sandstone is red, the slate grey), gives immense variety as well as majesty to the scene. Solitude, too, plays its part; between Combe Martin Bay and the Somerset border, a distance of 27km. as the crow flies, Lynmouth is the only sea-level settlement, because the abruptness of the cliffs leaves no room elsewhere for others.

The south coast of Devon, like that of Cornwall, is in full contrast with the north. Much of it consists of a low plateau, cut into by many wide river estuaries and made up of a great diversity of rocks – slate, sandstone, limestone, volcanic formations. The Dorset end of the coast is made up of chalk and greensand overlying limestone and shale; this is the area of spectacular collapse such as the Dowland landslip described in the gazetteer section under Seaton and Beer. These cliffs are blue and yellow; near Seaton they give place to the New Red Sandstone, which extends as far as Torbay, interrupted by grey, pink-tinged Devonian Limestone between Oddicombe Bay and Anstey's Cove, dark, igneous dolerite forming Black Head to the south of the Cove, and more limestone at Hope's Nose and along the northern strip of the Bay that includes the natural arch named London Bridge. The centre of the Bay is backed by New Red Sandstone, then we come again to limestone forming the southern shore through Brixham to Berry Head.

The land at Torbay and around the Dart estuary was formerly higher than it is today, and sank comparatively recently – probably during the New Stone Age. Torbay, for example, is only one of several areas along this coast where forests grew far out over what is now the sea-bed; during very low tides in the Bay the vestiges of the trees are plainly visible, trees among which the men and beasts whose remains were found in Kent's Cavern (*see* gazetteer section, Torquay) may once have walked. The 'drowning' of the River Dart is evidenced by the strange fact that its bed near the mouth is more than 30m. below sea-level. The beautiful valley that we admire today must therefore be just the top of a much deeper gorge of which the bottom was dramatically narrow and steepsided. The Dart Valley owes much of its loveliness to the circumstance that between Totnes and Dittisham it flows through a series of lavas and igneous rocks, each of which stands out in a bold forested crag, while between them the softer rock forms the gentler banks or has been worn away by a tributary into a branch estuary. Grits, hard slates, igneous rocks, and schists, all contribute to the rugged and romantic cliff scenery of the South Hams. Again, as on the Devon Exmoor coast, it is not only the formations but the diversity of colours that are striking, including as they do browns, yellows, reds, and a dull green reminiscent of the Lizard's serpentine. In Plymouth Sound the cliffs are again of various colours, though all made up of slates and schists, except Plymouth Hoe, which is limestone. The study of both Devon coasts has been made a great deal easier since the completion of the North and South Devon Coast Paths, two sections of the Master South-West Peninsula Coast Path of which the Cornish Coast Path is also a section.

Dartmoor needs a further word or two before we leave the Devonian geology. Although the heather- and bracken-clad barrenness of most of it invites comparison with Exmoor, fundamentally the two could hardly be more different. Exmoor's slate and sandstone rarely protrudes from the vegetation, even on the tops of hills. Moreover, much of the surface can be domesticated, to the extent that no little concern exists just now at the degree to which cultivation is making inroads that in the long term could alter the whole wild nature of the Moor. The soil that covers Dartmoor's granite, on the other hand, is not only all but impervious to cultivation, but, as if to emphasize the dominant character of the stone, is in many places thrust aside by the protrusion of bare tors and 'clitters', or lateral rocks. (A hill with exposed rocks on the summit is a tor, the word also being sometimes used to refer to the rocks alone; a hill with a smooth, vegetation-covered summit is a hill.) The granite, or moorstone as it is called locally, is a crystalline rock made up of mica, quartz, and felspar, formed by the consolidation of molten matter; it is not layered, but exists in an almost homogeneous mass extending down through the earth's crust to a depth that no one has yet succeeded in measuring. Tracts of peat, often forming bogs, cover parts of it, but only in the South-West has it become 'kaolinized' into china clay (*see* gazetteer section, Shaugh Prior). The reason why so much of its surface, even regions at present uninhabitable, carries so many relics of early man is twofold: first, the Moor was free of the dense forests that formerly choked the surrounding lands, and second, there is evidence that the climate was once more mellow than it is now.

Climate

In general, the Devon climate is still mellow; as part of the south-west peninsula, surrounded by the mild Atlantic, which also influences the estuaries, the county is bound to be temperate. But it is also bound to be wet. Emma Gifford, the future Mrs Thomas Hardy, wrote of the amount of 'soft, imperceptible-sprinkling rain' that fell in her native Plymouth, and before her Keats had described Devon as 'cursedly subject to sympathetic moisture'. In fact the climate varies bewilderingly from one small area to the next. The most rain – about 205cm. a year – falls on the highest parts of Dartmoor; at Princetown (as though the gaol were not dreary enough) the figure is actually 210cm. The average for Dartmoor as a whole and for Exmoor is about 160cm. The Exeter area, on the other hand, receives only about 89cm., the Exe estuary itself as little as 76cm. But even this figure is well above those for most of east and south-east England. Temperatures in the county, too, seldom reach extremes of either heat or cold – though anyone standing on the cliffs near, say, Hartland Quay during a January gale may be pardoned for doubting this. Summer warmth on the south coast, while not involving high thermometer readings, can be more relaxing, not to say debilitating, than many a hotter day by the Mediterranean. Contrary to a widespread belief outside the county, snow is neither frequent nor long-lying even in the highest regions of the two moors.

Rivers

Dartmoor's heavy rainfall has entailed the formation of many rivers, most of which flow into the English Channel. They include the Tavy (a tributary of the Tamar) and its tributary the Walkham, the Plym and its tributary the Meavy, the Yealm, the Erme, the

Avon, the Dart (union of the E. and W. Dart), and the Teign. The Exe, though making its way to the English Channel, rises in the Somerset part of Exmoor, and collects during its journey the northern Yeo, the Clyst, Creedy, and Kenn. Farther east, the Otter also rises in Somerset and the Axe in Dorset; the Axe's tributaries Yarty and Coly rise in Somerset and Devon respectively. The Devon rivers entering the Bristol Channel are far fewer. Unquestionably the most important are the Taw and the Torridge, which meet in a common outflow into Bideford or Barnstaple Bay. The Taw rises on Dartmoor and in its course through the gentle north-Devon lowlands collects the Mole, the confusingly-named Little Dart (no relation to East Dart, West Dart, or Dart), and southern Yeo. The Torridge is an extraordinary river. Rising in Cornwall, close to the source of the Tamar, it flows north, then east, then south-east, then east again, picking up the Waldon on its way; near Hatherleigh the Lew (one of two rivers of that name, both in west Devon) joins it and seems to steer it vaguely north-east, and a few km. later it is entered by the Okement, a combination of the Dartmoor-born East and West Okement. Only now does the Torridge resume its original direction northwards, finally turning north-west to flow in a series of huge, very pronounced loops toward Bideford. The only other river of any significance to debouch on the north coast is the Lyn, yet again an amalgam of East and West Lyn, the former rising as the Oare Water in Somerset. They are short streams, but both have several tributaries, which helps to explain the terrible floods that periodically afflict the Lyn, such as that which devastated Lynmouth in 1952 (*see* gazetteer section, Lynton and Lynmouth). The East Lyn's tributary, the Badgworthy Water, with *its* tributary the Hoccombe Water, form most of the northern end of the Devon–Somerset border, though their function in that respect is infinitely less significant than that of the famous demarcator the Tamar, which shares with the lower Severn and the Tweed the momentous task of keeping Celtic territory out of the clutches of the covetous English. A succession of tributaries empty into the Tamar from the Devon side: the Deer, the Claw, the Carey, the Lyd (which has earlier been joined by the other Lew, the Thrushel, and the Wolf), and, as already observed, the Tavy.

Flora and Fauna

Few of these rivers fail to run part of their course between steep wooded banks that constitute some of Devon's finest scenery. Both Dartmoor and Exmoor are unsuited to trees except in the sheltered valleys cut by the rivers; other rivers, all south-flowing, are at their timber-lined best where they open out in estuaries. Devon's 'natural' tree is the oak, varied in some regions by the birch. The Scots pine may have originated as an introduction, but it has spread widely by natural means, especially in the south. Large areas of Dartmoor have been planted with conifers by the Forestry Commission, not always to aesthetic advantage; the best of its forests is probably Fernworthy, south-west of Chagford, which has been growing long enough to have acquired a certain individuality, and where the Fernworthy Reservoir reflects the trees with a quasi-Alpine charm that makes nonsense of the conservationists' hysterical opposition to the planting of anything on Dartmoor larger than a sprig of heather, or the creation of any new body of water larger than a sheep trough. Britain can survive, at a price, without growing extra timber, because it can be imported, but we cannot import water, and in face of the increasing droughts of the 1970s, which many climatologists believe indicate a trend that will not be reversed, the frivolous obstructionism that delays every proposal to construct a new reservoir must increasingly be seen as constituting precisely the type of anti-social behaviour the obstructors profess to deplore.

The elms that were a feature of the red-sandstone regions have been subject to the same devastation by Dutch Elm Disease as in the rest of the country. Predators of another sort are the holidaymakers, who are particularly hard on the riverside ferns for which the Tamar, Lyd, and the two Okements were until recently famous; the ferns are pulled up for transplantation to private gardens, where the only specimens that do not die soon after planting are those already dead when they are put in. Away from the river valleys, the plants most characteristic of Dartmoor are the gorses, the heathers, the brooms, and in the boggy areas bog asphodel, Devon myrtle, and most of the smaller bog plants of southern England. The Devon myrtle, sometimes called the sweet gale, was a useful plant in the old days, its fragrant branches being used like lavender to sweeten stored linen, and its wax being extracted by boiling and fashioned into scented tapers. In spring the high, often vertical, banks of the lanes are hung with tapestries of primroses and violets, to be followed in early summer by foxgloves wherever they can find a foothold. In some parts of Devon foxgloves go by the enchanting name of 'flopadocks', but only at Hartland (qv in gazetteer section) do they figure in a ceremony (St Nectan's Day).

Coastal plants in the county have a special appeal for many botanists, because so many species proliferate only in one or two localities. Thus the blue squill is found in any numbers only near Hartland in the north and on Burgh Island off the South Hams in the south; the Jersey crocus all but limits itself to Dawlish Warren; the whiterock rose makes its only home at Berry Head; the place for strapwort and wild seakale is Slapton Sands. It was at Stoke Fleming, near the Sands, that seakale was first experimented with as a vegetable, rapidly to become popular throughout the country. Alongside Slapton Sands is Slapton Ley, a remarkable sheet of fresh water separated from the sea only by a 3km.-long strip of beach, and nowadays a nature reserve, with a field centre at Slapton village. As may be imagined, the Ley is of as much interest to bird-lovers as to botanists, and another area of common appeal is Braunton Burrows, the vast expanse of sand-dunes north of the Taw estuary, though here matters are complicated for the naturalist by the use of the terrain as an Army firing range. Such commandeering of areas of special beauty or other appeal by the Forces stimulates much argument; leaving aside the necessity for the military to train *somewhere*, on the one hand the regions they pick are usually denied thereafter to the public, but on the other hand the flora and fauna, except when actually destroyed by the missiles (which is more rarely than the civilian is apt to think – much less than where they are exposed to motorists), are protected as in a nature reserve.

Devon's fauna enjoys the distinction of having provided not one but two central characters in minor literary classics, the nameless hero of the Hon. J. W. Fortescue's *The Story of a Red Deer*, first published in 1897, and Tarka in Henry Williamson's *Tarka the Otter*, published just thirty years later; there are also Mr Williamson's other animal protagonists, such as Salar in *Salar the Salmon*. Probably Fortescue's masterpiece (which also brings in many other Exmoor species) is all but unread today, which is a pity, for behind its seemingly naïve anthropomorphism (all the animals talk) there is a very accurate observation of nature, and the climax, which could have been intensely sentimental, is almost unbearably moving simply because the presentation is so dignified. The little book should be compulsory preliminary reading for everyone proposing to take up stag-hunting. (Incidentally, the tale is specifically set in the Devon, not Somerset, part of Exmoor.) Henry Williamson's stories are, fortunately, still widely read.

There were also red deer on Dartmoor once, but today the only large mammals there with even a half-claim to be wild are the ponies. There are, however, fallow deer and a growing number of roe in east Devon. Smaller mammals offer no rarities, though the little Japanese deer, recently introduced to Dartmoor, is sometimes seen. The black rat, of former bubonic-plague notoriety, still flourishes on Lundy, because the brown rat has never reached there to drive it out. The Revd S. Baring-Gould helped his brother to kill what they believed was the last wildcat in Devon. The fox is hunted in many areas, the rabbit doubtless would be if common enough; but since myxomatosis it has been surprisingly – and to the farmer, gratifyingly – slow to re-establish itself in Devon. The county is rich in bird species because it is so rich in diversity of habitat. As for fish, the first mention of salmon in Dartmoor rivers was made more than a thousand years ago, and trout, both sea and freshwater, flourish mightily. There is a falconry centre, one of the few in England where public demonstrations are given, at Cheriton Fitzpaine, between Crediton and Tiverton.

The principal Devon industry based on livestock was formerly the wool and cloth trade, but is now dairy-farming. Yet on Dartmoor the sheep is still king; and where there are sheep there are those most accomplished of all domestic animals, the sheepdogs. When a sheepdog becomes too blind and stiff to do its job it is not humiliated by being left at the farm while the others set forth. Its master shoots it. Sheep and ponies are also very much part of the Exmoor scene. The cattle country is mainly synonymous with the lush red-sandstone areas of the south, especially the Exe Valley and the South Hams. The once-famous cider-apple orchards have shrunk dismally since the days when those around Chardstock used to help stock the orchards of Tasmania. Fishing as an industry, never having meant to Devon what it did to Cornwall, caused less disaster when it declined. It is not dead; there are still fishing-fleets, if small ones, at most of the ports on both coasts. Brixham occupies a position of special importance because of its tradition of pioneering new fishing methods; Brixham fishermen put trawling on the map before it was adopted by the North Sea ports. They were helped by two things: the adoption of the fore-and-aft rig (a system said to have been observed on some Continental craft by sailors fighting in the Seven Years' War), which gave ships the extra strength needed to haul the trawls; and the opening of the turnpike road to Bath and Bristol, where there was a good market for the sole and turbot that were most easily caught by trawling.

Roads and Railways

Roads have never been among the brightest jewels in the Devonian crown. The Romans laid, as we have seen, a negligible foundation west of Exeter, and later roads tended to be laid down without coordination by different landowners. Since the most prominent landowners were the monasteries, not unnaturally the best roads were liable to be those that connected the abbeys with ports or with one another. But all roads remained poor; there was congestion even in the days of the packhorse, and the joys of travel were not enhanced by the prevalence of bogs, sudden mists, fallen trees and rocks, overgrown hedges, and forgotten mine-workings. John Macadam's admirable improvements in road-building had hardly been experienced in Devon when the debut of the railway, latecomer though it was (the first line, to Exeter, began functioning in 1844), seems to have put a damper on further development. There was, of course, some progress, but it was really not until the second half of the twentieth century that Devon could claim any example of up-to-the-minute road engineering. The pioneer enterprise was the opening in 1961 of the Saltash road bridge, which suddenly made it as easy to cross the Tamar as the Thames, eliminating at a stroke the long hours of waiting for a ferry agonizingly endured by motorists who never reflected that by driving a very short distance up-river (to Gunnislake) they could have crossed by a bridge anyway.

Having thus opened the way from Plymouth into south Cornwall, the planners' next task was to improve the road between Exeter and Plymouth, a project eventually achieved by converting the existing A38 into a dual-carriageway, with new bypasses where needed round difficult towns. Meanwhile the network of motorways over England was steadily being pushed ahead, and in 1976 the M5 linked Exeter (except for two short stretches still to be completed near Taunton) with Bristol, the Midlands and North, and London. It is too soon to say to what extent the new through-way will affect Plymouth's fortunes as a commercial port, particularly if the search for undersea oil is extended shortly to the English Channel. At present the city's maritime commerce scarcely extends beyond the receipt of a little oil, and the car-ferry services to St Malo and Roscoff.

The Saltash road bridge was not, of course, the first spanning of the lower Tamar. Alongside it is the wondrous railway bridge created by the dying I. K. Brunel just over a century earlier. In 1849, ten years before the bridge's opening, the railway had extended itself from Exeter to Plymouth – a major engineering accomplishment in its own right, as anyone noting the many long, high viaducts can judge. From this line short branches peeled off to most of the ports and resorts of the south coast, the longest being from Newton Abbot to Torquay and Kingswear. Northward, branches ran to Moreton-hampstead, Ashburton, Princetown, and Tavistock. With the London & South-Western as well as the Great Western taking a hand, other lines brought in such towns as Okehampton, South Molton, Bideford and Barnstaple, Ilfracombe, and, by the un-forgettable Barnstaple & Lynton narrow-gauge line, Lynton and Lynmouth. Bude, Holsworthy, Tiverton, Crediton . . . in the heyday of the railway hardly a place of any note and some of no note at all had their stations. Today nearly all the branch lines have been closed, amid loud protests and scrambles for a place on the last train by people who had not used any branch line for years. However, in contrast to Cornwall, Devon savoured a little of the modern disposition to buy abandoned lines from British Rail, restore the stations and rolling-stock as far as possible to what they had been before the Second World War, and reopen the lines to traffic. Thus the Torbay line, truncated by BR at Paignton, has been re-extended (in summer) to Kingswear by the Torbay Steam Railway, and the Totnes-to-Ashburton line has been resuscitated between Totnes and Buckfastleigh by the Dart Valley Steam Railway, though its periods of operation are at present somewhat spasmodic.

Traditional Events

Widecombe Fair is the only Devon festival to have won renown beyond the county borders comparable with that of Helston's Flora Festival or Padstow's Hobby Horse junketings. But a number of quieter traditions are annually observed, among them the

Ram Festival at Kingsteignton, the Glove Fair at Honiton, the Proclamation of the Lammas Fair at Exeter, Barnstaple Sheep Fair, Brendon Horse Fair, Tavistock Goose Fair, Princetown Dartmoor Pony Fair, and Turning the Devil's Stone at Shebbear. In addition there is the usual assortment of art, flower, cattle, horse, and agricultural shows, together with regattas and their variants. From time to time Plymouth Sound is the setting for highly spectacular events, such as the gathering of the 'tall ships' – the cream of the world's surviving great sailing-ships – in order to set out on a race across the Atlantic or round the world.

A Few Devon Specialities

Cider Neither the orchards nor the product flourish on the scale of former days, but in addition to Whiteways well-known cider factory at Whimple there are still a few small family firms operating, such as Inch's at Winkleigh, where genuine scrumpy is produced as well as more sophisticated ciders.

Cream As famous as ever, but according to old people not as good as it was before the modern method of separating was introduced.

Ashburton Pop An eighteenth-century brew, the recipe for which died with the inventor in 1785. Described as 'far richer than the best small beer' and with the 'explosive quality of champagne'.

Laver Edible seaweed of the Porphyra species, gathered chiefly at Ilfracombe and prepared for sale by boiling and adding vinegar and butter or lard. Three weeks after purchase more of these are added, and the laver, now in jelly form, is eaten with mutton or sprinkled with flour and fried in little cakes.

White Ale A Kingsbridge brew, now long abandoned but of many centuries' standing. It included malt, eggs, flour, salt, and 'grouts', a secret ingredient known only to successive generations of one family. Very intoxicating.

Cornwall

Cornwall and Devon are together unique among English counties in that they are the only two with considerable lengths of coast facing each point of the compass. In Cornwall long stretches of the so-called north coast face approximately west, as do the cliffs on either side of Land's End and the 'south' coast from Porthleven to Lizard Point. From the Lizard to Falmouth (with the exception of Veryan Bay), from the Dodman to Charlestown, and from Lamorna Cove to Penzance the general facing direction is east. In this respect Cornwall is like an island, and another characteristic shared with many islands is the feeling inspired that the sea is never far away. In truth, only east of a line running approximately from Tintagel to Fowey, less than a third of the total distance from the Tamar to Land's End, is it possible to be more than 17km. from one coast or the other. Thus only in the southern half of Bodmin Moor, or between there and the Devon border, does one get any sense of being in the Cornish interior at all. Out of a county border totalling about 310km., 240km. are coastline; and if one traced all the irregularities – for example, the windings of the Tamar along the land border, the many coastal estuaries and inlets – the percentage of coast to land frontier would be still higher. The area of Cornwall is comparatively small, 356,260ha. (or 1,356 square miles) including the Isles of Scilly, whose shores are not included in the coastline figures just given.

Early Cultures

Tucked away in their remote, nearly sea-girt extremity of England, the Cornish people might well have developed a sense of apartness, of separate identity, without the circumstances of history. But history has played an even greater part than geography in inviting the Cornishman to feel that a different world lies across the Tamar, by adding considerations of race and language. There seems to have been little human activity in the area we call Cornwall before the New Stone Age (2500–1600 BC). During that long period a number of settlements were established: relics have been found at Carn Brea, south-west of Redruth, and several other points, nearly all in western Penwith (the district between Land's End and St Ives). At Carn Brea excavations have disclosed, belonging to this period (there is also later material), axeheads and leaf-shaped arrowheads, some much-broken pottery, and several rude rock shelters. These earlier New Stone Age settlers came across the sea from France and were hunters who gradually learned to keep cattle, grow crops, and make clay vessels. About 1700 BC they were joined by further immigrants, this time out of Holland and the Rhineland, rather whimsically known as the Beaker Folk, from their habit of burying pottery drinking-vessels with their dead. It was probably they who introduced the first objects made of metal, to whit copper and gold, which their traders had discovered in Ireland: and there is evidence that they soon dominated the settlers already established. Megalithic tombs, long barrows, flint-mines, and stone-axe factories belong to this era.

The Bronze Age is generally reckoned to cover the years 1600–600 BC, but it established itself very gradually, and overlapped the New Stone Age by several centuries, during which the Beaker Folk interbred and blended with those they had at first regarded as subjects. The Bronze Age is divided into Early, Middle, and Late; and in Cornwall the Early Bronze Age is not one showing evidence of much advance in civilization. Some of the clans, chiefly on Bodmin Moor, lived a pastoral life; others, again on Bodmin Moor and also near the north-west coast, practised agriculture. The Early and Middle Bronze Ages were the periods when burial took place in round barrows and cairns, and when cremation began to be practised alongside ordinary interment. The great stone circles and stone rows, some (but not all) hut circles and pounds, many standing stones, and some later flint-mines, are of the Early or Middle Bronze Age, as are the quoits or tombs consisting of a huge capstone laid on several massive uprights, and the astonishingly large number of simple 'entrance' graves found in the Isles of Scilly.

Now for the first time we find Cornish tin entering the picture, for it was needed in the manufacture of the bronze. That there was trade in tin with customers far outside Britain – the trade popularized in the stories about the 'Phoenicians' – is evidenced by the discovery of Mediterranean objects on Cornish sites, and Cornish vessels made in Mediterranean style. Meanwhile trade in igneous rock for axe-making continued, and agriculture became increasingly sophisticated, as one can see in especially fascinating form at Gwithian, west of Camborne, where a field-system has survived even to the furrows formed by the ploughshares. The Late Bronze Age continued all these features of a developing culture, adding to them rectangular embanked enclosures and even a few settled farmsteads; but, contrary to likelihood, very little of this epoch has survived in Cornwall.

This, then, was the state of the peninsula before the Celts took it over; much of it had already been inhabited for something like 2,000 years by successive waves of immigrants who had evolved a culture primitive enough when compared with the contemporary civilizations of the Mediterranean or China, but which included, as numerous gold and bronze relics show, an aesthetic sensitivity far above the purely utilitarian, and was not too parochial to have, through trade, an awareness of other peoples and lands. It is more than possible that Bronze Age Britons sometimes sailed back to their commercial visitors, but this is hard to establish. The Celts did not, like later invaders, arrive more or less out of the blue. They were probably small groups of Celtic settlers among the Middle Bronze Age inhabitants of Cornwall, and certainly among those of the Late Bronze Age. But as the culture of the latter declined, three successive waves of Celts invaded the peninsula, the first between 500 and 300 BC, the second between 300 and 200 BC, and the third between 200 and 50 BC. These Celts were Iron Age people, and the builders of the great hill-forts and cliff castles. They also constructed villages of round huts within an enclosure, accompanied by fields outside. Quite often their villages were a continuation of existing Bronze Age settlements. The profitable tin-streaming and export was continued, and the prevalence of Iberian-style brooches suggests that Spain was now a regular trading partner.

Most of the hill-forts were built by the third group of Celtic invaders, whose pottery shows them to have come both from Brittany and from Spain. At last the written word comes to supplement the evidence of archaeology, and it is from Latin records that we know the Romans were aware of the South-Western settlers before they set out to subjugate them. The Iron Age occupants of Cornwall and Devon, together with the Bronze Age peoples who continued to some extent to live a separate existence on the moors, were lumped together by the Romans as the Dumnonii. The great majority of settlements were now in the west-Penwith region. Though the Romans penetrated perhaps as far as Land's End in search of useful metals, their presence in Cornwall must have been very lightly felt. No Roman town was built west of Exeter (Isca Dumnoniorum), nor any major roads. Only one villa has been found west of the Tamar. Life for the Dumnonii must have gone on very much as before, and in the far west there was certainly no appreciable admixture of Roman blood, if any at all.

Cornish history, as distinct from pre-history, will be dealt with a little later in this account; here the concern is to outline the racial make-up of the Cornish people. After the Romans had departed at the beginning of the fifth century AD, leaving the Celts and their predecessors uncontaminated, the South-West's next invaders were the Irish, including the large and strange group of Irish missionary-saints. The missionaries, from the very nature of their calling, could hardly introduce a new strain into the race, but the less saintly immigrants undoubtedly did so. They came in two phases, the first in the late fifth and early sixth centuries from south Wales, to which their forebears had emigrated a few generations earlier; this group settled in north Cornwall and north Devon. The second phase came direct from Ireland at the start of the seventh century and settled in the already populous Penwith. Thus Celtic blood was added to Celtic. During the seventh century also another momentous event happened: the West Saxons occupied Devon. The occupation was not entirely a matter of conquest; the same century, or possibly the sixth, saw a considerable migration from both Devon and Cornwall into Brittany, occasioned, it is believed, by a series of plagues and famines. Famine or no, the emigrants left empty some fine agricultural land, which the West Saxons simply annexed. Only later was the occupation extended by force, and in the north, without the Tamar to provide a barrier, it was extended well into north Cornwall, the Saxons driving the Celts – or British, as they can equally properly be called – ahead of them. The old realm of the Dumnonii, once covering the two counties, was restricted to rather less than the whole of Cornwall.

The Anglo-Saxon Chronicle and other accounts record various subsequent incursions into the county, in which the invaders did not always have it all their own way. Nevertheless, under the Saxon King Egbert (802–39) 'independent' Dumnonia existed only west of the rivers Lynher and Ottery, and it is highly improbable that the British remaining east of that line failed to interbreed at all with their Saxon masters, although for a time each group continued to live under its own laws – the British still nominally under the kings of Cornwall. Even after Egbert's much later successor Athelstan had completed the political conquest of Cornwall, bringing the Cornish kingdom finally to an end, turning Cornwall into a Wessex shire and fixing the Tamar as its boundary, British and Saxons continued to maintain their own communities side by side, as they did still further east as far as Exeter. Just how the communities of each race were distributed is revealed by the place-names – Cornish where Celts were established, English where there were Saxons. By the time of the Domesday survey, however, it is apparent that the Saxons (or Anglo-Saxons) enjoyed almost a full monopoly of land ownership and were broadly speaking the masters while the majority of Cornish were the serfs. The Norman hold on Cornwall integrated it politically even more securely with the rest of England than Athelstan had done; the Saxon landowners were now dispossessed as the Cornish had been, and although evidence is lacking as to the effect of this sudden common subjection of former masters and servants, it is logical to assume that a fair amount of integration gradually took place, and that only in the extreme west and small pockets elsewhere did the Celtic strain of Cornish remain comparatively pure.

Language and Place-names

One thing that always binds a people together is language; this is why, throughout history, conquerors have tended to attempt suppression of the indigenous tongue of the conquered, and irredentist movements have always fostered the indigenous tongue (if there is one) as a major factor in impressing the subject community with a sense of national unity. This racialist exploitation of language is far from being a thing of the past; it accounts for the strenuous efforts to extend the use of the Irish tongue (including the changing of many county and place names) after the establishment of the republic; for the agitations of Welsh nationalists for more Welsh-language television and radio broadcasts, and for such symbolic gestures as the compulsory posting of road signs in both Welsh and English; and it is responsible for the efforts to revive Cornish. The great difference between the movements to encourage greater use of Irish and Welsh and the movement to resuscitate Cornish is that Irish and Welsh were still living languages, if minority ones, whereas Cornish died 200 years ago. Its resurrection is an intellectual exercise that, if it is to succeed, must take the form of entire replanting on bare soil, since there is not even the meagrest growing plant to cherish. The impetus towards revival dates from the formation of the Federation of Old Cornwall Societies in 1920 (with later additions), and after more than half a century the enthusiasm of the propagandists is greater than ever. Whether the extent of their success is commensurate is perhaps not the business of anyone from the wrong side of the Tamar to judge. One can state only that in statistical terms, despite the publication of manuals of instruction, the holding of 'live' classes and correspondence courses, occasional broadcasts, and church services, the estimated number of persons able to speak Cornish has still to reach four figures, in a population of slightly over 380,000. (The detailed estimate in 1976 was between 200 and 300 speakers, of whom about 100 were fluent, plus 150 to 200 learners in organized classes and possibly as many more in outside classes.)

The chief benefit brought about by the revival movement (for all but Little Cornwallers wholly obsessed with politics) is the fillip given to the study of Cornish and its influence on the county's history and culture. For the traveller the readiest acquaintance with these matters, indeed one he can hardly avoid, is in place-names. Already by the eighth century the Cornish-speakers, except for small pockets, had been pushed by the Saxons into the area west of the Ottery and Lynher rivers. From then onwards the dominant language in east Cornwall was English, so the place-names in the east and especially the north-east of the county are nearly all of English (i.e. Anglo-Saxon) origin. How the Celtic tongue afterwards retreated further west is demonstrated by changes in the form of certain names. For example, the Cornish word for 'dwelling' was originally 'bod', but by the thirteenth century had changed to 'bos', and later still to 'boj'. Bodmin, in east-central Cornwall, displays the early form of the word, showing that English had ousted Cornish before the change to 'bos', or the name would have been changed to Bosmin instead of being left like a piece of seaweed grown rigid after the retreat of the tide. To the north, however, we have Boscastle and Bossiney, showing that although these towns are so close to the first area of Cornwall to be Anglicized, the old tongue persisted well into the Middle Ages, a circumstance not unconnected with the uninviting nature of the north coast and Bodmin Moor as viewed by the Anglo-Norman settler. Further west is a whole crop of 'bos' names: Bartholomew's *Gazetteer of Britain* lists about a dozen (to which must be added several too small for inclusion), but not one in the east or in the south to the east of St Austell. Of the nine 'bod' prefixes listed in the *Gazetteer*, only two are west of St Austell. As for the final modification 'boj', this is found only in west Penwith.

Other place-name prefixes and suffixes confirm the chronology indicated by 'bod–bos–boj', namely that the Cornish tongue, driven out of the north-east and east with the Saxon colonization, steadily retreated west and north until it remained in use only in the far west. It finally died out in the eighteenth century; by tradition, the last person to speak it (though many dispute the assertion) was Dolly Pentreath, of Mousehole, who died in 1777. A further tradition is that the last people to *understand* it were John Davey, of Zennor (1770–1884), and his son, also John (1812–91).

The Cornish Saints

The traveller interested in Cornish-language place-names will find a list of some of the commoner components and their meanings on p. 211. Another place-name feature highly typical of Cornwall is the number of unfamiliar saints represented in many names, saints virtually unheard of elsewhere in England, except in the dedication of churches in neighbouring Devon. These are the saints who, as stated earlier, swarmed across to the north coasts of Cornwall and Devon from Ireland and south Wales during the late fifth and early sixth centuries, to be followed by a second invasion around AD 600. Most of the saints were Irish, even those who came from Wales, where Pembrokeshire had been 'colonized' by Irish during the fourth century; but a few were Welsh, and a very few came from Brittany, mostly to Devon. Unfortunately the accounts of their coming and of their lives in Cornwall contain far more legend than history; yet they had an important bearing on Cornish development, for the forms of Christian belief and worship that they taught were not those of Rome, and it was the defence of their religious system as much as of their secular inheritance that inspired the dogged Cornish opposition to the strictly orthodox Saxons. Indeed, the Cornish were already well versed in resisting attempts by Rome to bring them to heel, for as early as the beginning of the seventh century St Augustine had convened a conference beside the Severn at which he tried unsuccessfully to Romanize the Celtic bishops. In about 700 Abbot Aldhelm of Malmesbury, in Wiltshire, wrote a letter to King Gereint of Dumnonia and all the clergy of his realm urging them to adopt Roman practices, and implying that if they failed any disaster that should come to them would be their own fault.

The Irish saints, then, however mythical the tales that they arrived drifting in exactly the right direction on a leaf or briskly paddling a millstone, had a very real impact on Cornish life and religion. Not that their appearance went unopposed: some on landing were involved in fights, others accomplished some or all of what they had set out to do but finished up as martyrs. One of the most eminent of the saints, if one dare use such a term of men and women professionally dedicated to humility, was, at it happens, not Irish but Welsh. This was St Petroc, or Petrock, whose story is relatively well documented by accounts in French, Welsh, and Northumbrian chronicles. He was one of the saints known as the Children of Brychan, or Brocan, a half-mythical King of Brecon; following an education in Ireland he came to Padstow (a corruption of Petrocstow) in about 560 and took over the small monastery lately founded there by St Samson, who wished to travel further afield. Later Petroc moved on to Bodmin, where he took over the hermit's cell founded by St Guron, and from there he journeyed widely in Cornwall and west Devon, founding monastic communities and not so much converting the heathen as reviving an already established but flagging Christianity, much as Wesley was to do in the same area twelve centuries later; and just as Wesley's recipe for Christian worship was not that of the Church of England, so Petroc's was not that of Rome. Even though this schism now belongs to the remote past, more churches in Cornwall and west Devon are dedicated to St Petroc than to any other saint.

Like Padstow, most place-names based on those of saints involve a corruption, sometimes considerable, of the prototype. Appendix I (*see* p. 209) gives a selected list of place-names and the original saints' names.

Geology

Broadly and somewhat non-technically speaking, Cornwall consists of four granite moorlands surrounded by a scarcely-interrupted cliff coastline extremely inimical to shipping. Granite is an igneous, i.e. originally molten, rock of a crystalline nature; the four moorlands are, from east to west, Bodmin Moor (by far the largest), the St Austell highlands, Carnmenellis (including Carn Marth and Carn Brea) between the Fal estuary and St Ives, and the St Just uplands north of Land's End. The Isles of Scilly are in a sense a fifth granite moor, of which only the highest points remain above the sea; this is consistent with the steady drop in the elevation of the moors from east to west, and brings us to the question of whether there is any real basis for the legend of Lyonesse, the land believed to have once extended between Land's End and Scilly. The answer is that there are good grounds for assuming a subsidence, but far back in geological time, many millenia before the age of man, let alone of historical man.

Cornwall reaches its greatest height in Brown Willy (420m.) on Bodmin Moor, closely followed by the neighbouring Rough Tor: not great heights, compared with four peaks of over 600m. and several above 550m. on Dartmoor, but the views from them cover the whole county, missing only the river valleys and areas hidden behind the other granite masses. A profile of the Moor shows these heights to be projections above a tableland, dissected over the ages by river valleys, but easily recognizable, about 330m. above sea-level; and the rest of the Moor to consist of a much larger tableland at a height of some 250m., broken into by a succession of summits down its eastern edge, of which the highest is Kilmar Tor (390m.).

The St Austell granite mass is especially interesting because in much of the area the rock has become 'kaolinized', or broken down into china clay by the chemical alteration of its crystalline felspar into a white clay or kaolin. (This has happened, too, in small areas of Bodmin Moor, notably in the south-west.) Dramatic visible evidence of this, or rather of man's exploitation of it, is the bizarre pyramids of gleaming white waste that cover much of the landscape, where until 200 years ago there were only rounded hills dotted with huge half-buried boulders, the remains of ancient tors. Just *why* the St Austell granite turned into kaolin has yet to be satisfactorily explained. All granite undergoes changes as the result of weathering, but nowhere else, on anything like a comparable scale, is the changed material arranged in parallel belts as here, nor associated with veins of tin. The explanation must lie somewhere in the particular chemical conditions brought about by the original consolidation and cooling of the granite, when fluorine-bearing gases caused alteration of the felspars and the formation of, among other products, the beautiful mineral tourmaline.

The Carnmenellis, or Wendron Moor, granite is notable, like the St Just mass, for the number of its veins of tin, or more properly oxide of tin (cassiterite), many of which extend beyond the granite into the adjacent slate. The tin veins are really fissures that have become choked by deposits borne on the gases, such as fluorine and boron, emanating from the granite just before it hardened. In many instances weathering of the veins in the remote past gave rise to alluvial cassiterte deposits in the beds of rivers and streams. This was the first tin to be extracted by man, as long ago as the Bronze Age, the process being known as tin-streaming. Not surprisingly, most of the alluvial tin sources eventually became worked out, though at least one firm in Camborne operates a modern streaming process.

The St Just granite is separated from the rest of Cornwall by the broad depression that runs from St Ives Bay to Mount's Bay (in which, incidentally, St Michael's Mount is itself an isolated granite outcrop); this wide vale was once a strait, and the distance between one sea and the other is only 6km. The coastal part of the granite area is flat-surfaced except where cut into by valley-forming streams, but a short distance inland one is confronted in many places by a line of antique cliffs that used to be the coastline when the land was about 120m. lower than it is today, and the present coastal plateau was part of the sea-bed. Behind the cliffs the land is more undulating. In the St Just region the tin-bearing veins extend under the sea, and in pursuit of them more than one mine has been pushed out far from the shore. Farther east along the north coast the sea-cliffs consist of igneous greenstone rock and unusually hard slate where the ocean has not yet encroached as far as the granite. Its failure to reach the granite is attributable to the slate and greenstone having been baked when in contact with the hot granite.

Slate – locally called killa – is a much commoner constituent of the Cornish cliffs than granite. From Newquay to St Ives in the north, and from Looe to Falmouth in the south, the cliffs are nearly all of slate, varying in colour but generally very dark. Mingled with the slate is some grit or quartz, and shale. Other parts of the north coast consist of green-stone, hardened schist, and culm (a grit, sandstone, and shale mixture); other stretches of the south coast consist of limestones and sandstones. In appearance the two coasts could hardly differ more. Along the north coast, from Cape Cornwall all the way to the Devon border, are cliffs hardly broken except by areas of blown sand, with few bays or inlets and fewer harbours; along the south coast, between Looe and Gillan Harbour, are numerous inlets and estuaries and several stretches of much gentler seaboard. South and west of the Gillan estuary, however, the coast and the country behind it change, sediment-ary Devonian rocks – sandstones and limestones – giving place to metamorphic, the term used when heat and pressure have so altered either igneous or sedimentary rock since it was formed that its properties are now markedly different. Schist is metamorphic rock, so is gneiss, and until a few years ago a type of schist known locally as blue elvan was blasted out of two huge quarries between Porthallow and Porthoustock for road-making.

At Porthoustock (*pron.* Proustock) the rock changes to a fairly rare type called gabbro, or locally crousa. This, like granite, is igneous and coarsely crystalline, but the crystals differ from those of granite. When the road-metal firm ceased quarrying the schist, they turned to gabbro at Porthoustock instead. Five km. south, Chynalls Point marks the boundary of the most remarkable rock formation in either Cornwall or Devon, the fam-ous Lizard serpentine. A very 'basic' igneous rock consisting of the mineral olivine altered in the dim past by contact with water, this beautiful grey-green stone used to be widely exported for building purposes, as well as used locally for buildings. Being very durable and easily trimmed, it is today the basis of a thriving souvenir industry based on Lizard Town, whose craftsmen spend their lives turning out ornaments as remarkable in quantity as they are in substance. The serpentine is not plain in colouring, but seamed with veins of olivine and hornblende in which the metamorphosis is not complete, giving an effect something like marble.

As one rounds the southernmost tip of Britain the rocks become more and more fascinating in their complexity. The celebrated beauty-spots Kynance Cove and Mul-lion Cove both consist of serpentine cliffs, but at Kynance the serpentine is a chromite (double oxide of chromium and iron) variety called tremolite, and is interrupted by 'dykes' – vertical intruded masses of black epidiorite (a variety of gabbro) – and areas of banded gneiss (metamorphic, granite-like rock with its constituents tending to be arranged in bands). Kynance Cove also contains soap-stone or 'French chalk', a kind of soapy-feeling talc that used to be quarried here for the making of Worcester china until the firm found something better. Mullion's cliffs are of orthodox serpentine, as are the off-shore stacks Scovard and Henscath. The serpentine extends far enough inland to form the underlying substance of the Goonhilly Downs. Covered by coarse, unproductive

clay, and virtually undrainable by artificial means, this tableland is impossible to culti-
vate and would be wholly abandoned to Nature were not an unnecessarily large part of
it abandoned to the Navy instead for its Predannack Airfield.

North of Mullion Cliff and about Mullion village, however, the rock is schist, which
makes the earth on top of it extremely fertile; and another oasis of fertility is to be seen
above the cliffs at and around Lizard Point itself, where the rock is again schist. This
account of the rock formations, which include some of the oldest and some of the rarest
rocks in Britain within a tiny area of Cornwall, let alone England, is still incomplete, for
there has been no mention of the curious intrusion round Black Head, south of Chynalls
Point, of a gabbro variant called flasser, a 'pepper-and-salt' rock of large black and white
crystals; nor of the 'Kennack granite', the pink granite of the Lizard Peninsula named
after the Kennack Sands between Black Head and Cadgwith (although the Caerver-
racks Reef that runs out to sea from halfway along the Sands is made of serpentine).

Greenstone has been mentioned in connexion with the coast between Cape Cornwall
and St Ives. It also occurs in isolated fragments on the western part of the south coast. St
Michael's Mount, as stated, is an isolated block of granite, but Chapel Rock, at the
shoreward end of its causeway, is of greenstone; and off Land's End itself the Longships
shoal, where the lighthouse stands, consists of porphyritic greenstone mingled with
quartz. In the extreme north-east of the county, where the culm measures are, the layers
of the earth's crust have shrunk so that they are wildly contorted, as one may see in
cross-section in the cliffs. The creased and folded rock is mostly the sandstone element of
the culm.

Of minerals locked in the Cornish formations the best known is, of course, tin; but
copper (in some quantity), iron, lead, gold, silver, arsenic, wolfram, manganese, zinc,
antimony, cobalt, bismuth, and even uranium are all present – the greatest variety of
minerals in one area anywhere in the kingdom.

Landscape

Scenically Cornwall is made up of large areas of pastureland and a smaller amount of
arable, both divided into many little fields by stone walls (called 'hedges'); and of the
granite moors covered with heather, rough grass, boulders (notably in west Penwith),
and bog flora (notably on Bodmin Moor, where the bogs are rather worse than those of
Dartmoor). In addition to those already described there are several smaller moors, or
downs, the majority on the fringe of Bodmin Moor, but including a large one south of the
Camel estuary, and Hingston Down north of Callington. Natural woods and forests,
except along the river valleys, in particular those of the Tamar, Fowey, Fal, and Helford, are extremely few: in fact it is no exaggeration to say that if it were not for the
plantations laid down mainly in the eighteenth century by estate owners and in the
twentieth by the Forestry Commission, there would be no Cornish woods of any size
away from the rivers at all.

From the configuration of Cornwall it follows that few rivers can by general English
standards be called long. The longest is the Tamar (94km.), and except in its uppermost
reaches even that is only half Cornish, its left bank being part of Devon; the Tamar is the
Great Divide, separating Cornwall from the rest of England, or as many Cornish would
have it, just from England, the alien world 'up-country'. The longest wholly Cornish

rivers are the Fowey (35km.) in the south and the Camel (50km.) in the north. Other rivers are the Ottery, Tiddy, and Lynher, all tributaries of the Tamar; the East and West Looe, the Fal and its tributaries, the Helford, and the Cober, all debouching on the south coast; the Camel's tributary the Allen; and the Hayle, the Valency, and the Strat, or Leet, all debouching on the north – and all three, compared with the south-flowing rivers, mere streams. But what the rivers of Cornwall lack in length they make up for in beauty, and in most cases in the wholly disproportionate size of the estuaries. Those of the Tamar and Lynher (also called the St Germans) are part of the complex forming Plymouth Sound. The combined Looes, the Hayle, even the Camel and Fowey, open out in their lower reaches in a manner suggesting far longer waterways, while the Fal and the Helford could without much exaggeration be called all estuary and nothing else. One factor in the beauty of all these rivers has already been indicated, the rich woodland covering much of their banks, which are often high and steep; another is the extreme irregularity of the estuaries, the shores of which not only wind but are broken by numerous subsidiary inlets, many of considerable size: the Fal and the Helford are outstanding examples. The tiny River Valency has a claim on the traveller beyond that of its intrinsic loveliness – the fame given it in prose and verse by Thomas Hardy.

The beauty of the enormous coastline lies chiefly, as must have already become apparent, in the height and ruggedness of the cliffs, but to give the full picture this needs amplification. Part of the attraction of the cliffs lies in the variety of their colours, from the restful grey-green of the Lizard's serpentine to the sinister – in wild weather extremely sinister – jet black of the towering heights near Boscastle. Another factor is the profusion of islets, stacks, and rocks of all shapes and sizes that rise out of the sea, in some cases as far as a km. and more from shore: an aesthetic asset even as they are a navigational nightmare. The coastal contour, too, gives rise to numberless coves and bays, many sheltered and sandy. Nor does the coast consist wholly of cliffs: there are lowland stretches, sometimes backed by large expanses of towans, or dunes, such as occur at intervals along the great stretch of north coast from Hayle to Bude, on the south coast near Par and at several points round the Lizard promontory, and in Scilly, notably on Tresco. In very recent times the opportunity to savour the Cornish coast – as those of the other South-Western counties – has been greatly enhanced by the establishment, under the auspices of the Countryside Commission, of the Cornwall Coastal Path, one of the series of magnificent long-distance routes for pedestrians (and in some instances riders and cyclists) that are being established throughout the country.

The Path is part of the South-West Peninsula Coast Path from Studland in Dorset to Minehead in Somerset, and the Cornish section alone measures 432km., some of it over rough and rocky terrain, some of it over plain turf but involving steep gradients. Where necessary, steps have been cut; where the path runs near the cliff-edge it has in some instances (but not all) been fenced; in one or two places it follows the shore below the cliffs. Some stretches adopt the old coastguard paths in use for centuries, others are brand-new tracks over ground that the public has never been allowed to walk on before. Several thousand oak signposts bearing the words 'Coast Path' or just the Commission's acorn 'trade-mark' have been erected. Some of the estuaries encountered can be crossed by the regular ferry services, for others the walker is recommended to negotiate with a local boatman, in one or two cases it is necessary to walk round the head of the estuary, while to cross Gillan Creek, in Roseland, you can, if you wish, wait for low tide and wade!

Several maps, guide-books, and details of accommodation along the route are published either by the Countryside Commission or the Cornwall Tourist Board.

The disproportionate amount of coast to land surface, and the alluring nature of so much of that coast, tend to make the visitor overlook the Cornish hinterland. By this is meant those districts far enough from the sea (including the headwaters of deep-penetrating estuaries) to give a 'feel' of being really inland, which virtually limits the application of the term to Bodmin Moor from Rough Tor southward, and the middle reaches of the Tamar. Yet Bodmin Moor has a personality as individual as that of Dartmoor. Like Hardy's 'Egdon Heath' before the Forestry Commission turned it into a conifer forest, the Moor's bleak and solitary expanses give an impression of size far in excess of the reality. Nor is the bleakness without beauty, for when the mists are not swirling, the quality of the light is startling. The broken outline of Rough Tor and the gentler one of Brown Willy look five minutes' walk away, though they may be several km. distant. In hot weather the shadows in the valleys are purple, and on a day of dappled cloud and fresh wind the patterns chase one another gloriously across the great sweeps. There is excitement in the knowledge that dangerous bogs wait to trap the heedless, a sense of eeriness, in the right conditions, about such features as Dozmary Pool or even man-made Fernworthy Reservoir. Here on the Moor, even on the summit of Rough Tor, are some of Cornwall's best relics of prehistoric man, peopling the solitudes like the very ghosts of their Stone or Bronze Age creators. Here, too, because the greatest mineral wealth tends to lie on the fringes of the county's granite outcrops, are the 'knackt bals', the abandoned mines of the last century, cheek-by-jowl with the traces of tin-working in both prehistoric and medieval times. It is strange that in certain guide-books to Cornwall published well after the Second World War the stacks and engine-houses of the Georgian and Victorian mines are deplored as blots and eyesores, for today they inspire most of us with the same sense of romance that our eighteenth-century forebears found in ruined castles, and few contemporary guides fail to offer approvingly at least one photograph.

As for the Cornish side of the middle Tamar, from east of Boyton, say, to the great loop north of Latchley, this is a countryside of fields and waterside woods – the largest, the wondrously-named Carthamartha and its neighbours, border the river for more than 6km. and are in parts more than 1km. deep – of large mansions and estates, such as Werrington Park and Landue, of villages whose charm would be an unfailing draw were they near the seaside resorts, and of some splendid old bridges.

Climate

The lushness of so much of Cornwall's vegetation is, of course, due largely to the climate. Being to all intents an island, and the sea with which it is girt being to all intents the broad Atlantic, the climate is nearly as equable as that of, say, Madeira: nearly, because snow and frost, even untimely spring frost, are not unknown, nor are droughts and heat-waves. There are also variations between different areas, small though the county is. The coldest month is January, when in the north-east the mean temperature is 6·3°C, but in the south-west 6·9°C. This difference may not seem great, but the north coast often feels much colder because of the westerly Atlantic gales, which blow with greatest frequency in autumn and winter and against which the high, exposed northern tablelands offer no protection except in a few bays or valleys. In the summer, on the other hand, the northern resorts are far more bracing than the southern, and not just for visitors; a Cornishman living in the 'neutral' interior, where local loyalties do not involve automatic disparagement of the other seaboard, is well aware of the differing physical effects on him of a spell at, say, Falmouth and a day at, say, Bude. In rainfall the divisions are vertical rather than horizontal on the map, and the variations are unexpectedly wide. The east, especially the north-east, gets least rain – 85cm. at Bude – the centre receives the most – 126cm. at Bodmin – but in the west the figures drop again to 110cm. at Falmouth. Even the Bude figure is above the national average. A further source of moisture is the heavy mists that come in off the sea, and those that too often blanket Bodmin Moor.

Flora and Fauna

Amid such mildness and warmth the vegetation is not merely rich but in the southern bays and valleys subtropical. Palms are common, and not a few Mediterranean species have their northern limits in Cornwall, whereas there are no alpine varieties, as there might be if the granite extrusions were higher. Lime-haters such as gorse and heathers cover much of the moors and northern cliffs; only the northern dunes and a tiny area of limestone north of Millbrook in the Tamar estuary produce lime-lovers. In gardens and parks rhododendrons, some of immense height and the great majority for some reason with bright-red flowers, are a familiar sight; and in the grounds of Cotehele, beside the Tamar, are two of what must surely be the largest magnolias in the country. In spring the high banks of the Cornish lanes (as of the Devonian) that make driving a continuous test of nerve are ablaze with primroses and violets. Among the humbler botanical orders ferns, mosses, liverworts, lichens, and fungi are abundant, some of them exotic species inadvertently introduced with imported specimens of higher plants. In the wettest Bodmin Moor bogs the sphagnum, or bog, moss is found.

A joy of many northern cliffs and the rocks at their foot, including some off-shore islands, are the golden and rock samphires (the rock samphire is common all round the Cornish coast). In past times the golden samphire was much sought for pickling, and many a life was lost trying to gather it. Shakespeare knew of both the custom and its hazards, referring in *King Lear* to the 'dreadful trade'. The golden samphire has survived better than some of those who gathered it, but the same cannot be said of the once well-established juniper, which has disappeared as a result of the custom (still prevalent) of extensive heath-burning during the winter. A much sadder disappearance, not yet complete but seemingly inevitable, is that of the elm. In addition to the common elm and the wych elm, Cornwall has its own species, the Cornish elm, which is the variety most frequently seen in the hedgerows and a great favourite with the planters of avenues; its great stronghold is the Roseland Peninsula. But, alas, the Cornish elm is no more immune to the deadly Dutch Elm Disease than the common elm, and unless botanical science can come up with some last-minute miracle it seems that the elms of Cornwall are destined to suffer the fate of those in the rest of the country. The authorities have offered free replacement of lost elms with seeds of a quick-growing conifer – but who wants them?

The appearance of trees in Cornwall varies with the part of the county. In the voluptuous valleys of the south they grow normally – especially the oak, which forms fine woodlands. But in the north and north-east the prevalence of strong winds always from the same direction – off the sea – tends to make the boughs of every tree stream out like flying hair, with the trunks leaning in sympathy. On the summit of Dizzard Point, south of Widemouth, the spectacle is still odder, for here is a wood of dwarf oaks, some of them less than 1m. high: fully grown, but stunted by the gales. These oaks are much smaller than those of the well-known Wistman's Wood on Dartmoor.

A catalogue of Cornwall's flower species, even of her rare species, so numerous are they, is outside the scope of this introduction; but mention must certainly be made of the botanist's most rewarding area, which is the same as the geologist's – the Lizard Peninsula. Indeed, the two aspects are interlinked, for much of the botanical interest is due to the presence of the serpentine and the soils to which it gives rise. Here, on Goon-hilly Downs, grows the Cornish heath (*Erica vagrans*) interspersed with gorse and black-thorn. On and near the cliffs are mesembryanthemums, butcher's broom (a woodland plant elsewhere in southern England!), the rare early meadow-grass, various clovers, including the large lizard clover otherwise known only in the Channel Islands, lesser bird's-foot trefoil, rare sea-stock, brookweed, yellow wallpepper, prostrate dyer's green-weed, rare spotted cat's-ear and rarer prostrate asparagus (Asparagus Island, in Kynance Cove, is so named because of it), autumn squills, Babington's leek, autumn ladies' tresses, and many more. Some of these are found in a few other Cornish locations, a minority are common. Nearly all, together with certain further rarities, occur also in the Isles of Scilly, particularly Tresco and St Martin's. Tempted by the climate, a num-ber of estate owners and public authorities have laid out gardens filled with subtropical plants, or with a blend of subtropical and indigenous species.

In contrast with the flora, Cornish fauna offer no great rarities or surprises. Of larger mammals, since the Goonhilly ponies ceased to roam Goonhilly Downs, none remains in the wild state outside the wildlife parks. None on dry land, that is; for the coastal waters abound in seals, which climb upon the rocks at the foot of the cliffs and endear themselves to all except the fishermen. Porpoises are not rare, and whales are sometimes seen. If Cornwall had a fish in its coat-of-arms it would have to be the pilchard, but this is only the most prominent of the dozen or more species of marine fish that have been com-mercially fished throughout the centuries. The latest tourist lure, which has headquarters at Looe, is shark-fishing. Cornish rivers contain good trout, and at the proper time sal-mon come up the Camel, the Fowey, and the Tamar. Bird life, understandably, means predominantly sea-bird life. The broad tidal estuaries give great opportunities to waders, and marshland species frequent the bogs of Bodmin Moor. But the county's armorial bird, the Cornish chough, black and sleek, with red bill and legs, died out some years ago, and to see it today the traveller must journey to Newquay Zoo, into which a breeding-pair was recently imported in the hope of eventually reintroducing the bird to the wild.

History

The early phases of Cornish history have already been touched upon in our quest for the origins of the Cornish race. We have seen how successive invaders down to and including the Romans subjugated the existing inhabitants without driving them from the territory they occupied, except in the sense that the savage Celts probably drove a good many of their predecessors into the next world. But the testimony of heredity, of present-day physical appearance, proves that they fell a long way short of exterminating all the Bronze Age dwellers, and that the Cornish claim to be of Celtic blood is only partly true. We have noted the considerable degree of culture attained in Bronze Age Cornwall, derived partly from intercourse with Mediterranean traders but possessing a distinctive British flavour. There was at least one Greek visitor – Pytheas, who late in the fourth century BC sailed through the Straits of Gibraltar, landed near Land's End and established good relations with the tin-streamers, then circumnavigated Britain and called again at Land's End before departing. Except perhaps by sea, it appears likely that the pre-Roman Cornish did not have the contact with the other settlements in Britain that these had with one another: the ancient trackways such as the Ridgeway that link other parts of south and east England have no extension into Cornwall that has so far been discovered. Nor, in this cosmopolitan south-west corner of the land, where men had learnt to fashion pottery and decorated metalware as fine as any in Europe, was there a single town; a situation left unchanged by the Romans, whose mantle, spread over Cornwall light as gauze, did not provide for the building of any town west of Isca (Exeter).

Nevertheless, it was through the Romans that Christianity reached Cornwall. Of the local religion before that we know next to nothing, except that in the words of G. M. Trevelyan, 'the paganism of the Celts in France and Britain was a religion of fear and priestcraft' – the priests being the Druids. The completeness of their ascendancy (attested by Julius Caesar himself) and the indelibility of the mark that it has left to this day is evinced in the popular attribution of practically every ancient monument and not a few traditional customs to 'The Druids', no matter how impossible. The Romans, tolerant of every form of faith provided they did not deem it a threat to their political authority, considered the Druids a threat of the first order and suppressed them. Until the reign of Constantine Christianity was also regarded as politically dangerous and was persecuted, as we all know, but it does not seem there was much persecution in Britain, perhaps none in Cornwall, where the people continued the same form of probably pan-theistic worship that they had practised under the Druids, and were hardly if at all touched by the new faith. Even after it had become the official religion of Rome a century before the Romans left, its advance was very slow, and after the Roman departure it was mainly the Welsh whose missionary work re-established it. But with the end of the Roman era began at least two centuries of the darkest part of the Dark Ages – dark not only in the absence of written records, but in the breakdown of the Romano-British civilization under the attacks both of invading Angles and Saxons and of the unsubjugated tribes of the north of our island.

Much of this chaos would have escaped the Cornish in their backwater. The earliest Church established by the Welsh missionaries was almost certainly monastic, a form continued by the cohorts of saints-in-training that subsequently arrived in waves from Ireland. Meanwhile the Saxon pirates were steadily ravaging what was left of Roman Britain, followed, paradoxically, by earnest settlers and their wives whose only aim was to till the land and reorganize it on a civilized footing. But in many regions there was a long interval between the destruction and the resettlement, and during this period the Welsh and then Irish church-based organization of Cornwall must have shone like a light, had anyone in the rest of the country been in a position to perceive it. This was a Celtic light, not a Roman one, for in Cornwall there had never been a Roman culture. There is irony in the fact that the only part of central and southern England that might have been too remote for the marauders to penetrate in their lust to destroy everything Roman, was the only one that had nothing Roman to destroy. Yet even the Celtic Church could not prevent a great cultural decline in Cornwall; its own exponents were too primitive. The great influx of British refugees, deprived of their Roman towns and outer trappings, and finding themselves among an indigenous population that had never had those things, inevitably sank back, if not into barbarism, at best to the lower cultural level of their involuntary hosts. But if the Celtic clergy were primitive in terms of Roman culture, they were men of intelligence and some learning, as witness their ability to defend their version of Christian belief and practice against the demands that it should defer to that of Rome. They kept barbarism at bay until the general raising of cultural levels removed its threat.

Politically, Celtic kings continued to rule long after the Saxons, having mastered Devon, colonized the east of Cornwall. The colonists, whom by now we may call English, were administered by two reeves appointed by the King of Wessex. The native Cornish dynasty finally ceased contemporaneously with Athelstan. The persistence of this dual harness reflects the long-lasting hatred of the Cornish Britons – or West Welsh, as the English called them – for the invaders; a hatred still reflected in the dislike of all who live 'up-country' felt by the more fanatical Little Cornwallers of today. This early hatred was the chief reason why the Christianizing of the Anglo-Saxons was not initiated by the Celtic Church.

In 836 the Cornish – or West Welsh – took advantage of a Danish raid to ally themselves with the invaders in a revolt against the English, but were defeated by King Egbert in 838 in a great battle on Hingston Down.

This might be called the only serious contact between the Cornish and the Danes. Whether a combined victory would have paved the way for a complete Danish conquest of Wessex, such as so nearly occurred a mere forty years later when only the genius of Alfred averted it, is material for interesting if academic speculation. But Alfred defeated the Danes, who, settling in large numbers in an area far from Cornwall, turned quickly from marauders into farmers and traders; and when the second wave of Danish attacks under Sweyn and Canute resulted in the latter becoming king of the whole country, the event must have been hardly known, let alone felt, in Cornwall. In the meantime Athelstan had consolidated Anglo-Saxon authority by awarding most of the Cornish land holdings to English landlords, and by moving the Celtic Church in the county toward acceptance of Rome with the creation of a bishopric at St Germans and the provision of other ecclesiastical endowments.

The Normans invaded England, and after the Cornish had helped the men of Exeter to hold out for eighteen days against William, the Conqueror, like Athelstan nearly two centuries earlier, assigned the Cornish estates to leading men of his own race, much of the territory going to his half-brother, William de Mortain, whom he created Earl of Cornwall. This earldom became customarily held by the King's eldest son; and in 1337 its status was elevated to that of a dukedom, the oldest in the country. The first Duke was the Black Prince, and since then the Sovereign's eldest son has always been Duke of Cornwall. But despite this rather naïve attempt to tie them to the Crown, the Cornish remained by temperament rebels and supporters of lost causes; almost the only exception was their support of the Lancastrian cause in the Wars of the Roses. But hardly had the Lancastrian victor, Henry VII, ascended the throne than in 1486 a body of Cornishmen, incensed at the weight of taxation imposed by him for the Scottish wars, rose under one Thomas Flumank and marched to Blackheath, where the royal troops in a brutal rout killed 2,000. Wholly undeterred, and no doubt nursing vengeance, a year later another Cornish body rose in support of the pretender Perkin Warbeck, who had landed near St Ives and been proclaimed King Richard IV. This time the rebels got no further than Exeter before disaster overtook them. In 1549 the order to the churches to adopt Cranmer's Prayer-Book and conduct services in English provoked the Cornish, to many of whom English was still as much a foreign language as Latin, into an armed rising in which, egged on by the Catholic priesthood, the peasantry of Devon joined. But the Protestants of Exeter, despite many Catholic sympathizers in their midst, withstood a six-week siege, which gave the government time to organize an army under Lord John Russell. Crosses, holy banners, censers, and candlesticks were no match for military experience, and after defeating the rebels in three successive encounters Russell indulged in the type of savage vengeance that in the sixteenth and seventeenth centuries was one of the hallmarks of Christianity, whether Catholic or Protestant.

During the Civil War Cornwall on the whole was fervently Royalist, especially the estate owners. There were exceptions, such as the Eliots of St Germans – Sir John Eliot had died in the Tower rather than forswear his championship of English law – and Robartes of Lanhydrock; and one or two towns, such as St Ives, were always pro-Parliament. But the conflict continued in the county until well after its termination everywhere else, and in Scilly longer still; the islands, which in 1645 had been the last English refuge of Prince Charles, did not surrender to Parliament until 1651, two years after the official end of the renewed hostilities. The extent to which battles and sieges took place all over the county may be gathered by the many references in the gazetteer section. Many lives were lost, but the principal outcome was the severe impoverishment of the people by the heavy financial exactions of both sides. Yet even this was less long-lasting than the impoverishment of the churches by Puritan vandalism. However, neither of these misfortunes was limited to Cornwall; for though many did not realize it and would not have acknowledged it if they had, in most respects the county had long been an integral part of England.

The eighteenth century began as a quiet period of fishing, mining, smuggling, and spiritual apathy; and so it would probably have continued, at all events until the war that followed the French Revolution, had it not been for the explosive arrival of John Wesley in 1743. It has been said that no one individual throughout history has ever made such an impression on Cornwall; and in our own day experts on the working of the mind have suggested that Wesley knew all the techniques used by the great dictators and demagogues of the twentieth century to sway the masses, with the difference that he employed them to better ends. Cornwall that had held out for the Celtic Church against the Roman and the Roman against the Reformation and the Puritans, now became the greatest Wesleyan stronghold in the land. Methodist chapels burst out like spring blossoms all over the place. Audiences of rough miners and fisherfolk, to the tune of tens of thousands at a time, listened spellbound in such open-air theatres as Gwennap Pit near Redruth, oblivious of heat or cold, mist or rain. The convulsions, screams, and raptures of the converted were such as have not been seen before or since in this island, and scandalized the Established Church and upper classes.

If the coming of Methodism was the great Cornish happening of the eighteenth century, the coming of the railway was that of the nineteenth; and it came only just in time, for before the end of the century all three staples of the Cornish economy – fishing, mining, and smuggling – had collapsed. Only china clay was left, and although a near-monopoly in the country, it could not sustain the county. Still less could the relatively new early-flower industry. Salvation came with tourism, and tourism (in contrast with parts of south Devon, where it began during the Napoleonic wars) came with the trains. Nor has it ever diminished; on the contrary, when the motor-car added itself to the locomotive it was the signal for the summer influx to become a serious embarrassment. 'The Cornish don't want you, but they want your money' is a phrase currently heard. The rather churlish assertion, certainly belied by the warm and courteous hospitality of nearly all the Cornish people a visitor is likely to meet, does cover a dilemma, which is, quite simply, how to fit everyone in without life becoming unendurable. Cornwall is small and cornet-shaped, with nothing beyond it but the Isles of Scilly and the Atlantic. Devon is not only much larger, but – bearing in mind that nearly every holidaymaker enters from the east – enjoys the comfort of knowing there is still one county further west that the visitor can move on into. But Cornwall is the end of the line, and in the height of the season only the Channel Islands are more densely thronged.

The trend to better main roads, with bypasses round towns, accentuates the problem by simply encouraging more motorists, who find that the minor roads on which many resorts depend cannot accommodate the press of cars, nor can fishing-ports built on the flanks of steep and narrow clefts provide parking-space. Yet what is the alternative? Certainly not the railway, which in the whole county consists of one main line (subject to constant rumours that it is to be closed) with a few short branches. The very development that originally turned Cornwall into a tourist centre by making it so easy for people to come and go has now forsworn its responsibilities. Modern maps abound in unintentionally apt broken lines and the words 'track [or 'course'] of old railway'. True, some of these lines were built only to carry granite or mineral ore to the nearest port, but many were intended for passengers as well, such as the route that, after crossing the Tamar near Lifton, ran through Launceston to Hallworthy, Camelford, Wadebridge, and Padstow, or the Redruth–Perranporth–Newquay branch, or Camborne to Helston, or the two lines (one from Okehampton, one from Launceston) that used to serve Bude.

Before the railway fully extended itself in Cornwall, coastal shipping played a large part in the conveyance of passengers and goods. Ships from Bristol and south Wales plied regularly to several of the northern ports, and in the south it was regarded as a pleasant and cheap variation on land travel to take the steamer to Plymouth from Southampton or even London. To arrive at Plymouth by a regular passenger service today it is necessary to cross first to France. There are direct air services from London and other centres to the civil airport at Newquay, and helicopter as well as aeroplane services nowadays connect Penzance with the Isles of Scilly for those unwilling to face the notoriously rough sea voyage.

Towns

Cornwall is not a county of large towns. Until a century ago, when Truro was promoted in deference to its new cathedral, there was no *city* at all. And the town showing the largest population at the last census is really two towns, Camborne and Redruth, whose combined population is barely over 42,000. St Austell and Fowey, also combined, show just over 32,000, and then comes a drop to 19,500 in Penzance and 18,000 in Falmouth. The City of Truro musters not quite 15,000. No one built a town in the south-west peninsula west of Exeter before the Saxons, nor is it easy to define precisely what constituted a town in the earliest stages. Probably it is best defined as a place with a larger population than the average settlement, and a market, implying some kind of activity other than agriculture. The Saxons themselves in their scanty literature have left us no specific mention of Cornish towns, nor has archaeology yet unearthed unmistakable urban remains (whether Saxon or Celtic) except where the existence of a town was already known through other sources. Chief of these sources is the Domesday survey, for any town recorded in its pages almost certainly existed twenty years earlier, that is to say before the Conquest. The towns noted in Cornwall are Bodmin (the largest, with sixty-eight houses), Liskeard, St Stephen's-by-Launceston, Trematon (where Trematon Castle now stands, near Saltash), and Methleigh (now Porthleven). In addition Domesday implies embryonic towns at Stratton and Helston, and other sources record a market centre at St Michael's Mount. Such were the first recorded towns in Cornwall, and of the brief list Trematon and St Michael's Mount cannot be numbered among the towns of today. But kings and noblemen also founded towns; good natural harbours engender them as shipping develops, so does the establishment of fixed mines. Two centuries after Domesday the number of Cornish towns had grown to forty, though again some were destined not to stay the course: such places as Tregoney, with a present population of about 300, and Wick St Mary (385) have never really grown, while Mitchell, now a hamlet, and Cergoll, now a mere farm, have shrunk.

The importance of individual towns in different periods, as expressed in other ways than by population figures, is often harder to assess. Was a port such as Fowey, now a flourishing tourist centre with a sideline in shipping china clay, more important when it was a major English trading and naval centre from early-medieval to late-Tudor times? We can say that in the heyday of mining St Just-in-Penwith, for instance, was more important than it is now, and that Truro, now a cathedral city, is more important than it was before the nineteenth century. St Austell was less important when it was just one of many towns concerned with tin than now that it has become the china-clay capital of the United Kingdom. St Germans, on the other hand, has but a shadow of the status it enjoyed when it was (with Bodmin) the seat of the old Cornish bishopric. But with many towns, since the majority are on the coast, it is a straight question of whether they gain more in prosperity and general quality of life from today's holiday trade than they gained of old from fishing; for in the history of Cornwall fishing has been a way of life at least as long as the extraction of tin; and both, as stated earlier, have suffered a disastrous decline.

The Fishing Industry

For the modern traveller, seeing the handful of fishing craft, half lost among the more numerous holiday yachts, which are all that put out from any but two or three Cornish ports today, it is hard to picture the huge scale of the fishing industry in its prime (and it had a long prime). Many types of fish were sought, but the most important was undoubtedly the pilchard, which would appear in about July in huge shoals off Land's End and spread along both coasts. The season normally lasted until October, but occasionally it extended to Christmas or even into the New Year. The statistics of pilchards caught would be unbelievable if they were not so well authenticated. Between 1747 and 1756, for instance, the number of pilchards sent off from the four main ports alone – Fowey, Falmouth, Penzance, and St Ives – averaged 90,000,000 a year, and for the remainder of the century this average was exceeded. The peak year was 1796, when more than 200,000,000 pilchards were exported. But during the nineteenth century even these figures were beggared. Between 1829 and 1838 St Ives by itself exported to Italy alone an annual average of 27,000,000 fish. The all-time high in catches occurred on a November day in 1834, when the seine-fishing fleet from St Ives caught 30,000,000 pilchards in *one hour*.

A seine-net was an enormous sheet of mesh, generally made at Bridport, in Dorset (though at the height of the fishing boom St Ives had its own factory), and measuring some 400m. × 21m., with cork floats along one edge and lead weights along the other. At the beginning of the season the great fleet of boats (400 at St Ives) would be taken down to the water – every boat filled with children singing traditional songs; the children would get out, the fishermen in, and each seine unit of three boats would be rowed to its allotted station in the bay. Meanwhile on the headland the 'huer' or look-out man would keep watch until a disturbance and discoloration of the sea told him a shoal was approaching. He would then sound a blast on his long trumpet, and from the watchers on shore would go up a shout of 'Hevva, hevva!' (from the Cornish word for a shoal). While such women and children as were not already on the beach turned out of their houses in readiness to handle the landed catch, the huer would take up a pair of 'bushes', small tufted branches, and standing on top of his (stone) hedge would signal to the seine-masters exactly whither the shoal was heading. The oarsmen manoeuvred the boats into position, the huer would give the word through a speaking-tube to shoot the seine, and each net-carrying boat would pay it out in a near-circle. The second boat in the unit then dropped a smaller net to close the circle, the fish now being inside. The third boat, carrying the seine-master, then joined the nets together, following which tow-ropes attached to capstans on shore carefully drew the circles of net with their millions of trapped fish into shallow water.

Into each circle a 'tuck-net' was now lowered, one edge remaining attached to the boats and the other having fitted to it long ropes that at the proper moment were drawn up to the surface so that the tuck-net emerged laden with pilchards. Baskets were used to scoop them into boats appointed to ferry the catch ashore. Here carts, or at ports where carts could not reach the waterside, boxes on long poles, sedan-chair fashion, received the fish and conveyed them to the various cellars or 'pilchard palaces' still to be seen in many former pilchard-fishing ports, where the waiting children handed the fish to the women to stack in rows, a layer of salt being placed above each row until the stack became too high to raise any further. If the catch was big enough the work went on all night, possibly several nights; the word went around, bringing in helpers from villages perhaps far inland. After some weeks the pilchards were put into hogsheads and pressed down with stones to extract the oil (formerly used for lighting), and only then did the town-crier summon the seiners to an inn to be paid. Most of the fish, as already indicated, was exported, but some was sold fresh in the surrounding country.

Seine-fishing for pilchards was an inshore enterprise, and it ceased when the vast shoals ceased to swim into inshore waters. At St Ives, the greatest of the pilchard ports, it died before the general end, and all because of John Wesley. The fishermen, strict Methodists, would not in any circumstances fish on Sunday, so that if a shoal for which they had been waiting perhaps for weeks appeared on a Sunday, they let it go. But their rivals in Newlyn and Mousehole, broader-minded, took the view that if God sent them a shoal on Sunday he meant it to be caught on Sunday, and they caught it. The fish-merchants accordingly moved over from St Ives to Newlyn, and that was that. Of course many fishermen, not only in St Ives, attributed the end of the pilchard visits to the divine wrath. Others accounted for it by the introduction, just before the end, of the practice of curing in tanks instead of by the traditional method. Others again, the most practical, suggested that the huge annual catches had over-fished the grounds, or that the shoals no longer came because the collapse of tin-mining had removed the 'red' waste-water formerly discharged from the mines, which the pilchards were said to like. But the real explanation, or at any rate the one believed by all Cornish fishermen, is the increase in the number of deep-sea trawlers, which break up the shoals and destroy large numbers of immature fish. Not that pilchard-fishing has entirely gone; but such fish as are now caught are taken far out at sea by drift-net, in the same way as mackerel and herring.

A drift-net resembled a seine in having floats along one edge, but it had no weights on the other, for there was no question of it touching the sea bottom; it would be trailed in the water behind the boat, sometimes several nets attached end to end so that they trailed for a km. or so. The herring season followed that of the pilchards, and was in turn followed by that of the mackerel, though mackerel had a second season in the autumn. The herring-fishermen, who operated only from St Ives and the ports in Mount's Bay, sailed far afield, sometimes round the north of Scotland and back through the Irish Sea. The great boom in both herring and mackerel followed the advent of the railway in 1859, for now the fish could be sent off fresh to London. But this industry, too, was decimated by the 'foreign' trawlers, whose nets, dragged along the sea bottom, wrecked everything in their path. They also, of course, ultimately ruin an area for themselves, which is why the trawlers have to be ever seeking new grounds.

Where mackerel are fished from Cornish ports (such as Looe) nowadays, they are fished either by trawling three lines, fitted with baited hooks, from each boat (one from the stern, one from a rod projecting on either side) or by 'feathering', in which a length of line with a lead weight on the end and a dozen hooks ranged above it is dropped into the water, each hook being baited with a feather. The mackerel go for the feathers so fast that often every hook has secured a fish before the operator has finished paying out. The line is then rapidly hauled in, the fish are deftly removed, and the process is repeated. This strange but highly successful method was not discovered until the late 1950s. Another inshore fishing method in vogue today is long-lining; a line up to 15km. long, carrying a baited hook every 2½m., is trailed behind the boat. Conger eel, whiting, hake, skate, and several other larger fish are caught this way, which is much practised at (for instance) Mevagissey. But long-lining can be adapted to catch smaller fish, and is used at Polperro to catch pilchards.

In the main, however, the modern Cornish fishing industry is a microcosm of its old self. At Mevagissey the fishermen have their own cooperative, but perhaps only Newlyn does anything on a scale comparable with the old days (and certainly not comparable with the real boom periods). Here they have the facilities for fishing in the distant

Atlantic, where there are still pilchards as well as the popular tuna. Trawling, long-lining, and a method called ray-netting or tangle-netting are employed, and Newlyn has its own canning factory ashore. Also worthy of mention are the crab, lobster, and cray-fish industries in some ports (the threat here is from skin-divers, who denude any area in which they operate like a plague of locusts) and the oyster-beds in the ramifications of the Fal estuary. Here you may still experience the pleasant sight of fishing-boats under sail, for the plain reason that the use of motors would kill off the oysters in a couple of seasons. The oysters are dredged up in bag-shaped nets, the mouths of which are held open by iron frames, the bottom of each frame being fitted with teeth to prize the oysters off the bottom. It is a much more difficult operation than it may sound, for each boat has to be manoeuvred in the narrow creek while dragging the equivalent of a heavy anchor, and there is the tide as well as the wind to reckon with. Other oystermen dispense with sail and work by dropping an anchor, rowing away from it, and then hauling them-selves back by the anchor-cable while trailing the oyster-dredge behind them. The oysters cannot be sold for immediate consumption because the Fal bears a high content of poisonous copper in solution from old mine workings; so the catch is sold to middle-men who put it down in 'artificial' beds in the clearer waters of (e.g.) the Helford River, and when the oysters have got rid of their copper they are purified still further – under Government supervision – in special tanks.

Mining and Quarrying

The once-great Cornish tin industry is also a shadow of its former self, but it is pleasant to be able to record a modest revival, which there are plans to make immodest once the economic climate improves. During the first half of this century mine after mine was shut down until only the South Crofty Mine at Pool (Camborne) was still in operation. But today there are four – mining zinc and copper as well as tin: South Crofty and Wheal Pendarves, in the Camborne area, Wheal Jane at Baldhu (between Redruth and Truro), and the combined Geevor–Levant Mine running under the sea near St Just. There are also three tin-streaming or surface-dressing works: Tolgus Tin at Redruth, Hydraulic Tin at Bissoe, and Wheal Josiah over the Devon border near Tavistock. Tin-bearing lodes have a habit of running in nearly vertical diagonals in the granite. From the main shaft tunnels called levels are driven across each lode, and above each level is a sub-level. The miners go into the sub-levels and with pneumatic drills bore holes in the lodes above their heads. Blasting-charges are put in, and down comes the ore. Most of it is shovelled through a hole at the far end of the sub-level floor into trucks in the main level, which take it to the shaft to be carried to the surface, but enough is left for the miners to stand on and be able to reach to drill the next hole. When the blasting has gone through the lode and the granite on the other side is reached, all the ore below is pushed through the hole. Not all lodes run in a direction to make this method practicable, and modifications are made as required. There is a certain amount of danger, the chief being that of developing silicosis, though water-bearing drill-bits and other dust-laying devices have greatly lessened the risk. The Cornish miner of former times had the shortest working life of any calling in the country including coal-mining.

The slate quarries once so numerous in the country were reduced in number when the coming of the railway to north Cornwall gave the huge Delabole complex such an advantage over its rivals (nearly all of which, as it happened, produced slate of inferior quality) that they were forced to close. Today the threat, even to Delabole, comes from the use of plastic 'slates' and other artificial roofing materials. With so many means of livelihood failing in the nineteenth century, it is not surprising that there was a great deal of emigration, particularly among miners. At the very time when the Cornish mines were closing, the great gold, copper, and diamond mines of Rhodesia and South Africa were opening up. Between 1811 and 1841 the population of the county rose by more than 121,000, and altogether between 1801 and 1861 it rose from 192,000 to 369,000. But between 1861 and 1891 it fell back to below 323,000, and not until 1971 was the 1861 figure again reached. A few of the emigrants eventually returned, almost always with their health broken; the majority did not, and as a result there was a period when the people of Cornwall knew more about events in South Africa than about those beyond the Tamar at home, and a journey to Durban or Jo'burg was a more familiar event than one 'up-country' to London. Even today, though mass emigration has long ceased, the ties between Cornish people at home and kinsfolk in South Africa are numerous and strong.

Smuggling and Wrecking

To the 'foreigner' whose knowledge of Cornwall is derived from the sillier and therefore most popular sort of 'historical' novel (whether actually read or just seen in televised adaptation), the commonest activities of the Cornishman in past centuries, particularly the eighteenth, were smuggling and wrecking. The 'wrecking' can be dismissed with brevity because it is nearly all myth, one more of the many legends with which Cornwall is bedizened. All the talk of luring ships to their doom by false lights and other tricks is moonshine, as the total absence of any charges in the Assize reports bear witness. Undoubtedly the coast-dwellers regarded the spoil from a wreck as fair takings; so did the seashore dwellers round the whole of Britain and much of the world. And no doubt, since the looters were tough folk, there was the occasional murder of a shipwrecked mariner who tried to defend the cargo; but far from guiding ships on to the rocks, the Cornish record for saving lives is admirable, and is fitly symbolized by the achievement of Henry Trengrouse, the cabinet-maker of Helston, who after witnessing an inshore wreck that cost a hundred lives, devoted much of his own and all his £3,500 fortune to perfecting a life-saving rocket apparatus, for which a grateful Government gave him £50.

Theoretically the right to all wreckage belonged originally to the Crown, but as time went on the owners of estates bordering the sea put forward their own claims, and such illustrious families as the Arundells and the Godolphins did not hesitate to contest the intervention of royal officials. In due course a system emerged under which the Crown retained the right of wrecks but paid out royalties; and the Arundells, among others, made a regular and handsome income by this. The nearest to deliberate wrecking is to be found in a single incident in which Lady Killigrew, of the family that virtually founded Falmouth, in 1582 ordered the seizure of a Spanish ship in Carrick Roads, had its cargo removed to her own home, and saw to it that most of the crew were drowned. Otherwise the popular attitude is best summed up in the prayer that Parson Troutbeck, of Scilly, is alleged to have added to the Litany: 'We pray thee, O Lord, not that wrecks should happen, but that if wrecks do happen, Thou wilt guide them into the Scilly Isles, for the benefit of the poor inhabitants'. This may be apocryphal, but the sentiment is not.

Smuggling has a much firmer basis of fact than deliberate wrecking. For one thing, few people – and by no means only in Cornwall – regarded it as 'wrong', and customers for the smuggled goods belonged to all classes including the clergy ('brandy for the parson' is not a songwriter's figment), just as today not many people draw back from a bargain just because they suspect it may have 'fallen off the back of a lorry'. But the vast majority of beneficiaries from the smuggled goods were the very poor, and for them it sometimes meant literally the difference between subsistence and slow death from under-nourishment. Knowing this, many smugglers regarded themselves as fit and proper free-traders; one even forbade all bad language among his crew, and later, when a fugitive in Brittany, conducted regular Sunday services for his fellow-exiles. At the same time, smuggling was no kid-glove affair, and armed fights with the Excisemen were both fierce and frequent. On occasions, too, one side or the other mistook some inoffensive third party for an opponent. Probably only one smuggler went to the length of mounting a battery of guns on the cliffs to cover the illicit landings; this was John Carter, known from his likeness to Frederick the Great as the King of Prussia, and his guns were sited above the inlet near Perranuthnoe still called Prussia Cove.

This is but one of a host of smuggling stories, many invented, some true, some a mixture of truth and fiction, that surround this once common activity. No one knows when it developed: probably not to any marked extent before the eighteenth century, and it began its slow decline only in about 1840, finally dying out before the end of the century. Most of the contraband came from France, and most of it consisted of brandy and other spirits; but tobacco, fine-quality textiles, and a few other commodities were involved from time to time. The notion that Wesley killed smuggling is one of the smuggling myths; for a long time Methodism and the contraband trade went happily hand in hand.

Traditions and Legends

The Cornish of the eighteenth and nineteenth centuries not only smuggled much liquor, they drank vast quantities: primarily the tinners, who seem to have earned the greatest reputation for hard drinking, but men – and to a lesser extent women – in all spheres. Drunkenness was not only common but well-nigh universal and led to much brutality, especially in the home. One of the readiest occasions for getting drunk was the day or days of the local fair, when the public houses and kiddleywinks (beer houses) were allowed to remain continuously open. The purpose of the fairs was the marketing of live-stock and other goods and the hiring of farm employees, but amusements were not over-looked, including displays of the once celebrated Cornish wrestling. The largest fair was that of Summercourt, now just an insignificant hamlet near St Enoder. Another of equal importance was the Corpus Christi Fair at Penzance, which lasted three days. Next came St Peter's Fair at Camborne, where the drunken fights toward the close of the day were worse than at Summercourt or Penzance because of the perpetual rivalry be-tween Camborne and Redruth men. As in other counties, nearly all the fairs have either vanished or become debased into mere mechanized fun fairs, the marketing that was formerly their *raison d'être* having passed to the cattle markets and agricultural shows.

Festivals likewise have fallen from their former estate. Some died out because their pagan origins and unseemly practices were inveighed against by Wesley, others, more recently, because of the advent of cheap mass entertainment in its various forms. Of those that remain, the most widely known are the 'Obby-'Oss ceremonies at Padstow and the Furry at Helston. Another is the annual hurling game at St Columb Major; all these are described under the appropriate entries in the gazetteer section. The hurling game is also observed at St Ives. At St Cleer, near Liskeard, a 10m.-high pyre is lit on St John's eve, into which herbs and other plants that are known to guard against witches have been placed. In August Marhamchurch near Bude holds a Revel Sunday. A festival of a rather different type is the Gorsedd of the Cornish Bards, the counterpart of the Welsh Gorsedd except for the trifling matter of a gap of perhaps 2,000 years in the continuity of the Cornish ceremony. Revived in 1928 by the indefatigable Old Cornish Societies, and repeated every year since except during the Second World War, the Gorsedd is an occasion for the exercise of the Cornish language and fraternization with the Welsh Druidical leaders and those of the Celtic communities in Brittany and elsewhere. Each year the venue is a different spot believed to be associated with similar ceremonies in antiquity.

Cornish legends, traditions, and superstitions are less individualistic than the long semi-isolation of the peninsula would justify one in expecting; that is to say, many are shared with other parts of the British Isles and indeed of continental Europe. Even the most important of all the legends, those surrounding King Arthur, are a long way from being exclusive to Cornwall, much as the Cornish would like to claim Arthur for their own. Somerset, Wales, Scotland, Brittany – all have their Arthurian associations. The best argument for believing that the shadowy Romano-British chieftain we call Arthur was probably born in Cornwall, even if his exploits later led him elsewhere, is the strength of the tradition that this was so, the undoubted reverence felt by Cornish people in the past for Arthur's memory, and their belief that one day he would return. This may not be the stuff of which well-footnoted biographies are compiled, but tradition when strong enough and old enough is not to be scorned. If Arthur had lived either earlier or later one might have hoped to find some clue in contemporary writing. But he flourished in the very darkest part of the Dark Ages, and his figure remains shrouded in mists even thicker than those that so often shroud Bodmin Moor.

Perhaps the most interesting legends after the Arthurian are those attaching to Squire Tregeagle, for John Tregeagle, steward at Lanhydrock only 300 years ago, is a real personage of relatively modern times, yet the stories that have become associated with him go back to the very dawn of history. How, one wonders, did the association begin, and why have similar clusters of ancient superstitions not surrounded a score of other figures? (*See* Dozmary Pool in the gazetteer section.)

A Few Cornish Dishes, Past and Present

Star-gazy Pie   Made with whole pilchards, their heads sticking up through the crust.

Muggety Pie   Filled with the entrails of calves or sheep, sometimes with cream added.

Squab Pie   Contains apple, bacon, mutton, onions, and cream, formerly with a 'squab' or young pigeon included.

Likky Pie   Leek pie, with pastry underneath as well as above, and an egg included. The Cornish saints were said to prefer it to ambrosia.

Cornish Pasty   The original formula was 'potatoes or leeks or turnips or pepper grass, rolled up in black barley crust and baked under the ashes'. Meat is a comparatively modern addition.

Cornish Broth   Pork or beef scraps mixed with swedes, carrots, cabbage, shallots, or leeks. Formerly the staple Sunday dinner of the poor.

Scrowlers   Dried pilchards peppered and cooked over an open fire.

Kiddley Broth   Made by pouring boiling water over bread already garnished with pepper, salt, and butter. Once universally known in poor mining families.

Fair Maids and Mahogany   Pilchards and gin-and-treacle.
Scrolls   Cooked bacon-rind chopped into tiny pieces.
Shenagrum   Jamaica rum, a slice of lemon, soft brown sugar, and grated nutmeg, all added to a half-pint of home-brewed beer brought to the boil. There were variations in different regions.

Short-stay Guide

These pages are intended for the traveller whose time in Devon and Cornwall is limited to a few days. What, out of all that is described in this book, is most worth visiting? The question is a hard one, not just because it is clearly invidious, but because so much depends on *when* the traveller is making his or her visit. For example, a person would be ill advised to attempt Clovelly or Polperro in July or August, but out of season no one should miss them. Again, since not even the most energetic traveller could hope to get to all the places listed below in 'a few days', selection might be influenced by the calendar of events obtainable from any tourist office and many hotel foyers. In a toss-up to decide whether to visit, say, Falmouth or Helston, it would be prudent to check the date of Helston's Flora Festival. Even where a place is not listed, such as Padstow, the traveller finding himself near when the Hobby Horse celebrations are due might prefer to go there at the expense of somewhere listed. Finally, there is the weather: if Bodmin Moor, Exmoor, or Dartmoor is shrouded in mist, forget any recommendation dependent on natural scenery. The lists are alphabetical and not in order of preference or of geographical sequence; but by chance many of the entries are quite close to one another, which may also influence the choice.

Many of the items on the list are not the subject of a separate gazetteer entry: it is suggested that the index will provide the most convenient way of tracing descriptions.

Cities
Exeter (Devon)
Plymouth (Devon)

Coastal Towns
Brixham (Devon)
Falmouth (Cornwall)
Fowey (Cornwall)
Lynmouth (Devon)
St Ives (Cornwall)
Salcombe (Devon)

Inland Towns
Barnstaple (Devon)
Bideford (Devon)
Helston (Cornwall)
Stratton (Cornwall)
Tavistock (Devon)
Totnes (Devon)

Coastal Villages
Branscombe (Devon)
Clovelly (Devon)
Coverack (Cornwall)
Polperro (Cornwall)
St Just-in-Roseland (Cornwall)

Inland Villages
Chagford (Devon)
Gidleigh (Devon)
Golant (Cornwall)
Lawhitton (Cornwall)

Buildings (ecclesiastical)
Blisland church (Cornwall)
Exeter Cathedral (Devon)
Hartland church (Devon)
Kenton church (Devon)
Launcells church (Cornwall)

Ottery St Mary church (Devon)
Poughill church (Cornwall)
Little Petherick church (Cornwall)
Spiceland Meeting House (Devon)

Buildings (secular)
Berry Pomeroy Castle (Devon)
Castle Drogo (Devon)
Compton Castle (Devon)
Cotehele (Cornwall)
Lanhydrock (Cornwall)
Restormel Castle (Cornwall)
Saltram (Devon)
Sidmouth seafront (Devon)
Tintagel Castle (Cornwall)
Trematon Castle (Cornwall)
Truro: Lemon Street (Cornwall)

Feats of Engineering
Morwhellham Quay (Devon)
Plymouth Breakwater (Devon)
Saltash Bridges (Devon and Cornwall)
Treffry Viaduct (Cornwall)

Museums and Galleries
Camborne: Holman Museum and East
    Pool Engine House (Cornwall)
Dartington Hall Textile Mill (Devon)
Exeter Maritime Museum (Devon)
Penzance: Penlee House (Cornwall)
Plymouth Museum and Art Gallery
    (Devon)
St Ives: all galleries (Cornwall)
Sticklepath: Finch's Foundry (Devon)
Zennor Folk Museum (Cornwall)

Prehistory
Chysauster Village (Cornwall)
Halligye Fogou (Cornwall)
Lanyon Quoit and Men-an-Tol
    (Cornwall)

Spinsters' Rock (Devon)
Trethevy Quoit (Cornwall)
Trowlesworthy Warren (Devon)
Hembury Fort (Devon)

Gardens
Bicton (Devon)
Mt Edgcumbe (Cornwall)
Sharpitor (Devon)
Trelissick (Cornwall)
Trengwainton (Cornwall)

Animal Reserves, Sanctuaries, etc.
Braunton Burrows (Devon)
Brixham Marine Aquarium (Devon)
Dartmoor Wildlife Park (Devon)
Slapton Ley (Devon)

Coastal Scenery
Hartland Quay (Devon)
Helford estuary (Cornwall)
Kynance Cove (Cornwall)
Lowland Point (Cornwall)
Pentire Point (Cornwall)
Woody Bay (Devon)

Inland Scenery
Cheesewring (Cornwall)
Coombe Valley (Cornwall)
Dartmeet (Devon)
Dart Valley (Devon)
Luxulyan Valley (Cornwall)
Lydford Gorge (Devon)
Lyn Valley (Devon)
Tamar Valley (Devon and Cornwall)
Teign Gorge (Devon)

Miscellaneous
Minack Open-Air Theatre, Porthcurno
(Cornwall) – preferably attend a
performance

Gazetteer

Abbreviations
NT for National Trust

Entries in the Gazetteer
The first figure of the map reference supplied to each entry refers to a page number in the map section at the back of the book. The subsequent letter and figure give the grid reference.

Population figures are based on the 1971 Census.

Altarnun (*pron.* Altar-nún)   Cornwall   3G1
(*pop.* 718)
In the north-eastern part of Bodmin Moor, and mercifully just *off* the A30, the town consists mainly of one
narrow street winding between slate-roofed stone cottages. At the end farthest from the highway, beside a
stream called Penpont Water, rises the very tall (33m.)
tower of the church of St Non, or Nonna, mother of St
David, the patron saint of Wales. Otherwise the main
interest of the church lies in its large and splendid Norman font and its timberwork, particularly the sixteenth-
century carved bench-ends – nearly eighty in all – by a
Cornish carver, Robert Daye; there is also a fine screen
and altar rail. Altarnun contains a Wesleyan chapel
(Georgian) bearing a stone likeness of Wesley cut by N.
Burnard, a native of the town.

Just south of the church a branch road running to the
north-west leads after a few km. (turn right at Tregue
crossroads) through beautiful scenery to St Clether, a
village with a celebrated Holy Well where the fifth-
century Welsh saint built his cell by the River Inny. The
small chapel, through which the well-water flows, is of
the fifteenth century, restored in the nineteenth; but
some of the stones might have been used by the saint
himself.

Antony House   Cornwall   3H3
Overlooking the estuary of the Lynher before it empties
itself into the Hamoaze below Saltash Bridge, Antony

LEFT: *The font in the church of St Nonna, Altarnun*
BELOW: *Antony House: the Saloon. Furnished in walnut in the
early C18. The 'Earl of Westmorland' (full-length portrait)
and the 'Piping Shepherd' (centre) are by Reynolds*

House (NT) stands in its own park, nearer to Torpoint than to Antony village. The house, begun in 1711 to the plans of an unidentified architect and not subsequently altered (a trumpery Victorian *addition* was later removed), is often cited as the finest Queen Anne building in the West Country. The design is severely classical, the north or principal front showing nine bays or windows in the upper of its two storeys, with a columned portico below the centre three and a pediment above them. Six dormers break the line of the roof. Inside, period furniture and decorations harmonize with the original panelling, and there are portraits by Reynolds and others commemorating the Carew family who, prior to the NT, were the sole owners of the estate from medieval times. In the grounds stands a dovecote as old as the house, and the yew-hedged gardens afford glorious views across the estuary.

Three km. from the south entrance lies ST JOHN, sometimes called St John-in-Cornwall, a place of medieval houses and much charm at the head of an impressive sheet of tidal water, 2km. long and nearly 1km. wide, known as St John's Lake, though in reality it is an inlet of the Hamoaze. Students of sea-birds love it.

Appledore Devon 6D2 (*pop.* 2,172)
Considering its extremely busy shipbuilding yards – with a speciality, almost unique in the kingdom, in making replicas of the ships of other centuries, such as the *Golden Hind* – Appledore manages to remain astonishingly unspoilt, and even to look sleepy. This is because the yards are apart from the village, higher up the Torridge estuary; and also because the village streets are not wide enough for cars. The result is a place of pollution-free quiet, the many Georgian and early-Victorian cottages giving an impression of little change from one century to another. Some have very large upper windows to give a good light, in former times, for sail-making. The more ambitious houses face the estuary. Facing it too is Chanter's Folly, a reproduction of a medieval churchtower built by a merchant in 1800 so that he might watch his ships appear over the horizon. The church itself (1838) has nothing to detain the traveller. Salmon-netting was once a major activity, but as pollution of the water makes the fish scarcer and the fishing-fleet is dwindling. The yard where the wooden ships are made is a splendid sight, for tools and methods are employed that have long disappeared from the modern yard building steel ships (and there is one of these yards in Appledore as well – one of the largest *covered* shipyards in Europe). Not only replicas, but wooden fishing-vessels of large size are turned out. The pilots who guide ships past Bideford Bar (*see* Bideford) operate from Appledore, and there is a ferry service across the Torridge to Instow. Every August a regatta is held. On the great silt-formed plain between river-mouth and sea (NORTHAM BURROWS) are a lifeboat and a coastguard station, and behind them a golf course.

South of the golf course, facing the sea, is WESTWARD HO! (*pop.* 2,192), the only town in England to be named after a novel and the only one to have an exclamation mark after it. This might well be due to its uninspiring appearance, twentieth-century seaside architecture at its worst round a Victorian nucleus that is a long way from the best work of the period. It is interesting that Charles Kingsley himself protested vigorously at the project to put houses and hotels on this lovely piece of coast, and to 'defile . . . with chicken bones and sandwich scraps' the Pebble Ridge that for nearly 4km. fringes the beautiful wide sands. The ridge, faintly reminiscent of Dorset's Chesil Bank, consists of large flat stones torn, some experts believe, from the cliffs at distant Hartland Point and carried here by the current, becoming rounded in the process. Under the sands, out to sea, archaeologists have found Neolithic remains, including the bones or shells of an extraordinary variety of Stone Age foods. Some of these finds are in the North Devon Athenaeum at Barnstaple (qv). From 1874 until its sponsors took it elsewhere the United Services College was at Westward Ho!, and among its pupils was Rudyard Kipling; he used the experience, and the setting, for *Stalky & Co.* KIPLING TORS, the cliffs west of the town, are a NT property. The NT also own BURROUGH FARM, a small piece of wooded cliff on the Torridge estuary 2½km. due east of Westward Ho!, beyond Northam. Burrough House (now replaced) was used by Kingsley for the home of Amyas Leigh. A point not far from the NT patch is still named BLOODY CORNER, in commemoration of a victory by King Alfred's forces over the Danes, who had landed near this point. An inscribed stone set in the wall beside the main road bears the words 'Stop! Stranger Stop!' (fortunately not where this is likely to be mistaken for a traffic injunction), and testifies that after the battle King Hubba the Dane was buried nearby.

Arlington Court Devon 7E2
About 10km. from Barnstaple on A39 to Lynton (NT). The home of the Chichesters from the fourteenth century until the death of the last of the line, an elderly spinster, in 1947, after sixty-six years as mistress of the house. The present mansion dates only from 1822, with additions made in 1864, when it was in its heyday and patronized by the upper strata of Victorian society. The exterior is plain, the inside dazzling and almost overpoweringly filled with the personality of the last Miss Chichester, which the NT, a body that sometimes has an unfortunate tendency to decharacterize its properties, has not eliminated. On the contrary, it is fair to say the NT has acquitted itself well in keeping the house as nearly as possible as the old lady left it, which in turn was as nearly as possible as she found it, except that she amassed a great collection of pewter, ship models, and *objets d'art*. The stables contain a good assembly of horse-drawn vehicles; the gardens are not outstanding, but the

surrounding park by the River Yeo contains Shetland ponies and the rare Jacob's sheep, wildfowl of many sorts on the lake, and ravens and buzzards in the woods. The church, inevitably, is full of Chichester monuments; that to Miss Rosalie Chichester was designed by John Piper.

Ashburton Devon 4D4 *(pop* 3,518)

Successively a stannary town and a wool town, and always a market town, it was (until the administrative changes of 1974 did away with such aids to civic pride) the only urban district to be included wholly within the Dartmoor National Park – a deserved distinction, for it is little spoilt, which is more than can be said for its mainly fifteenth-century parish church after G. E. Street's restoration. The exterior of the church does not reveal too much heavyhandedness and there is an impressive tower; but inside Street's excess of zeal is only too evident. As an example, the removal of the pews revealed a superb early-Tudor carved and painted screen, damaged but not beyond renovation. The architect, however, made no attempts to restore it, preferring to design a monstrosity of his own. One piece of fine carving salvaged from a much earlier threat was formerly in the chantry. Hearing of King Henry VII's suppression of chantries, one John Prowse reckoned that it would be a pity to lose this fine decoration, particularly as he himself had executed it, so he took it all away and re-erected it in his own house in West Street. There it remained, together with some elegant panelling, until 1905, but on the death of their owner all the old woodwork was torn from the walls and sold to a London dealer before the people of Ashburton had a chance to keep it in the town. Is it still surviving, one wonders, and if so where?

The other ecclesiastical building of note is St Lawrence's Chapel, or rather its fourteenth-century tower, which is all that remains. In 1314 the tower was given to the Ashburton civil authorities and became a school, which was enlarged in 1593 and remained a school until 1938. The Old Court House at the back of it was probably the schoolmaster's residence. The town is well endowed with pre-Georgian, Georgian, and early-Victorian houses; 4 North Street was once the Mermaid Inn, General Fairfax's HQ for a time during the Civil War. No. 10 used to be a seventeenth-century gaming house nicknamed the Pack of Cards because of the slates on its frontage, which are cut in the form of hearts, diamonds, clubs, and spades.

At the west end of the town, near a Saxon cross, is St Gudula's Well, dedicated to this patroness of the blind because its waters were thought beneficial to ailing eyes. The Ashburton Museum contains, among many other exhibits, a model of the old market that used to be held on the site of the present car park. In former days a virtual museum of antique furniture and china was displayed at the (still flourishing) early-eighteenth-century Golden Lion Inn.

Atherington Devon 6D3

At the crossing of the B3217 and the B3227 10km. south of Barnstaple; the B3217 is the old Barnstaple–Crediton coach road. The village is attractive enough, but it is the church that qualifies it for entry here. Though the thirteenth- to fifteenth-century original was over-restored in the 1880s (by J. L. Pearson, the architect of Truro Cathedral), the monuments – some very old – remain, with their evocations of the Bassets, the Chichesters, the Champernownes, and several of the other great families that figure so prominently in Devon history. But the highlight of the church is the rood-screen and the gallery, in perfect condition and as rare in this part of the world as they are beautiful. The period is very early sixteenth century, and it is believed that the screen was once in the private chapel of UMBERLEIGH HOUSE, a mansion of the Bassets, 1km. north of Atherington. This house has now vanished, and all that is left of its chapel, apart from the possibly transferred screen, is a thirteenth-century doorway now hidden inside a garden shed belonging to the present Umberleigh House.

Axminster Devon 5H1 *(pop.* 4,515)

The easternmost market town in Devon, and a very lively one: the original home of Axminster carpets, the great factory for which still stands, near the church; manufacture was begun in 1755, ended when the firm went bankrupt in 1835, and was revived during the twentieth century; but 'Axminster' carpets are now made in many other factories as well. The town is on the River Axe, but owes more to being at the intersection of two roads, today the A358 (the Fosse Way) and the A35, both of importance since Roman times. The minster of the name was in being at latest by the mid eighth century, and two centuries later King Athelstan founded a college to celebrate his victory over the Danes and Scots in a great battle nearby. Axminster was knocked about a bit during the Civil War, but its only subsequent nod from history was when in 1688 William of Orange stayed a night at the Dolphin Inn (now vanished) after landing at Brixham on his way to chase James II from the throne.

The streets show a fair number of Georgian and early-Victorian buildings, the most outstanding being the municipal office block, Oak House, built in 1758, and Victoria Place, a nineteenth-century terrace with a single unbroken balcony along the first floor. The church, mainly Perpendicular, is not of great interest apart from a Norman doorway in the south aisle and a Jacobean pulpit. A number of small industries continue to operate in factories of various degrees of antiquity.

Of NEWENHAM ABBEY, founded in 1245 for the Cistercians, there are a few fragments 1km. south, near the A358: mainly parts of the nave and refectory. The best relic, if its alleged provenance is genuine, is an archway now forming the entrance to a bookshop near Axminster church. Several large mansions adorn the countryside within two or three km. of the town. Most are not open to visitors, but those named here can be seen from public roads. To the north, in the Axe Valley, CLOAKHAM or Clocombe House is a hardly altered building of 1832; north-east, WEYCROFT MANOR, a delightful survival from the fifteenth century; west, close to Kilminster, CORYTON PARK, 1756, brick with stone embellishments; south-west, SHUTE BARTON, a NT property, the outside of which can be seen at any time in daylight, the inside by application to the tenant: it is a stone manor-house begun in the fourteenth century and completed in the sixteenth, with a tower and many fascinating interior features; finally south, past Newenham Abbey, ASHE HOUSE, fifteenth-century, with an old tiltyard: here in Tudor times lived the Drake family, but not the Drakes who produced Sir Francis, so that when the latter 'borrowed' the coat of arms of Sir Bernard Drake of Ashe, Queen Elizabeth had to intervene.

At a later date (1650) the famous Duke of Marlborough, whose mother was a Drake, was born at Ashe House: a statement that perhaps needs amplification, since several authorities, including W. G. Hoskins, aver that the Duke was almost certainly born at Great Trill, another mansion (now vanished) 2km. east of Ashe. The argument is that Ashe, where on the outbreak of the Civil War Lady Drake, the Duke's widowed grandmother, had declared for Parliament, was burnt down by the Royalists in 1643 and not rebuilt by Lady Drake's son (the Duke's uncle) until well after the Restoration; meanwhile Lady Drake is said to have resided at Trill and been joined there by her daughter and son-in-law – the Duke's parents – who were consequently at Trill when the Duke, and before him his elder sister Arabella, were born. But in *The Early Churchills* A. L. Rowse tells us that before Ashe was burnt down Lady Drake went to Lyme Regis, where she remained during the Royalist siege. On the raising of the siege she betook herself to London, from which she returned to Ashe in 1647 and was joined by her daughter (the Duke's mother). In the same year, the war being over, the Duke's father also repaired to Ashe, where in due course Arabella and the Duke were born and baptized (as the registers show) in the private chapel.

From this it seems clear that the fire of 1643 did not destroy the whole of Ashe, so that although Lady Drake's son, who resided throughout at Great Trill, did indeed not repair Ashe until after the Restoration, part of the mansion must always have remained habitable. Today it is not open to the public, but a good view of the outside can be had from the Axminster–Seaton road (A358).

Four and a half km. west of Axminster, at LOUGHWOOD FARM just north of the A35, stands a small, heavily-buttressed Baptist chapel (though named Loughwood Meeting House). Built in 1653, this is among the earliest

RIGHT: *Atherington: rood-screen and loft*

Church of St Peter and St Paul, Barnstaple, from the E. The lead-covered broach spire, twisted by the sun's heat, is a fine example of its kind

priory. The latter he founded at Pilton (then a separate entity, today an integral part of Barnstaple) on the opposite bank of Barnstaple's second river, the Yeo. The principal river is the Taw, and, like Truro, the town was founded where the highest point of navigability touched the lowest point at which the river could be forded. The Normans reached the town in 1068, and some years later built a castle to defend it, of which only the central mound, fragments of the circular keep, and part of the line of the moat – now incorporated in a small public garden – remain. In the thirteenth century, at which time much of the town belonged to the Tracey family (an earlier member had been among the four knights who murdered Becket), the first bridge was built across the Taw, and although today's Long Bridge of sixteen arches represents the sixth rebuilding, the pier-bases are still those of the original. In the same period a priory – a colony or 'cell' of Malmesbury in Wiltshire – was established in Pilton. The wool trade, which formed a major element in Barnstaple's steadily growing prosperity, was becoming well established, and one interesting outcome of this and the profits accruing from running a prosperous port was that in Elizabethan times the town was one of a very few in the West to have a theatre, in which Shakespeare and his company performed in 1605.

Before that Barnstaple had contributed five ships to fight the Armada, and also her own hero, John Wilson, a ship's captain. Taken by the Spaniards while Philip II was preparing his onslaught, he was bidden to act as pilot, but despite fearful threats Wilson refused so staunchly that at last Philip with unwonted magnanimity freed him as a reward for his patriotism. During the Civil War the town, as might be expected, sided with Parliament and changed hands no fewer than four times, an architectural casualty being the church of St Mary at Pilton. This is the only relic of the former priory, but nearly all of it except the north aisle dates from the post-Restoration rebuilding. On the outside of the north wall you can still trace the roof-line of the monastic buildings. The altar rails, pulpit, and one or two tombs, however, predate the Civil War.

In 1685 Louis XIV of France revoked the Edict of Nantes – by which Henry IV had in 1598 recognized the right of Huguenots to their own form of worship – and as a consequence many Huguenots settled in Barnstaple. After that, commerce, to which in the nineteenth century was added shipbuilding, more or less took over Barnstaple's history, and is consistent with the prosperous eighteenth-century appearance of so much of the present town. Indeed, even the streets in which seventeenth-, eighteenth-, or early-nineteenth-century buildings survive are too numerous to list without engendering confusion, and only the highlights can be enumerated here. In many streets the houses remain unaltered; in others, more commercial, modern shopfronts have taken over the ground floors, and it is necessary to look above these. Right in the centre of the urban bustle, but

of its kind in the country, and the fittings installed in the eighteenth century remain fascinatingly unaltered. There are box pews, a gallery, and a plain waggon-roof. Below the pulpit the floorboards can be lifted to reveal the original bath for total immersion. In 1969 the chapel was given to the NT and carefully repaired. The key is at the farm.

Barnstaple Devon 6D2 *(pop. 17,317)*
The largest town in north Devon, the chief market centre, and one of the oldest boroughs in Great Britain, having received the first of its four charters in 930 from Athelstan, who also established a mint and a

in a cunningly planned oasis of quiet, stands the parish church of St Peter and St Paul, in company with St Anne's Chapel and some seventeenth-century almshouses. The church probably dates from the twelfth century, but was so heavily restored by Gilbert Scott that it might as well be Victorian except for its seventeenth-century spire, which is lead-covered and leans slightly. St Anne's Chapel is a fourteenth-century chantry chapel that became a grammar school (cf. Ashburton) and so remained until 1908. It is now a small museum of local-interest items. John Gay, author of the *Beggar's Opera*, was born in Barnstaple and educated at the school. The Guildhall of 1826, in the High Street, contains portraits of civic worthies painted in 1738 by Thomas Hudson (1701–79), a Barnstaple man who acquired a national reputation and taught Reynolds. At the back of this is a rather charming mid-nineteenth-century market, with twin rows of small and identical shops. In addition to the almshouses (Horwood's) by St Peter's church there are two other groups, Penrose's (1627) in Litchdon Street, and Salem (1834) in Trinity Street. The former has a handsome granite colonnade and a door with a bullet-hole in it from the Civil War. The Westminster Bank in Boutport Street was once the mansion of the Spanish

Merchants stationed in Barnstaple, and contains two early-seventeenth-century plaster ceilings of almost indigestible richness, which the bank people do not seem to mind you going in to goggle at.

In Litchdon Street again is the pottery works – modern representative of an industry practised in Barnstaple since the Middle Ages – where Barum Ware is made. (Barnstaple is familiarly called 'Barum' as Salisbury is called 'Sarum'.) The works may be visited in summer. At the north end of the Long Bridge, facing the Square, is the North Devon Athenaeum, founded in 1845 and now housing the public library and the town's principal museum.

By the river, too, is Queen Anne's Walk (1796), a colonnade of 1708 surmounted by a statue of the Queen. Originally called Merchants' Walk, the colonnade, which is very ornate, once served as a commercial exchange, the merchants sealing their transactions by placing their money on a mushroom-shaped pillar, still there, called the Tome Stone – exactly as their counterparts in Bristol placed their money on 'nails' and gave rise to the expression 'to pay on the nail'. The great commercial event nowadays is Barnstaple Fair, a three-day event every September that preserves a number of

Acland Barton: late-medieval wing. The Aclands originated here in the C12

old traditions, among them the hanging of a glove at a window of the Guildhall throughout the fair to indicate that all are welcome.

Pilton retains a number of attractive old houses, from Tudor to early-nineteenth-century, grouped round St Mary's; but the apparently 'Tudor' almshouses through which the church is approached are a happy imitation of 1849. A manuscript Book of Hours, drawn up in 1521 while the church was still the priory chapel, is now in the Bodleian Library at Oxford.

In the vicinity of Barnstaple, TAWSTOCK (*pop.* 1,978), 3km. up the Taw in lush countryside, is a village that throughout most of its existence was entirely owned by the great family reigning at Tawstock Court, which means successively the Martins down to the mid fifteenth century, then the Bourchiers, who became the Earls of Bath in 1536, and finally the Wrays, who married into the Bourchier family in 1652. The splendid Tudor mansion, as imposing as befitted such august owners, was burnt to the ground in 1787, only the rather handsome 1574 gateway remaining. A new house was built in the prevailing Gothic style, battlemented and turreted, and is now a school. Of more interest today is the church, which stands on a hilltop in the grounds, is cruciform in pattern, and has a 'landmark' central tower. Much of the building dates from the fourteenth century, with fine waggon-roofs, some prettily plastered Tudor bench-ends, an extraordinary ceilinged pew, a sundial giving the time in various European cities (not to mention Cairo and Babylon), but above all a fantastic wealth of monuments to the three owning families. The study of these alone would repay a long visit.

Another great Devon family associated with the area is that of the Aclands, and their manor, ACLAND BARTON, lies about 3km. east of Barnstaple, near Landkey. The house was probably built in about 1475, and certainly enlarged in 1591. There was some Victorian refacing and refurbishing, but much of the Tudor appearance remains, especially in the chapel wing. Not open to visitors, but visible externally. The final approach is best made on foot.

Bere Ferrers   Devon 4B4   (*pop.* 2,346)
Situated on the Tavy side of the peninsula formed by the union of the rivers Tavy and Tamar, Bere Ferrers is one of the many Devon places given extra interest by association for many centuries with a single dominant family, in this case the Ferrers. But it is also interesting for its peaceful, other-worldly silence. There is no through traffic, because there is nowhere further down the peninsula to go to. There is a railway (the Calstock branch-line), but this passes well behind the village, and the bridge by which it crosses the Tavy is 2km. south. Opposite Bere the Tavy is more than ½km. wide, and nearly deserted. Nearby are old quays, quite deserted, that once served the booming mineral trade in the Tavistock area. It is extremely hard to believe that the

fringe of Plymouth's continuous built-up zone is only 3km. away. The church dates from 1243, but was rebuilt and turned into a collegiate church by William de Ferrers in the 1330s. The strength consisted of a deacon, archpriest, and four priests, and the title of archpriest remains with the rector to this day. Despite Victorian restoration, a good deal of interest remains in the fabric, and more in the medieval tombs – though possibly less for the more imaginative traveller than in a number of anonymous gravestones in the churchyard that simply say 'Cholera 1849' and nothing more. Some fragments of the Ferrers family castle exist in an adjoining farmyard.

Berrynarbor   Devon 6D1   (*pop.* 711)
A Saxon name meaning the fortress of the Nereberts, who owned the manor in the early Middle Ages. The Nereberts became the Berrys, and it was they who in about 1480 built the manor-house that still stands near the church, albeit reduced in size by the demolition of a wing and the spiriting-away of the porch in 1889 to a mansion called Westaway, 1km. north of Barnstaple. For a time after the Berry interest had ended in 1708, the manor-house served as the village school. The 24m. church-tower was built at the same time as the house, and the rest of the church was largely refashioned during the same century. It contains some interesting wall-tablets, to the Berrys and others. The village lies in a pleasant valley, and because the bungalow-builders have preferred to put up their boxes where there is a view of the sea, the old nucleus remains pretty and hardly spoilt. At the coastal end of the valley is WATERMOUTH CASTLE, built in the reign of George IV, standing in a gracious park and Gothic in style. Originally a home of the Bassets, it passed in 1920 to Ernest Cairns, an eccentric 'sugar baron' who claimed to be both a US citizen and an English peer. It is now a museum. Of deeper historical interest is BOWDEN, a splendid old farmhouse, much of it still of the fifteenth century, tucked away in a side-coombe about 2km. south of the village (not open, and inadvisable to seek except on foot). Here in 1522 was born John Jewel, Bishop of Salisbury, author of *Apologia pro Ecclesia Anglicana* (1562), which Queen Elizabeth ordered to be read in every church in her realm.

The coast north of Berrynarbor is magnificent, and one must not begrudge the holiday camps and caravan sites that occupy some of it. The mighty, moor-crowned cliff-mass known as the GREAT HANGMAN (318m.), a recent NT acquisition, is the summit of the magnificence, in both senses. Between it and Combe Martin (a resort) is KNAP DOWN. From the thirteenth century onwards extremely lucrative silver-lead mines were worked here – it is claimed locally that Henry V could never have financed his French wars without them. A huge cup made from Knap Down silver was presented to a Tudor Lord Mayor of London, and in 1731 was converted into three goodly tankards, which are still in use at Lord

Mayor's banquets. The mines were abandoned in 1875, and the Down shows many ruined engine-houses and stacks. East of the Great Hangman, HOLDSTONE DOWN and its cliffs, parts of which are also NT-owned, is at 349m. even higher than its neighbour.

Bideford (*pron*. Biddyford)   Devon   6C3   (*pop*. 11,802)

Though smaller, the estuary of the Torridge is to Bideford what the estuary of the Taw is to Barnstaple (qv). Just before they reach the sea the two estuaries unite, and across their joint mouth lies BIDEFORD BAR, as dangerous a sandbank as any navigator could wish to be spared, and the doom of many a ship. Charles Kingsley's well-known lines 'But men must work, and women must weep, / Though storms be sudden and waters deep, / And the harbour bar be moaning' refer to Bideford Bar. Kingsley made Bideford famous, partly because its appearance charmed him, as it must still charm any but the most insensitive, and partly because, like Stowe Barton (*see* Combe Valley) in north Cornwall, Bideford was for centuries closely associated with the illustrious Grenvilles. William the Conqueror gave the manor to his queen, Matilda, but his successor Rufus bestowed it on the first Sir Richard Grenville, and it remained a Grenville possession until the Corporation acquired it in 1711.

The 'ford' in the name – probably a corruption of 'Byda's Ford' – refers to a pre-Norman crossing, the Bideford end of which is still commemorated in the name Ford House (*see below*). It must have been an important ford, since it formed part of a very ancient trackway extending across most of Devon. But Bideford's showpiece is its bridge, which replaced the ford in the thirteenth century. The first bridge was of wood; 200 years later the reigning Grenville paid for this to be enclosed in stone – enclosed, not replaced, for in our own century some of the original wood was found inside the stonework. Since the enclosure, as might be expected, there have been many repairs, two widenings in 1865 and 1925, and extensive rebuilding after the severe floods of 1968; but even if one is reminded of the axe that was still the genuine original despite having had two new blades and three new handles, much of the bridgework of earlier periods survives in the present structure. Its length is more than 206m., and it has twenty-four arches.

A charter to hold a market was granted to Bideford in 1272, but it was with the opening up of the Americas that commercial prosperity really came here. This was the first port to import tobacco in quantity, timber – much of it for local shipbuilding – was brought in from Newfoundland, and the weaving industry set up by the Huguenots caused a thriving trade in Spanish wool imports. From the late seventeenth century to the late eighteenth the town was very prosperous indeed. But the tobacco trade became diverted to Bristol, the French

encroached on the Newfoundland scene while their privateers preyed on Bideford ships, and boat-building tailed off as ships became too large for Torridge waters. Nevertheless, the port remains busy in a modest way, there are several light industries, and with the coming of the railway came the tourists. The principal street is still the Quay, long, wide, bordered with trees on the river side and a series of handsome frontages over the shops on the other. From it the rest of the main streets run at right angles up a steep hillside. The best is Bridgeland Street, designed all of a piece in 1690 by Nathaniel Gascoyne, and not too ruthlessly altered since; in addition to several of the original houses, the old tobacco warehouses still stand here.

The town has a zoo, a museum – containing among other things, pottery, shipwrights' tools, and prints and maps – in the Town Hall, and the Burton Art Gallery in Victoria Park, at the northern end of the Quay. In the park also are eight sixteenth-century Spanish cannon, probably captured from the Armada; quite properly, Bideford never lets you forget that Sir Richard Grenville of the *Revenge* was a Bideford man. Except for its Norman tower, the church, St Mary, was entirely rebuilt in 1864. There is one good Grenville tomb, but unfortunately the churchyard no longer displays the gravestone on which once appeared the well-authenticated epitaph:

> Here lies the body of Mary Sexton
> Who pleased many a man, but ne'er vexed one:
> Not like the woman who lies under the next stone.

The bridge leads to an east-bank suburb called EAST-THE-WATER, where the not very attractive Victorian courtyard of the Royal Hotel conceals a merchant's mansion of 1688. In this the original grand staircase leads to a room with one of the most beautiful plaster ceilings in the county. In this house Kingsley lived during his Bideford years. Most other rich merchants' houses of the town's palmy days are strung along the Northam road past Victoria Park. At the south end of the town FORD HOUSE already alluded to is a medieval stone farmhouse, considerably altered but still most agreeable to look at, with an original barn. Another handsome house some 4km. south of Bideford is ORLEIGH COURT. The manor of Orleigh was founded in 981 and was part of the endowment of Tavistock Abbey, which, however, granted it to the Dennis, or Dennys, family before 1200, from whom it passed in 1684 to John Davie, a Bideford merchant. In 1870 it came into the hands of a Mr Rogers, whose son sold it to the present owner, Mr Sanders, in 1939. The arched entrance is a fourteenth-century feature, the hall and remaining wing date from a rebuilding in 1580, and the rest is largely the work of Davie and his son after 1684, with a Victorian gable and mullioned windows where the other wing used to be. Towards the end of the nineteenth century the house fell into a state of dilapidation, but although now occupied by several households, it is a scheduled building and is being rehabilitated by the owner. John Hanning Speke, the explorer of the Nile, was born here in 1827, and a portrait of the house during the Civil War appears in Daphne du Maurier's novel *The King's General*. Orleigh Court is not open to the public, but can be studied from the Bideford–Buckland Brewer road.

Blisland Cornwall 3F1 (*pop.* 446)

A remote village on the Saxon pattern, that is to say grouped about a village green, on the western fringe of Bodmin Moor, not far from one of the principal heights, Hawks Tor (*see* Dozmary Pool). Tall trees (fortunately not doom-laden elms) make the green unusually handsome. Near it stands the slate-and-granite, basically Norman, church, pleasant outside (even to the dedication – St Protus and St Hyacinth) and truly breathtaking within, having richly-carved woodwork to its barrel roofs, a huge, astonishingly magnificent wooden rood-screen erected only in 1896, when restoration of the church began, but painted in the dazzling medieval style, old benches, fluted pillars disconcertingly out of the perpendicular, and several other evidences that restoration need not remove all personality and sense of antiquity from a church, even in Cornwall. F. C. Eden was the enlightened architect responsible.

At one corner of the green stands a mellow manor-house, mellower still before the porch gable was removed in the early 1960s. This is but one of a group of fine old manor-houses, now mostly farms, within 4km. of Blisland: on the village's western fringes is LAVETHAN, home of the Kempes, built in 1653 but incorporating parts of a predecessor 200 years older; then, beyond the River Camel, HELLIGAN, a part-seventeenth-century house with some older farm buildings; and south of Helligan, TREDETHY, similarly venerable. South of Blisland, just short of the A30, TREWARDALE is rather newer, having been built in 1773 and enlarged in the 1830s. All these hoary former manor-houses are closed to the public, but to glimpse an exterior as one explores the lovely wooded valleys west and south of the moor, is to realize how perfectly the work of man – his past handiwork, at any rate – blends with that of nature.

Boconnoc Cornwall 3F2 (*pop.* 141)

1½km. N of Couchsmill

Noted for its eighteenth-century house (replacing a medieval predecessor, and in truth rather plain) and its 120ha. (300 acres) of finely landscaped, exceptionally beautiful gardens and park (terraces, lake, beech avenues, flowering shrubs). The list of owners of Boconnoc should satisfy the keenest devotee of history and romance, for they include the last Lord Mohun, the wicked duellist featured in Thackeray's *Henry Esmond*; the second Lord Camelford, also noted for duelling; Thomas Pitt of India, owner of the fabulous Pitt Diamond; and William Pitt the Elder, who was brought up here. The house is not open to the public, but the park and gardens are, in

aid of the National Gardens Scheme, on one or two Sundays in the summer. COUCHSMILL, or Couch's Mill, itself is a delightful hamlet in the steep, wooded valley of the River Lerryn. Near BRADDOCK, or Bradoc, just north of Boconnoc, Sir Ralph Hopton (who was later to surrender Truro) defeated a Cromwellian force in 1644. Nearby, too, are an Iron Age fort, with numerous barrows, and by contrast several majestic railway viaducts.

Bodmin Cornwall 3F2 (*pop.* 9,207)

Though overtaken in size by Camborne–Redruth, St Austell, Penzance, Truro, and several other towns, though it has lost the county administrative offices to Truro, though Truro was chosen in the nineteenth century for the site of Cornwall's only cathedral and thereby promoted to a city, and though probably four out of five visitors look on Truro as the Cornish capital, Bodmin nevertheless remains the official County Town and historically, at least, the principal religious centre. The very name, a corruption of 'bod-minachan', means 'the abode of monks'; and it was at Bodmin that St Petroc, the virtual (as well as virtuous) patron saint of Cornwall, founded a priory in the sixth century. Converted and educated in Ireland, though born in either Wales or Cornwall itself, according to which authority you prefer, Petroc's first foundation on his return was at Padstow (Petrocstow); nor was his priory the earliest Christian manifestation on the spot that was to become Bodmin. Credit for this belongs to Guron, a hermit who a few years before Petroc's arrival had built himself a little cell beside a well that is still preserved near the church. After St Petroc's death his bones gained a not uncommon reputation for facilitating miracles, as a result of which in 1177 an Augustinian canon with more zeal than honesty carried them off to Brittany. The Prior, one Roger, was obliged to cross the Channel to retrieve them, which he did, it is said, in the fine ivory casket displayed today in St Petroc's church.

This church, at the eastern end of the town, is (except for an older tower) a reconstruction in Perpendicular style dating from 1469–72, when nearly every adult in the parish contributed either money or labour toward the work. And a fine job they made of it, for St Petroc's is now the largest church in Cornwall and the best Perpendicular example. A less fine job, as so often, was made by the Victorian restorers, whose ruthless interior alterations have, however, been partly counteracted by some imaginative modifications since the Second World War. In form the church appears threefold, north aisle, nave, and south aisle being all of the same width and divided by slender pillars. Of monuments there is really only one to interest any but the most dedicated, the altar tomb of one of the last priors, Thomas Vyvyan (d. 1533). This is magnificent indeed. Fashioned out of blue-black slate called Catacleuse – quarried at Cataclew Point, near Padstow – and grey marble, it shows the Prior recumbent on a sarcophagus decorated with cherubs and apostles. Outside, there is good carving on the roof of the porch, and in the churchyard, in addition to St Guron's Well, stands the Chapel of St Thomas, built in 1377, converted to a school after the Reformation, and restored in 1935.

The Priory was not the only reason for Bodmin's former ecclesiastical pre-eminence. During the short-lived Cornish see (909–1040, when it was merged with Exeter) the Bishops, whose main centre was St Germans, used Bodmin as a kind of second-string, and for a time it may even have been their only headquarters. In those days, when the town was still called Petrocstow (causing great confusion with Petrocstow-Padstow) there were at least a dozen churches.

As to later history, Bodmin rivals Oxford as a City of Lost Causes. In 1496 two Bodmin citizens led an armed uprising in protest at Henry VII's heavy taxation; the rebels marched all the way to London, and either perished in a fight with the troops on Blackheath or survived to meet an even uglier retribution. Not content with this, within weeks 3,000 Cornishmen gathered round the Pretender Perkin Warbeck, proclaimed him King at Bodmin, lost a battle at Exeter, and were deserted by him (the survivors, that is) at Taunton. Little more than half a century later the Bodmin folk were conspicuous in the West Country revolt against the newly-dominant Protestant religion. After camping outside the town the rebels, accompanied by Bodmin's Mayor, a certain Boyer, marched on Exeter, where they were hopelessly defeated. Sent from London to administer chastisement, the King's man Sir Anthony Kingston ordered Boyer to prepare and join him in a sumptuous banquet, at the end of which the unsuspecting Mayor was invited to step outside and see if the gallows, newly erected for those who were to be executed, were strong enough, and was immediately hanged. After this, though it played a part in the Civil War, Bodmin's active role in history dwindled, perhaps not surprisingly. No fewer than eight charters were granted it between Richard I's reign and that of George III.

The town, whose ghastly traffic problem is destined for relief shortly by the opening of a by-pass, is built around two main streets, charmingly called Fore Street and Bore Street, and except where prefabricated building materials have taken over, the predominant material is the buff-grey of another indigenous stone, elvan, with dressings of Bodmin Moor granite. The most conspicuous secular building is the Assize Court of 1837–8, granite in substance, neo-classical in style, the work of a Launceston architect, Burt, who also designed the nearby Judge's Lodgings, or Shire House. If you lift your eyes to the hills, the prominent obelisk that you will observe was put up in 1856 to commemorate Walter Raleigh Gilbert (d. 1853), a lieutenant general in the Bengal Army and – of course – a native of Bodmin.

There is a railway station, Bodmin Road, 5km. away on Cornwall's only surviving main passenger line

(Paddington–Penzance), but more interesting is the old line from Bodmin to Wadebridge, opened as a passenger line in 1834, one of the first in the country, and still used for carrying goods. The Great Western Society run a Railway Museum, open at weekends. Of houses in the Bodmin area the most rewarding are LANHYDROCK (qv), GLYNN, or Glynne, near Bodmin Road Station, stone, neo-classical, built in 1805 for Lord Vivian, one of Wellington's generals; and ST BENET'S, Lanivet, sometimes called St Benet's Abbey, 4km. along the St Austell road. Built in 1411 as a leper hospital, it had a chapel added a few years later. Some time after 1545 it became a mansion of the Courtenays, since when it has been put to many uses and much altered. Parts of the original can still be seen, also the tower of the chapel. The rather Gothic look of the house accords well with the description of it given by the first Mrs Thomas Hardy when she stayed there in the late 1860s: 'dark, gloomy, and not very healthy. . . . Everywhere an old-time sadness prevailed'.

Bodmin Moor Cornwall *see* **Introduction**, and **Altarnun, Blisland, Camelford, The Cheesewring, Dozmary Pool, North Hill, St Cleer, St Neot**

Bolventor Cornwall *see* **Dozmary Pool**

Boscastle Cornwall 6A6 (*pop.* 691) (NT)
In the midst of a highly scenic part of the north coast, this is the base for exploring Thomas Hardy's sector of Cornwall. The castle – now vanished – belonged to the Bottreaux family, and the small harbour is little used, though as recently as the last century most of the coal and general supplies for the region were brought in by sea. Architecturally there is little to delay the traveller; it is the magnificence and diversity of the scenery that make the area worth coming a long way to visit. First, the coast: north of the harbour, Pentargan Bay with its coal-black cliffs and dainty waterfall; then a little farther, Buckator, also black, towering above rocks and islets where the seals sun themselves; and so on past the incredible rocky maze called The Strangles. West of Boscastle, where Willapark Point (not to be confused with Willapark itself, farther along towards Tintagel) hides the great slate shaft of Blackapit, the headland called Ladies' Window, and steep Long Island, the coast is perhaps even grander.

Inland lies a complete contrast. Boscastle Harbour is actually the mouth of the little River Valency, and to walk beside the chattering stream up the dreamlike Valency Valley is to pass between wooded slopes resembling those of a mountain gorge. Small churches – Forrabury, Minster, St Juliot, Lesnewth – hide in the folds of the hills, often with no more than a farm or two anywhere near them. Of these churches the most famous is St Juliot, for it was to supervise its restoration that in 1870 the young architect Thomas Hardy came down

Landscape near Boscastle: looking over Forrabury Common from near Willapark Point, showing the embattled tower of Forrabury church (St Symphorian)

from Dorset, and at St Juliot Vicarage met the girl who was to become his first wife and (after her death) inspire a host of poems set here, in Boscastle, or on the neighbouring cliffs. St Juliot, as 'West Endelstow', is also the central scene of Hardy's novel *A Pair of Blue Eyes*. Apart from its associations, it must be confessed that there is little of intrinsic interest in the church fabric; much more lies in Hardy's descriptions, and his own and his future wife's sketches (some of which are to be seen in the building) telling us what a fairly average country church was like in the nineteenth century before the restorers took over. We blame them (quite rightly: Hardy, a sensitive man, himself did so) for their gross indifference to the legacies of the past, but, goodness, they certainly faced a huge task.

Botus Fleming (*pron.* Bo Fleming)   Cornwall   4B4 (*pop.* 290)
But for the intervening Tamar this would undoubtedly have become by now another dreary Plymouth suburb. Little has spoiled an unassumingly pleasant place that looks its best in springtime, when the orchards that rather unexpectedly surround it are in bloom. At the foot of the slope on which Botus stands is Kingsmill Lake, an inlet of the Tamar estuary with a miniature quay at

Moditonham and near to it MODITONHAM HOUSE, Georgian, stone, and, as if to make the most of the splendid view, three storeys high. Northward, beside the water, quiet and lovely countryside encompasses a string of pretty hamlets making up the parish of LANDULPH, whose church, not architecturally of much interest, contains perhaps the most fascinating grave in Cornwall – that of Theodore Palaeologus, last direct descendant of the medieval Christian emperors of Byzantium. Seemingly he spent his life travelling Europe in a forlorn endeavour to rouse the Christian powers to a kind of new Crusade, until finally he settled here, married, and in 1636 ended his days – and with them the imperial line.

Bovey Tracey   Devon   4D3   (*pop.* 3,834)
'Bovey' because it is on the river of that name, 'Tracey' because in the early Middle Ages the Traceys or Tracys held the manor. The original church of St Thomas of Canterbury was allegedly built by Sir William de Tracy to expiate his share in the murder of Becket (*see also* Barnstaple), but 150 years later all but the tower was burnt down, and the body of the present church is of the fifteenth century, including many of the furnishings. There is a carved and painted stone pulpit, a good

Stone pulpit, C15, Bovey Tracey church

screen of the period, some earlier miserere seats, and one or two ambitious later monuments. In the town on its hillside are a few Tudor and a few Georgian houses.

BOVEY HEATH, 3km. south-east, is a silted-up lake, yielding clay for local pottery and brick works, lignite, and – more interestingly for the traveller – many species of fossil plants and trees. Ornithologists also find it rewarding. It was here that in 1646 Cromwell surprised a force under Lord Wentworth so unexpectedly that the Royalist officers were still playing cards. They escaped by throwing their wagers at the Parliamentary troops, who stopped to pick up the money; but 400 horses were lost. Four km. from the town on the opposite side stands LUSTLEIGH (*pop.* 555), pretty, if somewhat over-touristy. The big day of the year here is May Day, when

elaborate traditional ceremonies take place. Among those who watched them earlier in the century was Cecil Torr, who lived in Lustleigh's eastern suburb of Wreyland and has bequeathed us a most congenial portrait of this corner of Devon in his three volumes of *Small Talk at Wreyland*. Too often ignored are the various manor-houses-turned-farmhouses in which the area north of Bovey is well endowed, such as at Pullabrook and Elsford. These cannot as a rule be entered, but their outsides are a perfect complement to the rich countryside. At a house called HIGHER KNOWLE, ½km. south-east of Lustleigh, a steep woodland garden of azaleas, magnolias, rhododendrons, and suchlike is open to the public every Sunday in April and May. It also has superb views.

Braddock Cornwall *see* **Boconnoc**

Branscombe Devon 8A5 (*pop.* 477)
A mere 3km. west of Beer, but a place of such rare charm and interest that it merits a separate entry. Straggling back from the sea along a leafy valley that presently branches into two, it is a series of man-made as well as natural delights. At the seaward end, great chalk cliffs tower 120m. and 150m. on either side of the combe. Like Dowland Cliffs (*see* Seaton and Beer), they are subject to spectacular landslips – nearly 4ha. (10 acres) once dropped an average of 70m. in one fall – yet close at hand a prehistoric earthwork (period unidentified) has managed to survive. The recorded history of Branscombe is itself pretty long: in the ninth century it was a personal possession of King Alfred, and in the tenth King Athelstan gave it to the Benedictine abbey at Exeter; the Domesday Book records it as still belonging to the then abbot. The Branscombe family who gave it their name lived until the fourteenth century at EDGE BARTON, which continues to stand in solitary grandeur alone on a hillside, with much medieval work showing in its make-up. The most illustrious Branscombe was Walter Branscombe, or Bronescombe, Bishop of Exeter 1258–80 and a leading builder of the present cathedral. After the Branscombes came the Wadhams, of whom the last was Nicholas Wadham, founder in 1610 of Wadham College at Oxford.

Among the other likeable old houses in which the combe is rich are Hole, the home of seven generations of Holcombes and several more of Bartletts, and one or two near the church such as Lower House, present and past home of the Fords, and the quaintly-named Church Living, of medieval origin. Nearer the shore, Great Seaside Farm is Tudor. The village contains a Tudor forge, a rather self-consciously splendid inn claiming to date from 1360, another inn, delightfully unpretentious, and an ancient bakery where the ovens are still fired by faggots. Bakery, forge, and a goodly stretch of the shore, where the beautiful semi-precious stone chalcedony is common, are all in the hands of the NT.

The church is of a calibre worthy of its graceful and historic surroundings. Cruciform, with a tower at the centre, it shows Saxon work on the inner walls of the tower, and other parts of the fabric represent every century from the eleventh to the sixteenth. There is a priest's room in the tower, one of only fourteen such surviving in all England; the west end has an Elizabethan gallery, at the east end Jacobean altar-rails enclose the altar on all four sides. For the rest, barrel-roofs, a three-tiered eighteenth-century pulpit – parson at the top, clerk below, lectern halfway up alongside – a little medieval wall-painting, a fair number of interesting monuments, mostly to the families associated with the neighbouring bartons. Among writers who have praised Branscombe are H. J. Massingham in *In Praise of England* and the great nature-lover W. H. Hudson in *Afoot in England*.

Bratton Clovelly   Devon   6D5   (*pop.* 372)

Not on Dartmoor, but contemplating a huge tableau of it, culminating in the twin 620m. summits of Black Tor and Yes Tor, from a hilltop of its own. In the forefront is the valley of a tributary of the Thrushel, opening out immediately south into the Thrushel Valley itself: altogether a magnificent position, and not yet discovered by the tourists. The church is a restored building dating in parts from the thirteenth or even the twelfth century; the most remarkable thing about it is that at some unknown date the floor was lowered, so that the interior has the height of a cathedral. There are some wall-paintings high up in the north aisle. Three km. south, beyond the Thrushel, is ORCHARD, now a farmhouse, once a manor-house: a pleasant sight from the road, but in some ways more interesting for what it lacks than for what it has, since this was one of the buildings from which the Revd S. Baring-Gould helped himself to any features he fancied to improve his home at Lewtrenchard (qv).

Brendon   Devon   7F1   (*pop.* 160)

In Devon's wildest north, only 2km. from where Exmoor meets the sea and about the same distance from the Somerset border: part of the *Lorna Doone* country. Here the uplands are deeply scored by the lovely valley of the River Lynn, most of it thickly wooded. Brendon church, dedicated to St Brendan the Voyager, an Irish saint who would seem to belong more rightly to Cornwall, is unique in Devon, in that apparently it began its existence somewhere else, namely Cheriton (4km. south-west), from which it was seemingly transported stone by stone in about 1738; but there is much mystery about the whole affair. The fabric dates mainly from the thirteenth and fourteenth centuries, with a Victorian rebuilt tower.

The uplands are well stocked with relics of prehistory. Six and a half km. south-west, on FURZEHILL COMMON, are several rows of short standing stones; on CHERITON RIDGE and the ridge east of it are tumuli and

hut circles; at BRENDON TWO GATES, 6km. south of Brendon where the county boundary runs east–west for a stretch, is a mysterious square with 9m. sides, marked by a stone at each corner. The Romans, too, have left their mark, a signal station (long thought to be an Iron Age fort), built late in the Roman period, on OLD BARROW HILL between the Lyn and the coast. In time of danger – for example, from Irish pirates – a beacon fire lit here would with luck be seen by the large garrison across the sea at Cardiff.

Brixham   Devon   5E5   (*pop.* 12,000)

Understandably the fishing port best known to the outsider, at least by name, on either Devon coast; and very rightly too, for early in the nineteenth century it was Brixham that developed the first major trawling fleet in the world. Not that it was then a new town; it was already known to be a Roman settlement when bones of men and animals found in a local cave proved it to have been an ancient scene of habitation even then, and on nearby BERRY HEAD at the southern tip of Torbay there is an Iron Age fort. Yet for so ancient a place the port has had surprisingly little 'history'. It was an important commercial harbour before fishing took over, its ships specializing in taking English goods to Newfoundland, Newfoundland salted cod to the Mediterranean, and Mediterranean fruit back to England. In 1688 William of Orange landed at Brixham to take over the country, as his statue by the Inner Harbour testifies. In 1843 work was begun on the great breakwater that was to turn what up till then had been successively a natural creek and a 'half-tide port' into a real deep-water one. It took until 1916 to complete this huge wall, which extends out to sea for 830m. from the eastern end of the town, but as a result much larger trawlers can now operate from the port. In 1940 many Belgian skippers brought their vessels here to escape the Germans, and some remained, like the Huguenots before them.

Today, after many ups and downs – a big 'down' during both world wars, an even bigger one in the 1950s and early '60s – the industry is holding its own, even managing to dominate the vast hordes of tourists who throng the harbour in the holiday months. This harbour is likewise much patronized by artists, even real ones. Indeed, it is a far greater focus of attention than the town, which, although picturesque enough, arranged in steep tiers up the hillside, has – like its history – very little that is outstanding in it. Properly there are Higher and Lower Brixham, each with its church. That of Higher Brixham, St Mary's, is a clifftop building, Perpendicular (restored), with a 32m. tower and a rather fine south porch; All Saints, Lower Brixham, is modern, replacing an earlier church of which the most notable feature was that one of its vicars (1823–47) was the Revd H. F. Lyte, who wrote a number of 'best-seller' hymns including 'Abide with Me'. In 1929 a carillon was installed, on which the hymns are frequently played. Close by is the entrance to the cavern in which the early remains were found. The 175m.-long cavern is cleverly lit to show off the stalactites and stalagmites.

The railway arrived in Brixham in 1868 – but only just. The branch-line owed its existence entirely to the enterprise of Richard Wolston, a native of Brixham; the line, in financial terms a distinct failure, was bought by the GWR in 1883. Wolston's Victorian-Gothic station at Brixham (though no longer a station) can still be seen. Such local history can be followed in the excellent Brixham Museum in High Street, although the emphasis there is naturally on marine subjects. Down on the quay there is also an exceptionally well-stocked aquarium, including such creatures as sharks and octopus, some of them luxuriating in the longest tank in Great Britain. A trawling exhibition is thrown in for good measure.

South of BERRY HEAD, with its lighthouse, isolated rocks, and heathy summit, Brixham has spread to the coast again at St Mary's Bay, but more rewarding is the next bay to the south, ending in Crabrock Point: for just short of the Point are MAN SANDS, marking the mouth of an agreeable valley in which, just behind the beach, is a freshwater lagoon, part of a 2km.-long stream. At high tide the stream-water is pent up, but at low tide, the little river having no proper mouth, it gushes out of the beach like a burst main.

Broadwoodwidger Devon 4B2 (*pop.* 565)
In the heart of Unknown Devon, as the guide-books say, on a promontory overlooking the River Wolf, a tributary of the Lyd that within 2km. of their union empties into the Tamar. There are first-rate views of Dartmoor, and a central green on which cattle browse. The name derives from the Wyger family, who acquired the manor in 1273. The church is a wonderful amalgam of styles from Early English onward, and possesses two interesting features, the bench-ends of 1529 in the north transept, and the waggon-roof, a gratifying example of how these things are restored nowadays, the work having been done in 1966. There is also a tomb-effigy of William Shilston, of UPCOTT, 2km. north-west (and not to be confounded with its namesake near Barnstaple), a little, lonely, and likeable mansion, fully visible from the road. Three and a half km. south-west of Broadwoodwidger a mansion of rather more consequence is WORTHAM, or Wortham Manor. Fifteenth-century Tudor (i.e. Henry VII), it was clearly once most impressive, and may well become so again when it has had a little time to mellow; for after a period of desertion and decay it has very recently been taken in hand and (of necessity) drastically restored by the Landmark Trust, which has converted it into three flats. The last owners of it as a mansion were the Berridges, the very last a Miss Berridge. (How often is the last occupant of a great house to keep up the style of former times a solitary and, in the end, elderly lady: one thinks of Miss Chichester of Arlington House, Lady Vyvyan of Trelowarren.) The

house is L-shaped, with a polygonal stair-turret and fine stone-mullioned windows, and it can be seen clearly and at close range from the lane outside. At the time of writing it is not yet open for public visits, but the Trust intends to offer facilities as soon as practicable. Well within living memory the interior contained a fifteenth-century screen and linenfold panelling in the lower storey of the hall, which had, as often happened, been divided into two floors. When the Trust took over Wortham the panelling had been removed, but the screen and the beamed and braced roof of the upper storey or 'summer' hall have been conscientiously preserved. Outside, the once fine grounds have also been rehabilitated.

Brushford Devon 7E4 (*pop.* 52)
A small village with a diminutive church, smaller than many a chapel, perched on a hilltop in the little-explored countryside between Dartmoor and Exmoor. The church is Norman, with an uncommon shingled

Chancel screen in the church of St Mary, Brushford

spire, the interior exciting no comment except for the pleasantly-carved beams of the waggon-roof and a remarkable screen – doubly so in such an out-of-the-way spot. More reminiscent of Brittany than of England, its design includes tracery so fine that some of the wood is only ½cm. thick – too fragile, alas, to have escaped damage. The screen appears to be early-Tudor, and may have been intended for the chantry chapel of Sir John Evans at COLDRIDGE (*pop*. 334), 2km. to the east, where there is also an admirable church with a parclose screen very similar to Brushford's separating the chantry. If the Brushford screen was meant for here, why was it rejected in favour of one so like it? The chantry contains Sir John's canopied tomb and effigy and his well-carved prayer-desk. But the finest piece of woodwork, as at Brushford, is the rood-screen, yet another of those magnificent specimens that in Devon and Cornwall crop up in the least likely places. This screen is uncoloured; the whole excellent impression of the church interior stems from the natural colours of the many wooden furnishings, from the carved roof-bosses to the very ancient benches in the north aisle.

Outside, the village is of typical Saxon pattern round a central square, and being on a ridge (the fine church-tower is a landmark) gets a splendid look at Dartmoor. On the other side of the Taw, 6km. north, is CHULMLEIGH (*pop*. 934), a little ghost-town on a hill-top above the last reach of the Little Dart before it joins the larger river. Until their downfall in 1539 Chulmleigh belonged for three and a half centuries to the Courtenays, who made it a borough in 1253. The wool trade, cattle markets, and fairs made and kept it wealthy until the end of the eighteenth century, after which the general decline of the wool industry, the building of a new road along the Taw Valley, which took away the previously profitable through-traffic between Barnstaple and Exeter, and finally the opening of the north-Devon railway, also along the valley, reduced it to its present high-and-dry state. But in addition to its old houses and Charles I inn it has a splendid church, rebuilt in the fifteenth century and restored in the nineteenth, but retaining a barrel-roof with carved angels and – the showpiece – an elaborately-carved rood-screen spanning the whole 16m. width of the building.

The surrounding country is rich in fine houses, among them COLLETON BARTON, 1½km. west, which includes some fifteenth-century vestiges but is otherwise of 1612: E-shaped, Elizabethan in style, with very fine, large transomed windows. Unfortunately it is not open, so that one cannot see the fine panelling, plaster ceilings, or pilastered drawing-room. But to add to the impressive exterior there is a gatehouse with a little chapel above it from the time of the earlier house. Through most of its history Colleton was the home of the Burys. Less than 2km. south, the fine interior of RASHLEIGH BARTON, another Jacobean mansion, is similarly not on public display, but the traveller is compensated with an agreeable exterior view. The house, now partly incorporated into a farmhouse of later date, was the ancestral home of the Clotworthy family. Nearby in Eggsford Forest two Iron Age hillforts stand by the Taw, and there are two Nature Trails. Finally, there are the ruins of EGGSFORD HOUSE. The original mansion belonged to the Chichesters, but this was completely rebuilt in 1830–2. During the latter part of the century Lord and Lady Portsmouth entertained London high society there; then in 1917 the second mansion was partly pulled down, leaving what has become a very romantic-looking ruin ripe for the filming of a Victorian ghost story.

Buckfast Abbey Devon 4D4
(*pop*. – Buckfastleigh – 2,656)

The Abbey stands about 1½km. north of Buckfastleigh, in exquisite surroundings beside the River Dart, and is one of very few examples in England of a foundation that has been re-established on the site of a predecessor suppressed at the Dissolution. It is thought by some historians that in the sixth century St Petroc, turning his attention for once from Cornwall, established a Celtic cell here, but Buckfast's firm history began when the Benedictine order settled here in 1018, during Canute's reign, and by 1066 had acquired large estates. After the Conquest it came under the control of Savigny, Normandy, then in 1147 it was made over to the Cistercians. After the Dissolution of 1539 the Dennys family of Holcombe Burnell acquired it (one of them was a Privy Councillor to Henry VIII), but as time passed it went through many changes of secular ownership, growing more and more dilapidated, until in 1805 the last owner, Samuel Berry, pulled it down and used the stones to build himself a Gothic mansion on the site. But in 1882 the estate was sold again, to a group of French Benedictines exiled in Ireland. They refounded the abbey, and in 1902 it acquired its first independent abbot for 363 years; but shortly afterwards he was lost at sea, and in 1907 the community set about building a new abbey as a memorial.

They did employ an outside architect, F. A. Walters, but otherwise all the work was done by the monks themselves, led by a brother who was a trained mason. It proved to be a 25-year slog, and even since the dedication of the main structure in 1932 much has been added, such as the Chapel of the Blessed Sacrament (designed by one of the order) completed in 1966. The main church is Norman in style, with an impressively simple interior in which many of the furnishings were also designed and made by the monks. There are a lantern tower with painted panels, and a mosaic floor copied from one in Ravenna. A link with the original foundation is provided by the incorporation into the living-quarters of part of Samuel Berry's mansion, built as I have said with the stones of the ancient abbey.

BUCKFASTLEIGH is most likely to appeal to the traveller

Hembury Castle

interested in industrial archaeology, for it has grown up around many old textile mills and workshops, using the wool of Dartmoor sheep. The church is of less note than the churchyard, which contains a thirteenth-century chapel (now ruined) unconnected with the church, and also a strange tomb with a sort of pent-house over it and an iron grille. This is the grave of Sir Richard Cubell, so wicked, they say, that when he died devils and black dogs left the moor to howl and cavort around his last resting-place; and just in case he failed to rest there, but arose to haunt them, the villagers put up this inelegant contraption to keep him in. There is evidence that the dog element of the story gave Conan Doyle his idea for *The Hound of the Baskervilles* (but *see also* Manaton). The Dart Valley Railway, which uses original GWR steam locomotives and rolling-stock, has a station at Buckfastleigh, postered as in the 1920s and '30s; much earlier is the fifteenth-century bridge across the Dart; and far earlier still is NT-owned HEMBURY CASTLE, 2km. north through fairy-tale woodland rides: an Iron Age fort on 150m. Hembury Hill, with tremendous views.

At the same distance on the south side of the town, west of the Dart Valley, stands DEAN PRIOR, spoilt as a village by the A38 dual carriageway, but of interest because for thirty-four years the seventeenth-century poet Robert Herrick was its reluctant vicar. The church contains lines by him on a memorial to his early friends Sir Edward Giles and Lady Giles, and the register records the burial (without headstone) of his housekeeper Prudence Baldwin, 'an old maid'. Herrick composed these rather movingly simple lines to her memory:

> In this little urn is laid
> Prudence Baldwin (once my maid),
> From whose happy spark here let
> Spring the purple violet.

But as no one knows the site of her grave, no one can tell if his wish has been granted.

Bude Canal (Bude Aqueduct)   Cornwall and Devon
6B4/C5/C6
The interest of this waterway is quite disproportionate to its short length and short life. Built between 1819 and

1826, at the then high cost of £128,000, its original length was 61km. from Bude via Marhamchurch and Hobbacott Down to Blagdonmoor Wharf, near Holsworthy. Near the Down a feeder entered from the Tamar Lakes to the north, and a little farther inland a branch turned southward to Druxton Wharf near Launceston. The first 1½km. from Bude to Helebridge, near Marhamchurch, were for normal wide barges; all the remainder was for special vessels called tub-boats – smallish, box-shaped craft fitted with wheels and carrying about 4,000kg. apiece. The reason for the wheels was that, although there were three locks on the canal, most of the changes of level were effected by raising or lowering the tub-boats on inclines fitted with rails. Motive-power was hydraulic: at the top of each incline a deep shaft was sunk into the ground, and to haul up the boats a large water-filled tank descended the shaft, pulling a chain to which the vessels were hitched. At the bottom the water was run out of the tank into a pipe that opened on to the lower level, and descending craft hauled the tank up again. Enough water could be retained in the tank to prevent the descending tub-boat from running away.

For more than sixty years the Bude Canal was a profitable proposition, taking coal (Bude was a small port in those days) and sand rich in lime – valued by farmers – inland and bringing back grain and slate for export. But, as everywhere else, the railway rapidly killed the canal trade. All but the brief wide-barge stretch to Helebridge was closed in 1891, the rest abandoned ten years later; the wide-barge part is now cleaned and navigable for pleasure-craft. But a good deal of the old canal and its appurtenances remain to be seen. At Bude itself, in addition to the sea lock, the old storehouses still stand above Falcon Bridge; at Roddsbridge, between Bude and Helebridge, is one of the two inland locks, and at Helebridge itself are a warehouse, the engineer's house, and an overgrown wharf; at Blagdonmoor Wharf, the Holsworthy terminal, contemporary farm buildings contrast with the old warehouses and stables: near Moreton Mill, east of the road from Stratton to the Tamar Lakes, Moreton Bridge, which once carried the feeder, is still in position with its original cast-iron arches; and on the Launceston branch, the terminal basin at Druxton is overgrown but still visible, flanked by the wharfinger's cottage, a warehouse, and the stables.

In addition, a great many stretches of the tub-boat canal are discernible, some indeed still containing water. But the *pièce de résistance* must be the remaining inclines. There were originally six, of which the most impressive today are those at Marhamchurch, Hobbacott Down (south of A3072 2km. west of its intersection with B3254), and Werrington. None of the rails for the tubs, nor the haulage chains, remain in position, nor has any machinery been discovered so far at the bottom of any of the shafts. But the mere inclines, overgrown as some

ABOVE, LEFT *and* RIGHT: *Bench-ends in All Saints' church, East Budleigh*

are, are a sight to see. That at Marhamchurch (reached by a short walk along the towpath from Helebridge) raised the boats 36½m. along a great ramp stretching overhead for 225m. The Hobbacott incline is even greater – a lift of 68m. by a ramp 255m. long. The Werrington incline (2km. north-east of the village at a hamlet called Bridgetown) is interesting because, although much shorter, it crosses over the lane, which passes under it through a tunnel.

Three of the tub-boats have been retrieved from the canal bottom, including a lead-boat with pointed bows. One, renovated, is in the Maritime Museum at Exeter.

Budleigh Salterton Devon 7H6 (*pop.* 4,157)
On its own straight-backed bay adjoining the mouth of the River Otter with its maze of channels. No one contemplating this most dignified of resorts and places of retirement would realize that for most of its history Budleigh's main interest in life was smuggling. As a

2km. north-west of that the gabled, mullioned, and thatched HAYES BARTON in which Sir Walter Raleigh was born in 1552. Hayes Barton can be visited from June to September (but not at weekends). Properly the house is part of EAST BUDLEIGH, a village that still manages to look as most people feel a Devon village ought to look, and has an essentially thirteenth-century church with plenty of good bench-ends (some carved, it is thought, by sailors), and Raleigh family memorials. Also open to visitors are the BICTON GARDENS, once the grounds of a 'stately home' now destroyed. Laid out in 1735 by the man who planned the gardens of Versailles, they now include a pinetum and a small country-life museum. Finally, on the western outskirts of Budleigh Salterton one may pay afternoon visits to the extensive parkland, woods, shrubberies, and flower gardens of Georgian LEE FORD. The house, noted for its French and English furniture, is also open.

Bulkworthy   6C4   (*pop.* 68)
Sir William Hankford, Chief Justice of the King's Bench under Henry V (whom as Prince Hal he had put in gaol), built the little church, though the inscription testifying to this has disappeared, probably during the restoration of 1873 that destroyed nearly everything else that may have been of interest. The pulpit, however, is a delight, composed of old carved panels salvaged, presumably, from another part of the building. The south porch has a room over it reached by a quaint outside staircase, but the modest exterior of the church is overshadowed in interest by a majestic tithe barn of venerable age standing opposite. For the rest, this parish in the valley of the Torridge less than a dozen km. from Cornwall consists mainly of old and mellow clusters of farm buildings and one subsidiary hamlet, HAYTOWN, nearer the river, in which the cottages are grouped around a chapel with a splendid Georgian entrance.

Cadgwith   Cornwall   2C6
One of the most captivating fishing villages or mini-ports on the Lizard Peninsula, amid some of its best coastal scenery. Built in typical Cornish fashion on the steep slopes bordering a stream, the cottages are nearly all of the local dark-green stone called serpentine; many are thatched. The showpiece of the coastal attractions is the DEVIL'S FRYING PAN (NT) just south of the village: originally an enormous cavern, in 1868 the roof fell in, turning it into a basin that makes you dizzy to look down at, especially when the sea foams in at high tide through what is now an archway. There are many other caverns, including DOLAR and RAVEN'S HUGO; and at POLTESCO, 1km. north, where you can see the ruins of a factory that used to process the serpentine stone for French shop-fronts, the local stream reaches the sea by a series of waterfalls. Beyond, in contrast with so much savagery, lie the km.-long silver-grey Kennack Sands, with excellent bathing. There is a beacon on the sands just

'front' it went in, of course, for fishing, and the second part of the name derives from the salt pans that used to be worked in the estuary of the Otter by the monks of the now vanished Otterton Priory. As a resort the place scarcely came into its own before Edwardian times, though it had had its distinguished residents: Anthony Trollope for a while, and John Millais, who painted his celebrated 'Boyhood of Raleigh' on the beach here. (Raleigh was a local – *see below*.) Some quiet Georgian terraces remain, and plenty of Edwardian villas, comely and comfortable. The modern church is rather dull, and so, really, is the beach; LADRAM BAY, a few km. north, is much more exciting with its eroded cliffs, large caves, and pillar-like rocks beloved of seabirds. But as an alternative to the beach Budleigh Salterton is backed by a nicely wooded hinterland, including pines, where there are plenty of public paths.

Just behind the town is the large, handsome, eighteenth-century bulk of TIDWELL BARTON (not open), and

A Camborne tin mine, C19 engraving

bearing the word 'Cable'. It belongs to the Post Office, and the other end of the cable is in Spain. Fishing at Cadgwith is for pilchards, but it has declined, as in so many places. Until 1963 there was a lifeboat station with a record of 400 lives saved, not to mention sterling service in 1940 by the lifeboat of the day at Dunkirk.

Calstock   Cornwall   4B4   (*pop.* 3,884)
On the steep right bank of the Tamar where its course twists so sharply that from the top of the town you can see the water on both sides. Hardly known to most travellers, this is one of the most rewarding parts of inland Cornwall, whether your interests lie in scenic beauty, horticulture, the history of our so-called Dark Ages, or the newer history of Victorian industry. The river-banks, thickly wooded for many miles on the Devon side, wooded in part on the Cornish, are in places high and abrupt enough to form gorges. On the Cornish side, too, are the orchards where strawberries, gooseberries, and sweet cherries (here called mazzards) are grown: Calstock should be seen in the spring! In the eastern semi-distance are the first tors of Dartmoor, and to the north-west the twin heights of HINGSTON DOWN rising to 333m. at Kit Hill. Industrially the most striking item is the twelve-arched viaduct that soars above the river by Calstock to carry the little branch railway from Plymouth to Callington (now only to Gunnislake). But more haunting are the scores of tall ruined engine-houses and taller chimneys of abandoned tin mines,

especially on the slopes of the Down: one is on the very summit of Kit Hill. On this hill, in 835, the Saxon army of King Edgar of Wessex fought and eventually won a furious battle against a combined force of Cornishmen and Danes; and relics of a still earlier age are the groups of tumuli all along the Down. Perhaps some of those buried in the tumuli knew DUPATH WELL, a spring subsequently adjudged holy and enclosed during the fifteenth century in a small granite baptistery that survives.

Camborne and **Redruth**   Cornwall   2C4
(*pop.* 33,416)
Apart from St Austell, these twin towns now officially classed as one form the only major centre in Cornwall devoted almost exclusively to industry. Once the county's tin-mining 'capital', they exist today mainly on light engineering and brewing, though mining never entirely ceased and today there are even signs of a modest revival (*see* introduction, p. 43). In one respect, indeed, it could be said that their pre-eminence in mining has remained unimpaired, for the School of Metalliferous Mining at Pool (now joined with the Cornwall College of Technology), in the eastern part of Camborne, still enjoys world fame. Several of the historic beam-engines in the mines – one of the first applications of steam-power to industry – were recently acquired by the NT. All but one are at Camborne, and at present three can be seen at appropriate times by the public: two at East Pool and Agar Mine, beside the A30, and one at the Holman

Gwennap Pit, near Redruth

Museum. This museum also contains an absorbing collection of engineering and industrial relics as well as working models. The Tolgus Tin Company, of Redruth, who run one of Cornwall's two surviving tin-streaming works, allow weekday visits. Camborne/Redruth and their environs abound in other reminders of the industrial pioneers. Pool, already mentioned, was the birthplace in 1771 of Richard Trevithick, inventor of the high-pressure steam-engine. On Christmas Eve, 1801, he put a wheeled version of his engine on the road at Camborne, and saw it chug successfully up Beacon Hill. (Two years later, over in Glamorgan, he was to build the first locomotive to run successfully on rails, and in 1808 he exhibited one on a circular track at – prophetically! – Euston.) Trevithick's birthplace in Station Road is marked by a plaque, his statue is opposite the public library, and his later home at LOWER PENPONDS, on the southern edge of Camborne, is now a NT property. A contemporary steam pioneer, Arthur Woolf, was also a Camborne man; and ILLOGAN (*pron.* Illúggan), midway along the short road to Portreath and today a sprawl of dreary council estates, was the birthplace of William Bickford, who in 1831 invented the safety-fuse for blasting, an achievement commemorated by a tablet on the wall of a factory at TUCKINGMILL, a district on the Redruth side of Camborne. Illogan, too, was the native heath of the Tangye brothers, inventors of the sort of pumping machinery without which the tin-mines could never have got off the ground, or to be more precise far

below it – at 900m. the Old Dolcoath was once the deepest mine in the world – and whose name and occupation are today preserved in Tangye's Cornwall Works at Birmingham. Finally, Redruth was at one time the home of William Murdock, builder of a steam locomotive way back in 1784, and inventor of the gas-engine, who in 1792, when everyone's thoughts were on the French wars, became the first man to experiment with gas-lighting in his house. The building, which had previously been a chapel and then a prison, survives in Cross Street behind Druid's Hall. As a result of Murdock's experiments the streets of Redruth were lit by gas as early as 1827.

Architecturally and aesthetically neither Camborne nor Redruth has a great deal to offer, Redruth being the more rewarding with its Georgian houses around the church (*see below*), on Station Hill, and in a few other streets. In both towns Methodist chapels, once catering for almost every known sub-sect but mainly Wesleyan (Wesley spent much time preaching hereabouts), are conspicuous, nor should one ignore the Quaker Meeting House of 1833; George Fox himself, the founder of the Friends, was imprisoned during a visit to Redruth in 1655. A more tragic figure was the once celebrated Cornish sculptor, Nevill Burnard (1818–78), who died in utter misery in the workhouse. The most interesting older building in Redruth is the parish church of St Euny, or Uny, set in what almost amounts to a separate village of tree-girt Georgian houses south-west of the

ABOVE, LEFT *and* RIGHT: *The crosses at Lanteglos-by-Camel-ford*

town proper, under the shadow of the hill Carn Brea. Except for its fifteenth-century tower, the granite church is Classical, dating from 1756–68. The church-yard gateway, on the other hand, is eighteenth-century Gothic. The large whitewashed interior of the church was made to look even larger when the west gallery was removed in 1878.

CARN BREA (Brea *pron.* Bray), 220m. high, offers about everything a hill can offer: huge granite rocks and deep caves, a Neolithic hill-fort, Stone Age hut circles, the remains of a castle, a hint of treasure (a sack of gold coins was found in 1749), views over most of Cornwall, an obelisk erected in 1837 to Lord de Dunstanville (*see* Godrevy Point), and a 'leisure centre'. One or two other places in the vicinity deserve mention. One km. east of Redruth lies GWENNAP PIT, a huge amphitheatre, formed by mining subsidence, where in 1762 and on several later occasions – the last when he was eighty-five – Wesley preached, amid perfect accoustics, to congregations of up to 20,000. In 1803 the Pit was im-proved somewhat, and to the present day great numbers of Methodists gather there every Whitsun. Somewhat further east, along the A390 to Truro, is CHACEWATER, a

Georgian and Victorian ex-mining village of some ele-gance, where James Watt lived while he was supervising the first steam pumping-engine used in a Cornish mine. On the subject of roads, traffic conditions in the twin towns have been immensely eased by a new by-pass. And as a valedictory note, no piece about Camborne should be written without a mention of the Town Band, the only brass band in the southern half of England that can match the famous bands of the industrial North.

Camelford Cornwall 3F1, 6A6 (*pop.* 1,544)
A little grey town beside the River Camel and astride the busy A39 that would be very pleasant if it were not for the traffic, and even now is a good centre from which to explore the northern half of Bodmin Moor. Although various etymologies have been furnished, needless to say the name 'Camel' is seized on by local enthusiasts as stemming from 'Camelot', and SLAUGHTERBRIDGE, which spans the river 2km. to the north, is pointed out as the spot where in 542 King Arthur was mortally wounded in a fierce battle against the forces of Modred, his nephew. A large granite slab nearby is said to mark the King's grave – and woe betide any authority who

says that the battle was really fought at Camelon, in Scotland, or that Arthur's grave is at Glastonbury in Somerset! A better authenticated battle at Slaughterbridge (though even in this case the location is not quite certain) was fought between the Britons or Cornishmen and the Saxons in 823.

A curious feature of Camelford is that until the present century the only church was at LANTEGLOS, 2km. down the road. This church has a fifteenth-century tower incorporating a fourteenth-century doorway, a fifteenth-century aisle, and a partly Norman chancel; but everything else has been subjected to one of the more ruthless Victorian restorations; there is a better flavour of originality about the gabled vicarage, reputedly designed by Pugin, and the early crosses. To the west are two large Iron Age forts, CASTLE GOFF and NEWBURY: and further west and north respectively the great slate quarries of DELABOLE and PENPETHY. Some of these are still worked, some abandoned. Those that are abandoned are eerie indeed, especially in twilight; all, worked or not, suggest landscapes on another planet.

Chagford Devon 7E6 (*pop.* 1,250)
Of old, one of Dartmoor's four stannary towns for assessing and stamping the product of the tin-mines; to-day, largely a holiday centre, though (as its small population indicates) managing to avoid modern spread. It has, indeed, remained surprisingly unspoilt notwithstanding 'discovery' by the holidaymaker at least a century ago. At that time, before the motor car had induced near-universal atrophy of the legs, it was walkers who came here, attracted by the remarkable array of tumuli, hut-circles, standing stones, and other evidences of vigorous life in this north-east corner of the moor in ages long past. Many old towns and villages have been dominated by one family: Chagford was dominated by the Whyddons, or Whiddons, who dwelt in WHIDDONPARK HOUSE, or Whiddon Manor as it used to be, set in a beautiful park overlooking the western end of the even more beautiful Teign Gorge about 3km. north-east of the town. The house is a picturesque granite affair with square chimneys and mullioned windows, mainly built around the turn of the sixteenth and seventeenth centuries. It has a fine thatched barn. The last Whiddon died in 1720. The house is not for viewing, but a public footpath crosses the park very close to it.

Chagford's fifteenth-century church lost much of its historical interest when it underwent its Victorian restoration, and it is appropriate that its chief surviving attraction is a Whiddon tomb, intriguingly decorated, that of Sir John (d. 1575). Secular buildings are a pleasant blend of the Victorian and the older thatched – reflecting, in a way, the harmonious juxtaposition of bare moorland and lush woods in the surrounding landscape. A distinguished member of the thatched group is the early-Tudor Three Crowns Inn, with mullioned windows and grand porch; here one of the Godolphin

family (Sidney) was killed in a skirmish with Parliamentary troops early in the Civil War. As to the prehistoric remains, most of these lie several km. south and are dealt with under either Gidleigh (qv) or Postbridge (qv). An exception is the group of hill-forts commanding the Teign Gorge north-east of the town: CRANBROOK, PRESTONBURY, and WOOSTON. These were all built by the Iron Age invaders of the first century BC.

One natural feature, so isolated that it is not really near any of the places in this gazetteer, may be considered with Chagford because for more than a century it has been a tradition to walk there from the town. This is CRANMERE POOL, a dried-up depression in the midst of nowhere at all (except the Army's danger zone when there is artillery practice), surrounded by bogs that are the source of many of Devon's rivers, and reached, no matter from which direction, only across at least 6 or 7km. of Dartmoor's highest uplands. In 1864 a Chagford man built a cairn in the middle of the 'pool' and placed a bottle on it for walkers' cards. The bottle was succeeded by visitors' books, which when full went to Plymouth City Library, and the cairn became a granite pillar containing a cupboard. Everyone arriving there had to address an envelope, stamp it, and leave it in the cupboard for the next comer to take away and post, himself taking the envelope left by his predecessor. Today, alas, people can motor to within a km. or so of Cranmere Pool by an Army-built road from Okehampton. But the cupboard is still there, and the more masochistically-minded still plod out to it.

The Cheesewring Cornwall 3G1
1½km. N of Minions
On Stowe's Hill, Bodmin Moor. In a region of fantastic granite formations, this is the most striking: a natural pile of huge stone slabs supported on smaller slabs. (Recently an artificial support has been added to keep the group from toppling.) Scarcely less striking is the view from the 381m. hill – a panorama that stretches from the Atlantic to the Channel, including virtually the whole of Cornwall, west Devon as far as Dartmoor, and north Devon as far, on a clear day, as Exmoor. The neighbourhood abounds in evidences of early man, and of men not so early but equally remote from our own pursuits. In Stowe hillside itself, sliced into by huge abandoned slate quarries, is DANIEL GUMB'S CAVERN, the 'home' for many years of Daniel Gumb, eccentric philosopher, mathematician, and stone-carver (d. 1776), whose handiwork is to be seen in a number of Cornish churchyards. Quarrying caused the cavern to fall in, but the same stones have been used to restore it. South of the hill is a cist, unnamed, in which less than a century ago was found a beautiful Bronze Age golden cup, now in the British Museum. South again are THE HURLERS, three large stone circles almost certainly associated with pagan religion, but which according to legend are the bodies of a party of wicked characters who

The Bronze Age cup (8½cm. high) found S of Stowe's Hill. Now in the B.M.

dared to play 'hurling' on the Sabbath. Similar stories are told of stone groupings in many parts of England, and originated in the anxiety of the infant Church to break the popular hold exerted by these rival temples. Circles were commonly picked on because of the prevalence of 'round' games.

South-west of The Cheesewring the land dips, then rises to CARADON TOR, its summit crowned by television masts, its flanks dotted with the ruined engine-houses of former copper mines, matching in their silence the Stowe's Hill quarries: only the television masts, the SIBLYBACK RESERVOIR, a few km. to the east, and the Dept of the Environment's wire fence round The Hurlers remind one that life continues at all in this vast dead landscape.

Cheriton Fitzpaine   Devon   7F4   (*pop.* 571)
A village that just misses being as attractive as its name, set on a hillside above one of the headstreams of the River Creedy, which lower down gives its name to Crediton. Many of the houses are Georgian, Stuart, or even Tudor; there is an excellent row of late-Tudor almshouses, 1594. The fifteenth-century church is large, and of red sandstone in pleasant harmony with the buff-coloured cob walls of many of the cottages. Inside, restoration has not been too unkind and has spared the old waggon-roofs of nave and both aisles. But one is disappointed not to see splendid monuments everywhere to the Fitzpaines. Two km. north, in a valley near the junction of two streams, is POUGHILL. Its namesake in

Cornwall is pronounced Poffle, but the Devon example calls itself Poil. (Dorset Poughill, just for the record, is pronounced Puffle.) A dreary little village that does not deserve its pleasant church (eighteenth-century waggon-roofs, box pews, some faded and therefore harmonious colouring, original floors – but all stonework glaringly over-restored) and still less deserves UPCOTT BARTON, up a gentle slope outside the village. This late-medieval mansion was given in Tudor times one of the most agreeable frontages of any house of its size in Devon. Of warm-coloured stone, with mullioned windows, its appearance is 'made' by the broad central upper window, in which the part of the transom between the two mullions is surmounted by a rounded stone arch. The house belonged to the Upcotts in the early Middle Ages, and in the mid fifteenth century its owner was Nicholas Radford, a notary. But Radford had incurred the anger of some of the Earl of Devon's family, and in 1455 a group led by the Earl's son, Sir Thomas Courtenay, broke into Upcott and murdered the notary. The Courtenays then took over the house. Today a farmhouse, it is not open to visitors, but a footpath over the top of the hill east of it gives a view of its attractive exterior.

Chulmleigh   Devon   *see* **Brushford**

Chysauster   Cornwall   *see* **Gulval**

Clovelly   Devon   6C3   (*pop.* 434)
Go to this north-coast showplace in spring, autumn, or a mellow patch of winter, for during a longer and longer stretch of summer each year it is the most overcrowded spot in Devon. And it is worth going to, for it *is* very pretty, and hardly spoilt – perhaps because there is hardly room to spoil it; for it consists of just one cobbled street that descends the cliff so steeply that (praise be) no motor vehicle could use it if it tried: donkeys and sleds are the only transport. (There is a rough track running down to the harbour well outside the village, limited to vehicles transporting beer down to the pub and the more fragile tourists – not necessarily patrons of the pub – back to the top.) The presiding Clovelly family, whose mansion, Clovelly Court, stands back from the top of the cliff, was successively that of the Giffards, the Careys, and (since 1738) the Hamlyns: and it is to two Hamlyn ladies, Mrs Patricia and her daughter Christine, that the embellishment and preservation of Clovelly is due. Much of the improvement of the cottages, not to mention the siting of all tourist amenities on the cliff-top, well clear of the street, is due to Mrs Hamlyn, who had 'reigned' over the scene for fifty-two years when she died in 1936; and that a good deal of further cottage beautification is due to her daughter can be deduced from the initials 'C.H.' on many houses. The cottages, which all but stand on one another's roofs, are a jumble of angles and projections, white or colour-washed, most of them thatched, and

Clovelly

with pocket-handkerchief gardens agleam with flowers. In view of the Hamlyns' good work, it seems unjust that Clovelly Court – Georgian, after a fire had destroyed its predecessor – should itself have been nearly wrecked by another fire not many years ago.

The little harbour is the only refuge for ships between Westward Ho! and Bude, and was once a busy fishing centre, mainly for herrings, which are still caught by the few boats continuing to operate. An impressive crop of artists and authors have depicted Clovelly: painters from Turner to Rex Whistler, novelists Charles Kingsley in *Westward Ho!* and Charles Dickens in 'A Message from the Sea' (*Christmas Stories*), in which he called it 'Steepways'. Kingsley's father was curate and then vicar here in the 1830s, and could apparently handle a herring-boat and its gear as well as any professional fisherman. The church, near Clovelly Court, is a mixture of Norman, Early English, and Perpendicular, and full of monuments to the Careys and Hamlyns. Also near the Court grounds is a sizeable tract of woods and farmland belonging to the NT; part of it is a Nature

Reserve. The viewpoint and miniature park called Mount Pleasant is also NT property, given by Mrs Hamlyn in 1921 as a memorial to the Clovelly dead in the First World War.

East of the village Hobby Drive, a 5km. paved ride along the cliffs between beeches and other trees, was devised by Sir James Hamlyn-Williams and his wife between 1811 and 1829, as a hobby – and one with very pleasant results. The Drive comes out on the main road (A39), but 2km. farther on this passes the head of a very attractive wooded valley leading past the tiny, white-washed hamlet of BUCK'S MILLS to a little beach with lime-kilns and a few fishing-boats: in summer a restful change from the crowds at Clovelly, to which, incidentally, it is possible to walk at low tide. Another fine walk is provided on the west of Clovelly by GALLANTRY BOWER, a curious name that has a near-counterpart near Dartmouth and is perhaps a corruption of the Cornish *col-an-veor*, 'the great ridge'. Certainly this is a great ridge, with a sloping landward flank but on the seaward side a sheer drop of well over 100m. It ends with

St Andrew's church, Colyton, from the NW

a descent to MOUTH MILL, another small beach at the opening of a larger and more indented valley than that of Buck's Mills. At Mouth Mill the rocks look especially wicked even for this grim coast, being eroded into the form of huge teeth.

South of Clovelly, inland, where its own road joins the A39, is CLOVELLY DYKES, a triple earthwork covering in all about 7ha. (20 acres), with banks averaging 6m. high. Of Iron Age construction, the complex continued in use by the Romans and perhaps the Saxons.

Coldridge   Devon   *see* **Brushford**

Colyton   Devon   5G2   (*pop.* 2,112)
On the Coly, a tributary of the Axe, between Axminster and the coast. Its position so far east and so near the Axe estuary meant that West Saxons sailing along the coast westward founded a settlement here probably before 700. Its first Norman lords were the Bassets, who obtained a royal grant of a seven-day fair in 1208 and soon afterwards founded a borough about 1km. south at COLYFORD. But this was not a long-term commercial success – it probably 'died' after about 200 years – whereas Colyton survived and is now the seat of various light industries. It is a delightful little town of sloping, winding streets in a gracious countryside strewn with old and handsome farms, a number of which, in reversal of the commoner process, were taken over by the 'squirearchy' two or three centuries ago and promoted into mansions, usually with constructional embellishments to suit. Other farms are replacements of manor-houses mentioned in Domesday. In the town itself some of the more notable among many historic buildings are the Vicarage (1529), built by the learned Doctor Brereward who gave the church its fine screen; The Great House, former home of the Yonge family, Elizabethan though partly rebuilt; Colyton Cottage (1610), larger than its name implies; Oroolong House, once the home of Captain Henry Wilson, Pacific Ocean explorer; and the Old Court House in which Judge Jeffreys is reputed to have held an assize. Colyton was long in the ownership of the Courtenays, and after their downfall in 1539 twenty local merchants purchased the confiscated estates for £1,000, the transaction being legalized by a Deed of Feoffment as a result of which the new owners called themselves the Chamber of Feoffees. The Feoffees' aim was to use the revenue from their land for the town's good, and they have been doing so ever since. The main initial achievement was to found a grammar school in the building today called the Church House.

The church itself is fully worthy of its handsome and historic setting. Though a mixture of periods – a little thirteenth century, much fourteenth, aisles rebuilt in 1765 and 1816 respectively, many late-nineteenth-century repairs, new roof and seats following a fire in 1933 – it is handsome, spacious, and full of interesting things. One such thing – outside – is the late-fifteenth-century octagonal lantern surmounting the Norman tower, another the very large fourteenth-century west window. The chancel was built in 1383, a good example of Early English style; the screen, as stated, was the gift of Dr Brereward, vicar from 1524 to 1544. The oldest feature is a Saxon cross, now in the south transept, found in pieces in the tower after the 1933 fire. The newest feature is the fine classical organ, formerly in a Baptist church and brought here in 1974. Fine tombs and monuments are exceptionally numerous; the oldest, in the chancel, is the tomb of Margaret Countess of Devon (d. 1449), John of Gaunt's granddaughter. There are seventeenth-century monuments in the Pole Chapel, and in the Lady Chapel or Yonge Chapel many Yonge tombs as well as a Jacobean stone screen bearing their arms.

The seat of the Courtenays (among their many) was COLCOMBE CASTLE, 1km. north of the town, first built in the reign of Edward I and just rebuilt on a far more sumptuous scale by Henry Courtenay, Marquess of Exeter, when his attainder in 1539 ended his ownership.

The monument to Sir John (1658) and Lady Elizabeth Pole in the Pole Chapel, St Andrew's church, Colyton. It is perhaps the work of Gerard Johnson of Southwark

Cotehele : the King's Bedroom

Colcombe was not among the acquisitions of the Feoffees, and was already falling into ruin when in Elizabeth's reign it was bought by William Pole, of Shute, for his son, who proceeded to rebuild it but (although he took up residence) never completed the work. After playing a part in the Civil War the mansion became a farmhouse, which it continues to be. There is no public admission, which is a pity, for the interior is still of much interest; but the exterior, also rewarding, is visible at a distance of ½km. from the B3154.

Combe Raleigh Devon *see* **Honiton**

Coombe Valley Cornwall 6B4 (NT)
Halfway between Bude and the Devon border, this superb partly-wooded valley with its stream and Nature Trail is not entirely in NT hands, but probably enough of it is to prevent spoliation, except perhaps by cars, which can unfortunately reach DUCKPOOL, the little bathing-cove at the valley mouth, crowding it out in the season and ruining the enjoyment of pedestrians. This is the country of R. S. Hawker, the eccentric vicar-poet of Morwenstow (qv). He spent his honeymoon with his first wife at Coombe Cottage, or Hall Barn as it was then named. Also belonging to the NT, on the hill-slope south of the valley, lies STOWE BARTON (not open to the public), part Tudor, part 1701, one of a number of magnificent old farmhouses in this area of Cornwall and Devon. Its name preserves that of Stowe House, once alongside, the ancestral home of that celebrated Elizabethan mariner Sir Richard Grenville – the 'Chapel' from which he set forth in 1591 to embark on his last voyage as so finely described by Kingsley in *Westward Ho!*

As a result of his descendant Sir Bevil Grenville's Civil War victory at Stamford Hill (*see* Stratton and Bude), Charles II agreed to finance a new home for the Grenvilles. Accordingly Stowe House was pulled down and replaced in 1680 by another on an adjoining site; but this, although it won high praise from the Cornish antiquarian William Borlase, was generally adjudged to be so hideous that in 1739 it was pulled down in its turn. Today only a flat, raised piece of meadow marks the site of the earlier house, but of the later, in the next field, the bases of various walls, a flight of steps, the tennis court (converted to a yard), and the terraces that were once gardens are all clearly visible, and excavation may uncover more. Various fittings from this house survive: panelling at Houndapit Farm, 1km. south-east; the grand staircase (a splendid affair) and other fragments at Cross, a mansion of the 1680s just north of Little Torrington, Devon; woodwork and a painting by Verrio at Prideaux Place, Padstow (qv).

At the very head of Coombe Valley stands KILK-HAMPTON (*pop.* 840), an agreeable village notwithstanding its situation astride the A39. The manor was first granted to the Grenville family in 1088, and the patronage of the church in 1238 – a right that the family still

holds. The church is among the many to have been re-built in the late fifteenth or early sixteenth century, but there is a magnificent south doorway of about 1130, probably built by the masons who erected Tewkesbury Abbey, Gloucestershire, which at that time held the patronage. The interior consists of nave, chancel, and two aisles; the most interesting features are the eight monuments (including Sir Bevil Grenville's) by Michael Chuke, a Kilkhampton-born pupil of Grinling Gibbons, and little if at all inferior to his master; and the outstanding collection of 157 carved bench-ends and pew fronts, the earliest 1380, the most recent a small number of very competent replacements made during the 1860 restoration. This last, though typically harsh in other respects, did produce some good wood carving, including the present rood and screen. Characteristically, the restorers threw out the fine Jacobean pulpit, also decorated by Michael Chuke, but not before a visitor had made a careful sketch of it. This sketch then disappeared from view, but was discovered by chance in London in 1950.

In the upper part of the valley slightly west of Kilkhampton stands PENSTOWE MANOR, an early-nineteenth-century mansion built for Arthur Christopher Thynne, a grandson of the then Earl of Bath and therefore a member of the Grenville family. The house is now a hotel, and, contrary to some statements, does not contain any fitments from the former Stowe House.

Cotehele Cornwall 3H2 (NT)
W of Calstock, from which it is 3km. by footpath but 13km. by road.
For centuries the seat of the Earls of Mount Edgcumbe, the house was built during the reigns of Henry VII and VIII, and remains one of the least altered late-medieval residences in the country. Some fragments of an earlier house are incorporated. Of grey granite with stone-mullioned and transomed windows, it surrounds two courtyards, the first entered through an arched gateway, and contains all the expected features of a mansion of its time: a great hall (this separates the courtyards), a chapel, and seemingly endless rooms all leading one out of the other. The furniture, tapestries, and armour have always been in the house, and therefore, though the reason is hard to define, give a much more satisfying impression than in some other NT properties where the contents have been assembled from a variety of 'alien' sources.

But rivalling the house itself is its setting. The terraced gardens, with ponds and little waterfalls, shelve down between woodlands to the Tamar far below. There is a medieval dovecote; and high above the river, in the woods, stands the Chapel on the Hill, built by Richard Edgcumbe to mark the spot where he escaped arrest under Richard III (he was an active supporter of Henry Tudor) by throwing his cap and a large boulder into the river. Hearing the splash and later seeing the cap afloat,

Cotehele : the main entrance

the pursuing soldiers concluded he was drowned and rode off. Beneath, some distance apart, are MORDEN MILL, the manorial water mill, once more in working condition; and COTEHELE QUAY, where the valley opens into the Tamar.

Couchsmill   Cornwall   *see* **Boconnoc**

Coverack   Cornwall   2D6
Like Cadgwith, a fishing village of increasing attraction to holiday-makers but so far reasonably unspoilt, on the same wild and exciting east coast of the Lizard Peninsula. It is partly this wildness and the large number of caves that in the past made Coverack a favourite port with smugglers. Today the highlight of the year is not the arrival of a spectacular smuggling haul but the no less spectacular ceremony on a Sunday every August when the Methodists hold a huge meeting at the harbour, complete with brass band and hymn-singing choirs foregathered from many places.

To the north the coast curves out to LOWLAND POINT, a NT headland, interesting geographically because it is really a raised beach of the last Ice Age. Its summit affords a good view, when the tide is low enough, of the most dreaded rocks off the Lizard coast, the MANACLES, more than a km. out to sea, widely scattered, all but one invisible at high water, and lying right in the path of ships making for Falmouth. The name has nothing to do with handcuffs, but is a corruption of 'Maen Eglos',

the Church Stones. The nearest church, in fact, is that of ST KEVERNE 2km. inland, a building with many unusual features and an octagon spire that formerly served as a landmark to sailors trying to avoid the Manacles. But more than 400 who failed are buried in the churchyard.

To the south of Coverack the coast runs south past the CHYNALLS POINT promontory to BLACK HEAD, then turns west. Several stretches of the impressive coast here are preserved by the NT, which is pleasant not only for the holiday-maker but for the geologist, whether professional or amateur; green serpentine, black-and-white gabbro, and red granite are all nearly unique to this area and afford fascinating evidences of the strange way in which our planet assumed its present form.

Crantock   Cornwall   *see* **Newquay**

Crediton   Devon   7F5   *(pop.* 5,161)
A town with a great place in Devon history, for between 909 and 1050 it was the seat of the Devon bishopric, and during the last decade of that period the seat of the united Cornish bishopric as well. In 1050 the see was transferred to Exeter, which could be more easily defended against invading Danes. Long before that, in 680, St Boniface (called Winfrith in England) had been born here: a man of great energy, he went as a missionary to Germany and converted many of the heathens, as well as re-converting to orthodox Catholicism others whom

earlier Celtic missionaries had converted to their own Christian practice. It was at the hand of a pagan tribe that Boniface met his death, after becoming Archbishop of Mainz. There is a statue to him in Crediton's town park.

The parish church (which is not dedicated to St Boniface) has had an unusual history. Large and grand, as befits a town where there was a monastic foundation 170 years before there was a bishopric, it is at least the third building on its site, although incorporating earlier features dating as far back as 1150; most of the present fabric was erected *c*. 1410. Being a collegiate church, it was in peril of destruction after the Dissolution, but was bought by the townspeople for £200. Twelve 'Governors' were appointed to preserve the building, and their successors still do. It is very long, cruciform, with a tower at the centre of the cross, resting on Norman piers. The Lady Chapel was a grammar school from 1572 to 1860. The Governors' Room leading off the east transept used to contain a very valuable library, but this has been removed to Exeter. There is a good west window, and a similar east window that used to display a unique and striking pattern of its own until a Victorian vandal named Hayward, in charge of 'restoration', destroyed this in the interests of conformity.

The best feature of the interior is the very large number of monuments, ranging from the tomb of a fourteenth-century knight and his lady to a positive triumphal arch in honour of Gen. Sir Redvers Buller, hero of the Relief of Ladysmith in 1900. Buller was a local boy; his birthplace, DOWNES, is a Georgian mansion just to the east of Crediton and visible from the Exeter road (A377). The secular buildings of the town, where not modern, are predominantly Georgian and Victorian, the result of the extensive destruction of their predecessors in two fires, 1743 and 1769, which particularly affected the western end. In the previous century the Civil War had seen Crediton change hands a number of times, both armies making it their headquarters; but damage from the fighting was relatively slight. The citizens' income in the past derived mainly from cloth-making and a market; today it comes from light industries and cider.

Crediton is surrounded by rivers. The Creedy flows to the east of it, the Yeo to the south, and both have a number of tributaries. Two km. north, above the Creedy and one of its satellites, is SANDFORD (*pop.* 1,061), a picture-village of eighteenth-century houses and cottages, an old Tudor inn, The Lamb, a George IV classical mansion (now a school), and a satisfying church containing

Crediton church from the SW: built of red sandstone, it is in essence a C12 cruciform church, remodelled early C15

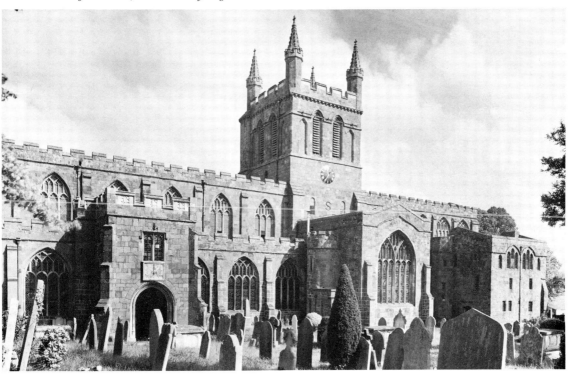

fifteenth-century bench-ends, a carved west gallery dated, surprisingly, 1657 – during the Commonwealth – and memorials of local 'great families'. A little farther from Crediton, north-east beside a tributary of the Yeo misleadingly named Shobrooke Lake, and backed by the 240m. Raddon Hills, is STOCKLEIGH POMEROY (*pop.* 108), an agreeable village with a church very well off for carving, especially of bench-ends. The Pomeroy family (better known in association with Berry Pomeroy – *see* Totnes) lost the manor after being implicated in the Catholic rising of 1549. Beside the main road midway between here and Crediton is GREAT GUTTON, a large Tudor farmhouse as elegant as its name is otherwise.

Cullompton Devon 7G4 (*pop.* 3,745)
An old market town astride the formerly fiendishly busy A38 Exeter–Taunton road, but now enabled by the opening of the M5 motorway to enjoy at last its place beside the pleasant River Culm. The town's long connexion with the wool trade is reflected in the survival of several expensive mansions built by the wool merchants, and in the opulence of the church. One such mansion is the so-called manor-house, now a hotel, a mixture of styles and periods but with parts dating back to the year of the first Queen Elizabeth's death. Another is Walronds, completed in 1605. At the opposite end of the social scale John Trott's Almshouses form a well-designed row. The church possesses a tall and elaborately adorned tower built in 1549 and following years. Lane's Chapel, really a second south aisle, the gift of John Lane, a wool magnate in Henry VIII's reign, has much carving outside and good fan tracery inside. Roofs of chancel and nave are carved and coloured, as is the great rood-screen.

Five km. east of Cullompton is KENTISBEARE, in whose church is a magnificent west gallery of 1632 and a more magnificent screen of exceptionally skilled design and execution, perhaps the work of monks from Tavistock after the Dissolution. In the chancel there is a tablet to the Revd G. W. Scott with verses by his kinsman Sir Walter Scott. Near the church is Priest Hall, a highly interesting priest's house of about 700 years ago. Two km. south, at a farm on the outskirts of Kerswell, are the remains of KERSWELL PRIORY, once a cell of the Cluniac order at Montacute (Somerset). A barn, still containing a huge chimney at one end, was probably the monks' refectory, and the farmhouse itself incorporates linen-fold panelling, a Norman doorway, and other items rescued after the Dissolution. At the same distance north-west of Kentisbeare stands BRADFIELD HOUSE, which, with its predecessor, was for many centuries the home of the Walronds. The present house is Tudor, with later modifications, and is an impressive sight from the road south of it. The house is not open, so that one must miss the great hall, wealth of Tudor carving and ornamental plasterwork, and fine tapestries; but a good notion of the carving may be had from some of it that

The clapper bridge, Dartmeet

was transferred to the Walrond Chapel in Uffculme church (3½km. north-east).

Dartmeet Devon 4C3/D3
A hamlet on the Ashburton–Tavistock road (A384) close to the point where the East and West Dart rivers unite. Beside the present road bridge is the thirteenth-century clapper-bridge that served the packhorses; but more interesting and far less noticed by the thousands who motor out here on summer weekends is the COFFIN STONE about ¾km. east of the bridge, up the steep main-road hill that leads to where the Widecombe-in-the-Moor road branches off. In the old days, when someone in one of the isolated moorland settlements died, his or her coffin was borne by relays of men all the way to Widecombe or Ashburton churchyard; here by the Coffin Stone they rested after the climb, and while they rested they carved a cross and the initials of the dead on the stone. It is split in two now, but several crosses and initials can still be deciphered.

On every side of Dartmeet are standing stones, hut circles, cists, and other Bronze Age relics; Dartmoor has 1,350 hut sites alone, and most of them are in the south. Each hut consisted of a low, circular stone wall surmounted by a conical roof of turf or heather, and with an entrance between two stone jambs rising to a more convenient height than the walls. The entrance was nearly always on the south or south-west side because of Dartmoor's north-west gales. The huts were grouped into villages, some of which were enclosed in a protective earth wall or 'pound' – though this word on the map sometimes refers to a pound in the modern sense of an enclosure for strayed animals; Dunnabridge Pound, beside the main road 3km. west of Dartmeet, is one such.

DARTMOUTH

One km. west of Dartmeet a branch-road leads south to
Huccaby, and less than another km. along it, just beyond the bridge over the West Dart, is Jolly Lane Cott,
the house built in a single day. In past centuries (including the last) anyone who could build a house on Dartmoor common land between sunrise and sunset on a
single day had perpetual security against eviction. The
privilege also carried the right to free grazing, peat for
fuel, and bracken for bedding. In 1832 one Tom Sutter-
ley, an ostler at the inn at Two Bridges, with his bride
and a party of friends, used the granite stones of the
Moor and heather for thatching to build Jolly Lane
Cott. At first it was only one storey high and had no
chimney, but it fulfilled the conditions, and was in fact
the last house on Dartmoor ever to do so. The line where
the roof sloped down to the original single storey can
easily be seen today. The modern roof is of slate. Tom's
bride and eventually widow lived here until her death in
1901, when her coffin was carried to Widecombe and
duly laid upon the Coffin Stone on the way.

Dartmoor, Devon *see* **Introduction**, and **Buckfast
Abbey**, **Chagford**, **Dartmeet**, **Drewsteignton**, **Gidleigh**, **Ilsington**, **Lydford Gorge**, **Manaton**, **Moretonhampstead**, **Okehampton**, **Petertavy**, **Postbridge**, **Princetown**, **Rattery**, **Shaugh Prior**,
Sticklepath, **Tavistock**, **Widecombe-in-the-Moor**.
Although the Moor is not mentioned in the articles, **Ashburton** and **Bovey Tracey** also belong to Dartmoor.

Dartmouth   Devon   5E5   (*pop.* 5,707)
The naval tradition of this old town goes back long before the establishment in 1905 of the Royal Naval College, or even of its forerunner the training-ship HMS
Britannia in 1863. Before the close of the twelfth century
Richard I, Coeur de Lion, assembled over 100 ships and
nearly 2,000 men to take on his Crusade; 31 ships and
750 men sailed from Dartmouth to assist Edward III's
siege of Calais; and a contribution was made to Drake's
fleet against the Spanish Armada, though by then
modesty seems to have overtaken the authorities, for the
ships numbered only two. In a wider sense, too, Dartmouth was a major shipping (and piracy) centre
throughout the Middle Ages – Chaucer's pilgrim Shipman came from 'Dertemouth'; later it took a leading
part in the growing cod-fishing trade off Newfoundland.
Several of the Tudor explorers of the western and north-
western Atlantic used Dartmouth as a base. During the
Second World War a contingent of the forces for the
invasion of Normandy sailed from the estuary. Today it
is a very upstage yachting centre, with an important
annual Royal Regatta.

Like Falmouth and Fowey, Dartmouth lies a little
way up its estuary and relied for its defence on a fortress

RIGHT: *Stone pulpit, St Saviour's church, Dartmouth*

Dartmouth Castle and part of St Petroc's church (Gothic style, 1641–2)

either side of the mouth; and, like Fowey, it was further protected in time of danger by a chain slung from fort to fort. Dartmouth Castle was not one of Henry VIII's constructions, but was built in 1481, the successor to a modest fortress erected a century earlier. During the Civil War, when the town declared for Cromwell, the Castle was besieged for a month by Prince Rupert, captured, then recaptured by Fairfax. A small collection of Civil War arms are among the things to be seen there; the Castle is open throughout the year.

With one or two exceptions, Dartmouth streets, as in most ancient ports, consist mainly of a medley of narrow thoroughfares extending back from a fairly wide waterside embankment. The town centre is the Butterwalk,

essentially a row of seventeenth-century houses-over-offices, the domestic storeys projecting over the footwalk and supported on granite pillars. It suffered severe damage in an air-raid in 1943. The colonnade was the scene of the old pannier market, and is now the forecourt, so to speak, of the town museum, which occupies the Butterwalk with a collection of maritime souvenirs including more than 100 model ships. The building itself exhibits much fine carving and plasterwork; and there is more of this in the former Mansion House (1732), which is also open, but by appointment only. Another museum is the Henley in Anzac Street, open all the year in the afternoons and housing a varied display covering most of Dartmouth's history; and finally there is Newcomen

House, adjoining the Butterwalk, in which one of Newcomen's original atmospheric pressure engines (1717) may be seen working. The inventor was born in Dartmouth in 1663, and his engines were extensively used for pumping water out of mines.

The church (St Saviour), dating from 1372, is notable for its massive and resplendent south door, equally resplendent fifteenth-century rood-screen, carved, gilded, and coloured stone pulpit, Jacobean west gallery, and chancel brass of 1408 to Sir John Hawley, who had founded the church and was probably Chaucer's prototype for the Shipman. There is a second old church, St Petroc, outside the town by the castle. The present building is a curiosity, an almost wholly seventeenth-century construction in the Gothic style, only some arches and the font surviving from the preceding edifice. Its earlier history is misted over by uncertainty: the much-travelled St Petroc himself perhaps began the story by founding a cell, and later in the Middle Ages it is thought monks resident here may have operated the lighthouse.

Two of the oldest secular buildings are a house called The Cherub (1380), in Higher Street, and Agincourt House (1413) in Lower Street. There are many seventeenth-century houses. BAYARD'S COVE, near St Petroc's, where the ships tied up in the Middle Ages, shows the ruins of a castle that *was* built by Henry VIII, and another row of old houses, including the Old Custom House (1739). Near the castle too is GALLANT'S BOWER (a corruption of Galleons' Bower), also part of the old defences. The cliffs at the mouth of the Dart estuary on this side, from a point south of the castle round to the rocks at the tip of Start Bay known as the Dancing Beggars, belong to the NT. On the east bank of the river, gracefully grouped round a wooded headland, is KINGSWEAR (*pop.* 1,301), terminus of the steam trains from Paignton that have succeeded the British Rail service. A car-ferry links it with Dartmouth.

Kingswear Castle, like Dartmouth's, is some distance down the estuary. Believed to date from King John's reign, it was rebuilt (or built) in 1491, slightly later than its opposite number, and strengthened by Henry VIII. But the Castle was abandoned as artillery grew in power, and is today a private house. On this side you can still see the point of attachment of the defensive chain. Kingswear has a very wealthy air, and hardly a stretch of level street, but no outstanding buildings. The church, with the exception of its tower, is a reconstruction; its churchyard has had to be cut into the slope. The sea-coast on this side of the river-mouth is very majestic, with EASTERN BLACK ROCK rising from the sea a km. from shore, and, nearer in, the massive conglomeration of rock called the MEW STONE.

Dean Prior Devon *see* **Buckfast Abbey**

Denbury Devon *see* **Newton Abbot**

Dozmary Pool (*pron.* Dozemary) Cornwall 3F1
In the bleakest and most silent part of Bodmin Moor, this great dark sheet of sinister-looking water, over 1km. in circumference, has inevitably given rise to many myths: it is bottomless; no life can endure in it; it is the lake associated with the sword Excalibur in Arthurian legend; a wicked steward of Lanhydrock (or was it St Breward?), one Tregeagle, was condemned by the powers controlling the next world to toil night and day for ever trying to bale the Pool dry with a leaky limpet shell if he would save his soul from eternal damnation; and so on. Well, the lake has been found to have a bottom, it sports plenty of fish, on topographical grounds Loe Pool near Helston, a rival claimant to the Excalibur story, has a much better case, and as for Tregeagle . . . the age of television has not encouraged the survival of nocturnal fears, yet on a stormy winter's night near Dozmary it is not too difficult to fancy that the wind bears on it the terrible cry of poor Tregeagle as the Devil turns up to give him a prod or two.

Fiction of another kind is associated with JAMAICA INN, almost the only building in the tiny hamlet of Bolventor, 2½km. north beside the A30. When Daphne du Maurier wrote her well-known novel the rambling group of buildings were part of a farm, and were turned into an inn only as a result of the success of the book. They are genuinely Georgian, though spoilt inside with much simulated Tudor, and even more over-popularity. On the other side of the A30, 3½km. south-west of Bolventor, is HAWK'S TOR, more than 300m. high; and on Hawk's Tor Downs hard by are the STRIPPLE STONES, a once magnificent prehistoric stone henge or circle nearly 70m. across, with a centre pillar 3¾m. high and a surrounding earthen bank. The site has suffered during the centuries, but still repays a visit, particularly since it is one of a remarkable wealth of stone circles, hut circles, barrows, and standing stones between here and Blisland – an area that also includes at BRADFORD, due west of Hawk's Tor, two very fine clapper bridges, one large and one small (the former widened in 1927) over separate channels of the River De Lank.

Drewsteignton Devon 7E6
A travel-poster thatched village with the loveliest reach of the Teign in its foreground and the expanse of north Dartmoor for a backdrop. There is nothing very much to single out in the place, it is the setting and *tout ensemble* that make the impression; however, there are a number of points of interest in the vicinity. The three Iron Age forts, Cranbrook, Wooston, and Prestonbury, are noticed under Chagford, but 4km. to the west is a much more unusual antiquity: SPINSTERS' ROCK, one of only four Stone (as opposed to Bronze or Iron) Age tombs in the whole of Devon, and the only one on or near Dartmoor. It is in fact a quoit, the upright stones rising 1½m. and supporting a capstone roughly 3m. by 2½m. There are other standing stones near it. Down in

Castle Drogo, Lutyens's tour de force

the valley below the village is the seventeenth-century FINGLE BRIDGE over the Teign, comparatively new in this region of very old bridges, but a great favourite with the weekend motorist, especially from Exeter or Torquay. Yet the greatest sensation in the Drewsteignton area is wholly modern: CASTLE DROGO, the last castle or private house on the 'stately home' scale to be built in England, and likely to remain so. It was designed in 1910 for Mr Julius Drewe, founder of the Home and Colonial Stores, by Sir Edwin Lutyens, the distinguished creator of New Delhi, and construction lasted until 1930; it is now owned by the NT, although Mr Drewe's grandson continues to occupy part of it. Built of granite, on a granite outcrop above the Teign Gorge, the irregularity of its shape skilfully avoiding monotony in its huge façade, and with enormous, multi-paned bay and bow windows breaking up the expanse of stone, it is a dramatic sight. The surroundings are in proportion – large terraced gardens surrounded by seemingly endless private grounds. The principal rooms can be visited between March and October; so can the chapel and kitchens, both cut into the rock. The beholder's chief impression is likely to be one of bewilderment that so much splendour (and, within the context, good taste) should be allied, in a twentieth-century house, with kitchen, bathroom, and bedroom fittings that seem to date from at least a full 100 years earlier.

Dunchideock Devon 7F6 (*pop.* 116)
A minute place only 6km. from the centre of Exeter, yet as rural as you please, and of no small charm, on the

fringe of very hilly and well-wooded country. The name means 'wooded fort', and there are indeed remains of an Iron Age hill fort, Cotley Castle, 2km. to the north-west. The late-fourteenth-century church, despite *two* Victorian restorations, is of great merit if only for what it contains: some fine bench-ends, both Tudor and modern, a restored but beautiful rood-screen, a monument to one Aaron Baker (d. 1683), who waxed rich in trade with the East Indies and spent part of his wealth on rebuilding the chancel aisle, and another monument to General Stringer Lawrence (d. 1775), who for twenty years had commanded the forces of the East India Company and has been called (by people who insist on this sort of epithet) the father of the Indian Army. Of at least equal interest with the General is the author of his epitaph, Hannah More (1745–1833), the poetess, dramatist, and religious reformer whose efforts in the last-named field were responsible for the formation of the Religious Tract Society.

General Lawrence bequeathed his large fortune to Sir Robert Palk, Governor of Madras (of the same Palk family that was later to make another fortune out of 'creating' Torquay on land that it owned). Sir Robert, who after his retirement lived close to Dunchideock at Haldon House (rebuilt 1900), thereupon commemorated his benefactor by building a triangular 'folly' tower, HALDON BELVEDERE, on an adjacent hilltop. A statue of the General, with an inscription, surmounts the tower, but anyone minded to toil up the hill to read it should be warned that it is in Persian. Near Dunchideock church is the former priest's house, medieval but

St Mary's church, Luppitt: the Norman font

restored to an extent just short of the disastrous. Dunchideock House, opposite, part Georgian, part earlier, is beautifully sited and magnificently mellow.

Dunkeswell Abbey   Devon   7H4

A rather Wordsworthian sight, this: a group of thatched cottages round a small square, and in the garden of one of them the gatehouse of the vanished abbey. Founded in 1201 by Lord William de Brewer, the Cistercian foundation remained in being until the Dissolution. Either the original Norman or Early English buildings were replaced, or the gatehouse was added later, for its style is Perpendicular. The outline of the abbey church and buildings is easily discernible in aerial photographs, and in dry weather on the ground. Some of the old stones were used to build the cottage in whose garden the gatehouse stands, and indeed many other cottages besides. On the site of the abbey church a new church, not without its early-Victorian charm, was erected by the owner of the site, Mrs Simcoe, in 1842, also using stones from the ruins. Inside is a collection of abbey documents, plans, and relics, including two thirteenth-century stone coffins found while digging the church foundations, and containing the bodies of a man and woman, probably Lord William and his lady. A young tree marks the spot where they were reinterred in the churchyard. There are some pleasant carving and painted glass in the church, all the work of Mrs Simcoe's seven daughters: a touch that is not the least factor in the Victorian charm. Dunkeswell Abbey should not be confused with Dunkeswell itself, a village lying 3km. to the south.

The same distance south-east of Dunkeswell, on a steep hillside above the valley of a River Otter tributary, is the delightfully-named LUPPITT (*pop.* 395). A pleasant village with extensive views down the river to the earth-fortress on the top of Dumpdon Hill, it possesses a church of well above average merit. Some two dozen pairs of massive curved beams or braces form a shallow-pointed arched roof over the chancel, and four more make a large, arched cross where nave, chancel, and transepts intersect – something of an architectural *tour de force* for its period (fourteenth century). There is a Norman font, engagingly carved, and in the north wall of the chancel a very rich tomb, that of Sir John Carew, who fought at Crecy (d. 1320). There used to be a stone rood-screen, but it was broken up, and pieces of it now form mantelpieces and other features in some of the Luppitt houses. The Carew arms also figure at MOHUNS OTTERY, on the other side of the hill facing Luppitt, in the Otter Valley proper. Of this mansion, built by Sir Reginald de Mohun, a richly ornamental gatehouse survives, along with some lesser fragments incorporated in a farmhouse. It is only poorly visible from the lane.

Three km. south-east of Dunkeswell is BROAD-HEMBURY, of which Thomas Toplady, who wrote the hymn 'Rock of Ages', was vicar for a time. South-east of the village, HEMBURY FORT is the largest earthwork in Devon. Majestically situated on a spur of hill, and offering some of the widest views in Devon, it must have been in use for many centuries; as it stands, its triple row of oval ramparts belongs to the Iron Age, but excavation has shown the existence of a New Stone Age enclosure before that, and the discovery of Roman coins and a small statue indicate Roman occupation afterwards. Curiously, no evidence has been found of occupation during the fifteen hundred years of the Bronze Age that separated the Stone from the Iron Age. Hembury Fort (not to be muddled with Hembury Castle near Buckfast Abbey, qv) measures 317m. by 109m. Between the ramparts the ditches are deep, and there is a fine inturned entrance at the northern end. Masses of bracken cover much of the site, and woods clothe the rest of the hill.

Dunsford Devon 7F6 (*pop.* 586)

A comely place of cob, thatch, and stone, facing Dartmoor across the Teign Gorge, part of the opposite bank of which belongs to the NT. The church soon makes one aware that this is another village dominated through the centuries by one family, the Fulfords; the best of their many monuments in this Perpendicular building (restored 1840, but gallery, pulpit, and altar rails spared) is that to Thomas Fulford (d. 1610). The Fulfords lived at GREAT FULFORD, 4km. north-west – and they lived there a long time, being the only family in Devon who could claim uninterrupted male descent since the time of the first King Richard. Perhaps it was the love of tradition encouraged by such a pedigree that made them the last household in England to employ a professional jester. The present house, which stands in its own park just outside Dartmoor National Park, was built in Henry VIII's reign, fairly drastically altered later but preserving its quadrangular layout. It had the distinction of experiencing a special siege by Fairfax in 1645, eventually capitulating. The chapel was licensed in 1402, and finally abandoned for worship only in the nineteenth century.

This is a region of manors, now farms, old enough to figure in the Domesday Book. CLIFFORD BARTON, between Great Fulford and the Teign, is one that still shows some work of past centuries; CLIFFORD BRIDGE, nearby, is a 'modern' reconstruction made in the seventeenth century. A km. or so east of Dunsford, SOWTON BARTON, dating from the thirteenth century, has also retained some medieval parts. Both can be seen from the road. Again, 6km. north-east of Dunsford HOLCOMBE BURNELL has a very fine barton, built in 1480 by Sir Thomas Dennis, or Dennys (*see* Bideford), alongside the church; possibly because of the latter's proximity the private chapel of the barton was demolished in 1700. The church underwent restoration in 1843. The village (*pop.* 184) is at a little distance.

East Budleigh Devon *see* Budleigh Salterton

East Down Devon 6D1 (*pop.* 214)

In the gorgeously wooded valley of the Yeo north of Barnstaple is a village associated with two great families, the Northcotes who became the Earls of Iddesleigh and the Pines who became the Pine-Coffins. The Northcote

ancestral mansion stood 1½km. north-east, and is represented today only by rebuilt Northcote Farm; but the Pine mansion, East Down House, beside the church, is a handsome building of 1700 and in parts earlier, with white angle pilasters against a grey stone front. The church contains a remarkable font and a screen restored by Herbert Read with his usual care. The village in general is pretty. WEST DOWN (*pop.* 471) is 8km. from its counterpart, with another village in between. Here the countryside is more the downland implied by the name, and the village shares the spacious impression with its wide streets. There is an Elizabethan manorhouse beside an early-fourteenth-century cruciform church with a chancel rebuilt in 1675 to the old plan and a tower replaced in 1712. The 'great man' of the parish in early days was Sir John Stowford, who was Justice of the Common Pleas in the fourteenth century and whose chapel occupied the north transept. His effigy in wood, life-size, stands here, repainted in 1873; the colours are garish, but so would the originals have been.

The village between the two Downs is BILTADON (*pop.* 39). It looks most picturesque from across its valley, but on closer inspection has nothing to offer, the little church being ruined (by restorers, not decrepitude, which might have been preferable). There is, however, a notable collection of eight Bronze Age round barrows just over 1km. north.

Exeter: The City Devon 5E2, 7G5
(*pop.* – excluding Topsham (qv) – 90,900)

Exeter, like Plymouth, is not the same city that existed before the air-raids; but whereas Plymouth was refashioned fairly swiftly, and certainly with panache, the redevelopment of Exeter has been slow and much more piecemeal. To some extent this is not Exeter's fault: the destruction, too, was more piecemeal, denying her the chance that Plymouth had to replan the entire central area as a single unit. The result for the visitor, in purely aesthetic terms, is that Plymouth now consists of a postwar city surrounded by a pre-war one, with surprisingly little overlap, while in Exeter the new and the old are almost inseparably interwoven.

When the Romans pushed as far west as the head of the Exe estuary they found there the tribal capital of the Dumnonii, who occupied what are now Devon, Cornwall, and part of Somerset. It was they who had built the great Iron Age hill-forts, in which lived not only the warriors but the farmers who grew the crops and tended the cattle below. Some of the Dumnonii were international traders, and there is evidence that trading centres existed in both Exeter and Topsham. The Romans were therefore confronted by a well-developed community, and the tradition, probably based on truth, is that in AD 49 the Second Legion had to lay siege to Exeter and fight a major battle before the Dumnonii gave in. At any rate, when the invaders turned the settlement into a typical Roman town they held their

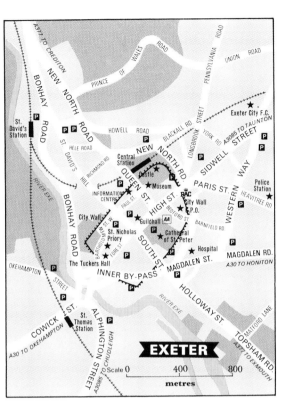

subjugated opponents in sufficient respect to call the place Isca Dumnoniorum, or 'Exeter of the Dumnonii'. Until very recently it was thought they left their new subjects more or less alone until, in about 200, it was decided to turn Isca into a proper Roman town, with a forum, rectilineal paved streets, public buildings, and – of greatest subsequent significance – an enclosing wall. But now excavations have revealed a military bath-house dating from a few years after the conquest, so that much of the Roman city has had to be antedated. The excavations have also brought to light the existence of an early graveyard, from the form of which the archaeologists have deduced the possible existence of an adjacent church even before the coming of the Saxons. The Dumnonii, or Celts, or British, probably with an admixture by now of 'Roman' blood (the Romans were drawn from many parts), continued to occupy the abandoned buildings after their conquerors had left (c. 410), and may have continued trading with mainland Europe; many, it is believed, emigrated. Whatever the unknown history of these obscure years, contact with Christianized peoples and Christian missionaries must have taken place. Meanwhile the Saxons advanced steadily west, and in 658 won a decisive battle at Pinhoe, on the fringe of Exeter, which enabled them to occupy

the city. Whether they found the monastery, known to be flourishing by 670, already established or whether they themselves established it almost at once, the work of excavation has not yet revealed. By now the Saxons were certainly Christian, and that they shared the city with the British is indicated by the different saints to whom the churches in the northern and southern halves are dedicated.

The graveyard remained in use right through the Saxon period, and a change in the alignment of the graves during the tenth century marks the probable building of a new church. There is even one set of foundations that suggest the erection of a free-standing tower. If the hypothesis is correct, this would fairly certainly have formed part of the early abbey. One reason why so much conjecture comes into all these interpretations is the depredations of the Danes. The first Danish raids on Devon came in the ninth century, and in 876, after a siege, one army of marauders captured Exeter, where they remained, robbing, roystering, and raping, until driven out by King Alfred in 879. But the raids went on, the last and worst being in 1003, when the invaders, admitted by the treachery of the city's Reeve (a Frenchman, not a Devon man), sacked and burnt the whole town, including the abbey whose scanty remnants may now be in course of discovery.* These occurrences must have been particularly damaging to Saxon *amour-propre*, because from the outset Exeter had been a personal possession of the Crown. The later Saxon kings, from Ethelred II (d. 1016), made a custom of handing their Exeter revenues to their queens as a wedding-gift, a practice continued by the early Normans; and it may have been as much to bolster up the city's prestige as for safety that in 1050 Edward the Confessor allowed Bishop Leofric to transfer the see of Devon and Cornwall to Exeter from Crediton. By that time the city had been rebuilt, but it had no industry yet, and little cause for prestige except what could be given it by the Church; long before the transfer of the see, the monastery or abbey already referred to was noted for its school, and had been generously endowed by King Athelstan.

Exeter proved a hard nut for William the Conqueror to crack. No 1066 here. In 1068 the citizens strengthened the city defences, and led by the late King Harold's mother Gytha, told William they would neither admit him nor swear allegiance. He came down to confront them. The authorities went out and promised to do all he wished, but on returning were promptly disowned. For eighteen mid-winter days the new King was

---

* The archaeological work, which is taking place on the site of the demolished Victorian church of St Mary Major and adjacent ground in the Cathedral Close, is being advanced each year. Pending the accumulation of sufficient funds to conserve the Roman baths and other finds so that they can safely remain exposed as an open-air museum, they have been covered-in again with easily removable sand.

*St Martin's church and Mol's Coffee House in the Cathedral
Close, Exeter*

obliged to lay siege to the city: both sides were conscious
that all the rest of Devon and Cornwall would act according to the outcome. Eventually the citizens surrendered, but only on condition that there should be no
plundering or retribution. Gytha and her immediate
following were allowed to leave. William kept to the
terms, but took the precaution of building a castle on the
mound known as Rougemont. Of this castle the gateway
remains today; the rest, largely in ruin, was removed in
1784. Nearby is the shell of a tower built by Athelstan.

Charters were granted to Exeter under Henry II,
Richard I, and John. The first mayor was appointed in
John's reign; and Edward I held a Parliament here,
under which the Statute of Coroners was passed. During
the Wars of the Roses the city supported both sides by
turns, a sort of civic forerunner of the Vicar of Bray. In
1497 the pretender Perkin Warbeck besieged it, twice
entered, and was twice driven out. Forty years later the
glow of royal gratitude still shone; for Henry VIII
granted county powers to the city. In 1549 Exeter found
itself besieged by the Roman Catholic insurgents, who
included among their captains the Vicar of the city
church of St Thomas. The siege went on for five weeks
before relief arrived. The defeated Catholic leaders
were sent for trial to London, except the Vicar, who out
of regard for his cloth was hanged, in full vestments,
from a gallows erected on the top of his own church-
tower. Three ships were fitted out at the city's expense

to oppose the Armada: not many, one might think, compared with the record of several much smaller centres in Devon and Cornwall, particularly since all the great Elizabethan sea-captains from Drake downward seem to have frequented Exeter nearly as much as London or Plymouth. (They used to foregather at Mol's Coffee House in the Close; it escaped the air-raids and is now an art shop.)

At the outset of the Civil War Parliament tried to neutralize Exeter's Royalist sympathies by appointing the pro-Parliament Earl of Bedford as Lord Lieutenant. The citizens then had to endure a Royalist siege until their Cromwellian masters surrendered, and later, after the war had swung in Parliament's favour, a siege by Fairfax until their Royalist masters surrendered. On each occasion the victors exacted huge sums of money on behalf of the Cause. During the Royalist occupation Charles I and Queen Henrietta Maria stayed for a time at Bedford House (now vanished), and here the Princess Henrietta was born. After the Restoration Charles II, generous as ever, gave the impoverished citizens a portrait of his sister by Lely.

The war had done damage harder to repair than that to people's pockets. The Puritan troops, fired by their Christian fervour, set out to destroy as much as they could of the ecclesiastical art that other Christian fervour had created. The Royalist officers contented themselves with extremely insanitary habits in the houses in which they were billeted. Many Exeter men joined Monmouth's uprising, and afterwards eighty were hanged at Heavitree. Possibly because of this experience, the authorities three years later were chary of welcoming William of Orange, who had reached Exeter from Brixham after a stop at Axminster. But the populace welcomed him, and it was probably his sojourn of no less than twelve days in the city that enabled him to gauge popular reactions sufficiently to feel confident of success. The eighteenth century passed in relative tranquillity, if not the torpor that often goes with easy commercial prosperity. The French wars, up to the Peace of Amiens in 1802, touched Exeter only in the matter of rocketing food prices; but the Napoleonic wars that followed the interlude produced the same invasion scare that Thomas Hardy has pictured so well in respect of neighbouring Dorset, in his novel *The Trumpet-Major*. Prices rose still higher, just when the breadwinner of most families was being drafted into the forces. Pitched battles were fought with the press-gangs, but the inroads on the male population continued. The younger and prettier women were lucky: they could turn to prostitution. The rest, with their children, half-starved on a poor-relief pittance. The cloth trade, which in Tudor times had made Exeter the wealthiest town in Devon and had lasted in reasonably good health ever since, was killed off by the Napoleonic wars, and there was nothing else. The place became just a somnolent cathedral city. The advent of the railway brought the

usual influx of tourists, most of whom either paused in Exeter on their way to the coast, or visited it from their holiday bases. Then the motor-bus appeared, and the motor-lorry, making it suddenly much more convenient to sell and buy in the county capital. Exeter again became a major marketing centre.

Ironically, it was the devastation wrought by the Second World War that really provided the combination of incentive and opportunity to go beyond this. Progress was slow, as stated earlier, but gradually new industrial areas (and many office blocks) have appeared quite close to the city centre, complemented by trading estates, such as at Pinhoe and Marsh Barton, on the perimeter. That latest, and most welcome, urban phenomenon, the shopping or pedestrian precinct, has come to Exeter, taking the dual form of barring all traffic except buses from certain existing thoroughfares, and the designing of certain new ones (Princesshay is a good example) for walkers only.

Considering the extent of the 1942 bombing, it is remarkable how many old buildings have survived. Mol's Coffee House, in the Cathedral Close, has been mentioned. Belonging to the Cathedral are the Bishop's Palace, the Choir School, and the Deanery. The Palace was founded in the thirteenth century, but what the traveller sees today is Butterfield's nineteenth-century rebuilding. Its most interesting feature is the Cathedral Library, now housed here: about 20,000 books and 9,000 manuscripts, collected ever since Leofric started the library in 1072 with (*inter alia*) the Exeter Book written in 950. Another early treasure is the Exon Domesday of 1086 – the original report on Devon and other south-western counties before it was edited down for the Domesday Book itself. The library is open in the afternoon, Monday to Friday. A section of the Roman city wall stands in the Palace garden. The Choir School is also Butterfield's work. The Deanery's main attraction is its fourteenth-century hall, with minstrels' gallery and timbered roof. Other buildings in the Close that survived the raids include the Royal Clarence Hotel, 1770, the Annuellars Refectory (1380: part of a building for monks who sang annual masses for the dead), a whole row of Tudor or Tudor/Georgian houses along the north side, and St Martin's church, dating from Leofric's time, rebuilt in the fifteenth century. The church is as quaint as it is historical, the chancel being at an angle to the nave. It contains box pews and a number of worthwhile features. Behind the church is St Martin's Well, perhaps Roman, perhaps not; but this was very much the heart of Roman Exeter, or Isca, as the earlier references to current archaeological activities must have made clear. Also close to St Martin's church, in St Martin's Lane, is the Ship Inn frequented by Drake.

Another fine row to have survived not far from the Close is Southernhay, a Georgian terrace of 1805 reminiscent of some of those in London's Inns of Court. Leading off it are Dix's Field and Barnfield Crescent, both built a few years later. Southernhay is one of the two best places from which to see what is left of the city walls, the other being the Castle (Rougemont).

A short distance north-west of the Close is the High Street, much of it rebuilt, but in which the Guildhall still stands. Claimed by Devonians as the oldest guildhall in the land, it was referred to in a deed of 1160. Restored in 1330 and again in the following century, it was given its present frontage projecting over the pavement in 1593. The main hall has a timbered roof of 1468–70, and panelled walls of which no two panels are alike. There is a picture collection, including the Lely portrait of Charles II's sister, given by the King. The Guildhall is open on weekdays when not required for official ceremonies. Next door is the Turk's Head, an inn with Dickensian associations, and there are several other old buildings remaining. In Fore Street, the continuation of High Street, the best building is Tucker's Hall, 1471, still, as it has always been, the property of the Incorporated Company of Tuckers, Weavers, and Shearmen, the last survivor among the city's old craft guilds. In the seventeenth century the Hall was divided into two storeys, but the upper retains its splendid hammer-beam roof. Below are pieces of armour that were found among the beams when a plaster ceiling, which for long had hidden them, was removed.

Leading off Fore Street is Mary Arches Street, containing the church of St Mary Arches, the only Devon church with a double row of Norman arches, c. 1130. Here are tombs and memorials of many mayors. In 1942 bombs damaged the roof, which has been repaired with timbers from a barge used in the Normandy landings of 1944. A little farther along Fore Street is a passage called The Mint, and here will be found St Nicholas Priory. Founded in 1087, this is a Benedictine guest house, the only one in the country surviving *in toto*, and the only remaining part of the old Priory of Exeter destroyed and built over after the Dissolution. Cellars, a two-fireplace kitchen, and guests' and priests' rooms are to be seen. A plaster ceiling in one room is a reminder that for a time after being secularized the building was a private house. It is open Tuesday to Saturday, April to September inclusive. At the far end of Fore Street, West Street leads to Stepcote Hill and the church of St Mary Steps. The church contains another of Devon's magnificent rood-screens, originally in St Mary Major and transferred when the latter was rebuilt in the last century; but St Mary Steps is better (if less deservedly) known for its chiming clock (called the Matthew Miller clock) in which the bells are struck by moving figures, one of them representing Henry VIII. In West Street, too, is the much-publicized House that Moved, a tall, narrow, Walt Disneyish timber building of the fourteenth century that in 1961 was moved bodily from another site to make way for road-widening. It is now a gift shop specializing in semi-precious stones.

West Street leads on across Western Way to Quay Hill and then to the Quay (*see below* under Maritime Museum). Western Way itself passes the end of South Street – in which is another very ancient tavern, the fourteenth-century White Hart, with a noted wine room – and continues as Magdalen Street, noted for Wynard's Almshouses (1436, restored in 1692 and 1864), built round a central court and including a chapel. They remained almshouses until 1970, when they became offices for the Citizens' Advice Bureau, the Exeter Samaritans, and other social bodies. In the opposite direction Western Way brings you to the Exe bridges. The first bridge over the river was constructed at the instigation of Walter Gervase, Mayor of Exeter in 1231 and 1239, and consisted of seventeen arches – for the river was much wider and shallower than it is today. At the east end stood a chapel, St Edmund's. Recently the part of the bridge that has been overtaken by dry land has been excavated, and eight and a half arches, or exactly half the bridge, have been exposed, together with the remains of the original chapel, which had been several times enlarged and finally rebuilt in 1830 after a fire. The exhibits will remain on permanent view.

North-west of here, in what was the south-west corner of the walled city, the Bartholomew Burial Ground, disused since 1871, is now a pleasant, park-like area, with tall trees, tombstones remaining here and there, fine views across the river, and a number of good Georgian houses flanking it. The other park area on this side of the High Street–Fore Street axis is that around Rougemont Castle, where the old outer ditch was converted into a public garden – Northernhay Gardens – in Charles II's reign, making it one of the oldest parks in the land. Immediately adjoining, south of the Castle's rocky mound, are the Rougemont Gardens. Here are the Assize Courts and Rougemont House, built in the mid eighteenth century in what was then the castle yard, and now housing the Exeter Museum of Archaeology and Local History (open weekdays). Close by is the County Library, a brand-new building with (in an annexe) a comprehensive collection of works on Cornwall as well as Devon. Also on this side of the High Street, but a good deal farther out where there was space to build, are the spacious modern buildings of the University of Exeter and the even more modern Northcott Theatre.

Other museums include the Royal Albert Memorial Museum and Art Gallery in Queen Street, inaugurated in 1868 and several times expanded (open weekdays); and the Underground Passages (entered from Princesshay), remarkable tunnels either cut from rock or built of stone, by means of which fresh water from springs in a nearby vale was conducted through the town. Until recently it was thought that the oldest channel was one built by the Dean and Chapter of the Cathedral in the fourteenth century; now it is believed some of the passages may be Roman. There was a public outlet at the South Street–North Street junction, but houses above the conduits could let buckets down through holes until the flow of water was encased in lead pipes. At intervals there were inspection adits. The system continued in use until the eighteenth century. The Underground Passages are open on weekday afternoons; the guide who takes you round tells you beneath which bit of the city you are standing at any given moment.

Only one museum could compete with anything so unusual as this, and that is the Maritime Museum, created by the International Sailing Craft Association (ISCA – as Isca Dumnoniorum) and arguably the best of its kind in the world. Formed out of the old port of Exeter, it uses the Basin and Quay for floating exhibits, the massive nineteenth-century dockside warehouses for undercover items. The range is astonishing, and constantly being added to – and there is room not just for models, but real ships, even quite big ones. Open daily except Christmas; the facilities include a launch trip through the Basin and on into the EXETER SHIP CANAL, which would assuredly be in the museum if it were movable, and is in any event close by. The building of Countess Weir or Wear across the Exe in 1290 is noticed under TOPSHAM. By the time it was removed the river above it had become silted up, and in 1564–6 a canal was cut by a Welshman named Trew and equipped with three sets of the first proper locks in Britain. At first it could take only ships of less than 10 tons, but in 1698 it was enlarged to take vessels of 300 tons, the work being done entirely by women, dressed in white and encouraged by the City Band. The final improvement came in 1831, when the canal was extended to its present mouth at Turf, a total length of nearly 9km. The railway, of course, soon made it irrelevant, but it continues to handle a little commercial traffic in addition to museum vessels being tried out. Trew's original locks were replaced in time by a lock (called Double Locks) of an equally interesting pioneer design, employing turf instead of masonry.

South-west of river and canal lies the suburb of ALPHINGTON (*pop.* 5,531 – included in Exeter total). Once a separate village, it has a Georgian inn, the Double Locks, and a fifteenth-century church with a superb Norman font and fifteenth-century screen; nearby the Rectory is dated 1609. Apart from this nucleus Alphington is largely a modern trading estate. Equally utilitarian is COWICK (*pop.* 4,794 – also in Exeter total), immediately to the north, except for Cowick Barton, a former manor-house of 1540, open to the public because it is now an inn. Another outlying former manor-house, even older, is Bowhill, alongside Dunsford Road (the A30) on the eastern edge of the city. The house was built for Richard Holland, Devon's Member of Parliament, but is now in a sad state of dilapidation despite several commercial attempts to set up business there. Its great hall, in particular, should be saved before it is too late. Other suburban mansions of note are Bellair, built in chequered brick about 1700, in Topsham Road: now County

Council offices; Cleve House, of the same date, in Exwick (west of St David's railway station), now a Guide Dogs for the Blind centre; Matford House, probably dating from before 1620, near Bellair and occupied by the South-Western Water Authority; Whipton Barton, in the north-west district of Whipton, one of the few surviving Tudor farmhouses in the immediate Exeter area: now a primary school; and Pynes, 4km. north of the city centre, set amid woodlands between the converging rivers Exe and Culm. On the site of an earlier mansion long occupied by the Larder family, the present house was built by Inigo Jones for the Northcotes (later Earls of Iddesleigh), who still occupy it. It is not open to the public, but a public footpath to the south gives a view of the exterior.

Exeter Cathedral   Devon   5E2, 7G5

It is an oddity of history that all the sees of the South-West, with the exception of Wells, were either carved out of other sees or began with their cathedrals in other towns. The see of Bristol was created out of Gloucester in 1542; Salisbury replaced Old Sarum in 1258; the see of Truro was created in 1876 out of Exeter (the early medieval Cornish see had been based on St Germans); and the Devon see was moved to Exeter from Crediton in 1050. There had been a monastery church very near the site of Exeter Cathedral nearly 400 years earlier, at a point that excavations during the 1970s have shown to be the centre of the Roman city. Then a minster (a church for use by monks) was authorized by King Athelstan and completed in 932, probably where the Lady Chapel now stands. This was burnt down by the Danes in the last of their ferocious raids on Exeter, in 1003, but rebuilt between 1017 and 1019 by Canute, himself a Dane but by then England's king. The times continued very troubled, however, and despite the disaster of 1003 Exeter was at least walled, which Crediton, at that time the seat of the bishopric, was not; so in 1050 Edward the Confessor sanctioned the transfer of the see by Bishop Leofric. The King himself came to Cnut's church to enthrone Leofric as first Bishop of Exeter.

Leofric at once organized twenty-four canons to superintend the daily worship in the new cathedral. He himself lived to see the Norman invaders firmly established throughout England before he died in 1072. The Normans, great cathedral men, finding Canute's modest church wholly inadequate for Exeter's new responsibilities and dignity, in due course ordered Bishop Warelwast (in office 1107–37) to do something about it; and he decided on a new, very dignified fane on a site alongside the existing church, which would be demolished (and was). This first cathedral built as such was of the same size as the present one without the Lady Chapel, and we can judge of its magnificence from what we know of other Norman work and from the two west towers that still stand; most regrettably, however, notwithstanding the exquisite quality of the present edifice,

nearly all the remainder of this great and obviously splendid Norman building has vanished. Only a little stonework at the base of the later walls and some buttresses to the nave remain. Yet no one individual pulled down Bishop Warelwast's cathedral; it disappeared piecemeal, almost imperceptibly one feels, as successive bishops each contributed his improvement. For some 130 years after the dedication in 1133 there were no changes at all. Then, in 1258, two things happened; Bishop Walter Bronescombe was elevated to the Exeter see, and in the same year he attended the consecration of the brand-new cathedral at New Sarum, or Salisbury. This had been designed in the prevailing Early English style, and Bronescombe found he greatly preferred it to the Norman. He resolved to use the now vacant site of the Saxon church to build a Lady Chapel, with a smaller chapel each side of it.

The work outlasted his life (he died in 1280), but he was buried in one of the smaller chapels (St Gabriel) in a tomb of extraordinary splendour, as one can see today. The achievements of his successors are probably most easily visualized from a bare summary: 1280–91, Bishop Peter Quivil – Lady Chapel finished and four eastern bays of the choir begun; the Norman towers converted into transepts by strengthening them with arches, removing their inner walls and substituting their small windows with large Decorated ones; 1292–1307, Bishop Bytton – choir completed, eastern part of new nave and chapels of St Paul and St John the Baptist built; 1307–26, Bishop Stapeldon – choir furnished with screen, reredos, and throne; 1327–69, the great Bishop John Grandisson (*see also* Ottery St Mary) – west front, remainder of nave (including the Minstrels' Gallery), and chapel in which Grandisson was later buried, all built; 1370–94, Bishop Brantyngham – east window replaced and Cathedral finally completed.

Like many of its kind, the great building has throughout the centuries suffered much bruising: removal of statues and damage to reredos and sedilia under Edward VI and Elizabeth I; destruction of the cloisters and removal of the organ during the Commonwealth; and thorough restoration during the 1870s by Sir Gilbert Scott, who, however, was a good deal less harmful at Exeter than he was at Salisbury. But no previous disaster can compare with what happened on the night of 3–4 May 1942, when Exeter became the target of one of the German so-called 'Baedeker' raids on cities of beauty. A bomb fell on St James's Chapel, bringing down thousands of tons of masonry and two south buttresses of the choir. Fortunately the fourteenth-century glass in the east window, and the Bishop's Throne, had previously been removed for safety, but both

the stone and wooden screens were shattered. Nevertheless, after the war Herbert Read, whose name occurs – usually linked with praise – in a number of entries in this gazetteer, collected all the pieces and reassembled them with such skill that the beholder might imagine the damage to have been only superficial. The restoration of the rest of the Chapel was made under the supervision of master-mason George Down, who personally carved some new corbels, one (as is the tradition in such cases) depicting himself, another showing a rugby football forward – a rugby match had helped to raise funds for the work – a third in the likeness of a cat, perhaps in recollection of the fact that there had been a Cathedral cat since at latest 1610, when a hole, still to be seen, was cut for it in one of the doors. George Down's ashes are interred beneath his portrait. The south aisle of the choir, in which there is a memorial to Herbert Read, to this day shows cracks in some of the monuments, but is otherwise as though the events of 1942 had never been.

Exeter Cathedral, apart from the towers, may have been inspired by Salisbury, but it ended up looking vastly different. Salisbury Cathedral is, except for one or two later chapels, Early English throughout, and relatively austere: Exeter's construction extended from Early English through Decorated well into the Perpendicular period, and the result is far softer, more ornate – feminine compared with masculine. Wren, who praised Salisbury's absence of too many ornaments to 'glut the eye', could never have said the same of Exeter. Yet Exeter's beauties harmonize so well both with one another and with the basic design that it is hard to visualize anything simpler that would not be less pleasing.

On approaching the west entrance the traveller is confronted by the vast Image Screen, with its many figures ranging from angels to plain soldiers. When it was fashioned it glowed with bright colours and must have presented a bizarre sight by our standards, accustomed to think of the outsides of churches as devoid of colour save that intrinsic to their materials. With the loss of its colours the screen became blackened, but it has recently been cleaned and its mass of detail is once more apparent. Bishop Grandisson's body was laid to rest in a small chapel behind the Screen, immediately to the right of the centre door, but was removed when the chapel was rifled under the Tudors.

Within the building the eye and mind are caught in wonder at the roof; through the length of nave and choir spray after spray of ribbing fans out from apparently slender columns like a double avenue of palm trees, the longest stretch of Gothic vaulting anywhere on earth. Yet any feeling of excess, of a tunnel effect, is prevented by the transverse line of the Choir Screen, and behind it the tall, brooding bulk of the organ. The stone used in the interior – of several different kinds and colours (eg Beer stone, Purbeck, yellowish sandstone, local red sandstone) – adds to the magnificence of the display.

Exeter Cathedral: the W front, c. 1346–75, also showing the Norman S tower (the battlements and square pinnacles of which are late-C15)

OPPOSITE: TOP: *Exeter Cathedral: detail from the W front;* BELOW: *Misericords*

One notices the pillars that rise from the floor, their massiveness completely disguised by the pretence that each is a cluster of sixteen slender shafts. Above them the arches are similarly treated. In the north-east corner is the little Chapel of St Edmund, so nearly hidden behind the oldest screen in the Cathedral that it is easily overlooked; it is of particular interest to the antiquarian because it contains one of the few remnants, other than the towers, of Bishop Warelwast's Norman building. Over the fourth arch of the nave on the same side is the fourteenth-century Minstrels' Gallery, put up for the Palm Sunday ceremonies and used today for the singing of Christmas carols. The front is beautifully carved in a series of statue-bearing niches, but from the ground the little figures are hard to appreciate in detail. The Choir Screen (1318–25) has a Moorish look, as though the designer had copied it from something in Seville or Granada: exquisite, but almost out of place. The paintings (not at all Moorish) in the panels along the top are

seventeenth-century additions; the two altars were restored in 1933. The choir, beyond the transepts, is in style a continuation of the nave – chronologically, of course, it was the nave that continued the choir. On the south side is the Bishop's Throne (1316), an 18m.-high pinnacle of elaborately-carved Devon oak. Similar in spirit are the three sedilia of about the same time; but the statues in their canopies are modern, and depict Edward the Confessor, Bishop Leofric, and Queen Edytha. The High Altar is surmounted by two candlesticks of Charles II's time and a graceful cross designed in 1962 by Louis Osman. The pillar behind is called the 'Exeter Pillar', and is the master or prototype of all the rest.

Lastly, working east, the traveller reaches the Lady Chapel, the visionary creation of three Bishops, Bronescombe, Quivil, and Bytton. How much did any of them foresee of the wonders that Grandisson and their other successors would perform? The Cathedral is such a homogeneous entity, one likes to believe that some

divine vision enabled even Bronescombe, who died before the Lady Chapel had taken form above the window sills, to foresee in every lovely detail all that was to follow. I have written nothing of the chapels and chantries that flank the choir and transepts, of most of the tombs and monuments, of quaint medieval bosses and corbels, of much other detail. A bare catalogue seems pointless, detailed descriptions would fill too much space; but the pleasure of a great church is to wander round and discover the smaller beauties for one-self. Explanatory literature is always to hand on the spot to explain their technicalities and history; only the eye can convey their worth.

Outside the Cathedral proper, but part of it, are the Chapter House and what is left of the cloisters. The Chapter House was built in 1225, but the upper part was raised and rebuilt by Bishop Lacy (1420–55), who gave it its elaborate carved and painted roof, as breath-taking as any of the more ornate features of the Cathedral itself. In the floor, appropriately, is the tomb of the first Dean, Serlo, appointed in 1225. The fourteenth-century cloisters were largely destroyed during the Common-wealth; most of what remains was converted in 1887 by J. L. Pearson (one of his first tasks after designing Truro Cathedral) into the Cloister Room, in the style of the original and with coloured window glass formerly in the Cathedral west window.

The Bishop's Palace, Deanery, and Close are dealt with in the article on Exeter City.

Exmoor, Devon *see* **Introduction**, and **Brendon**, **Lynton** and **Lynmouth**, **Parracombe**. (The greater part of Exmoor lies in Somerset.)

Falmouth   Cornwall   2D5   (*pop.* 18,041)
One of the county's half dozen largest towns and the only major port. Yet it is the reverse of ancient. The fine natural anchorage has probably been appreciated by seafaring folk ever since our shores first knew any, but until 1660 the very name of Falmouth did not exist. The early Celts put up a hamlet of fishing-booths, which they called 'Head of the Valley', or 'pen-y-cwm', to which the Saxons added 'wick', or village, so that the settlement became 'Pen-y-cwm-quick', or 'Penny-Come-Quick', a name now lost here but still found at Plymouth. The place was also for some reason called 'Smithwick', and it was 'Smithwick alias Penny-Come-Quick' that in 1660 Charles II at last decreed should thereafter be known as 'Falmouth'. Within thirty years it became a mail-packet terminus, which it remained until 1852. After that the prosperity it had acquired might well have declined, had it not been that as ships became bigger and bigger fewer and fewer of them could sail past it to Penryn or Truro. But any ships could get into Falmouth harbour, in any weather. For years sea-captains sailing to Britain had the instructions 'put into Falmouth for orders'. The great dock system was opened in 1859, and almost

exactly a century later the Queen Elizabeth Dock was reopened after being enlarged to take ships of up to 90,000 tons. During both world wars of this century the importance of the harbour was enormous, notably prior to the great Normandy invasion of 1944, when it was associated in particular with the navies of the United States and the Netherlands. Today its significance is perhaps greatest as a repair port, partly because it is the first to be reached by any ship in trouble on the Atlantic.

The town grew up on the south side of the harbour, where it was protected from the south-westerly gales. The land here happens to form quite a narrow penin-sula, and in the mid nineteenth century, helped by the coming of the railway, a second Falmouth grew up on the other side of the peninsula: a sun-facing holiday resort, enjoying (despite my mention of gales) one of the best sunshine records in the British Isles. This in turn stimulated an interest in the harbour by yachtsmen, and now in the summer it is possible at times to see CARRICK ROADS, as the great estuary of the River Fal is called, occupied not only by commercial vessels of all shapes and sizes but by up to 300 yachts.

It was Henry VIII who built the stout fortresses of PENDENNIS CASTLE, at the tip of the peninsula, and ST MAWES CASTLE on the other side of the Fal, but it was Sir Walter Raleigh who set Falmouth going, as it were. When he came back from Guiana there was just one mansion here: Arwenack Manor, belonging to the Killigrews; he suggested that they ought to develop so superb an anchorage, and being an enterprising family they did, taking the opposition of rival ports in their stride. Of their Elizabethan mansion barely a fragment survives, and of the family, sadly, even less. The mansion was almost entirely destroyed in the Civil War, and the Killigrews simply died out. There is a newer Arwenack House, of no intrinsic interest, on the old site at the far end of Grove Place, but the Killigrews are more notice-ably commemorated by the granite obelisk set up in front of it by one of their number, Martin, in 1737, and by Killigrew Street and Road, together forming one of the town's chief central thoroughfares.

The first street in Falmouth was Church Street, but such original houses as remain do not look as old as they are. The church itself, dedicated in 1665 (four years after the town had received its first charter) to Charles I, whose portrait is to be seen inside, is in the classic style (much mauled about by the Victorians) with gallery and barrel roof, but is of less interest for its architecture than for the exceptionally fine singing quality of its choir, and (to Scotsmen) the memorial to the fourteenth Earl of Glencairn, Robert Burns's friend and patron, who was buried here after dying at sea. Impressive eighteenth-century buildings are also few – Bank Place and Grove Place, toward the Killigrew Monument, are the best – but of early-nineteenth-century architecture, there are a number of good examples, both in terraced private houses (in Florence Terrace and Place, Tehidy Terrace,

Stratton Terrace and Place, Albert Terrace, and neighbouring streets) and in public buildings. The best of the public buildings are the Custom House, in the Greek Doric style *c.* 1820, where Custom House Quay joins Arwenack Street; the Royal Cornwall Polytechnic, 1833, in Church Street; the Synagogue, 1816, in Vernon Place; the Classical and Mathematical School (no longer such), 1824, in Killigrew Road; and the Royal Hotel, *c.* 1812. There is also Marlborough House, 1805–15, in Marlborough Avenue, with its pavilion and Ionic colonnade. At the entrance to Custom House Quay stands the King's Pipe, a chimneyed furnace in which the excise authorities used to burn contraband tobacco.

The 'other' Falmouth, the holiday resort, lies over the crest at the back of Falmouth the port. The beaches – there are several – are backed by a long line of those pleasant hotels of painted wood, with balconies and ornate barge-boards to their gables, so popular among the resort-designers of late-Victorian and Edwardian times. Here, too, are a number of expensive, well-conceived private houses of the last half-century, built for retired professional people. Falmouth may have a busy down-to-earth port, but as a holiday centre it is, on the whole, dignified and gracious despite the teapot-shaped tea hut on the principal beach. Valuable among the amenities are the Gyllyngdune Gardens, close to the front, where the wealth of sub-tropical plants is a reminder of Falmouth's warm climate. Other gardens, a little farther away, offer similar reminders: to the north, those at Tremough (*see* Penryn): to the south, on the road to Mawnan Smith, the gardens of PENJERRICK, a mansion built by the Quaker Foxes. The mansion is not open, but the gardens, on both sides of the valley leading down to the sea, may be visited. They, too, are almost wholly sub-tropical.

But above all Falmouth is a place of seascapes: in all the South-West only Plymouth Sound surpasses the Fal estuary for beauty of natural design. There are viewpoints without number, yet the one to be recommended most is Pendennis, for three reasons: the view itself embraces the whole of Carrick Roads and the Channel coast as far south as Manacle Point; Castle Drive, by which Pendennis is approached, is a magnificent scenic road; and the Castle, which can be entered at most normal times, merits a visit because of its Civil War associations: Queen Henrietta Maria and Prince Charles both sheltered here, briefly, in 1644–5, and the following year, when it was one of the last fortresses in the West to hold out for the King, Pendennis fell only after a six-month siege.

Farway Devon *see* **Honiton**

Fowey (*pron.* Foy) Cornwall 3F3 (*pop.* 2,369)
Today almost wholly devoted to the holiday trade and the export of St Austell's china clay, during the Middle Ages Fowey with its convenient natural harbour was one

Fowey: Place, the Treffry mansion

of the most important ports in England, sending ships and men to fight the French and the Scots, merchant vessels to exchange tin for Bordeaux wine, and privateers – less politely called pirates – to bring back anything they could get. The Fowey 'Gallants' became all but invincible, at one time defeating even the august Cinque Ports fleet. One outcome of these lawless goings-on was that both the Spanish in 1380 and the French in 1456 raided the town, the French burning half of it down, though Place, the mansion of the Treffrys in the heart of Fowey, was sternly (and successfully) defended by its master's lady during his absence. In Tudor times it was the Treffrys who built St Catherine's Castle to defend the harbour, paying for it with their share of the loot from the dissolution of Tywardreath Priory. A Fowey ship, the *Frances of Foye*, sailed with Frobisher to the Arctic, Drake to the West Indies, and Drake again to

*Landscape near Fowey: looking over Churchtown towards the
china-clay workings of St Austell*

meet the Spanish Armada. But with the coming of
Stuart times Fowey's power declined until Charles II
made it a base in the Dutch wars. Trade revived, mainly
with France and Spain, and a huge pilchard industry
developed, leading to commerce with the Mediterranean
countries and (as a change from piracy) a vast amount of
smuggling. A slump followed the Napoleonic wars, and
after a further revival later in the century Fowey gradually settled down to what it has remained, a leading
exporter of china clay, and a favourite haven for yachtsmen. Its most recent chance to revive its old fighting
days came in 1944, when part of the American landing
force sailed from here on D-Day.

The town has had a succession of charters, the first before 1225. In 1968, as a reflection of their common
china-clay interest, Fowey and St Austell were made
into a single borough. Essentially, Fowey consists of one
long street bordering the harbour, with steep and
narrow lesser streets that follow no discernible pattern.
Two buildings overshadow the rest, the church of St
Fimbarrus, or Finn Bar (an odd name even for a Cornish
saint; he later became Bishop of Cork), and its neighbour,
the Treffrys' mansion Place. The church is a fourteenth-
century building, with a fine carved waggon-roof and a
very tall fifteenth-century tower, much ornamented.

There are a font of 1150, made from the Catacleuse
stone quarried at Padstow, a carved pulpit made in 1601
from the oak of a Spanish galleon, the grand tomb of Sir
John Rashleigh (he owned the *Frances of Foye*), and
numerous monuments to the Treffrys. Place, apart from
a lovely sixteenth-century bay window in the courtyard (the house is not open to the public), is almost
wholly nineteenth-century Gothic, lofty, battlemented,
and – an interesting touch – with external ornamentation matching that on the church tower.

For the rest, the Ship Inn in Trafalgar Square, once
the town house of the Rashleighs (and named in honour
of the *Frances of Foye*), was built in the fifteenth century,
renovated in the sixteenth, and refronted in the nineteenth. Also in Trafalgar Square is the Town Hall of
1792, with some much earlier bits, and opposite this, part
of the old Broadgate, a relic of the medieval defences.
There are old houses, rewarding to nose out, in Webb
Street, Lostwithiel Street, Union Street, Custom House
Hill, Fore Street, and elsewhere. A well-stocked museum
inhabits the Town Hall. Many illustrious feet have
trodden Fowey's stones, from those of Warwick 'the
Kingmaker' to those of the present Queen; and few
towns of its size have figured so prominently in literature,
for it is the 'Troy Town' of Sir Arthur Quiller-Couch,

who lived for half a century at The Haven, beyond the landing stage, and the setting for several novels by Daphne du Maurier, who resided for some time at Menabilly (*see below*).

Around the harbour are various places of note. At the seaward tip is ST CATHERINE'S POINT, a NT area adjoining the Castle (itself administered by the Dept of the Environment) donated as a memorial to the fallen of Fowey in the two World Wars; from here the chain used to be hauled across the harbour mouth to keep out undesirable visitors. The chain's other end was at the twin castle of POLRUAN, opposite, where there is still a boatyard to perpetuate the boat-building tradition of the wooden-ship days. A ferry now plies to Polruan. Less than 2km. west of St Catherine's lies MENABILLY aforesaid, famous in fact as the Rashleighs' country mansion, in fiction as the setting of Daphne du Maurier's celebrated novel *Rebecca*. It is not open to the public, but its beautiful park can be seen from the magnificent cliff walk that runs from Fowey to GRIBBIN HEAD, with its huge beacon, and right round to POLKERRIS facing into St Austell Bay. Today Polkerris is just a charming miniresort, china-clay pollution having driven away the fish that formerly provided its livelihood. But you can still see the ruins of the pilchard warehouse or 'seine house', one of the biggest in Cornwall; and the very congenial local pub is virtually a museum of relics.

Opposite Fowey, divided from Polruan by the 'branch' creek called Pont Pill, is BODINNICK, a rather self-consciously picturesque yachting resort redeemed by a very interesting, though sadly uncared-for, medieval chapel at Hall Place. The picture-postcard appearance of all this side of the Fowey estuary makes it hard to visualize the grim fighting that took place here during the Civil War, when the Earl of Essex invaded Cornwall (then sternly Royalist) for the Parliament, and Royal guns at Polruan and Bodinnick bombarded Cromwell's ships unloading at Fowey's quay. Eventually Essex was defeated in one of the biggest Royalist victories of the war at CASTLE DORE, 3km. north of Fowey. This is an interesting spot in its own right, possessing a well-preserved and double-walled prehistoric earth fort with traces of huts inside; on the day before the battle Charles I slept there in his carriage. A very much earlier and more nebulous association connects Castle Dore with another monarch, King Mark of Cornwall, uncle of Sir Tristram, or Tristan (the subject of Wagner's *Tristan und Isolde*). Tristan and Isolda are said to be buried here, and King Mark is said to have had his palace, in which the Knights of the Round Table met, inside the earthworks.

Up the estuary, 3km. from Fowey past tiny SAW MILL CREEK, beloved of artists, the village of GOLANT peers from the steep wooded bank across to the slice of NT-owned bank opposite, adjoining Penpoll Creek. At water-level there are a little quay, an inn, and some cottages, over all of which the church keeps vigil from

halfway up the slope. The late-fifteenth-, early-sixteenth-century passion for rebuilding churches means here that the entire structure (not that there is overmuch of it) dates from about 1509, modified only slightly by unwontedly modest Victorian restoration. The design consists of a short granite tower with a holy well beside it, a nave, and one aisle. The nave has a fine waggon-roof, the aisle an equally fine cradle-roof. Box pews have replaced bench-pews, but the bench-ends have been kept and made into a pulpit and stalls; the carving shows a wonderful assortment of pictorial motifs. Some fifteenth-century stained glass shows St Sampson, to whom the church is dedicated, and St Anthony. A memorial tablet of 1716, to one Edmund Constable, bears the epitaph:

> Short blaze of life, meteor of human pride
> Essayed to live but liked it not and died.

Gidleigh Devon 7E6 (*pop.* 91)
To the traveller, breathless before the beauty of this area of north Dartmoor (especially if he happens to have climbed up from the Teign Valley far below) it must seem incredible that the population of this granite village should be markedly diminishing; but then visiting a very remote, very elevated spot is not the same as having to live in it the year round. Gidleigh has its own tor, Gidleigh Tor (332m.), forest-clad all over, and its own incredibly small early-fourteenth-century castle, long ruined but currently undergoing private restoration. The parkland, where the lords of the castle once hunted, could serve for the forest of *A Midsummer Night's Dream* or the last scene of Verdi's *Falstaff*. Hardwood trees of many species grow from a foundation of heather, berried shrubs, ferns, and wild flowers, interspersed with rocks of sometimes arresting formation. No wonder it all went to the head of a certain Mr Prinsep, who once tried to build himself a house on the extreme summit of Gidleigh Tor. He failed. The name 'Gidleigh' means Gydda's, or Gytha's, ley, referring to the mother of King Harold; yet history makes no mention of the place until the twelfth century. The date of the present church is as late as the sixteenth century, with a mildly notable screen, some venerable glass, but not a great deal else.

The countryside is almost an encyclopaedia of history, with hut circles, stone circles and rows, and burial cists, from the remote past, field systems and ancient crosses from the Middle Ages, and Tudor and Jacobean former manor-houses. Nearly all the prehistoric relics are on the southern, or Dartmoor, side, nearly all the manors to the north and east, and the crosses wherever a track has long existed. They are mainly of the 'wayside' variety. Some of the sites are dealt with under various gazetteer headings. Others of outstanding interest include FERNWORTHY FOREST, a very large plantation area from 4km. to 6km. south containing Fernworthy Circle, a Bronze Age ring of twenty-seven upright stones; several rows of standing stones (one row 45m. long); and several groups of hut circles. Here too is FERNWORTHY RESERVOIR, a km.-long man-made lake out of which the South Teign flows. Two and a half km. north of Gidleigh, but still well inside the National Park, THROWLEIGH (*pop.* 269) is a larger but equally tranquil hilltop village. The church, rebuilt in the fifteenth century, is notable for a very fine priest's door in the chancel. Beside the church is the church house, also of the fifteenth century; on Throwleigh Common are hut circles and there was, until its partial destruction, a well-preserved pound, in the 'hut-enclosure' meaning of the word; but the village is primarily mentioned here for the number of Tudor and even earlier manor-farms in the neighbourhood. One of the best of these is WONSON, about 1km. south-east, home of the Knapmans and then the Northmores. One of the latter, Member of Parliament for Okehampton in George I's reign, was a heavy gambler, and after losing a fortune (but not the house) on the turn of an ace of diamonds, he painted the card on the panelling of his bedroom and cursed it every night instead of praying. Unhappily the farm is not open to the public, for the card is still there. But the outside of the fine old house is easily seen from the road, as are SHILSTONE, ¾km. south-west of Throwleigh, with a hut circle nearby, and CLANNABOROUGH, ¾km. north-west; thirteenth-century Clannaborough can in fact sometimes be visited, for it contains an interesting private folk museum open most weekends subject to a preliminary telephone enquiry (Whiddon Down 238).

Godolphin House, or Hall   Godolphin Cross
Cornwall   2B5

One of the county's more ambitious 'stately homes' still in private hands, though no longer, as throughout most of its existence, the seat of the Godolphin family. It is open at limited times to the public. The Godolphins first came into their own under Henry VIII, but their most famous representative was the first Earl, Sidney, Queen Anne's Lord Treasurer. The house, built round three sides of a square, is a low, battlemented, partly Tudor, mainly seventeenth-century structure with an eighteenth-century hall. The north façade is embellished with a long loggia of great fat Tuscan-style columns. The once highly-decorative gardens, the silence of the large woods enfolding the place, and the general atmosphere of departed glory, give Godolphin House an air of melancholy that is not easily forgotten.

Tin-mining was the source of much of the Godolphin wealth, and the deserted workings so familiar in Cornwall litter the countryside. Two km. south of the Hall is TREGONNING HILL, surmounted by an earth fortress called Castle Pencaire and several prehistoric circles, but perhaps of greatest interest because here in 1768 William Cookworthy, a Plymouth chemist, discovered the substance (kaolin) from which, after experiment, he produced the true hardpaste porcelain that is the basis of England's porcelain industry.

Godrevy Point (*pron.* Godréevy)   Cornwall   2B4

Godrevy marks the western end of a notable stretch of cliff scenery between St Ives Bay and Portreath, all of it fortunately in NT hands. Equally fortunately the coast road is for the most part some distance inland, leaving the Cornwall North Coast Footpath well to seaward of it for all but a short stretch. Off the Point is GODREVY ISLAND (in reality a group of islands), on which, following the execution of Charles I, the ship carrying much of the King's personal property was wrecked with the loss of all but two of its crew. The royal effects were washed up all along the coast, and must have found their way into unexpected hands. In 1857 the lighthouse was built, and was probably the model used by Virginia Woolf in her celebrated novel *To the Lighthouse*, despite the fact that in the book she transferred it to Scotland. The island used to be rich in lobsters. These have mostly departed, but the NT coast is rich in other wildlife, particularly seabirds and seals. Caves, rocks, islets, and small sandy bays abound, and at some points such as Hell's Mouth the grey slate cliffs fall sheer for 30m. or more.

It is a pity PORTREATH did not come into NT hands as well, for 'development' in the worst sense of the term has ruined the appearance (and even the accessibility) of a very interesting little port built early in the nineteenth century by Lord de Dunstanville to import coal for nearby Camborne and Redruth and export their tin-bearing ore. Transport between harbour and cliff-top was effected by one of the world's earliest powered railways (1809), the power coming from a stationary engine at the top operating a cable; the line continued to the mines. This historic line has now been torn up, though you can follow its course up the cliff.

Inland of the cliffs the landscape is chiefly downland, with the notable exception of the extensive park and woods of TEHIDY HOUSE, south-west of Portreath, the home of the Basset family to which Lord de Dunstanville belonged. In 1819 the eighteenth-century mansion was largely burnt down, and its successor is now a hospital. East of Portreath, 2km. off the B3300 to Redruth, lies MAWLA, where the enterprise of a Mr Morse has assembled for public inspection a quite remarkable collection of historic farm vehicles, machinery, and implements. It deserves to be far better known.

Golant   Cornwall   *see* Fowey

Goonhilly Downs   Cornwall   2C6

The high central plateau of the Lizard Peninsula, fascinating alike to botanists, geologists, and students of prehistory. The botanists use the summer months to hunt for a wide range of the rarer Cornish flowers, the geologists study the otherwise rare green serpentine rocks here so prevalent, together with the greenstone and slate; and the prehistory students revel in the sites of three separate Celtic villages, numerous standing stones, and tumuli almost beyond counting. For the ordinary traveller the most agreeable seasons are the early summer, when the air is heavy with the scent of vast acres of gorse, and the early autumn, when the Cornish heath is blooming. Except for a few pines, trees are non-existent, thus leaving unimpeded the science-fiction-like spectacle of the Post Office's Satellite Tracking Station, the gigantic dish-aerial of which received, on 10 July 1962, the first television pictures ever to reach Britain 'live' from the United States.

Great Torrington Devon 6D3 (*pop.* 3,531)
On a hill above the Torridge (to which there is a sheer drop from the castle site), in the midst of a countryside of irregular green fields like the pieces in a patchwork quilt. The old castle, built by the Normans and rebuilt in 1340, has all but disappeared, and where it stood there is now an agreeable public park. The town has been a market centre from Saxon times; at one period a descendant of King Alfred owned it, then in the twelfth century it passed to William FitzRobert, who gave the townfolk some common pastureland that has remained corporate property ever since. By the fourteenth century Great Torrington was the most important mart north of Dartmoor, and in the Tudor period it was also a noted cloth centre. Its charter of incorporation was granted in 1553, preceded in Devon only by Exeter, Plymouth, and Totnes; and other Torrington charters followed. During the Civil War it was a Royalist stronghold until Fairfax took it, after a fierce battle in the streets, in 1646. Almost immediately afterwards an explosion (accidental, if your sympathies are Cromwellian; deliberate, if they are Royalist) blew up the church-tower while it was crammed with prisoners, causing some 200 deaths – of guards as well as captives. In 1724 a serious fire destroyed over eighty houses and all the borough records, but this does not seem to have affected prosperity for long, and it is interesting that nearly 200 years ago the population was within a thousand of today's figure. Today the traveller is likely to be attracted by the sleepy peace of the place, but the somnolence is to some extent deceptive, for gloves, glass (Dartington), and a variety of light industries now keep the town going, as well as a cattle market and twice-weekly pannier market.

Despite the fire of 1724, natural wear and tear, and deliberate modernization, there are a number of earlier buildings in the old town's predominantly Georgian streets, notably the Black Horse Inn (1681), parts of the Blue School (founded 1709), and 28 South Street, a highly distinguished William and Mary mansion. Important post-fire buildings include Palmer House in New Street, built in 1752 by John Palmer, who married a sister of Sir Joshua Reynolds and frequently entertained the artist and also Dr Johnson; this is one of the best examples of mid-eighteenth-century domestic architecture in Devon. Early-nineteenth-century buildings are the Globe Hotel (1830), the Wesleyan chapel (1832), and

the Market House or Pannier Market (1842). The Town Hall was Georgian, but rebuilt in 1861. Also Georgian is Castle Hill House, except for the castellated south wall, which was added as a kind of memorial to the old castle by Lord Rolle, head of the then leading local family, in the 1830s. He also built the bizarre Town Mills by New Bridge. As to the unfortunate parish church (St Michael), the enterprising citizenry rebuilt most of it within five years of the explosion, very much in its original Perpendicular style. The living was once held by Henry VIII's Thomas Wolsey, who founded Christ Church, Oxford; there are still links.

There is no town museum, but the Dartington Glass Works can be visited, except at weekends or Bank Holidays. Just outside the town on the Exeter road is ROSEMOOR, the ornamental gardens of which are open in the afternoon from April to September. LITTLE TORRINGTON is 3km. south, also with good views of the Torridge Valley but not much else. More rewarding is TADDIPORT, opposite Great Torrington, reached by a seventeenth-century bridge, guarded by an eighteenth-century tollhouse, and gratifying the traveller with a delightful little fourteenth-century chapel attached to an almshouse that was once a leper hospital. At FRITHELSTOCK, in a wooded landscape 2km. west of the town, are three walls (one with fine lancet windows) remaining from the church of the Augustinian priory – a cell of Hartland Abbey (qv) – founded here by William de Beauchamp in 1220. The ruins, which include the base of the tower, are still very impressive. Cloister Hall Farm, to the west, is a remodelling of what used to be the Prior's House. The parish church, immediately beside the Priory, has a high tower, an ornate fourteenth-century east window, waggon-roofs, and early carved bench-ends and bench fronts.

Gulval Cornwall 2B5
A parish to the north of Penzance containing some of the most remarkable Stone Age and Iron Age relics in the county. First in importance is CHYSAUSTER, where four pairs of roofless but otherwise well-preserved drystone houses stand on either side of a kind of street as they have stood for some 2,000 years. The pattern of each house is more Mediterranean than British: externally the building is roughly oval, and all the rooms are contained in the thickness of the immense outer wall, access to them being from a central courtyard. The largest room, also oval or round, is opposite the passage to the courtyard from outside. There were paved floors, built-in granite mortars, drains, and at the back of every house a walled and terraced garden. The villagers made their living by streaming the tin from the tiny river at the foot of their hill and conveying it to merchants at St Michael's Mount, who sent it across France to Mediterranean purchasers. Chysauster continued to be occupied into Roman times.

It was defended by a triple-ramparted fortress, CASTLE-AN-DINAS (not to be confused with its namesake

Chysauster, Gulval

near St Columb Major), still conspicuous on a 233m. summit of the Central Downs 1½km. east of Chysauster. Even more conspicuous, immediately south of the Castle, is ROGER'S TOWER, a 'folly' built about 1800, presumably for the grand views it provides. But it is the Stone Age and Iron Age relics – more numerous between St Just and St Ives than in any other part of Cornwall – that give the landscape its character. (For other important sites *see* Morvah, St Ives, St Just-in-Penwith, and Zennor.)

Hartland　Devon　6B3

(*pop.* – including Stoke – 1,363)
A name spread over a number of places that are far from cheek-by-jowl: Hartland Point, Hartland Quay, Hartland the town, Hartland Abbey, and Stoke, where you go to find Hartland parish church. HARTLAND POINT is the southern, or if you prefer western, tip of Bideford's large bay: a dark, scowling promontory with a coast-guard station and a lighthouse and very long views up and down the wild coast as well as out to Lundy and even, in the clearest weather, the coast of Wales. Principally one associates it with bitter gales, but it is sometimes possible to visit it in winter without needing

an overcoat and in some years primroses can be seen in bloom in early January. Three km. south, the coast at HARTLAND QUAY is even more vicious-looking, with great masses of rock rearing out of the sea wherever you look. This is because the strata and the cliff-line are at right angles, so that the softer rocks have been washed away and the harder left sticking up in ridges extending into the water. The cliff-faces, too, are fantastic, consisting of carboniferous rock that has become squeezed and folded, with the result that the layers go up and down diagonally, like gigantic dog-tooth ornamentation, or here and there in even weirder contortions. Human activity is nowadays represented by the Hartland Quay Hotel, but for a long time there really was a harbour at this unlikely spot. The monks of Hartland Abbey built it in the fifteenth century; in the sixteenth it was strengthened as the result of a Parliamentary Bill introduced by Raleigh, Drake, and Hawkins, no less; in 1887 it was damaged by a gale, and in 1896 another gale swept all of it away but the stump of quay to be seen there today.

If this part of the coast is harbourless, it is not devoid of inlets, most of them deep, narrow valleys, wooded and in spring carpeted with flowers, that have been cut by

Near Hartland Quay

streams generally terminating in waterfalls. These falls are due to the rapidity of the sea's encroachment; it bites away the mouth of each valley, leaving the stream 'hanging' in mid air. In the case of WARGERY WATER, which now cascades into the sea a few m. south of Hartland Quay, the valley used to run parallel with the coast to a point north of the Quay, taking the stream with it, but the sea breached its side of the depression and allowed the stream to take a short cut. Enough of the valley remains to make this easily traceable. A short distance farther south is SPEKE's MILL MOUTH, with a series of four falls; the valley behind this is a Nature Reserve. East of Hartland Point – for the coast turns a full right-angle here – SHIPLOAD BAY surprisingly offers a safe and sheltered bathing beach; the cliffs above it belong to the NT.

HARTLAND, the town, grew up as a market centre, and is mainly unspoilt Georgian. The Chapel of St John was built in 1839 as a chapel of ease: unremarkable, but very pleasant with its box pews. It stands on the site of the old Town Hall, and in fact has inherited the Town Hall clock, a venerable instrument made in Barnstaple in 1622 and improved by the same clockmaker thirty-five years later. HARTLAND ABBEY, 1½km. east, began as a college

of secular canons founded by King Harold's mother Gytha. A priory of Augustinian canons followed in the twelfth century, founded by a Fleming, Geoffrey of Dinant, but very little seems to be known about it until the Dissolution put an end to its function. Sir William Abbott then converted the Abbot's Lodge into a secular mansion, to which a wing was added in 1705. This mansion was replaced in 1779 by the Gothic house there today. But the Gothic house incorporates a good deal from its predecessors: the whole of the wing of 1705, a Tudor window and entrance-hall panelling, even substantial parts of the fourteenth-century abbey cloisters. The house is occasionally open to the public.

The parish church at STOKE, above the Abbey vale, compensates for any shortcomings in the Abbey, since there can be few, if any, lovelier churches in all Devon. Dedicated to St Nectan (to whom Gytha had dedicated her college), it has chancel, nave, transepts, and chapels, a north and south aisle, and the highest tower in the county (40m.). The inside seems spacious as a cathedral. Waggon-roofs, painted in different colours, cover most sections. An enormous but very handsome rood-screen, painted and gilded, spans the building and is probably a fifteenth-century work. The font is Norman, ornately carved. There are numerous monuments and one grand tomb. Over the north porch a priest's room called the Pope's Room is now a small museum. The body of the church dates from the fourteenth century, the tower probably from very early sixteenth; and of course there was a nineteenth-century restoration, during which the restorers removed the fourteenth-century windows and put in mock-Perpendicular ones of the wrong proportions. East of the church is the old Priest's House, altered but recognizable.

How did so large and splendid a church come into existence in so lonely a region, and side by side with an abbey at that? As far as the murky records of the Dark Ages can be trusted, it is recorded that when Nectan came over from Wales in the sixth century it was at Stoke that he established himself. Rather less credible is the account of his martyrdom, which states that after being beheaded he carried his head under his arm (thus anticipating Ann Boleyn by a thousand years) back to his cell, and that wherever a drop of blood fell a foxglove grew. His bones, or what all men believed were his bones – and they may have been – were preserved here until the Dissolution, and quite likely Stoke became a place of pilgrimage; if so, the offerings of the pilgrims would have done much to finance the building of the church. We may smile at the story of the foxgloves; but each year on St Nectan's Day in June children still bring foxgloves to the church, and who would wish to end the charming ceremony?

Hatherleigh Devon 6D4 (*pop.* 915)
A hillside village or small town overlooking the River Lew, a tributary of the Torridge. There is a cattle market, chartered since 1693, but Hatherleigh has never really developed since the eighteenth century; much of its elegance therefore remains unspoilt in spite of bad fires in 1840 and 1846. The showpiece is the George Hotel, dating from 1450 and in parts possibly earlier; there is some evidence, not conclusive, that the building once belonged to Tavistock Abbey, which certainly owned property in Hatherleigh. White Hart House is also largely a fifteenth-century building. The church, at the top of the hill, has a shingle spire, a good oak ribbed roof, and a little seventeenth-century Flemish stained glass in the west window. The screen was destroyed by restorers in 1820 (the top) and 1862 (the rest) and a pulpit and lectern were made up from the pieces. On the eastern edge of the town, where two roads fork, is an unmutilated medieval wayside cross.

Hatherleigh Moor, south-east of the town, with vast views, is common land, believed to have been granted by John of Gaunt in the fourteenth century. On it is St John's Well, once believed to cure eye ailments by miraculous means; water for baptisms was drawn from it. In the environs of Hatherleigh are many gracious Tudor manor-houses now serving as farmhouses: DECK-PORT, just east of the Moor, is a good example.

Hayle Cornwall 2B4 (*pop.* 5,378)
Makes no pretensions to cater for the holidaymaker, leaving that to its neighbour St Ives. It is the only commercial port on the north Cornish coast and provides a good deal of interest for the industrial archaeologist. It also provides a less visible interest for the ancient-history lover, for it was through Hayle that all those saints with the strange names came, seemingly in a body, from Ireland. (Those from Wales came through Padstow or via Devon.) Somewhere under the sand at Riviere, between Hayle and the open sea, lies buried, we are told, the palace of King Tewdrig, or Theodore, who reigned towards the end of the fifth century and 'received' many of the saints. Just how he received them is open to some doubt, since he is variously described as having sheltered them in his palace, and killed some. Maybe he did both. Their arrival, saints or no, must have seemed suspiciously like an Irish take-over. Hayle's more substantial history began to achieve importance early in the eighteenth century, with tin-smelting works and then copper smelting at the north-eastern end of the town still called COPPERHOUSE. The copper trade lasted about 100 years, but was then transferred to Swansea to be nearer the coal supply. As a port Hayle found itself serving the Redruth–Camborne area mines, bringing them coal as well as exporting their product. For this a railway was built as long ago as 1837–8, using a stationary engine, the ruined housing of which can still be seen. The main line to Penzance from London reached Hayle in 1859. The port is still busy, ships bringing in coal, sulphur, and oil for local factories and depôts. It is also busy in a less desirable sense, the town being strung along the traffic-hideous A30. There are many Georgian houses and cottages, and in some of them, notably in the northern suburb-village of St Phillack, the brownstone is varied with blocks of black scoria or slag from the copper-smelting. There are no churches of merit.

Helford River estuary Cornwall *see* **Helston**

Helston Cornwall 2C5 (*pop.* 9,978)
The name probably means 'Old Court Town', but of course the prestige all comes from the famous annual Furry Day – properly Flora Day – celebrations and dance. This takes place on 8 May, which is a public holiday in the town (it could hardly be anything else). Decorations are everywhere. Church bells peal out at an early hour, whereupon the inhabitants are supposed to go out *en masse* and gather garlands. At 7.0 am the town band strikes up for the dancing, which in the old days used to involve just about every inhabitant who could move on his or her feet, not to mention outsiders; and the unique aspect of the performance was that the dancers wound not only through the streets (which they still do), but through the houses, in at each front door and out at the back. At 10 o'clock children's dancing takes place, followed at noon by the *pièce de résistance*, a dance

by the town dignitaries in morning coats and top hats. Further general dancing ensues until 5.0 pm, though it used to continue longer and be succeeded in the evening by a parade of adults and children singing a traditional ditty to greet the summer. The whole ceremony probably stems from pre-Christian rites, and according to legend celebrates the joy of the townsfolk at being spared injury when a fiery dragon flew over and dropped a large stone. Helston has indeed a long history, having been a market town even in King Alfred's day; and the granting of its charter in 1201 made it the second borough in the county. Later it became a stannary town – that is, one where a court assayed and stamped the local tin. The layout is very pleasing; Coinagehall Street, the main thoroughfare, is on a slight curve, with clear water rippling down it in a conduit. There are little steep lanes, glimpses of gardens everywhere, and a goodly number of old houses, all built of the local stone and most of them eighteenth-century or Regency buildings. The best public building is the classical-style Market House of 1838; another eye-catching structure of the same decade is the Georgian-Gothic park gateway of 1834, at the foot of Coinagehall Street. The much-restored church of St Michael is disappointing but worth entering for the amusing east window of 1938, showing two angels dancing the Furry Dance. The Angel Hotel was once the town house of the Godolphin family (*see* Godolphin House); and the Blue Anchor Inn has a skittle alley and splendid painted ceiling.

Helston was described admiringly by Daniel Defoe; its Grammar School (vanished, alas) was associated with Coleridge's son (headmaster) and Charles Kingsley (a pupil); and its citizens include Henry Trengrouse, pioneer of rocket-apparatus for sea rescues, and Robert Fitzsimmons, the celebrated nineteenth-century barefist boxer. Trengrouse's device can be seen, along with many records of life in the whole Lizard Peninsula, in the Borough Museum in the Old Butter Market.

East of Helston lies the estuary of the HELFORD RIVER, beloved of yachtsmen and of all who respond to the sight of a waterway of intense beauty whose wooded banks (much of them belonging to the NT) are broken by many side-inlets. One of these is FRENCHMAN'S CREEK, another piece of Cornwall made famous by the popular fiction of Daphne du Maurier; a second contains PORTH NAVAS, headquarters of the important local oyster industry; and a third shelters HELFORD itself, a village of great charm, which is more than can be said of some of its 'artier' visitors.

Hembury Fort Devon *see* **Dunkeswell Abbey**

Holbeton Devon 4C5 (*pop.* 609)
On a hillside above the upper estuary of the River Erme, in the slice of south Devon known as the South Hams. Being nearly 1km. from the estuary and 4km. from the open sea, Holbeton has never been developed as a sea-

side resort and remains tranquil and unvandalized. Its chief aquatic interest is the large heronry beside the Erme, though of course the tidal waters attract seabirds and waders of many species. The village has stone cottages, the majority thatched, a pub called the Dartmoor Union that used to be the workhouse (workhouses were called 'unions' in the last century), and a Perpendicular cruciform church notable for its carving. The tower and spire were, as was common, not involved in the Victorian restoration, but had to be restored in 1930. Exquisite sixteenth-century screens divide off the chapels. The rood-screen is not the original, but a remarkably faithful copy made in the nineteenth century by Edmund Sedding, more of whose work can be seen in Cornwall than in Devon, and who made something of a speciality of church screens. If only all the Victorian restorers had been so sensitive!

Two km. up-river is FLETE, a mansion with a very odd history. The original building belonged to the Damerells and then the Heles. On the death of the last of these in 1761, the house – a Tudor reconstruction of a medieval manor-house – passed to the Bulteels, a later representative of whom managed somehow to convert it into neo-Gothic. In time it came into the ownership of Lord Mildmay of Flete, who did what he could to remove the Gothic monstrosities. Next Flete was bought by an Australian millionaire who in the 1870s engaged Norman Shaw, the designer of London's New Scotland Yard (now Norman Shaw House), to remodel it into the present great essay in Victorian Tudor. After this the house became for a time a hospital belonging to Plymouth Corporation; and today it is operated by the Mutual Households Association Ltd, who allow the public to visit it on Wednesday and Thursday afternoons from May to September inclusive. Nearer the mouth of the Erme, MOTHECOMBE (*pron.* Mother-cum, not Mothy-cum), to which the Mildmays moved from Flete, is a handsome mansion of 1710, on the site of a much earlier one, amid exquisite surroundings. It is open to the public on one weekend in May.

Holcombe Rogus Devon 7H3 (*pop.* 438)
A village that climbs a hillside facing Somerset and culminates in as attractive a grouping of church and grand mansion as one could wish for. The house, Holcombe Court, has a strange history. For centuries it was the home of the Bluett family, until in 1786 they ran out of heirs and willed it to a namesake, Peter Bluett of Falmouth, in the hope that he might be at least a distant relative. It was never established that he was, but in any case it would not have helped much, for after only seventy years or so the new Bluetts were forced by gambling debts to sell house and lands. Until then the early-Tudor building erected by the original Bluetts had been very little altered, except for the regrettable pulling-down of the north-west wing in 1845; but the new owner decided on extensive changes. Fortunately he kept them

to the interior and the back, leaving the imposing frontage, which, with its entrance tower, stair turret, transomed windows, and dovecote, all on a vast scale, is the most majestic Tudor façade in either of our two counties. Various internal features also survive, but since the house is not on view it is the exterior that concerns the traveller. Finely landscaped grounds, with woods and a twisting lake, stretch away at the back.

The church is by no means an anti-climax. Wholly Perpendicular, it came relatively well out of its Victorian restoration, and the interior is full of magnificent things: waggon-roofs, a fan-vaulted south porch, an attractive screen (originally at Tiverton), a great many monuments to the first lot of Bluetts, and the showpiece, the Bluett pew, Jacobean, untouched, with 'box' sides and front carved near the top, and above them a carved screen capped with carved medallions. Outside, the south porch (as graceful without as within, and dated 1343), opposite the vicarage, is the former priest's house, Tudor or perhaps earlier.

Two km. south-east by footpath, twice that by road, is CANONSLEIGH, now a farm, but exhibiting all that remains of an Augustinian house of canons founded in the twelfth century by Maud, Countess of Devon, and in 1284 made over to canonesses. There are parts of the fifteenth-century gatehouse and of the mill, on a tributary of the River Culm. Between the two are the wings and stables of an eighteenth-century house probably built with stones from the religious buildings.

Holy City Devon 8B4
1km.–2km. NW of Chardstock

This very un-Devonian name, highly impressive on headed notepaper, covers a somewhat ill-defined area of well-wooded, extremely steep hills traversed by the narrowest of lanes that stop creeping along a slope only to turn straight up or down it. The 'city' consists of a small number of cottages and about as many old and distinguished mansions, several of which, in reversal of the commoner process, have become 'mansionized' out of former farmhouses as the growth in the size of farms has made many of the latter redundant. Some of the most satisfying of these venerable buildings are RIDGE, OLD ORCHARD, WHITEHOUSE, WOONTON, and HOOK. With each of them the present edifice is mainly Tudor, but vestiges of earlier work exist. Hook, Ridge, and Woonton all date from the reign of Henry II, the origins of the other two are uncertain. Ridge, recently restored and no longer a farm despite the proximity of an ancient barn almost as large as the house, used to grow alder-trees for clog-making. Whitehouse, a rough-hewn old place, ceased to be a farm a few years ago. Old Orchard, also a farm no longer, was partly rebuilt and had a second storey added in the year 1600. Woonton, rather larger, continues to be a farmhouse, and is the only place in the list that cannot be seen at close range from the road, though it can from farther off. All this area (part of

Dorset until 1896) used to be great cider-apple country, and there is strong evidence that seedlings from around Chardstock started off some of the famous cider orchards of Tasmania. It was also great sheep country; a traveller towards the close of the last century complained that on one lane he encountered a flock 'nearly a mile long'. As to the origin of the name Holy City – first used in a cottage deed of 1734 – even the writers of the most authoritative works on Devon place-names cannot give it with certainty. Local belief is that the region was christened by the followers of the Duke of Monmouth, who certainly passed this way. Other suggestions are that it was named by the Puritans, or by the monks of Forde Abbey, near Chard ('Chardstock' means Chard cattleyard), or, less romantically, that 'Holy' is a corruption of 'holly', which grows in profusion in the hedges. But no one knows.

Honiton Devon 7H5, 8A4 (pop. 5,072)

One wide, sloping, pleasant (since they built the bypass!) street of Georgian houses holds just about all that matters, aesthetically and historically, in this town on the old London-to-Exeter coach-road (now the A30), which in turn was the still older Roman Icknield Street. There are several explanations of the name, of which the likeliest is the most prosaic – that stones for honing or sharpening instruments used to be quarried nearby and marketed in the town. In spite of their highway, the Romans left very little record of their presence. In Saxon times the manor belonged to the Earls of Devon, then, after the Conquest, William gave it to his half-brother. After reverting for nearly two centuries to the Earls, it passed to the Redvers and later the Courtenay families. It became a borough under a portreeve and bailiffs, and a municipal borough with a mayor in 1847.

In the Catholic rising of 1549 Honiton was the base from which Lord Russell set out to defeat the rebels at Fenny Bridges, 6km. to the west. In Civil War days King Charles and his army camped outside the town twice in 1644, Fairfax once in 1645. During the eighteenth century the main events in the municipal annals were fires: in 1747, when three-quarters of the houses were burnt down, 1765, 1790, and 1797. It is hardly surprising that nearly all the buildings on the main road are late-Georgian. However, despite these checks a diversity of industries flourished: malting and brewing, tanning, ornamental iron manufacture, and of course the making of Honiton lace. This last continues, on a much diminished scale, but for reminders of the great days of Honiton lace – two queens, Charlotte and Victoria, wore it at their weddings – one must look in the Honiton and All Hallows Public Museum in the High Street (weekdays, April to October), itself one of the oldest buildings in the town. Also in High Street is a shop that sells contemporary lace. Markets and fairs in which lace formerly featured have figured prominently since the early Middle Ages.

Marwood House (1619), Honiton

Of pre-Georgian buildings the most important (apart from the church) is Marwood House, at the east end of the town, built in 1619 by the son of Elizabeth I's physician. Charles I is said to have stayed here on his way to Exeter before the Civil War. The house may be visited, being now an antique shop. St Margaret's Hospital (now almshouses), along Exeter Road, is nineteenth-century Gothic, but the site has a long history, beginning with a fourteenth-century hospital for lepers. Some of Monmouth's followers executed by order of Judge Jeffreys are buried here. On the Axminster road is castellated 'Copper Castle', a nineteenth-century tollhouse of interest because the iron gates that used to bar the road are still on their hinges. The New Dolphin Hotel, near the Market, contains fragments of the Courtenays' fourteenth-century manor-house formerly on the site. The dolphin was their emblem.

The old parish church was St Michael's, on a hill south of the town. Built by a Courtenay who was Bishop of Exeter until his death in 1529, it was gutted by yet another fire as recently as 1911. It has been rather well restored, but has no pews. There is a monument to physician Marwood, who was a doctor for seventy-five years and died aged 105. St Paul's, the present parish church, was begun in the year of Queen Victoria's accession to save the climb to St Michael's. For some reason, this simple gesture of commonsense required an Act of Parliament of thirty-eight printed pages to sanction it.

Five km. south is FARWAY (*pop.* 208), a hill village that takes its name from *faer weg*, a prehistoric track still to be seen on the ridge, where there are also two notable groups of round barrows; but the greatest attraction is Farway Countryside Park (open Good Friday to

October, as a rule), 28ha. (70 acres) of, among other things, rare farm breeds, nature trails, and pony rides. Five km. east of Honiton, and mercifully clear of the A35 road, lies WIDWORTHY (*pop.* 202), a pretty village with a manor-house of 1591. North of the town and bypass COMBE RALEIGH (*pop.* 187) was the medieval home of the Raleighs, though their mansion has gone. There is, however, Chantry House, 1498, most attractive despite some philistine's destruction of nearly all the old windows in favour of larger, aggressively modern types. The house was probably built for the priest, whose church is today of small moment except for a ponderous medieval *folding* door. Combe Wood, near the village, is NT property.

Ilfracombe Devon 6D1
(*pop.* – including Lee – 9,859)
Holiday centre, winter resort, place of retirement, market town, and except for Bideford and Barnstaple, behind their dicey sand-bar, the only seaport for ships of any size on the whole north-Devon coast. The harbour has been important since at the latest King John's reign, especially to monarchs interested in invading Ireland, but its great days were in the nineteenth century, when steamers plied regularly to Bristol, Hayle, Boscastle, and the ports of south Wales, and occasionally to Ireland and France. This sort of trade declined as the tourist trade grew, and for the same reason: the coming of the railway, which reached Ilfracombe very late – 1874. Back in the days of sail, large numbers of the town's population had had a stake in the ownership of vessels, much as some people today club together to acquire a racehorse. Nowadays, about the only regular shipping service from the port is to Lundy, though the summer sees plenty of excursion steamers.

The town's setting is exceptionally beautiful, with its wooded hills rising from the shoreline to heights of more than 150m. On the west side the NT owns the cliffs for 2½km. Above the harbour is Lantern Hill, crowned by a small chapel dedicated to the patron saint of sailors, St Nicholas, and with a history as picturesque as its position. It began in the thirteenth century as the chapel and cell of a hermit who maintained a light to guide shipping; from the Dissolution to the late nineteenth century it was the abode of a secular light-keeper; then it was abandoned; and finally the Rotarians acquired it, spruced it up, re-opened it as a chapel, and revived the light.

Unsurprisingly, the oldest surviving residential buildings are the small and agreeable-looking houses that line the north and west of the harbour and the (much 're-vised') Georgian Manor House south of it. Next come the surviving traces of a curious and unsuccessful attempt to popularize Ilfracombe as a bathing centre in the 1830s: Tunnel Baths, 1836, and some residential terraces – Adelaide, Montpelier, Hillsborough. Otherwise nearly everything that is not of the twentieth century reflects the swift post-railway growth during the last

quarter of the nineteenth century, an exception being the *early*-Victorian Royal Britannia Hotel. Although parts of Holy Trinity church are Norman, the exterior is uninspiring, and the interior would be too were it not for the unexpectedly glorious waggon-roofs, richly carved and gorgeously painted. The thousands of visitors who annually spend their holidays at Ilfracombe without ever entering the church little realize what they are missing. In Wilder Street is the Ilfracombe Museum, where in addition to the kind of local exhibits one expects in all town museums there are some evocative pictures of Victorian and pre-Victorian Ilfracombe and its shipping, and a good collection of Victoriana. The museum is open from Spring Bank Holiday to the end of October.

West of Ilfracombe, just beyond the NT stretch of cliffs (along which runs a splendid footpath), lies LEE BAY with its marble-streaked rocks and sheltered combe noted for the fuchsia hedges lining the road. If you can ignore the hotels, the thatched village of LEE is still a pretty sight, and it is not hard to believe it once made its living by smuggling. There is an old water mill, now café, hard by the sea, and inland the Old Maids' Cottage where the 'three old maids of Lee' died elderly spinsters because they had never found any suitors up to their standard. On the opposite (east) side of Ilfracombe, at 1½km., CHAMBERCOMBE MANOR overlooks a partly wooded ravine with a stream, beside which is its own water-garden. The manor-house – open to the public from Easter to September – is largely a fifteenth-century building, though the site has been occupied since the twelfth, and is all angles and nooks, with secret rooms, its own oratory, an early-medieval cider-press, and old stained glass. The Rotarians who resuscitated St Nicholas Chapel have also restored eighteenth-century BICCLESCOMBE MILL in handsome Bicclescombe Park, south of the town. It is open on weekdays from Easter to the end of September.

Illogan Cornwall *see* **Camborne and Redruth**

Ilsington Devon 4D3 (*pop.* 1,397)
Lacks only a fair and a popular folk-song to have become another Widecombe, for in every other respect it is an easy match for its western neighbour. It perches on a steep hillside above a small tributary of the River Bovey, with a horseshoe of woods beneath it. The fourteenth-century church, enlarged in the fifteenth, has carved bosses on the nave roof and an ornately-carved rood-screen of about 1530 that once had painted panels depicting saints; but after surviving the iconoclastic zeal of the Puritans these were effaced, for no particular

OPPOSITE: *Looking over the harbour of Ilfracombe, from Hillsborough*

reason, during the 'improvements' of 1855. Nevertheless, the screen remains a splendid sight. In the manor-house of BAGTOR, 2km. south-west, the dramatist John Ford, called by Charles Lamb 'the last of the Elizabethans', and best known today for his recently-revived play '*Tis Pity She's a Whore*, was born in 1586. There had been a manor here since before Domesday, but the present house is a late-seventeenth-century building; it seems uncertain whether Ford was born in a predecessor on the same site or in the excellent Tudor house, now a farmhouse, next door. In 1663 another Ford, Miss Jane, willed some of her property to be invested, and the income used for the education of the children of the local poor: a pioneer gesture several generations in advance of its time, bearing in mind the fear and hostility that attended the introduction of the Ragged Schools nearly two centuries later.

The tors west of Ilsington include Hay Tor, Bag Tor, Saddle Tor, and Rippon Tor. Cairns and hut circles are numerous (*see also* Widecombe-in-the-Moor), and on Rippon Tor there is also, if you can find it, a block of granite with a great cross cut on it long ago by an Ilsington sculptor – no one knows why.

Kelly Devon 4B3 (*pop.* 122)
In the extreme west of mid Devon, 2½km. from Cornwall across the Tamar. For many centuries the life of the little settlement revolved around Kelly House, the home of the Kelly family since before the Norman Conquest. The house (not open), standing in very beautiful, partly wooded grounds far from a main road, is a mixture of Tudor and Georgian. It is equalled in interest by the adjacent eighteenth-century granary, with round window and elaborate entrance; for here the villagers had a long tradition of performing plays, a practice that inspired Mary Elfreda Kelly to found the Village Drama

The Shambles, Kingsbridge, with St Edmund's church behind

Society. There is a memorial to her in the church (dedicated 1259); the only other feature of interest in the church is a few pieces of fifteenth-century stained glass.

Four km. north-east, on the River Lyd, is SYDENHAM, a fairly unspoilt mansion (now a girls' school, and not on view unless you own a current or prospective pupil) built in James I's reign by Sir Thomas Wyse, or Wise. During the Civil War it was captured from the Royalists, who must have given a bad report of it, for such alteration as it has undergone was made soon after the Restoration. A pleasant view of it may be had from the Lyd bridge. Between Kelly and the Tamar is BRAD-STONE (*pop.* 48), a scrap of a place in which the interest lies not in the church (dedicated to St Nonna, mother of St David, and allegedly the scene of her martyrdom although in fact she died in Brittany), but in the manor-house, for several centuries (until 1740) the home of the Cloberrys. Much of the Tudor house was Georgianized, as may be observed through the elaborate late-Tudor gatehouse. Many farm buildings of mellowed granite complete the agreeable scene.

Kentisbeare   Devon   *see* **Cullompton**

Kilkhampton   Cornwall   *see* **Coombe Valley**

Kingsbridge   Devon   4D6   (*pop.* 3,545)
Often called (much to the annoyance of rivals) the 'capital' of the South Hams (the southward prolapse of Devon between the Dart estuary and Plymouth Sound), Kingsbridge is handsomely placed on the side of a moderate hill (moderate for Devon, that is) at the head of its own 7km.-long, very deeply indented estuary. This estuary differs from many in Devon in that instead of being steep-sided and wooded, it lies between gently rounded farmland slopes, with only the occasional wood here and there. No one seems to know which king provided the first half of the name; the bridge, at the customary point where fordability ends and navigation begins, links what for many centuries were two separate towns, Kingsbridge and Dodbrooke. At one time both belonged to Buckfast Abbey, which derived a nice profit from the export of wool, manufacture of cloth, and operation of flour mills. Kingsbridge has also always been a market town, and there are still a Charter Fair in July and an Agricultural Show in September.

For once the oldest part of the town is not down by the water, but midway up the hill and centred on the main street, Fore Street, immediately past the Victorian Town Hall with its ball clock on a slate-hung, tapering support like a head and neck in helmet and chain-mail. First comes The Shambles, a building reconstructed in 1796 on late-Tudor granite pillars. In rear of this stands the church – cruciform, with central spire – built by the Buckfast monks in the thirteenth century and to all intents rebuilt in the early fifteenth. There is little of

importance in it. Further up Fore Street comes the Old Grammar School, 1670, now dedicated to Kingsbridge's most illustrious scion, William Cookworthy (1705–80), who set in motion Britain's hardpaste-porcelain industry (*see* Godolphin Hall). The Kingsbridge Cookworthy Museum devotes one of the old school's panelled rooms entirely to Cookworthy, filling other rooms with costume, agricultural, and miscellaneous exhibits. It is open on weekdays, from Easter to October. In Wallingford Road is Well House, a Georgian mansion with a Tudor gateway. At the lower end of the town a promenade and model railway now extend along the quay, and inevitably the estuary is full of yachts. Across the water Dodbrooke, which might be expected to offer some interest, does not.

The rolling countryside all about is well stocked with fine old farmhouses, formerly manor-houses. Few can be seen inside, but their exteriors are generally visible from the nearest road or footpath. Among the more rewarding are several close to Sherford, the next village eastward.

HOLMFIELD, on the southern edge of Sherford, possesses a fourteenth-century window that certainly never started where it is now – in the front garden, looking down on the road – and was perhaps taken from the church during the restoration; KEYNEDON BARTON, ¾km. further south, is recognizably early-Tudor in part; it was the home of the Hals family, one of whom was Bishop of Lichfield and Coventry before 1500; two centuries later the Halses died out. Easily seen from the road, the house presents a most striking façade. One and a half km. west of Kingsbridge, BOWRINGSLEIGH was built in the thirteenth century, rebuilt in the sixteenth, and 'amended' during the nineteenth, but with the Tudor element predominating today. It can be seen from the lane that bounds the eastern side of its park. Bowrings, Pikes, Webbers, and Ilberts successively lived in it, and it was an Ilbert who, when South Huish church was abandoned in 1869 as no longer necessary, brought to Bowringsleigh the magnificent fifteenth-century screen now in the chapel of the house. Another fine screen, as well as several ornate plaster ceilings, are in the mansion itself, and therefore also shut away from our gaze. But the outside of the house is a worthwhile sight. Finally, 3km. north-west of Kingsbridge, near Churchstow, LEIGH was once a monastic 'cell' of Buckland Abbey. The present farmhouse, mainly fifteenth- and sixteenth-century, includes the monks' dormitory and refectory, and in front is a complete fifteenth-century gatehouse.

Kingswear   Devon   *see* **Dartmouth**

Knowstone   Devon   7F3   (*pop.* 182)
In the little-known moorland country south of Exmoor, but close to the even less known wooded valley of a stream improbably called the Crooked Oak, the waters

of which eventually find their way into the Taw. Its church has some Norman work and pleasant late-Georgian pews, but it is chiefly of interest because for just under half a century one of its vicars was the Revd John Froude, as strange a representative of his calling as even Devon history has provided. So irascible was he that he kept a gang of criminals to set fire to the houses and farm property of anyone who dared to cross his path, and eventually he died of rage because a local farmer had destroyed a favourite bush in the vicarage garden. No wonder R. D. Blackmore, author of *Lorna Doone*, put him in a novel ('Parson Chowne' in *The Maid of Sker*). WADHAM, 1km. north-east across the valley, was the home before they moved to Branscombe (qv) of the Wadhams, of whom Sir Nicholas, in 1610, became the founder of Wadham College, Oxford. The original house has been replaced. Two km. east of Knowstone, and well visible, is sixteenth-century – and older – SHAPCOTT BARTON: a former manor-house held by the Shapcotts possibly from before the Norman conquest until the last of them died in 1770.

Landewednack   Cornwall   *see* **The Lizard**

Landulph   Cornwall   *see* **Botus Fleming**

Land's End   Cornwall   2A5
A pity it no longer looks as it did when Turner painted it. Today the cliffs and rocks remain grand enough – though many other parts of the Cornish coast are grander – but the rather dreary land on top has suffered greatly from the lavish installation of all the tawdrier 'amenities'. More interesting, except as a symbol, than the granite headland itself – 'Penwith' in the Cornish tongue – are some of the neighbouring formations, whether at the sea's edge or encompassed by it. Both CAPE CORNWALL, 7km. to the north, and GWENNAP HEAD, 4½km. south, are at 'corners' of the general coastal contour and give a similar impression of being at the end of England, without the commercialized detraction from their grandeur. One and a half km. south of Gwennap Head a solitary rock, the RUNNELSTONE, rises wickedly out of the sea, to the detriment of many a ship before the obstruction was equipped with a warning light and bell. Close to the Head is TOL-PEDN-PENWITH, 'the Penwith headland with a hole', a magnificent cliff scene with a huge crater formed by a cave whose roof has fallen in. From here on, towards Land's End, is a succession of sinister caves in fairly sinister cliffs, with enormous rocks littering the water's edge. Nearer Land's End the rocks tend to be farther out in the water, and have been given weird and wonderful names such as The Armed Knight, Dr Johnson's Head, Dr Syntax's Head, Irish Lady, and Kettle's Bottom. Out beyond Kettle's Bottom the Carn Bras group includes the LONGSHIPS LIGHTHOUSE, where the height of the building added to that of the rock on which it stands gives the light an

altitude of some 33m. above the sea. Farther out still, 12km. from Land's End, is the WOLF ROCK LIGHTHOUSE, and beyond that, 40km. from Land's End, are the nearest of the Isles of Scilly (qv); but contrary to the tourist publicity, it is only on days of rare clarity that Scilly is visible from the mainland.

Immediately north of Land's End is SENNEN COVE, between which and Scilly the sea is said to cover the lost land of Lyonesse. What it very definitely covers, 11km. north-east of Scilly, is a group of rocks called THE SEVEN STONES, on which in 1967 the 61,000-ton oil-tanker *Torrey Canyon* wedged herself in one of the most publicized wreckings of modern times because of the prodigal spillage of oil. Sennen Cove is a pretty little bay with a breakwater, though increasing villa-building is eating into its solitude; the cliffs on the Land's End side of it are a NT property and include MAEN CASTLE, the most westerly Iron Age fortress in Britain as SENNEN itself, though 1km. inland, is the most westerly village. Here King Arthur crops up once more, being supposed to have defeated the Danes on the site of the village in a battle so gory that the wheel of the local mill was allegedly driven for a time by their blood. After the battle Arthur and his Knights feasted, it is said, on the flat rock called Table-men, near the church. This church retains a measure of thirteenth- and fifteenth-century work, and the tower looks out over the buildings round the Cove towards its nearest ecclesiastical neighbour in the United States.

Lanhydrock   Cornwall   3F2   (NT)
4km. S of Bodmin on B3268
One of the half-dozen most important houses in Cornwall, set in a well-designed park amid the beautiful and verdant scenery of the Fowey Valley. The house, which is open at most seasons to the public, was largely built by the first Lord Robartes of Truro in Charles I's reign and was completed by his son John, who during the Civil War was an exception to most Cornish 'stately home' owners by holding it for the Parliament. Two-storeyed and battlemented, it originally filled all four sides of a large central court, but the front or eastern side was later removed. Some distance before the courtyard is reached, the magnificent sycamore-lined approach ends in a graceful gateway, two-storeyed and battlemented like the house, completed in 1658. Internally the most striking feature is a picture-gallery occupying 36m. of the upper floor of the north wing. It has a curved plaster ceiling decorated throughout its length with ornate patterns and scenes from the Old Testament. Unfortunately the artists cannot be identified, though work in Barnstaple and elsewhere also appears to be theirs. In 1881 a fire destroyed most of the house but spared the north wing with the gallery; and the rest was rebuilt to the original plans, plus some inconspicuous additions at the back. On a slight rise behind the mansion stands the church (St Hyderoc), older than the

Lanhydrock : the gardens and church

house, since the tower is fifteenth-century, but of no especial merit. The house contains many shelves of anti-Catholic literature.

Lanhydrock was the principal model for 'Endelstow House' in Thomas Hardy's novel *A Pair of Blue Eyes*, though he embellished it with features from Athelhampton, the Dorset mansion near his birthplace.

Lanteglos-by-Camelford   Cornwall
see **Camelford**

Launceston (*sometimes pron.* Larnson)   Cornwall
4A2, 6C6   (*pop.* 4,741)
The original name of the town round the castle was Dunheved, Launceston (Lan-Stephen) being that of the 'rival' settlement round the important monastery on the next hilltop. In the thirteenth and fourteenth centuries, after the mint and market had already been transferred from the sacred town to the secular, the Lan-Stephen folk began, no doubt with all due respect, to feel that the physical protection of the castle was a safer proposition than the purely spiritual protection of the monks, and so they shifted, taking the name 'Launceston' with them; but the 1971 official census report still apologizes, in a special footnote, for not calling modern Launceston Dunheved. The first fortress was Celtic, the next Saxon, when it was already of major standing, being latterly a personal stronghold of King Harold. The Normans

Launceston: the church of St Mary Magdalene

erect. The rest of the present church was built between 1511 and 1524, at the expense of Sir Henry Trecarel; and the elaborately carved granite stones are those really intended by him to adorn a new manor-house, until a bereavement turned his thoughts heavenward instead. Apart from all this carving, the most striking thing about the church is that it is separated far enough from the tower to allow a secular building to stand in between – a building that until 1881 served as the town hall. Inside the church the best thing is the woodwork of different periods.

The church of St Stephen, though it remains the mother-church of Launceston, is now in a residential, predominantly Georgian suburb today called Newport. Yet its sixteenth-century tower still commands attention, which is just as well, for the late-Norman interior, rebuilt before 1420, has suffered the common fate of excessive and insensitive Victorian restoration. In the valley between the two hills flows the small River Kensey, crossed by two bridges, an eighteenth-century one carrying the present road, and a splendid low medieval one hardly more than 1m. wide. Down here, elegantly situated near the gasworks, is all that is left of the Augustinian priory that in 1126 replaced the original monastery of St Stephen. What little there is was rediscovered only by accident during the building of the railway in 1886. Close by is the third church of note, St Thomas, once a chapel to St Stephen's and also the place of burial for any Castle captives who died during their imprisonment. There is some good panelling, but, again, all the signs of far too zealous a restoration. The Norman font, probably from the priory, is the largest in Cornwall.

There are a medieval South Gate, sole survivor of three, an old inn, the White Hart, with a doorway that originated in either the priory or the castle chapel, and Georgian houses too many to list: suffice it that the best (some say the best in Cornwall) are in Castle Street, but that is not to disparage the others; until 1835 Launceston claimed to be the County Town, and building standards were in keeping with that status.

Obviously, a town built on two hills is a place for views, but they are particularly varied, since Bodmin Moor lies close on the west side, and Dartmoor not far off to the east. Between them, and including the lovely valley of the upper Tamar, lies some of the best and least-known inland scenery in the county, rich in woods and unspoilt villages. Barely 2km. south-east of Launceston, for example, is LAWHITTON, a most gracious spot in surroundings that look like a landscaped park but are just 'normal' land. Even closer, north of the town, the River Ottery is crossed at YEOLMBRIDGE by a fourteenth-century bridge that is among the oldest in Cornwall.

improved it, and so did the Black Prince, but after his date it declined, though remaining in the direct ownership of the Duchy of Cornwall, as it still does, administered today by the Dept of the Environment. Most of what remains is of the twelfth or thirteenth century: the great outer wall, the frowning keep on its central mount, and between them the bailey, which became a public park as long ago as 1840.

The other predominant building in this town of so much interest is the parish church of St Mary Magdalene, externally the most lavishly decorated church in Cornwall. Only the late-fourteenth-century tower is old, the surviving portion of the modest chapel that was all the authorities in St Stephen would allow Dunheved to

OPPOSITE: *Launceston from the N, showing the castle*

St Peter's church, Lewtrenchard. The reconstructed screen (1899)
is a good example of modern carving. The pulpit, modelled on
those of Kenton and Launceston, is early-C20

Lewtrenchard Devon 4B2 (*pop.* 131)
A diminishing village south of the London–Land's End
road (A30) above the beautiful valley of the River Lew,
a tributary of the Lyd, which itself empties into the
Tamar. This is the place in which lived the notable
chronicler, novelist, poet, parson, and writer of the
hymn 'Onward Christian Soldiers', the Revd Sabine
Baring-Gould (1834–1924); and the spot to which, a
lesser Lord Elgin, he took such architectural treasures

as happened to catch his eye in the course of his travels.
Admittedly this refined looting was limited to local
Tudor and Jacobean manors, but Orchard, in particular (*see* Bratton Clovelly), was denuded of mullioned
windows and even its datestone of 1620. Baring-
Gould's highly synthetic home (Lew House) is now a
hotel. The church, on the site of one perhaps founded
by St Petroc, is late-Perpendicular, or was: Baring-
Gould's grandfather restored it in 1835, and he himself

had a further go in the 1890s, introducing some of his 'pickings'. He also rebuilt the screen, which seems to have been destroyed during his grandfather's restoration. Many bench-ends were lost at that season, but a few good ones remain. Some memorial tablets to earlier Goulds came from Staverton church, where – for once – they had been genuinely discarded. The Revd Sabine inherited the manor in 1872, and was appointed to the living in 1881. Originally, as the name implies, the manor had belonged to the Trenchards.

One km. through the woods east of the village, at LEW MILL, is a small and attractive Elizabethan Dower House. In the opposite direction, and on the other side of the A30, lies STOWFORD (*pop.* 247), grouped about its nobly-towered Perpendicular church, restored in 1874 by the distinguished but not always happy hand of Sir Gilbert Scott. Here the hand was quite happy, and even the addition of a north aisle by it does not spoil the church. There are five original waggon-roofs, and a wonderful seventeenth-century monument to Christopher Harris of Haine and his wife, the husband in the get-up of a Roman legionary except for a large wig instead of a helmet, and both spouses with legs of a shortness that suggests the sculptor, by a considerable feat of anticipation, modelled his figures on Toulouse-Lautrec. By the churchyard gate is a Romano-British stone, and

in the comely village two houses stand out: Shepherds, near the church, thatched, irregularly gabled, and perhaps Tudor; and Stowford House, once the fairly plain rectory, but with startling neo-Gothic additions. HAINE, the Harris seat, lies 1½km. west, again mercifully off the main road: Tudor, but largely rebuilt by the well-known late-Georgian architect Wyattville. Fine trees, a shell grotto, and a cascade adorn the grounds.

Three km. north-west of Lewtrenchard, near Combebow Bridge, which carries the A30 over the River Lew, stands BIDLAKE MILL, a scheduled medieval corn-mill, the history of which goes back to at least 1268. The mill is complete with large water-wheel, and the scene is embellished by rock- and water-gardens laid out in terraces some twenty years ago. It is open on Wednesday afternoons from April to October, or by appointment at other times of the year.

Liskeard (*pron.* Liskard)   Cornwall   3G2
(*pop.* 5,264)
A market town, slung between two hills, whose days of greatest prosperity came when the coppermines north of it were at their zenith. There is much unpretentious Georgian and pre-Georgian housing still to be seen, and some rather grander Regency and Victorian houses overlooking the valley of the River Looe, around the

View of Liskeard by Rowlandson

street called The Parade. The grandest is Webb's Hotel, 1833. Other buildings of the same era are the Market Hall, 1821, and, south of the town, Lamellion Hospital, 1839, formerly the Workhouse. Some of the larger houses are stuccoed, though the chief impression is of slate roofs and slate-hung walls; but this applies only to the older part of Liskeard below the A38 trunk road. The flanks of that sordid highway are as uninviting as the traffic that thunders along its surface.

The church is, after Bodmin, the largest in Cornwall: it is a fifteenth-century building, much modified, and, for once, with a tower (1893) that is newer instead of older than the body of the building. Inside there are pleasant vistas of granite arcades.

Two km. north of Liskeard stands the seventeenth-century manor-house of TREWORGEY, not on display, but standing in a garden conspicuous for its enormous yew trees and yew and box topiary. The garden also contains a quaint timber-hung clock tower, probably Georgian, with a pagoda-style roof.

The Lizard   Cornwall   2C6

Nothing to do with reptiles, but a corruption of Lis-Arth, the 'Holy Palace'; properly the name should be limited to Lizard Point, but often nowadays it is applied to all the area nearly islanded by Loe Pool and the Helford River. Here it is used for a survey of the coast from the Devil's Frying Pan (*see* Cadgwith) to Mullion Cove (*see* Mullion). A well-known guidebook of 1897 described this, the southernmost part of England, and indeed all the hinterland to beyond Helston, as 'almost, if not quite, the most solitary district in Cornwall'. Alas, were the writer to return to it on a fine July or August day in the present era, he might well call it the most congested! However, the fascination lies in the shore-line, and here, except for the occasional cove, the grandeur of the cliffs dwarfs the human intruder where they do not actually bar him by their inaccessibility. The virtual death of the pilchard industry in these parts has resulted in a number of deserted fish-warehouses and small ports. At LANDMARK, 2km. south of Cadgwith, the old fish 'palace' has been turned into a villa, and you can still see the abandoned quay and winch: Landmark was the port for LANDEWEDNACK, just inland in one of the few wooded vales hereabouts, and so far not too much spoilt. The cottages are painted in washes of various pastel colours, and even the church tower is a mixture of pinkish granite blocks and the dark-green local serpentine. The church contains Norman and Perpendicular features and some of Britain's oldest bells, but catches the imagination mainly because it is the most southerly church in the United Kingdom apart from the Channel Islands.

Close to Landewednack is KILCOBBEN COVE, where the lifeboat formerly at Cadgwith is now kept. Since there is no professional fishing fleet left in the area, it is a heart-warming sight, when the maroon sounds, to see

the farmer, newsagent, and others who earn their livelihood on land and fish only for recreation hurrying to join the two professional fishermen in launching the vessel into the storm. South of Kilcobben, BASS POINT is an outpost of NT territory; here at least, as in the other NT zones west of Lizard Point, the land behind the cliffs is spared the litter of boarding-houses, booths, bungalows, with all their attendant rubbish of masts, cables, aerials, and so on that have made hideous the area between the Point and LIZARDTOWN, once a fairly picturesque village devoted (as in part it still is) to the carving of ornaments from the easily-worked serpentine. The presence of the serpentine is one cause of the extraordinary beauty and variety of colouring of the cliffs round the Lizard Peninsula – as though their ruggedness were not beauty enough! Though predominantly dark green, it is often veined with 'undigested' streaks of the olivine and hornblende that went into its composition. In other parts the cliffs are black, or show the local red granite. The whole area entrances geologists, for the rocks are among the oldest on the earth's surface.

Contrary to popular belief, Lizard Point itself is not Britain's most southerly point, which is to be found much nearer the lighthouse, forming the western horn of POLBREAM COVE. Also further south than the Point is the headland ½km. east of Polbream, close to THE LION'S DEN, another version of the Devil's Frying Pan. The lighthouse was erected in 1753 and modernized in 1903. It can be visited at suitable hours. The sea facing it contains an incredible mass of rocks, extending nearly 1km. from the shore. North of Lizard Point the NT again owns a stretch of clifftop that includes part of KYNANCE COVE, a beauty spot that for once deserves all the praise given it. The rock is nearly all serpentine, and therefore green, and the numberless rocks and caves have such names as Asparagus Island, the Kitchen, Parlour, and Drawing Room, the Devil's Letterbox, and the Bellows (a blowhole). On the cliffs, in due season, are masses of wild flowers, including many mesembryanthemums. The majesty of the cliffs continues past PREDANNACK HEAD, through further areas afforded the valuable protection of the NT.

Looe   Cornwall   3G3   (*pop.* 4,090)

Properly divided into East and West Looe, with the estuary of the River Looe – quite narrow for Cornwall – between. Both towns rise steeply up their respective hillsides and contain many narrow winding streets. The harbour is another favourite of yachtsmen, but here, happily, the pilchard-fishing industry has not died out; nor is the fishing limited to pilchards, but includes a variety of other fish as well as lobsters and crabs. Like Fowey (qv), Looe was an important medieval port and time and again made a sizeable contribution of men and ships for service in the French wars. East Looe received a charter in 1237 and West Looe in 1243; and there were later charters for both under Elizabeth I and for East

St Bartholomew's church, Lostwithiel, from the E: the early-C14 octagonal spire is the outstanding feature; the E window, of the same date, is one of the most elaborate in Cornwall

Looe under the Stuarts. The two boroughs were not united until 1886. The eighteenth century was passed in trading and smuggling, the nineteenth largely in torpor, though the fishing never died out, and there was always a trade in shipping granite for such constructions as London's Victoria Embankment and Plymouth Breakwater. But it was the growth of the holiday trade that restored the twin towns' energies.

East Looe is the larger and retains many of its old houses, though in Fore Street and other commercial thoroughfares you have to lift your eyes above the dreary same-everywhere shopfronts to notice them. In other streets loving owners have made the picturesque houses *too* picturesque, rather 'twee'. The church, St Mary, is not impressive, having been rebuilt by G. E. Street, seldom one of the better church architects. The sixteenth-century Old Guildhall (restored) now houses a historical museum, and is something of a museum itself, retaining many features from the days when the Corporation met there. In an elegant house dated 1652, in the same quarter, lived Thomas Bond (d. 1837), town clerk and local historian. After his death an immense horde of gold coins was found in a cupboard, and removed quite casually in a farmer's waggon. Where the river reaches the sea is the quaint Banjo Pier, and on it an aquarium and shark museum – Looe is one of Britain's most important centres for shark-angling.

West Looe, once called Porthbyhan, is joined to East Looe by a dull Victorian bridge that replaced a magnificent fifteen-arch affair completed in 1436. The church of St Nicholas looks almost too small for its various changes of use. Built in the fourteenth century as a chapel, under the Commonwealth it became the town's Guildhall, then at the Restoration reverted to a chapel, only to become the Guildhall again in 1679; finally it was restored and reopened as a church in 1852. Its unusual composite belfry was for a time the 'Scolds' Cage' for incarcerating nagging women. The Jolly Sailor inn is a sixteenth-century building.

Out to sea south of West Looe lies LOOE ISLAND, or St George's Island; there, according to the magnificent old legend, St Joseph of Arimathea landed with the infant Jesus on their way to Glastonbury. In the twelfth century a group of monastic cells was set up there, opposite a similar group on the mainland. For a time they belonged to the Abbot of Glastonbury, but as the centuries passed they dropped out of the records. But the ruins of both mainland and island settlements can still be seen. A somewhat later story, perhaps as legendary as the other, avers that when Looe Island was unexpectedly bombed during the Second World War it was because the Germans thought it was a battleship!

Up-river the Looe divides into the East Looe and West Looe, both bordered by green and pleasant scenery. On the northern outskirts of West Looe a large sheet of water, the Mill Pool, is cut off from the tidal river by a sea wall, built in 1614. The pool is now used

Landscape near Lostwithiel, showing Restormel Castle

as a boating-lake. Opposite, on the high, wooded spur separating the two rivers, is a temple; this stands in the landscaped grounds of TRENANT PARK.

Lostwithiel Cornwall 3F2 (*pop.* 1,905)
Small but ancient, having acquired its first charter in 1189; nor has it grown very much since, in spite of having been for a time the capital of the county and the only stannary town for assaying the tin. But if it is no longer important it certainly remains attractive, in a manner that some commentators have called Breton rather than British; and its attractiveness is considerably improved by the diversion of through traffic along a bypass. There is also a new bridge to take most of the traffic over the River Fowey, otherwise crossed by a truly splendid five-arched bridge built at the beginning of the fourteenth

century, with parapets added in 1676. The Fowey was navigable then – as it still is for very small craft – and remained so until late-Tudor times. But the most important feature of the town is the church of St Bartholomew, and the most important feature of the church is its early-fourteenth-century octagonal spire. This, with the delicate stone tracery of its eight pointed 'windows', one to each side, is unlike any other in Cornwall. G. E. Street, the Victorian church restorer, called St Bartholomew 'the glory of Cornwall'. After the capture of the town by the Parliamentarians they housed their prisoners in the church, and much damage was done later when the guards let off a bomb to dislodge two captives who had hidden in the spire. Fortunately the spire itself escaped harm, as, for that matter, did the fugitives. The lovely Early English east window also escaped. The body of the church is of late-fourteenth-century date, but has been re-roofed.

Down by the old bridge are the even older Great Hall of 1280, usually miscalled the Old Duchy Palace, and various other remnants of the old Stannary Court. The town contains a small Guildhall, c. 1740; other Georgian buildings include the Grammar School, the Municipal Offices with panelled walls and a good plaster ceiling, and several mansions. These are all in or near the main thoroughfare, Fore Street, where a house of 1688 is also to be seen at No. 9.

One and a half km. upstream from Lostwithiel, high on a hill-crest, is the castle of RESTORMEL, easily the county's best piece of military architecture. A fragment of the gate dates from about 1100, but most of the building is twelfth- or thirteenth-century. The castle belonged first of all to the Cardinham family, then the Traceys, then Simon de Montfort, and finally the Dukes of Cornwall, who still own it, administration being by the Dept of the Environment. It is open to the public. The lofty position, sheer walls, and steep hillside, the single point of approach, make Restormel most impressive to look at (though less romantic than before the ruins were cleared of creeper) and also to look from, for the views are tremendous. During the early part of the Civil War Restormel was held for the Parliament, but despite its seeming impregnability it was captured by the redoubtable Sir Bevil Grenville, descendant of famous Sir Richard. Between the castle hill and the river is Restormel House, a delightful Gothic Revival mansion of the 1760s; and in contrast to these works of man, 4km. to the west, on the far side of Red Moor, is HELMAN TOR (209m.), on which there is a good example of one of Cornwall's several logan stones.

Returning to the Fowey, above Restormel the river becomes increasingly lovely, marred only (beyond Bodmin Road Station) by the presence of both the main railway-line and the busy A38 (Liskeard–Bodmin) road. The left bank is wooded almost continuously, the right, interrupted by the mouth of many small streams flowing down off Bodmin Moor, is part wooded, part meadowland. These reaches are greatly prized by anglers. South of Lostwithiel, that is to say downstream, the river soon widens, and here on the left bank is ST WINNOW, a name synonymous with the Llanwynog to whom several churches are dedicated in Wales. With the broad estuary immediately before it, the woods of Ethy alongside on its own bank and those of Lantyan opposite, the minute group of church, vicarage, and a single sixteenth-century barton looks like a poster-artist's fiction. The small church is Perpendicular, with a few Norman vestiges, all restored but retaining much of the original waggon-roof carving, some lovely fifteenth-century stained glass in the east window of the south aisle, and a number of Tudor carved 'picture' bench-ends, some displaying unusual subjects. There is a rather fine rood-screen, part original, part restored – with his customary appreciative care – by Edmund Sedding in 1907. This is very much Civil War terrain, but among the monuments is one to a hero of a later contest, Lieutenant Melville, who saved the Queen's Colours during a battle in the Zulu Wars, 1879. All very deliciously Victorian.

Lundy Devon 6A1 (*pop.* 49) (NT)
The well-known island in the Bristol Channel, bigger than it looks on all but the largest maps or from the mainland, the nearest tip of which is Hartland Point, 18km. distant. Lundy in fact measures 5km. by, at the widest part, 1·3km. Geologically it is a single outcrop of granite, and the natural flora is limited to grass, heath plants, and many wild flowers, but man has added a few trees, rhododendron thickets along the east coast, and has put about a quarter of the 47ha. (116 acres) under

cultivation. Animal life includes Soay sheep, Sika deer, ponies, wild goats, numerous smaller creatures and insect species, and of course myriads of sea birds, particularly the puffin, which is the island's symbol and from the Norse word for which it derives its name. Inevitably Lundy's history is a pretty black one, and its record of association with piracy, smuggling, and assorted thuggery makes the activities of the toughest mainland port seem like a vicarage bring-and-buy sale. Hut circles and at least one tumulus prove Neolithic occupation, there is a Romano-British inscribed stone, archaeological evidence of a Christian colony in the sixth or seventh century, and inevitably the piratical Vikings found the island a most convenient base, even if they did not actually start its freebooting tradition.

The first recorded lord of the island was Sir Jordan de Marisco, 1154, who built the first castle. The Knight's conduct, however, was so outrageous that Henry II confiscated castle and island and awarded them to the Knights Templar. But the Mariscos refused to let the Templars land, and continued in their regrettable ways until in 1242 William de Marisco and a bunch of accomplices were hanged for conspiring to cut Henry III's throat. Henry then built a newer and larger fortress, the remains of which are to be seen today, still under the name of Marisco Castle. Nevertheless, Lundy remained a pirate base, catering for Captain Kidd among other celebrities of the profession; French, Spanish, and even Turkish pirates used it. Charles I and later Cromwell both appointed governors, but without effecting improvement, for near the end of the century French privateers raided Lundy itself, killed all the livestock, and took the islanders' clothes. Half a century later the island was in charge of Thomas Benson, pirate, smuggler, slave-owner, and Member of Parliament, who carried on the old tradition so vigorously that finally he had to flee to the Continent or be hanged. He fled. In 1836 the Heaven family acquired Lundy, and at last brought order, peace, and many improvements. In contrast with so much early skulduggery, it is pleasant to know that during the Second World War John Pennington Harman, a member of the last family to own Lundy privately, earned a posthumous Victoria Cross in Burma. The NT took over in 1969, and later leased Lundy to the Landmark Trust, who are pledged to preserve its beauty and natural amenities.

Apart from Marisco Castle the main buildings (nearly all in the south) include the late-seventeenth-century church or chapel, inside the old burial ground and now in ruins; the new church (1896), unfortunately devoid of architectural interest; a hotel; a pub (the 'Marisco', naturally); a general store; the Old Light (1819), a delightful piece of granite construction; the North and South Lights, which replaced the Old Light in 1894; the remains of several old gun batteries; Millcombe, the house built for the Heavens, with its rather gracious garden; and the islanders' cottages, some of which let rooms to visitors. The finest cliffs (up to 114m.) are on the west coast. Of some disused quarries – relic of a venture that never paid – one is now called V C Quarry, in memory of John Harman who played there as a boy. There is a bird sanctuary in the north, and plans exist for an underwater nature reserve. The port for Lundy is Ilfracombe, with services throughout the year.

Luppitt   Devon   *see* **Dunkeswell Abbey**

Lustleigh   Devon   *see* **Bovey Tracey**

Luxulyan Valley (*pron.* Luxillian)   Cornwall   3E2
One of the most unusual and delightful spots in the Cornish hinterland. Amid trees wide enough apart to allow long vistas, grow in profusion a mass of ferns and wild flowers. But this is not all; throughout the valley are scattered enormous boulders, some larger than the occasional cottages, of a variety of porphyry found only here. One great block of it was used to make the Duke of Wellington's sarcophagus in St Paul's Cathedral, at the then enormous cost of £1,000. There is a stream in the valley, milk-white with china-clay deposits; and dominating everything else there is the Treffry Viaduct, 30m. high and nearly 200m. long, built in 1839 by J. T. Treffry of Fowey to carry a railway and a canal from the Treffry granite quarries to the coast. Both are now disused and so, therefore, is the viaduct, which presides over the scene in a silence matching that of the valley itself. LUXULYAN village (*pop.* 1,028) is notable for its big church of the local granite, in which all the Cornish Stannary Court records were kept prior to the Civil War, when they were moved to Lostwithiel and vanished. The village also boasts a small neatly-enclosed Holy Well, that of St Cyr.

Lydford Gorge   Devon   4B2/B3   (NT)
It is ironical that this beautiful ravine of the River Lyd, with its miniature cataracts, rock-girt pools, and open-wooded sides, should lie so close to Lydford Castle, for centuries a place of such terror and injustice as a prison that its name struck more fear into the people of Dartmoor than ever the present Dartmoor Prison at Princetown has done. 'I oft have heard of Lydford Law', began William Browne's seventeenth-century ballad, 'How in the morn they hang and draw / And sit in judgment after'. It appears that on at least one occasion 'they' did exactly that. Lydford Castle was built in 1195 but intended from the outset as a prison for Stannary Law offenders; and not all the neatness imparted to the ruins by the Dept of the Environment can lessen the aura of darkness and cruelty.

Close to the prison, by a further unintended irony, stands the fifteenth-century church of St Petroc, granite, with a north aisle that was added in 1890. The building's chief claim to interest lies in its modern carving: an admirable rood-screen designed in 1904 by

Bligh Bond and carved by Miss Violet Pinwill of Ermington; and nearly seventy bench-ends portraying prophets, martyrs, saints, and God-fearing personages from Samuel to Archbishop Temple, set in borders depicting local flora and fauna, the whole designed in the 1920s by the renowned Herbert Read of Exeter and cut by two carvers, one for the figures and one for the borders. Of earlier vintage are the Norman font and the stained glass in the chancel south window nearest the screen, said to have once been in Salisbury Cathedral. In the churchyard is the gravestone of a watchmaker, George Routleigh, bearing an epitaph that makes ingenious use of horologists' terms.

For centuries Lydford Gorge was in private hands and not accessible to the public, until thrown open by Daniel Radford. The NT acquired it between 1943 and 1968, and today there is a path along its whole length of about 2½km., beyond which the river continues to flow between steep and forested banks for several km. more. The most dramatic reach is at the northern end, where for several hundred m. the river has cut a narrow cleft, 18m. deep and in places barely a m. wide, in the solid rock below the base of the ravine proper. Here, among the stone hollows the seething waters have worn, is the sensational Devil's Cauldron. At the other end of the Gorge, also sensational, though less so for some tastes than if projections split up the fall, is the White Lady Waterfall, a single cascade of 30m. The sides of the ravine are clothed all along in oak, beech, and sycamore above a green and floral carpet of, in spring, Disneyesque loveliness. The Gorge is open daily from April to October inclusive.

East of Lydford unfolds the whole huge panorama of really high Dartmoor. South of the Gorge are two westward outposts of the Moor: GIBBET HILL, scene of many a 'Lydford Law' hanging, of the burning of Lady Howard as a witch (true, she had probably murdered four husbands), and, if legend be based on truth, of the occasional dumping of a highwayman in an iron cage until he died of starvation; and the eye-catching, isolated NORTH BRENTOR, or just Brentor, on the extreme 345m. crest of which is perched the small church of St Michael, built *c.* 1140, rebuilt some 250 years later. It belonged to Tavistock Abbey, to which Henry VII granted the right to hold a three-day fair every September on this inconvenient hilltop. Along with the rest of the Abbey lands, Brentor passed to the Russell family after the Dissolution.

Lynton and **Lynmouth**   Devon   7E1   (*pop.* 1,984)
One whole, but with a vertical difference of 165m. between them. Virtually cut off from the rest of Devon and Somerset by the almost uninhabited wilderness of Exmoor, they remained poor villages (Lynmouth a fishing community) without much prospect of ever becoming anything else until the Napoleonic wars made Continental travel hazardous, and the fashionable

Coastal scenery near Lynton : Castle Rock is in the foreground

section of English society, generally the only people with enough money to travel anyway, bethought them of the current fashion for the Wild and Romantic and discovered this exceedingly wild and romantic coast of north-east Devon. Among visitors at that epoch were Shelley and Southey, who left a very vivid and detailed description of Lynmouth. As for Shelley, he so alarmed the authorities by a pamphlet defending the arch-radical Tom Paine that he had to leave in haste – some say in a fisherman's boat for Wales. The Lynmouth cottage in which it is believed he lodged was destroyed by fire in 1907, and on the site of it stands now the Shelley's Cottage Hotel.

Next it was Lynton's turn to receive the Wordsworths and their friend Coleridge. Among those drawn there by the poets' praise was Thomas Coutts, founder of Coutts Bank, and it was he, together with a local man named Litson, who saw that Lynton could be turned into a popular resort. But communications were the problem – the roads across the moor were terrible; and it was left

for another famous figure connected with literature, publisher Sir George Newnes, to remedy this in the 1890s. First he paid for the hydraulically-worked cliff railway that still connects Lynton and Lynmouth; then he created the Barnstaple–Lynton Railway, 30km. long, 61cm. (2ft.) in gauge, with four engines and sixteen coaches, and connecting with the main-line station at Barnstaple. This highly practical toy lasted until 1935, when it was closed and the equipment sold off. It is hard to imagine the railway fanatics of today allowing such a fate. Nevertheless, better roads and the motor-car have ensured that the twin villages have never looked back as resorts. Vestiges of the line, including bridges, can still be seen.

Lynton, if it lacks the pleasures afforded by the immediate proximity of the sea, also lacks its perils – Lynmouth was virtually wiped out by a terrible high tide in 1607, and many now alive recall the fearful night of 15 August 1952, when after weeks of rain 23cm. fell in a few hours, and in the night the overburdened East

Lyn river suddenly went mad, bringing down thousands of tons of earth, boulders as big as cottages, huge tree trunks, and masses of debris, all in a great surge of water 3m. high. The electricity went, and in pitch darkness, to a deafening roar, houses, cars, trees, and people were swept far out to sea. Thirty-four lives were lost. The scenery round about is arguably the most awe-inspiring in Devon, but perhaps nothing is more impressive than the mark on one of the houses in Lynmouth indicating the height reached by the floodwater on that occasion. The village has been rebuilt and is more popular than ever – the river has been made safer by widening – but with these repeated disasters old buildings are few: Rock House and Manor House are two pre-Victorian survivors. Another casualty of the sea was the early-nineteenth-century jetty, which for a time had allowed a prosperous herring-fishery. Lynton is predominantly, even overwhelmingly, Victorian, with all the rather endearing architectural whimsies of a new resort of the time. It also has the very entertaining Lyn and Exmoor Museum (open May–September, not Saturdays), containing pictures of old Lynmouth, souvenirs of the railway, local arts and crafts, and a replica of an Exmoor kitchen.

Local beauty-spots include the NT's WATERSMEET, where after tumbling through a steep and wooded gorge the East Lyn is joined by the Hoar Oak Water; FORE-LAND POINT, where the tremendous cliffs form the eastern end of Lynmouth Bay – this is also a NT property; the ancient earth fort on WIND HILL, COUNTISBURY, a magnificent viewpoint already centuries old when Odda of Devon defeated the Danes there in 873; and on the west side of Lynton the much-visited VALLEY OF THE ROCKS, a curious depression between two tors, one of which rises straight from the sea. On its windy and uncomfortable summit a hut stood during the last century,

Hound Tor, S of Manaton

in which lived an old hermit woman used by Blackmore as Mother Meldrum in *Lorna Doone*.

Manaton Devon 4D3, 7F6 (*pop.* 416)
A stone village on eastern Dartmoor, surrounded by many natural and prehistoric sites of interest and itself of note because for years the novelist and playwright John Galsworthy lived at a farm called WINGSTONE, on the south-western edge of the village; the uniform edition of his works is called the Manaton Edition. He died (in London) in 1933, but is still recalled with affection, for he was the reverse of aloof, not only riding about locally and sitting out of doors to write, but sometimes buying up the cottages of villagers who could not afford their rents so that he could ask them much less.

There is little deserving of individual notice (excepting perhaps the fifteenth-century church screen) in Manaton. Most striking and also nearest of the adjacent sights is THE BOWERMAN'S NOSE, 1km. south-west, an isolated rock-pile between 7m. and 9m. high (according to side) with the top part in the likeness of a head wearing a cloth cap. Nearby are hut circles – indeed, there are hut circles on nearly every tor in the neighbourhood. On HOUND TOR, 2km. south of Manaton – a great favourite with the tourists because of the views – there are in addition the remains of a medieval village, recently excavated. Here, too, in legend, the black hounds of darkness hid by day, coming out at night to ravage the livestock. Some say it was here that Conan Doyle picked up his idea for *The Hound of the Baskervilles* (but *see also* Buckfast Abbey). Hound Tor's western neighbour is HONEYBAG TOR, one of the Moor's most spectacular formations.

East of Manaton, including north-east and south-east, the landscape embraces large areas of woodland. A bare km. north-east, the River Bovey flows through MEADON CLEAVE, a handsome defile that continues downstream as LUSTLEIGH CLEAVE. One and a half km. south-east of the village, on a tributary of the Bovey, are the BECKA (or Becky) FALLS, much visited but worth it except in the full holiday season, when it is better to seek out some of the less publicized beauty spots. Some prefer that at any season.

Mawgan-in-Meneage Cornwall 2C5 (*pop.* 1,476)
Up a little creek of its own on the south side of the Helford River estuary: also called St Mawgan, after yet another Irish (or possibly Welsh) saint who was a tutor of other saints and also a bard. The church dedicated to him has an exceptionally impressive tower, with a figure of St Mawgan himself (or so they say) over the west window, and a most beguiling collection of monuments, due to the fact that no fewer than four great families lived or had interests nearby: the Carminows, Reskymers, Vyvyans, and Ferrers. All four coats of arms can be seen near the west door. It was the Vyvyans who built TRELOWARREN, 1½km. south-east, a large, low, rambling,

partly battlemented house amid woods and fronted by a huge lawn. Its stones span the centuries from the fifteenth to the nineteenth. Sir Richard Vyvyan was Charles I's Master of the Mint, and during the Civil War coined money at Trelowarren to pay the soldiers. As a reward Charles II gave him one of the portraits of his father by Van Dyck. The last Vyvyan to maintain house and grounds in the privacy they had always known was 'Clara Vyvyan', the writer, widow of the tenth baronet. For nearly half a century she helped to finance the estate by running a profitable market garden, but after she died, aged ninety, in 1976, the great house was converted into holiday flats (in one of which lives her nephew and heir) and the grounds were made available as a tent and caravan centre. Unless you know a tenant the house is not open, but you can read about it in the works of its last grand lady, *The Old Place* and *Letters from a Cornish Garden*.

Close by, to the west, is a spot called HALLIGYE, which has the largest 'fogou' in Cornwall, 27½m. long and nearly 2m. high, in excellent condition. Only the entrance has been modernized. These fogous, or subterranean passages, were perhaps used for storage (*see* Pendeen), but another suggestion is that they were refuges – very like Second World War air-raid shelters. They were not made by tunnelling, but dug as deep trenches and then roofed and earthed over. They are unique to Cornwall, and always occur near Iron Age villages or forts (here at Halligye it is a fort). In addition to serving as refuges from attack, if that was their use, they must also have been useful retreats from the worst winter weather.

Mevagissey Cornwall 3E4 (*pop.* 2,151)
The origin of the name is as unusual as the name itself, for 'Mevagissey' is an amalgam of two saints' names, the Welsh St Meven, or Mewan, and the Irish St Itha, or Ida. Mevagissey's story is that of so many Cornish south-coast settlements – a thriving pilchard-fishing port undergoing decline and then being saved by the growth of the tourist industry. Not that fishing here is dead or even continuing its decline, but what is left does sometimes give the impression of being retained mainly for the benefit of the artists who churn out their paintings for sale in the gift shops that were once fish-merchants' offices. This is a pity, because the port had the advantage of facing east, so that its boats could go out when the prevailing gales were making it too rough for harbours facing south and south-west; and furthermore the Mevagissey fishermen were not afraid of modernization, for example by substituting drift nets for seine fishing long before most of their rivals.

Though tourism has provoked a bad outbreak of bungalows and other alien encumbrances round the perimeter, the original village remains picturesquely jumbled above the harbour, with the little slate-hung cottages varied here and there by grand Georgian mansions to remind one of the days when tens of millions of pilchards were exported every year, most of them to Italy. The harbour consists of an inner and an outer enclosure, the pier of the inner dating from the 1770s. What was once the lifeboat house is now an aquarium. The church of St Peter, 1259 but heavily Victorianized by St Aubyn, stands on the site of earlier churches going back to 550. Some interesting monuments survive from the 1259 building.

The environs of Mevagissey include a splendid coastline, especially southward. Immediately south is Port-mellon, an artists' adoption looking like a slightly incredible reconstruction of a Cornish village for an international fair, but redeemed by a boatyard making fishing craft. Mevagissey Bay ends at Chapel Point, near which is NT-owned Bodrugan's Leap. During the 1480s Sir Henry Trenowth of Bodrugan (a mansion of which the remnants are now incorporated in a nearby farm), fleeing from the wrath of Richard III for having sided with the future Henry VII, rode his horse over this dizzy cliff, landed safely in the sea, was picked up by a passing ship, and escaped to France. (*See* Cotehele for the not dissimilar escape, in the same circumstances, of Sir Richard Edgcumbe.)

Next comes Gorran (Goran) Haven, supposedly founded by St Guron after he had given up his cell at Bodmin (qv) to St Petroc. Perhaps he built his new cell where the present church stands by the cliffs, despite its dedication to St Just. It is a small, simple, fifteenth-century building, no doubt of some charm until St Aubyn took it in hand, though if so the charm was less than infallible, for at one period the church was used as a fish store.

Farther south more NT land takes in much of Dodman Point (114m.) or just The Dodman, whose cliffs fall so sheer into the sea and way below it that large ships can safely sail close in. There is a prehistoric fort on top, and a cross erected to encourage the Second Coming.

Inland of Mevagissey, up the valley, lies Heligan, an impressive mansion dating from 1603, with several subsequent modifications and additions, in gardens once resplendent with tropical plants. But the house is now turned into flats and the gardens are neglected and overgrown. There is a public footpath through the park.

Moretonhampstead Devon 4D2 (*pop.* 1,140) One of the highest towns on Dartmoor where the Oke-hampton–Newton Abbot and upper Plymouth–Exeter roads cross: inevitably, in such a position, a market town, though somewhat outrivalled in this respect now that the motor-car has brought Exeter and Newton Abbot markets so much nearer. But that same ease of travel has made it all the busier as a halting-point for travellers. As with its neighbour Manaton, it is less the town than what lies about it that brings it into this gazetteer. Its own most interesting features are a row

The granite-built almshouses at Moretonhampstead (1637)

of seventeenth-century almshouses with a granite-pillared frontage, and the churchyard in which lie a number of French officers of Napoleon who were taken prisoner, incarcerated in Dartmoor Prison (it was a gaol for prisoners-of-war long before it was used for convicts: *see* Princetown), and died in this alien clime while on parole.

Within a few km. of Moretonhampstead are several of the ancient crosses so conspicuous on Dartmoor. In 1645 – *before* the Commonwealth was established – an ordnance was issued that all crosses in churches and open spaces should be destroyed, but a number escaped because they marked the way where tracks crossed or were obscure. Occasionally there was a compromise: the cross was destroyed but the easily recognizable shaft was left. Such a shaft is to be seen some 2km. north-east on Mardon Down. There is a complete cross the same distance south-east, near Hunter's Tor; and a very good one 1½km. south-west, on the way to North Bovey. This is HORSPIT CROSS, popularly called Stumpy Cross. It has a single letter on each face and on the ends of the horizontal arms, four letters in all, indicating that the respective surfaces face Bovey Tracey, Moretonhampstead, Okehampton, and Newton Abbot.

NORTH BOVEY (*pop.* 388), which has succeeded in preserving its own village cross on the edge of the green, is something of a model Dartmoor village, all unspoilt stone and thatch, most of the cottages dating from the eighteenth century or earlier, with oak-trees on the green. The church is not too drastically restored, and has some good bench-ends, and eighteenth-century paintings round the organ loft. Outside the village (fortunately) the Manor House Hotel was built in a Jacobean style in 1907 for Viscount Hambleden.

Morvah Cornwall 2A5 (*pop.* 77)
A tiny place on the bare land between St Ives and Land's End, but one of the focal points for as exciting an assembly of prehistoric remains as are to be found in either Cornwall or Devon. The best known (because most photogenic) of these is LANYON QUOIT (NT), beside the Morvah–Penzance road. The Quoit consists of a flat capstone, nearly 10¾m. long, resting horizontally on three other stones. These now raise it only 1½m. from the ground, but in the eighteenth century, it appears, a man on horseback could pass underneath it without bowing. In 1815 the Quoit, like Napoleon, took a tumble, and during the effort to re-erect it the restorers broke one or more of the uprights, forcing a general reduction in height. Two km. west is CHUN CASTLE, a round fort on a commanding hill that in its day must have been all but impregnable. A double ring of drystone walling was

Lanyon Quoit, Morvah

TOP: *Chun Castle, near Morvah*   BOTTOM: *Men-an-Tol, near Morvah*

faced with huge granite blocks. Today the walls are much mutilated, but within memory the inner wall still stood more than 3½m. high. As with Castle-an-Dinas and Chysauster (*see* Gulval), Chun defended villages whose inhabitants extracted the local tin: a smelting-furnace and a lump of tin slag were found some years ago in the fort itself. There are remains of one settlement a few dozen m. north-east of the Castle, and there were two more. West of Chun Castle is CHUN QUOIT: four uprights supporting a thick 2m.-square capstone. About 2km. north-east of Lanyon is MULFRA QUOIT, three surviving uprights bearing a capstone that has partly slipped.

MEN-AN-TOL means the stone with a hole through it; there are several in Cornwall, but the most impressive is the one that stands 1½km. north of Lanyon Quoit; a twin stone polygon with a perfectly round hole in the centre, standing on edge between two supporting pillars. It was part of a tomb, but no one is sure of its purpose. Until a few years ago sick people crawled through it to assuage their ills, and children were passed through to cure them of rickets. Nearby, a circle of eleven stones is somewhat inaccurately called THE NINE MAIDENS. Barrows, tumuli, and carns (the same as 'cairns') are found everywhere; of the last-named are HANNIBAL'S CARN and CARN GALVA, both north of Men-an-Tol, and CARN KENIDJACK, halfway between Morvah and St Just.

Morwenstow Cornwall 6B4 (*pop.* 534)
At the extreme northern edge of the county; a village famous beyond its own deserts because of its noted vicar-poet Robert Stephen Hawker (1803–75), one of England's great eccentrics. His eccentricities began when as a boy he sat on the seashore clad only in seaweed, and was nearly shot by a farmer who did not like mermaids. While he was at Oxford he learned that his father could no longer support him there, so he hurried on horseback to the home of the lady who had taught him to read, and asked her to marry him. This she did, though he was twenty and she was forty, and her money paid for the rest of his time at university. Astonishingly, the marriage gave both partners perfect happiness until the lady died nearly forty years later; whereupon Hawker, now sixty, married a Belgian Roman Catholic of twenty. This marriage, too, was happy, and the only shadow cast on it, the story that the wife and her priest pressurized the old parson on his deathbed into turning Catholic, is open to dispute.

Hawker held the Morwenstow living from 1834 to 1875, and stalked its wild acres in a brimless beaver hat, fisherman's jersey (marked with a cross where Christ had received the spear), long wine-red coat surmounted by a yellow cloak, and fisherman's long boots. He kept a pet pig, encouraged jackdaws in his chimney and cats in his church, and when he baptized a babe that he felt had been brought over-late to the font he would pinch it first to let out the Devil. Though his ecclesiastical masters

were Church of England, he had no love for the Church in its current state, and would have preferred to restore the old Celtic religion. But whatever his theological eccentricities, in his life he could put many a more orthodox divine to shame. He would give his own dinner to feed a starving parishioner, his own cloak to protect one from the cold. But above all he was concerned for the victims of the many shipwrecks on the terrible coast south of Hartland Point. He built a little hut on the cliffs – it is still there, on Vicarage Cliffs, now NT land – from which he watched the Atlantic in its many moods, and where he wrote many of his books and poems, though not his best-known ballad, the *Song of the Western Men* (refrain: 'And shall Trelawney die?'). He buried more than forty drowned persons in his churchyard; over the graves of the captain and crew of the *Caledonia* stands the ship's figurehead as a memorial.

The church is as interesting as its celebrated vicar. The fabric is predominantly Norman, with some beautiful dog-tooth work; Hawker liked to think of the zig-zags as representing the ripples when the Holy Spirit breathed on the waters of baptism. There are fifteenth- and six-teenth-century bench-ends, a Saxon font, a superbly-adorned fourteenth-century waggon-roof – all of these discerned gradually, as the eyes become used to the deliberate dimness of the light. Even the adjacent vicarage, which Hawker built, reflects his personality, for the chimneys represent aspects of his life, being in the form of two Oxford college towers, his mother's monument, and three little church towers.

A short distance south of the church is a most pleasing Tudor manor-house, TONACOMBE; and at a slightly longer distance north, almost on the Devon border, is another, MARSLAND, where there is also a fine inn, formerly the smithy. The sea opposite Marsland is ribbed at low tide by bizarre ridges of rock running far out at right-angles to the shore. No wonder there were so many wrecks.

Mount Edgcumbe Cornwall 4B5
½km. S of Cremyll
The seat of the Earls of that name, in a magnificent position facing Plymouth across the Sound. The beautiful Tudor house, visited by kings and princes from Cosmo di Medici to Napoleon III, was completely destroyed in one of the great air-raids that devastated Plymouth in the spring of 1941. It has now been rebuilt and even opened at specified times to the public, but to-day the interest lies in the park, with its beguiling views, and the gardens filled with cedars, cork trees, and many other trees, plants, and shrubs, rare and otherwise. There are also an Orangery and an Italian Garden, both long famous, an eighteenth-century 'ruin' (not without irony, this), a holy well, and a monument. The Cremyll ferry from Plymouth (Stonehouse) has its terminal near one of the park entrances. CREMYLL itself is pretty if unremarkable, but a tree-lined road leads from it along the edge of Millbrook Creek, or Lake, to MILLBROOK

St John the Baptist, Morwenstow: S porch, incorporating a Norman arch

(*pop.* 1,529), a place that might well have become a Plymouth dormitory but has remained a large Cornish village, now somewhat decayed and with a slightly pre-occupied air as though it were trying to remember something. South of Mount Edgcumbe lies CAWSAND BAY, with its twin villages of CAWSAND and KINGSAND. Here the future Henry VII landed before Bosworth, and from here the Fleet was victualled when it used to anchor in the Bay before the building of Plymouth Breakwater (completed 1841). After that the Navy docked at Devonport, but Kingsand and Cawsand maintained, as they still do, a brisk fishing industry, much assisted in the past by smuggling. Devon-red in colouring, both villages on their steep sub-tropical hillside are unspoilt and delightful. Wooded cliffs lead on south to RAME HEAD, where Plymouth Sound reaches the open sea. Rame is a limpet-shaped projection that is almost islanded; at its summit (nearly 120m.) stands a fourteenth-century chapel (rebuilt in 1881) that also carried a beacon to guide shipping. The views from Rame are among the best in this region of superb views.

Mousehole (*pron.* Mowzel)   Cornwall   2A5
(*pop.* inc. in figure for Penzance)
This fishing village on Mount's Bay, a few km. south of Newlyn, was formerly called Porth Enys (island port), from ST CLEMENT'S ISLE immediately opposite the small port. The island and the fact that Mousehole faces east, with its back to the prevailing gales, give it good shelter at most times; but when an easterly gale does blow, a

door is closed across the harbour-mouth, to the no small dismay of any navigator caught outside. Mousehole bears the rare distinction of having been raided and destroyed by Spaniards in 1595 (*after* the defeat of the Armada), when only the Manor House survived. This later became the Keigwin Arms and later still a number of flats: John Keigwin (killed in the Spanish raid) was an authority on the Cornish language, which – discounting its modern intellectual revival – was spoken longer hereabouts than anywhere else.

Mousehole is a shadow of its bygone self. Once west Cornwall's most important fishery, it was also the port from which many pilgrims sailed to the Holy Land and to the shrine of St James at Compostela, and into which came salt from Britanny for salting the pilchards. However, the tourists keep it going without, so far, having spoilt its attractiveness, except by choking its steep, narrow streets with their cars. In the 1930s a measure of transient fame came to Mousehole from radio broadcasts of its choir. Less transient, one hopes, will be the future of the hospital for injured and oil-smeared birds run for nearly half a century by Miss Dorothy Yalesias. But lack of money seriously jeopardizes the prospects of this admirable institution once its founder has been obliged to withdraw.

Up the hill is PAUL, Mousehole's church-town. The church was originally Decorated and Perpendicular, but had to be rebuilt after the 1595 raid. Today its barrel roof, box pews, eighteenth-century monuments (one worded partly in Cornish) and very tall tower render it of above-average interest. One monument is the tomb of Dolly Pentreath (d. 1778), alleged (against not a little contradiction) to have been the last person to speak pre-revival Cornish. Prince Louis Bonaparte had a hand in erecting the tomb. Alongside the church is a pleasant row, the Hutchens Almshouses of 1709.

Mullion Cornwall 2C6 (*pop.* 1,346)
A rather self-conscious village containing a high percentage of retired professional people, but possessing a notable church, with a striking 'black and white' tower, *c.* 1500, of mixed granite and serpentine, and a body basically of the same period. This was restored in 1870 by F. C. Eden, one of the most sensitive of the Victorian rebuilders, whose work, all too rarely come across (Blisland is another example), reminds one just what could have been achieved had other restorers showed his vision and touch. Thanks to him Mullion retains its original barrel-roof timbers, north and south doors, font, and its greatest glory, the carved bench-ends, hardly surpassed not only in the county but in the country. The carvings probably date from late Henry VIII or soon after, and show a fascinating pageant of Biblical scenes and symbols.

MULLION COVE, properly called Porth Mellin, shares with Kynance (qv) the advantage of cliffs composed mainly of serpentine – the most northerly outpost of it

on the western side of the Lizard. Looking at the small 'toy' harbour today, it is hard to believe that Mullion too was once a busy pilchard-fishing port. Harbour, winch house, and fishermen's store all belong to the NT, and so do MULLION ISLAND, slightly to the south – home of many species of seabirds – and various neighbouring stretches of cliff, including, 2km. north of Mullion Cove, POLDHU POINT. At this spot, on 12 December 1901, history was made when radio morse signals were transmitted, to be picked up by Marconi waiting in St John's, Newfoundland – the first-ever Transatlantic broadcast; later the same station was used to send the first short-wave signals to Australia. Today the old buildings have gone, but a monument put up by the Marconi Company marks the site.

In the days of sail the Porth Mellin fishermen did their share of smuggling, and of plundering the many craft wrecked on the neighbouring shores. But the

St Melanus's church, Mullion

Dartmoor Landscape, near Vixen Tor

The gardens at Cotehele

respectability that characterizes the place today must have been in evidence even then, for the plunderers never plundered on Sunday.

Newlyn Cornwall 2A5
(*pop*. inc. in figure for Penzance)
The south-coast's answer to St Ives as an artists' centre. In point of fact the Newlyn colony came first, around 1883, with the founding of the Newlyn School by a group of young painters who, after training in France, decided to settle here. Langley, Gotch, Forbes, Harris, and Garstin were among the pioneers, and later Newlyn artists included Ernest Proctor and Sir Alfred Munnings. Even one of the vicars of Newlyn, the Revd A. G. Wyon, was a sculptor, and executed the memorial plaque to Stanhope Forbes to be seen in the Art Gallery (on the Penzance boundary) given to Newlyn in 1895 by Passmore Edwards, who as a benefactor was to Cornwall what Tate was to London.

Newlyn is still the haunt of a few artists (St Ives is definitely preferred today), but it is also an important fishing centre, with the largest fishmarket in the county and its own cannery for pilchards and mackerel. Its fishermen's quarter was once as picturesque as the most ardent of the artists could desire, but was ruined when in 1937 Penzance Council decided, in the interests of progress, to pull down more than 85 per cent of the old cottages, notwithstanding the fishermen's desperate action in sailing a lugger all the 460 miles to Westminster with a petition of protest. However, other old cottages remain, and the town is still a typical Cornish maze of narrow streets, many of them steep. There is a Victorian church appropriately dedicated to St Peter, containing more sculpture by Wyon and a little Newlyn School work. Except for one fifteenth-century pier in the harbour, everything built before the seventeenth century was destroyed in the Spanish raid of 1595.

Newquay Cornwall 2D2 (*pop*. 15,017)
Notwithstanding its name and present appearance, Newquay is not new, for episcopal indulgences were handed out to those who should help to build a harbour at 'New Kaye' in 1439, and even before that there was a village here, called Towan Blystra. But contemporary Newquay can show only one old building, the dazzling-white Huer's House on the headland, from the turret of which in the days of pilchard-fishing the huer would raise hue and cry to tell the fishermen that a shoal was near. Today's story is the standard one of fishing almost vanished, and shoals of tourists providing a livelihood instead. There was a short period in the second half of the nineteenth century when the two phases overlapped, and Newquay was a big schooner port for the china-clay trade as well, owning 150 ships of her own. This was just after the coming of the railway in 1874 (goods) and 1876 (passengers). At the moment of writing, the line (a branch of the Paddington–Penzance route) still func-

tions, but of the extension to the jetty all that remains to be seen is the opening of the tunnel through the cliffs. The principal church was not completed until 1967, and even the present Wesleyan chapel not until 1904.

Newquay's peninsula site and long coastline deserve better architecture. On the south-west the town is bounded by the estuary of the River Gannel, beyond which lies CRANTOCK, an attractive village whose antiquity is refreshing after Newquay and whose fourteenth-century church, expanded from a thirteenth-century one, is of considerable interest despite the inevitable Victorian restoration – in this case really inevitable, since the old church had become almost a ruin. The south shore of the estuary, and the cliffs right round to Holywell, several km. south-west, belong to the NT. Included is an inlet called Porth or Polly Joke, 'joke' being a corruption of the Cornish word for jackdaw; so the only funny thing about Polly Joke is that it really means Jackdaw's Cove. To the east, Newquay merges into ST COLUMB MINOR, of which the church – it served Newquay as well until the latter's new church was built – was much spoilt inside by the Victorians, but retains a splendid granite tower. Just outside the suburb is RIALTON BARTON, a farmhouse that is really the main part of a country manor owned by the monks of Bodmin until the Dissolution. It was built by Prior Vivian, the last prior but one, in about 1510, and a number of rooms remain, together with the decorated waggon-roof of the hall. Unfortunately for the traveller, if not for the occupants, Rialton is not open to the public, but the exterior alone is of sufficient interest to deserve a glance. Four km. south-east of the town centre stands TRERICE (*pron*. Tre*rice*, to rhyme with mice), for long a principal seat of the widespread Arundell family, now belonging to the NT and recently restored. It consists of a three-storey, ornately-dormered mansion of 1571, built largely of elvan, a kind of schist or hornblende quarried nowadays mainly for road-building. The windows are all mullioned, and include one huge window, with two transoms, that lights the two-storey-high great hall. Several rooms have good plaster ceilings, and there are two fine Tudor fireplaces. The gardens have been lately redesigned. The house is open every afternoon from the end of March to the end of October.

Newton Abbot Devon 5E3/E4 (*pop*. 19,399)
Newton Abbot has been to Devon what Crewe has been to Cheshire or Swindon to Wiltshire – a historic railway-workshop town. However, its history started a good many centuries before the railway, when the manors of Wolborough and Teignwick (later named Newton Bushel) were established on either side of the River Lemon. In the twelfth century Wolborough came into the hands of William de Brewer, who had founded Torre Abbey; he bestowed the manor on the Abbey, and so it became the Abbot's new town, or Newton Abbot. For long the two towns existed independently; each was granted the right

to hold markets and fairs, and did hold them until Newton Abbot market (still enjoying a vigorous existence) absorbed its rival in 1633. Each town prospered from the wool, leather, clay, and pottery trades, and also played a large part in the Newfoundland cod trade: the Jolly Sailor inn in East Street was once a major haunt of the seamen engaged in this. Brunel set up his Atmospheric Railway in Newton Abbot, and it later became a major railway engineering centre. Newton Bushel, changing its name again to Highweek, was not amalgamated with its neighbour until 1901.

The feverish railway development swept away nearly all the town's old buildings. The chief church, St Leonard, was pulled down and a new one built in 1836 (ten years before the railway took over), only the fourteenth-century tower being left. Much more striking is St Luke's, near the Milber Pine Woods. The design for this came to the Revd Keble Martin, author of the

botanical masterpiece *The Concise British Flora in Colour*, in a dream in 1931, and on being told by an architect that it was practicable he collected the funds to build it. It was completed in 1963, a bizarre affair something like a huge arrow with the altar at its point. Unhappily the builders did not serve its creator too well, but because of its origin it has its place in local affections, and is invariably known as 'The Dream Church'.

Several important houses border on the town. BRADLEY MANOR, only 1km. south-west but in a beautiful rural setting, was the home of the Bushels and later the Yardes, a descendant of whom gave it in 1938 to the NT but continues to lease it, so that (except by special arrangement) it may be seen only on Wednesday afternoons between April and September inclusive. It is a small fifteenth-century fortified manor-house – small because of its original four sides only one remains: but this includes the great hall of 1419 with its handsome

Trerice, SE of Newquay: the Drawing Room ceiling

Bradley Manor, SW of Newton Abbot: central part of the E front (c. 1495), showing the oriel

beamed roof; a Tudor and a Jacobean screen, the latter brought from Ashburton; and the fourteenth-century chapel. The surrounding woods, mercifully devoid of cars, offer pleasant walks, especially beside the river.

FORDE HOUSE, in the heart of the town towards Milber, was completed by Sir Richard Reynell in 1610, in the shape of a short-armed E with mullioned windows and Dutch-style rounded gables. There are a grand entrance hall and staircase, and no fewer than seven plaster ceilings, often reckoned among the best in Devon. Sir Richard entertained Charles I here, and later William

of Orange also stayed on his progress to London. By that time the Courtenays had succeeded the Reynells, but Sir William Courtenay, though he left orders for William to be entertained, was himself diplomatically absent. The Courtenays relinquished the house in 1936 in order to concentrate on their other property, Powderham Castle. Today Forde House is not on view as such, but since part of it is used as antique showrooms, neither is it entirely closed.

Most of the once pretty villages round Newton Abbot have been or are being swallowed up in the town's suburban spread. Two, however, that have so far escaped, are DENBURY and TORBRYAN (combined *pop.* 547), respectively 4km. and 6km. south-west. Denbury is dominated by its seventeenth-century manor-house, given a new face in Georgian times and further titivated in 1825. The village is an example of the Town that Failed, having been granted a market and then made a borough in the Middle Ages, but never becoming more than a village. It retains some splendid Tudor cottages. On its south-west fringe is Denbury Camp, a massive hill-fort of unknown date, but whose name, 'fortress of the men of Devon', suggests that at some time it played a rôle that impressed. Torbryan is something of a gem of a village, with a definite gem of a church, full of light and colour, containing an altar-table exquisitely made from pieces of the carved medieval pulpit and a present pulpit strikingly made from pieces of the rood-screen. The fifteenth-century church is still equipped with the original pews boxed-in 300 years later and given brass candle-holders. Outside is the Church House Inn, converted, like that of Rattery, from the former priest's house, and nearly up to Rattery standard.

North Bovey   Devon   *see* **Moretonhampstead**

North Hill   Cornwall   3G1, 4A3   (*pop.* 650)
A village beside the River Lynher, beyond which, at no more than a km., is the fringe of Bodmin Moor rising quickly to Hawk's Tor (310m.) and Kilmar Tor (390m.). The immediate environment, however, is not barren, for a belt of woodland clothes the edge of the Moor. The village is built of slate and granite, all the cottages (hardly one of which looks less than two centuries old) having slate roofs and many slate-hung fronts. The church in their midst is distinctive, and without the forbidding air of some granite churches. It has a dignified fifteenth-century west tower, a nave and two aisles of the same period (clearly another outcome of the rebuilding fervour that swept over the country in the fifteenth century, mainly towards the close of it as a thanksgiving, no doubt, for the return of law and order after more than a century of war), and a fourteenth-century chancel. Monuments are elaborate and unexpectedly numerous, nearly all seventeenth- or eighteenth-century. The Victorians restored the church with their habitual devout insensitivity, but they spared

Okehampton Castle: apart from the keep (late-Norman?) the remains are largely from a rebuilding of c. 1300

the beautiful waggon-roofs and a family pew of 1724 with a wood inlay.

Until a few years ago TREBARTHA HALL was a mansion 1 km. north-west of North Hill. It has now been demolished, but its abandoned park is still beautiful. One km. south of the village the Lynher is spanned at BERIOWBRIDGE by a three-arched medieval bridge widened in 1890. On the Moor west of the two tors already named are several groups of hut circles (*see* Dozmary Pool).

Okehampton Devon 4C2, 6D5 (*pop.* 3,915)
Ancient market-town on the northern fringe of Dartmoor, just above the confluence of the East and West Okement rivers from which it gets its name. It is easy of access because of the many roads that meet there, but they do not help its peace and quiet, particularly the diabolically busy A30 that passes right through its centre. Okehampton began with a Saxon settlement slightly west of the present site, where the church now stands. This Saxon town was abandoned when Baldwin

de Brionne, the Conqueror's Sheriff of Devon, built a castle and founded the present town soon after the Normans had reached these parts. Before the end of William I's reign it already had a market, and by 1220 it had gained its first charter. The Courtenay family were by then its lords, and remained so until one of them, the Marquis of Exeter, incurred the wrath of Henry VIII, who executed him and caused the castle to be 'slighted', to use the word properly applied to partial dismantlings. The ruins, open daily, remain attractively 'romantic'. A further charter, granting borough status, was obtained from James I, and prosperity, mainly from wool, advanced in spite of setbacks during the Civil War until the general decline in the wool trade shifted the emphasis to the advantages of being a main-road staging post. Nevertheless, the eighteenth and nineteenth centuries saw lean times here as in most of Devon, until things revived with the advent of the railway in 1871 – rather late.

The parish church on the site of the Saxon town was burnt down, all but the fifteenth-century tower, in 1842, but rebuilt within two years; William Morris designed the windows. Often mistaken for the parish church because it is so much more central, is the Chapel of St James in Fore Street (the A30 under another name). This was originally a chantry chapel, which after the Dissolution passed to the corporation, and served as a chapel of ease. It was rebuilt in 1862, but the fourteenth-century tower and some early woodwork were allowed to survive. The Town Hall was converted in the mid nineteenth century from a large private house built in 1685.

Four km. south-east, BELSTONE TOR (478m.) has on it a circle of seventeen stones known as the Nine Maidens, Cornish style, representing the petrified figures of a group of girls who dared to dance on Sunday. Or so they say.

Ottery St Mary   Devon   5F2   (*pop.* 5,834)
Distinguished for having what many consider the most noble and lovely church in Devon. Set in a pleasant landscape beside the River Otter, the town goes back at least to Saxon times, when in 1061 the manor was given to the secular canons of the Cathedral of Rouen by Edward the Confessor for the good of his soul: a choice of beneficiary one might more readily have expected of William the Conqueror a few years later. It did indeed prove far from wise, for whatever the effect on Edward's soul, the Dean and Chapter of Rouen became increasingly oppressive and exacting towards the people of Ottery. The climax came in 1280; Rouen leased manor and church for life to one William de Lechlade, which meant that the more he could extract from the parish, the more he could keep after paying Rouen its dues; and one day as he left Exeter Cathedral he was murdered. This scarcely made the attitude of Rouen more benevolent, and even half a century later, when newly-consecrated Bishop Grandisson of Exeter decided to buy back Ottery, he had great difficulty before he succeeded (1334).

There had been a church here since at least 1190, but now it was to be transformed into the present magnificent building; and in view of the Bishop's part in the matter, it is not coincidental that the present church bears a distinct affinity with Exeter Cathedral. Not that Grandisson was responsible for the whole edifice: the eastern end, including the transepts, is a thirteenth-century enlargement of the Saxon building, and the north aisle, called the Dorset Aisle, was added by a Marchioness of Dorset in the sixteenth century. Bishop Grandisson was responsible for the nave and Lady Chapel. Yet for once it is as much to the Victorian restorer that we owe this church's present fine appearance. The man responsible was William Butterfield, who in 1850 took in hand what a few years earlier had been described as 'degraded and neglected' and transformed it, not, as customarily, into the Victorian idea of what it might have been if the original builders had had better taste, but into a genuine revival of the original.

St Mary's church, Ottery St Mary: the early-C16 Dorset Aisle

There are two towers, one with a short spire, one with none, and it is the lower parts of these that form the transepts. Inside, nave and chancel are beautifully vaulted, and there is superb fan tracery roofing the Dorset Aisle. Beautiful bosses, too, adorn the roof of the Lady Chapel, which otherwise is distinguished for its stone screen and fourteenth-century miserere-seat benches. Everywhere a striking attribute is the colour. Tombs bearing effigies include those of Sir Otto de Grandisson (d. 1358) and his wife, and of John Haydon of Cadhay (d. 1587). An eighteenth-century vicar of the church was the Revd John Taylor Coleridge, whose time when not in the church must have been spent largely in the bedroom, for he begat thirteen children, of whom the youngest, born in 1772, was Samuel Taylor Coleridge,

the poet. The houses of the town are congenial, and if devoid of showpieces are also devoid of eyesores.

Of country houses round about the most distinguished is CADHAY, 1½km. north-west, built about 1550 on the site of an earlier 'sub-manor' of Ottery by John Haydon, who had married the last Cadhay heiress. The great hall (1420) of the earlier house was kept, and Haydon's son added a 'long gallery'. The inner courtyard, the 'Court of Sovereigns', is of interest: it contains statues of Henry VIII, Edward VI, Mary I, and Elizabeth I. Some judicious alterations were made to Cadhay in 1760, some injudicious ones a century later, when the splendid hammer-beams were taken away from the upper of the two rooms into which the Georgian changes had divided the hall. The mansion was split into two farmhouses, and was not reunified until 1910. The grounds are limited but gracious, with the original 1420 fishponds and a fine avenue of limes leading to the entrance. Although the Powlett family, the owners since 1925, use every room, Cadhay is open to the public on summer Wednesdays and Thursdays and certain public holidays.

Another house, this time to be admired from the outside only, is the pre-Tudor thatched farmhouse at TIPTON ST JOHN, 3½km. down-river from Ottery. At HARPFORD, 1½km. farther on, something of a gem of a village with seemingly nothing but Georgian thatched houses and cottages, the incumbent for a time was the Revd Augustus Toplady, author of the hymn 'Rock of Ages'. Finally, 3km. north-east of Ottery, midway to Honiton, an equally 'intact' Georgian village is GRITTIS-HAM (*pop.* 220), in the pleasant valley of a tiny tributary of the Otter. The church, small and most pleasing, looks on to the village green and is surprisingly rich in endearing rustic monuments.

Padstow Cornwall 2D1 (*pop.* 2,802)
The original name for this settlement on the wide Camel estuary was Loderick, and here it was, they say, that St Samson established himself on landing from Wales. In about 560 St Petroc also landed here, from Ireland, took over St Samson's cell and founded one of his own, before going on to Bodmin (qv) and repeating the formula with the cell of St Guron. Padstow and Bodmin then both became known as Petrocstow, at the cost of no small confusion. Later, Padstow also enjoyed a spell as Aldestow, after the tenth-century King Athelstan. For many centuries the port did business both as a sole-fishing centre and a terminus for the transatlantic passenger trade; many of the ships were built in its own yards. But at some unspecified point in its story Padstow produced a citizen called Long Tom Yeo, who near the mouth of the estuary shot what he said

afterwards he thought was a seal, but which was a mermaid. Understandably annoyed, she threw a handful of sand across the water, and it grew into the Doom Bar, a nasty obstruction that ever afterwards severely limited the size of the ships that could use Padstow. So today there are no passenger vessels except pleasure launches and ferries, cargo activity (also formerly extensive) is limited to the odd small coaster, and fishing is confined mostly to crab- and lobster-catching.

The holiday trade, however, has deservedly grown, for in addition to the fascination of its setting Padstow is old, rather beautiful, and full of personality. To see it at its best it should be visited outside the season, when the vestiges of its old occupations (there is even a small boat-building yard still) give it just enough bustle to let any but the least imaginative traveller catch a glimpse of what it – and so many other Cornish ports – must once have been like. Its greatness began at latest in Tudor times. Queen Elizabeth I granted it a charter, and it was well known to Hawkins, Frobisher, and in particular Raleigh, who in his capacity as Warden of the Stannaries is said to have taken up residence and collected his dues in Raleigh's Court House, a building still standing beside the South Quay. Elizabeth's reign also saw the completion of Padstow's grand mansion, PRIDEAUX PLACE, on the northern outskirts. It is not open to the public, but its battlemented façade is a landmark for km. around. There Charles I was for a short time a guest of the Prideaux family after the Battle of Naseby (1645), when his sojourn nearly ended in his capture. The house, formerly Prideaux Castle and before that Gwarthandrea, occupies the site of St Petroc's monastery, which never recovered from destruction by the Danes in 981.

Old cottages of various styles, periods, and colours survive in the town's narrow streets and by the harbour; there is a fifteenth-century Abbey House by the North Quay; and in the Market Place stands St Petroc's church, much of it thirteenth- and fourteenth-century, full of Prideaux family monuments. On May Day the Market Place becomes the focal point of the 'Obby 'Oss (Hobby Horse) Celebrations, one of those quaint pre-Christian junketings, all music, dancing, and grotesque pageantry, in which our island is so rich. This particular event extols the coming of summer.

Opposite Padstow, across the estuary, is ROCK, a very stylish yachting centre, and behind Rock, across a golf course, is TREBETHERICK, beloved of Sir John Betjeman in his childhood and prominent in his works. Unhappily the Trebetherick of today is fast becoming engulfed in the great aesthetic wilderness of combined holiday resorts Polzeath and Pentireglaze. The isolated little church of St Enodoc, actually on the links, was buried under sand-drifts until 1863; but its presence was known, for one eighteenth-century parson used to have himself lowered through a hole in the roof so that he could conduct services and thus qualify for tithe. After the exhumation St Enodoc's suffered even greater

OPPOSITE TOP: *St Mary's church, Ottery St Mary, from the SE*
OPPOSITE BOTTOM: *Cadhay, Ottery St Mary: the 'Court of Sovereigns'*

indignity by being restored in his characteristic manner by J. P. St Aubyn. But once the traveller has circum-navigated the caravans and bungalows and reached the coast (of the open sea, not the estuary), he sees at Pentire Point as fine a cliff (luckily NT-protected) as any even north Cornwall can show. On Padstow's own side the rocky and cave-pitted coastal cliffs – note particularly the giant Butter Hole and Pepper Hole near the estuary mouth – culminate to the west in TREVOSE HEAD, which has just about everything – a coastguard lookout, a life-boat station, a lighthouse (which can be visited), islands far out to sea (the Quies Rocks and Gulland Rock), and a view that in the best weather extends from St Ives to Hartland Point.

But one of the most beautiful and certainly most un-common places in the Padstow area is not on the coast at all, but at the head of its own small creek off the Camel estuary. This is LITTLE PETHERICK (*pop.* – with St Issey – 599), or more properly St Petroc Minor of Nancefountain, a village with two sets of religious associations nearly a millenium and a half apart; for this is St Petroc's own territory, in which his little copper bell must have rung many times, and in which eventually he died; and at the other end of the long span of years the small church became closely associated with the noted early-twentieth-century Anglo-Catholic Athel-stan Riley and his circle. The church had been virtually rebuilt as long ago as 1858 for its rector, the Tractarian Sir Hugh Molesworth. But it was the work of Riley and the artist Sir Ninian Cooper during the first forty years of this century that gave the church its uncommon beauty, the *pièce de résistance* of which is the painted screen. Sir Ninian also built the Riley Chantry Chapel in which Athelstan Riley and his wife are buried. Once the Padstow–Wadebridge road is left, the country round about is intimate and pretty; but *its* showpiece, the old watermill that had turned for centuries, has gone.

Paignton   Devon   5E4   (*pop.* 35,000 approx.)
Although there was a settlement here in the Bronze Age and a town in Saxon times, this sprawling resort had no important fisheries, mining, wool-trading, or other activity to build it up before the coming of the railway and the tourists in 1859. All that remains of the old town, which is behind the new one, is the parish church, and one late-medieval house, Coverdale Tower, remain-ing from a medieval palace of the Bishops of Exeter. In this palace in Tudor times, Miles Coverdale, the trans-lator of the Bible, is believed to have lodged for a period, though the story that he made his translation here is false, for he had completed it long before he visited Devon. The church dates from Saxon times and was built on the Bronze Age site. A few paving-stones remain from this building; from its Norman successor, begun in 1100, we still have the west door, part of the chancel, and the font; but most of the church consists of the rebuilding carried out by Bishop Lacy of Exeter from 1420 onwards.

The highlight is the late-fifteenth-century Kirkham Chantry, with tombs and stone screen – the latter a really fine piece of work.

Before the tourist era there were two Paigntons, Paignton Well (the church and palace area) and Paign-ton Quay. There was minor fishing activity and a little trade, including the export of a once-famous local strain of cabbage. Among the modern resort amenities are the Seashore Aquarium (open June–September, inclusive) and Paignton Zoo, one of the best in England; it includes tropical flora as well as animals (open all the year). Not originally built as an exhibit, but now open all the year to be visited as such, is Oldway Mansion, a vast, fan-tastic building that might well have been a creation of the American William Randolph Hearst but was in fact put up in 1874 by a fellow-millionaire, Isaac Singer, of the sewing-machine company, and added to by his son. The building is somewhat like a miniature (and not so very miniature) Versailles in pale-pink stone; inside, a vast staircase sweeps up to a first floor with marble columns beneath a painted ceiling, and there are a hundred rooms. At the foot of the stair are two cannon supposed to have come from HMS *Victory*. There is an exhibition of early sewing-machines, and elsewhere art exhibitions are held. Woods and fine gardens (especially the Italian) surround this dream-palace, which Singer modestly called The Wigwam.

The Kirkhams, whose chantry embellishes the church, were the owners of nearby Kirkham House, a fifteenth-century stone building that has recently been restored as an example of a pre-Tudor town residence. Its principal feature is a hall extending from ground-level to timbered roof. Under the Dept of the Environ-ment, it is open from April to September, inclusive. But the Kirkhams' own home was BLAGDON BARTON, 2km. east, mid-Tudor with a later doorway; in one sense it is open to the public, since it is now a guest house. Blagdon is also the location of the TORBAY AIRCRAFT MUSEUM (open all the year), which has an extensive collection of aircraft from the days of Channel pioneer Bleriot on-wards, and a special Colditz feature. From Paignton south to Kingswear (*see* Dartmouth) the old Western Region line has been taken over by the Torbay Steam Railway. Original GWR locomotives are used.

Parracombe   Devon   7E1   (*pop.* 255)
One of the villages in Devon's part of Exmoor; the name is a corruption of Petroc's Combe, and the church, whose builders followed the frequent practice of choosing a site well away from the village, is dedicated to St Petroc. Ironically, no part of the church had been restored until the early-medieval tower was struck by lightning in 1908. In consequence the interior looks as so many of the Devon village churches must have looked before Victorian lack of imagination destroyed their personality. The chancel is thirteenth-century, the nave and south (or only) aisle late-fourteenth- or fifteenth-

century. A simple screen, with tympanum over, divides the latter, and the old box pews that the Victorians hated have been left undisturbed. In 1878 a new and more central church was built for Parracombe, but the villagers refused to let their old church be pulled down; and one wonders how many other 'unimproved' churches held a greater place in the affections of the worshippers than the brisk 'improvers' imagined.

The cottages are stone, tiered in a steep valley, giving an attractive picture. As throughout western Exmoor, there are a number of prehistoric sites in the vicinity. On the village threshold is HOLWELL CASTLE, an impressive hill-fort; PARRACOMBE BRIDGE has built into it an ancient inscribed stone; 2km. south-west, on Challacombe Common (nothing to do with its namesake on southeast Dartmoor), are CHAPMAN BARROWS, a collection of some ten grave-mounds 480m. above sea level, with a 3m.-high standing stone, the LONGSTONE, nearby; also on Challacombe Common, a triangle, with sides averaging 17m., marked out by stones; 2km. south-west of Parracombe, near BLACKMOOR GATE, a spot where large cattle-markets are held, are tumuli and an enclosure.

Paul Cornwall   *see* **Mousehole**

Pendeen Cornwall   2A5
Pendeen was, after St Just, the main centre of the tin- and copper-mining industry once so flourishing in these parts; what is more, one or two of the mines are still working. Even its church would not have existed but for the tinners, for they built it themselves to the design of the Revd R. Aitken, who modelled it on Iona Cathedral and in 1851 became its first incumbent. Many are the mine stories heard in these parts. There was Levant Mine, which ran 1½km. out under the sea, and in which the miners pursued one rich but ever-rising vein of ore until they were so close under the sea floor that they could hear the rocks being churned about during gales. The Levant was also the scene of a major disaster in 1919 (graphically portrayed in a recent television documentary), when the 'man-engine' that carried the miners up and down broke, with the loss of 31 lives. In 1930 this mine was closed – not before time, for later the sea really did break in – but recently gained a new lease of life by being drained and linked underground with Geevor Mine, one of those that had resumed operations. The surface paraphernalia of a working mine is a good deal less romantic to look at than the ruined, lonely, and often haunted-looking engine-houses of the abandoned mines, but the implications are romantic enough when you reflect that it symbolizes more than 2,000 years of continuous activity.

Unexpectedly in this bleak landscape, Pendeen also possesses, 1km. north of the village near PENDEEN WATCH with its lighthouse, a fine sixteenth- and seventeenth-century mansion, Pendeen House, now a farm. For generations it was the home of the Borlases, of whom

one, Dr William Borlase (1696–1772), became a noted antiquary. Among his works – and still of value – are *Natural History* and *Antiquities of Cornwall* (both recently republished). His Cornish collections are now in the Ashmolean Museum at Oxford. In the yard of Pendeen House is the entrance to an Iron Age fogou or underground passage, stone-lined and with two chambers opening out of it, probably used for stores. The fogou is 16m. long.

Penryn Cornwall   2D5   (*pop.* 5,135)
Although barely separated nowadays from Falmouth, the much smaller Penryn is no satellite or suburb, but a town in its own right, and a far older one than Falmouth, too, having received its first charter in 1236. It is built along a ridge, and its main road climbs steeply out of what might be called its own private creek between rows of unusually handsome Georgian houses that (equally unusually) no one has destroyed yet. Another surprise is that although founded by a bishop, the Italian Simon of Apulia, Bishop of Exeter, strictly it has no church of its own, the generally accepted parish church, St Gluvias, properly belonging to the adjacent village of that name. Drastically restored by the heavy-handed St Aubyn, who ruined so many Cornish churches, it has been partially redeemed by judicious work during the past quarter-century; but Penryn really pivots about the impressive tower (1839) of its Town Hall. A huge granite industry keeps the town going – the stones of London's former Waterloo Bridge, the Old Bailey, and New Scotland Yard came from here – and it is rare indeed not to see a granite boat in Penryn Creek. Killigrews were almost as prominent here as in Falmouth, especially the women, one of whom, Dame Mary, was tried for piracy, condemned to death, then pardoned and allowed to live out her days in Penryn. Another Killigrew, Lady Jane, bequeathed to the town a silver cup and cover (now in the Town Hall) 'when they received me in great misery' in 1633.

The best houses are in St Thomas Street, Broad Street, St Gluvias Street, West Street, and the Square, but to appreciate them fully it is necessary to go down some of the alleys between their long gardens: for the backs are usually much older than the fronts. On the outskirts of the town, in the parish of Mabe, is the Georgian mansion TREMOUGH, now a girls' boarding-school. In its grounds, which can be visited, is one of the best collections of rhododendrons in Britain, mainly Himalayan varieties of enormous size, together with camellias. Further out in the same direction, i.e. towards Stithians, two other notable Georgian houses are TRETHEAGUE, early, and TREVALES, late.

Penzance Cornwall   2A5
(*pop.* – inc. Newlyn – 19,415)
Penzance's position as the westernmost (and nearly the southernmost) town in England may give it a romantic cachet, but it has also provided it with a rough ride

through history. Raided and ruined, like its neighbours, by the Spaniards in 1595, it was then sacked by Parliamentary troops in 1646 and raided by pirates from France, Algeria, and Turkey on repeated occasions during the next century. (The *real* pirates of Penzance were less amusing than W. S. Gilbert's.) On the credit side it was granted a market in 1332, a Grant of Harbour Dues in 1512, its Charter of Incorporation in 1614, and the status of a stannary town, assaying the tin from all the West Penwith mines, in 1663. This last honour, incidentally, was attributed to the cost and inconvenience of carrying the metal to 'very far distant and remote' Helston, all of 21km. away. As a port Penzance has done business since the Middle Ages, dealing in imports and exports as well as the inevitable pilchard-fishing. Today it still does a little international trade, in addition to being the port for Scilly and popular with yachtsmen, particularly the French. There are a dry dock, begun in 1810, and a busy Trinity House depôt for servicing buoys. The railway from London – always the harbinger of the holiday trade – arrived in 1859, getting off, however, to a somewhat shaky start, for after only ten years a great storm destroyed 180m. of the viaduct that carried the line beside the beach.

The Domesday Book name for the Penzance–Newlyn areas was Alwareton; 'Penzance' means 'holy headland', and referred originally to a small Chapel of St Anthony, now vanished, on the promontory south of the harbour called Battery Rocks. Thanks to the Spaniards, nothing of the old town survives, and although Daniel Defoe admired the buildings he saw in 1724, the older parts of the town today nearly all belong to the first half of the nineteenth century. They are scattered fairly widely, but Chapel Street, Regent Square and Terrace, and Clarence Terrace contain some of the best houses. The 'Egyptian House' is in Chapel Street, and so are most of the art shops. The Market House dates from 1837, St Mary's church from 1834. There had been a chapel on the church site, but the mother-church of Penzance was really that of MADRON, 2km. to the north-west. In 1889 the grounds of a large house were laid out as the Morrab Gardens and filled with all manner of tropical trees and plants; the house itself is now the exceptionally good Public Library. There is a museum of local archaeology, history, and mining, at Penlee House; it includes a model of the remarkable Iron Age village at Chysauster (qv).

Reverting to Madron, the granite church is largely of the fourteenth and fifteenth centuries, but of greater historical interest are the remains of ST MADRON's WELL and the accompanying fourteenth-century baptistery, now a sad ruin; for the well was once among the most famous in Cornwall, resorted to from far and near for its healing properties even a century ago. Near Madron is TRENGWAINTON HOUSE (NT), not in itself of much interest and not open, but its extensive park and gardens can be visited from March onwards. They are particularly rich in rare rhododendrons and magnolias, and in

a series of walled gardens grow flowers not seen in the open anywhere else in England.

Petertavy Devon 4B3 (*pop.* 291)
On the west side of Dartmoor, between the River Tavy and the high tors. Also frequently spelt in two words, Peter Tavy. Not in itself a postcard gem, but surrounded by points of interest. The best building in the village is not the church, which except for a graceful spire is one more grim example of gross over-restoration, but the Peter Tavy Inn, a splendid seventeenth-century hostelry. Two km. north-west is Petertavy's sister village, MARYTAVY, or Mary Tavy (*pop.* 783), once a busy mining centre; for this was a great mining area, tin, copper, lead, iron, zinc, silver, and lesser products of the earth all being extracted from mines whose gaunt – and indeed haunting – remains rise up on every side like the gravestones of a vanished prosperity. Of one mine, WHEAL BETSY, beside the A386 on the slopes of Gibbet Hill (*see* Lydford Gorge), the engine-house has been preserved. Another mine, WHEAL FRIENDSHIP, was in operation for 130 years, during which time it produced £1,500,000 worth of metals. At Harndon, a hamlet 1½km. north-east of Marytavy, is a settlement built exclusively for workers in the DEVON AND FRIENDSHIP MINE, the remains of which also lie in idleness nearby. The ruined cottages of other former mine-workers are numerous in the Marytavy area. A more cheerful sight, 2km. north-east of Harndon, is WILLSWORTHY (not open), a sixteenth-century farmhouse, since altered but still predominantly Tudor, on the site of a Saxon farm. It once had a chapel. Two km. farther north-east, beyond the end of the road and well among the high tors, the River Tavy passes through TAVY CLEAVE, a wild and romantic gorge reminiscent of the Scottish Highlands. There is a weir at the lower end. No part of Dartmoor is more lavishly scattered with prehistoric sites than the tors east, and particularly south-east, of the two Tavys. White Tor, Petertavy Great Common, Cox Tor, and Little Mis Tor may be cited. There are also many rock basins on the tops of tors: not, as once thought, the work of Druids, but hollows formed by weather action.

Plymouth Devon 4B5 (*pop.* 239,452)
Overwhelmingly the largest city in the South-West after Bristol, Plymouth is nevertheless something of an upstart. It is, in fact, in the unusual position of having several outlying parts, originally separate entities, of greater antiquity than its core. At Mount Batten, east of the River Plym, there was an Iron Age trading-post by about 200 BC, but nothing that we know of at Plymouth. The Domesday surveyors found a squitty little hamlet called Sutone, or Sutton, behind the Hoe, but at Stoke a much larger settlement linked to a small estate of Edward the Confessor's at King's Tamerton. The major port of south Devon was then Dartmouth, and the only port in Plymouth Sound was at Plympton. In 1211 something

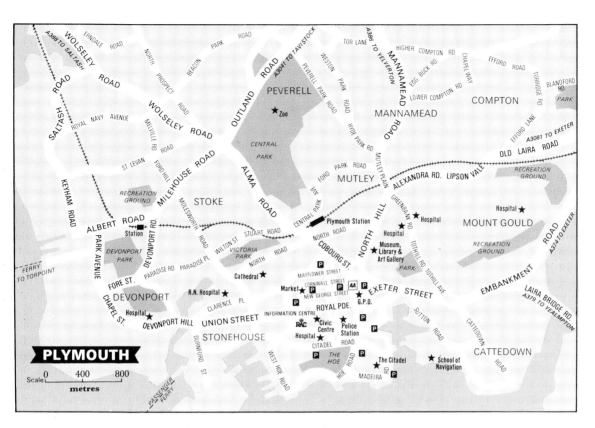

like a port at Plymouth is at last heard of – and under that name – but it enjoyed a very subsidiary status as a possession of Plympton Priory, which completely controlled it. The harbour was called Sutton Pool, as that particular inlet is today. Trade was given a considerable fillip by the development of tin-workings on Dartmoor, and then a further fillip by the silting-up of the Plym due to the tin-streaming, and the cessation of Plympton as a rival.

Military considerations also helped Plymouth, in common with other Devonian and Cornish ports, now that the English Crown controlled all western France down to the Pyrenees. However, there were still difficulties. The much safer Dartmouth continued to be a preferred harbour, and although in 1253 a weekly market and annual fair were established, the authority for them had been granted to the Priory, not to Plymouth. Yet Plymouth grew fast, and friction with the Priory kept pace. Neither the establishment of a major naval base at the port in 1295, nor serious attacks by French 'pyrats' in 1388 and 1403, entailing the burning of many houses, nor yet again petitions to the King to be allowed to elect a mayor, lessened the limpet grip of the Priors on their lucrative property. Not until 1440 was independence at last granted, and then only on condition

that annual compensation of £41 (later reduced to £29 6s 8d) be paid to the Priory. At the same time the name Plymouth was confirmed for the several parts of the town.

Earliest of the great sea-captains who brought Plymouth its period of high renown was William Hawkins, who in 1528 and subsequent years sailed three times to Brazil, and also to the Gulf of Guinea. His son John Hawkins, later an efficient Comptroller of the Navy, earned notice beforehand as the first Englishman to engage in the negro slave trade. It was largely due to him and to Francis Drake, a Tavistock man, who had already accomplished his astonishing voyage round the world, that Plymouth was chosen instead of the more reliable Dartmouth as the base for the war against Spain. It was a risky decision, but less risky now that Plymouth seamen (and ship designers) had mastered the art of sailing to windward: ships were less likely to be bottled up in the Sound by a sou'-wester. Nevertheless, they could get out only on an ebb tide, which is why when the Armada was sighted the experienced Drake knew he was losing nothing by remaining on the Hoe to finish his game of bowls.

The build-up of the fleet to face the Armada caused enormous activity in Plymouth and a great increase, albeit some of it only temporary, in her population.

Plymouth: a view of the city centre; Royal Parade is the main street in the foreground

Drake identified himself with the city, both before and after 1588, in far more than his capacity as Admiral of the fleet that happened to be based there. He became its Member of Parliament and twice its mayor, and in the 1590s, only a few years before his death, he brought a supply of fresh water to the citizens by causing a leat or channel to be dug from the West Plym on Dartmoor into the heart of Plymouth. Several portions of the leat are still traceable in the countryside.

In 1606 Sir Walter Raleigh sailed from Plymouth to found the colony of Virginia, and in 1620 the Pilgrim Fathers set forth in the *Mayflower*, though it should be remembered that they had only put into Plymouth for repairs. Through the succeeding centuries pioneer after pioneer, explorer after explorer, made this port his starting-point, including James Cook in 1772 and 1776 and Sir Francis Chichester in 1966. Small wonder that between them they named more than forty other Plymouths about the globe! After the Civil War, in which Puritan Plymouth was unsuccessfully besieged for three years by the Royalists, Charles II built the huge

Citadel on the Hoe. In 1688, losing no time, it seems, after his adoption as King, William III laid down the first naval dockyard on the Hamoaze. At the outset of the next century Defoe reported Plymouth to be a place devoted to seafarers and the shops serving them, though he conceded that there were also a few gentlemen about. Exactly a century later, on the other hand, another traveller, Joseph Farington, found Plymouth society among the country's best and most intelligent.

This was the time of the Napoleonic wars. Throughout the eighteenth century the early dockyard on the Hamoaze had been augmented by others, some the work of distinguished architects – Morrice Yard, for instance, was designed by Vanbrugh. As early as 1695 the naval base had been transferred from the Cattewater (the lowest reach of the Plym) to the Hamoaze (the lowest reach of the Tamar), alongside which a new town, simply called Dock, had grown until by 1800 it was actually bigger than Plymouth, resulting in much jealousy and rivalry. In the naval war against Napoleon the British fleet shared its attentions between Plymouth

Sound and Torbay (*see* Torquay); Nelson came to Plymouth only once. But prisoners-of-war came there in plenty, as they had during each of the eighteenth-century wars. The Millbay Prison, where conditions were hideous anyway, became so full that old ships – the 'hulks' made familiar (in other places) by Dickens – moored in the Hamoaze were used as well. In 1806 a new prison on Dartmoor was embarked upon to relieve the strain (*see* Princetown).

In 1812 it was decided at last that something must be done to protect the Sound from south-westerly gales, and the distinguished engineer John Rennie was commissioned to build a breakwater. Four million tons of limestone and three million tons of dressed granite were shipped into the Sound, and it took until 1841 to complete the 1½km.-long rampart. After Waterloo Napoleon was exhibited for a few days on board HMS *Bellerophon*, and it was a Plymouth artist, Charles Eastlake, who, after going out many times in a small boat to make sketches, painted the famous portrait of the shipbound Emperor that at one time was rivalled only by *The Stag At Bay* for pride of place on the walls of every English boarding-house. Dock soon afterwards changed its name to Devonport, and throughout the rest of the nineteenth century Devonport, Plymouth, and the newly-filled area between them, Stonehouse – the Three Towns, as they were called – merged slowly into one. The dockyard, and a long way behind that fishing, were the city's main activities, together with the necessary supply services. As to social life, a dazzlingly vivid picture of it between 1840 and 1860 appears in a small book called *Some Recollections*, written in her old age by Thomas Hardy's first wife, who had been born and brought up in Plymouth. (I have been using the word 'city', but in fact Plymouth became a city only in the twentieth century.)

In 1849 the railway arrived, and soon afterwards Millbay Docks were added to the rest. During the Second World War the air-raids came to Plymouth sooner than to Exeter, the worst occurring in March and April 1941. There was great loss of life, and virtually the whole of the city centre was destroyed; but by 1943 a plan for its reconstruction had already been worked out under the chairmanship of Sir Lascelles Abercrombie. The new centre is based on Royal Parade, a very wide thoroughfare (roughly on the line of pre-war Plymouth's principal street, Bedford Street), with some of the leading shops on one side and St Andrew's church, the Guildhall, and the Civic Centre on the other. There are trees, flower-beds, and broad pedestrian walks along the Parade, which is among Europe's finest streets. At right-angles to it is another broad avenue, Armada Way, similarly designed with a high regard for both beauty and pedestrians. The buildings lining these two thoroughfares are low, with slightly higher blocks at the intersection, thus adding to the sense of spaciousness and avoiding the competition of tower blocks with the towers of St Andrew's church, the Guildhall, and the Civic

Centre. The rest of new Plymouth takes its cue from these central arteries, including an elevated shopping centre, a large covered market, numerous traffic-free precincts, and parks and gardens. In the midst of the city is Central Park, a large, completely new open area that includes football and cricket grounds, a sports centre, and the Zoo. Altogether post-war central Plymouth is as good a piece of town-planning as this country has seen since the redesigning of Bath under the Georges, and yet in some respects the effect is very saddening. Not only those who remember the old pre-war city, but even those who just study a map of it, must be numbed by the mass of streets and landmarks that have simply disappeared, without a hint of a modern counterpart. By no means everything that has vanished was good, but it was the heart of a city that many loved, and neither in Exeter nor in London has so large a piece of the past been so utterly effaced, even to the names and whereabouts of the former streets.

Fortunately a fair amount of off-centre Plymouth was spared, and a very few historic buildings were heavily damaged, but not beyond restoration. Foremost of these is St Andrew's church. Fire-bombs gutted this, sparing (as so often) only the fifteenth-century tower. But the outside walls remained standing, and inside, although the general effect of the reconstruction reminds one of the over-restorative Victorians, here and there a battered pillar or arch proclaims its survival from the pre-war church. Most of the wall tablets also survived. Some very arresting stained-glass windows were designed by John Piper, and a personal note is struck by an Elizabethan drawing, roughly traced in wet plaster beside the window immediately west of the south door, and hidden before the bombing, that shows some sailing ships alongside a globe with a ring round it. Could this have been an impromptu commemoration of Drake's voyage round the world?

Behind St Andrew's, and connected with it by a Door of Unity restored by the American Daughters of 1812, is the Prysten, or Priest's, House. Built on the orders of Plympton Priory in 1490, it is reputedly Plymouth's oldest house, and since it somehow escaped bomb damage it seems a pity it had to be rescued quite so drastically from the normal effects of time. To go inside, apply to the nearby Parish Office between 9.30 am and 12.30 pm.

Beside the church the new Italianate Guildhall replaces one, itself a replacement, erected only in the 1870s. The Civic Centre, completed in 1962, has a thirteen-storey tower with a public viewing-gallery (windy but worth it) and café. In the opposite direction from St Andrew's, down Exeter Street, what used to be the city's second church, the Charles church (1640–58), was also reduced to a shell by bombs, but has been kept in its ruined state as a memorial to Plymouth's civilian dead. It looks suitably impressive, especially when flood-lit, but to see the interior, which retains a few tombstones and wall tablets, the traveller must take his life in his

Plymouth: part of the Hoe

hands, or rather his feet, for the church now stands islanded in the centre of a busy roundabout, with neither subway nor pedestrian crossing to afford access.

A few minutes' walk south from Royal Parade brings one to Plymouth's best-known feature, the Hoe. Until the mid nineteenth century this was a wild jumble of rocks (Drake's bowling-green, it is thought, was on a site now covered by the Citadel), which were laboriously blasted to make a foundation for the present area now partly turf, partly a large expanse of asphalt. Nature and Man between them have shaped the Hoe cunningly, for it remains slightly above the level of the streets behind it, thus enabling the newcomer to breast the rise unprepared for the sight beyond. This is Plymouth Sound, unquestionably (though the champions of other harbours naturally question it) the most beautiful inlet on the English coast. Here is no smooth-curving bay or trumpet-shaped estuary, but a majestic and gradually widening sheet of water between coasts of varying height, much indented with subsidiary inlets, and on the Cornish side richly wooded. Breaking up the expanse of

sea are Drake's Island at a km. or so from shore, and 2km. beyond that the long line of the Breakwater with its lighthouse and central fort. Drake's (formerly St Nicholas) Island was fortified in the fifteenth century and strengthened by Drake. After being a fortress it became a prison and then reverted to a fortress, the last garrison being withdrawn after the Second World War. In 1964 the Crown granted it on a 99-year lease to the NT, which inaugurated an Adventure Training Centre there. In 1976 the NT lease was taken over by the Mayflower Centre Trust, which continues to operate the Centre. Drake's Island may be visited during the summer months by special launch (four times daily) from the Mayflower Steps, Barbican.

Along the irregular rim of the Hoe are parades at two levels, and on its hinterland is a great crop of monuments, mostly very large. Among the less large is the copy of the Tavistock statue of Drake, but without the frieze (*see* Tavistock). Also here is the upper part of the former Eddystone Lighthouse – the Eddystone shoal lies 21km. out to sea opposite Plymouth – the third of four to have been built on the shoal, and erected by John Smeaton in 1759. It was replaced in 1882 only because the sea was undermining the rock on which it stood. Smeaton's Tower, as it is now called, is open daily. At the back of the Hoe is the Hoe Theatre, and at the eastern end is Charles II's elephantine mass of stonework, the Royal Citadel, some of the walls of which are more than 6m. thick. There are conducted afternoon tours from mid April to late September, and public Sunday services in the chapel all the year. Not far from the Citadel is Plymouth's excellent Aquarium (open all the year), and down the slope to the east lies what even before the raids was the oldest surviving part of Plymouth, the Barbican area behind Sutton Pool. Incredibly, the attacks that shattered so much elsewhere did minimal damage here. New Street, Notte Street, and Looe Street all have a few Tudor houses; in New Street the splendid Elizabethan House, furnished by London's Victoria and Albert Museum, is open daily throughout the year. Almost opposite is a frontage hardly less imposing. In the Parade, the main street when this was the whole harbour-town, is the Tudor Old Custom House, and opposite it stands the colonnaded New Custom House of 1810. Southside Street contains a Jacobean house and – incorporated in Messrs Coates' gin distillery – the refectory of a small Dominican friary formerly on the site; visitors are welcome. Old warehouses, the ground floor of one now converted into a pleasant wine bar, face the Pool. The Mayflower Stone marks the spot from which the Pilgrim Fathers finally set out for America. A rash of plaques records the start of other ventures. Only the inns in this quarter disappoint. Very surprising to some visitors is the great number of art, antique, and old bookshops that line several streets with hardly a break, a display unequalled for concentration even in the art districts of London. Plymouth's City Museum and Art Gallery, however (open daily all the year), is at Drake Circus, in the new city.

On the western side of new Plymouth lies Devonport with its docks, and between the two Stonehouse, the area filled in during the residential boom caused by the Napoleonic wars. Not that Stonehouse had no buildings at all earlier: the most elegant surviving street, Durnford Street, dates from about 1775. But pre-bombing Stonehouse is mainly the child of John Foulston, a London architect who in 1811 won a competition, set by Plymouth Corporation, for a combined hotel, theatre, and assembly room. The raids destroyed many of his streets, but Emma, Adelaide, and Caroline Places survived fairly intact, and there are isolated houses elsewhere. In Plymouth itself the Crescent is the best extant example of his handiwork. In Devonport he designed the Civic Centre (1824) in Ker Street, to celebrate incorporation and the change of the name from Dock.

Rennie, who built the Breakwater, simultaneously had his own part in compiling Stonehouse; the huge and

aesthetically satisfying Royal William Victualling Yard (William being William IV) was designed by him between 1826 and 1835. Being by the rules of war a legitimate military target, it escaped the bombs and (since it is closed to the public) is well worth looking at by going to the end of the little cul-de-sac off Durnford Street called Admiral's Hard, and preferably extending the journey by taking the Cremyll ferry right past the frontage.

Devonport, like many ports, hides its docks behind high walls. Some remain shrouded in secrecy, but others are open at times to the public. To see them from the seaward side it is best to cross to Torpoint by the ferry and make north. Outside the dockyard walls are many small nineteenth-century houses, and in the extreme south, at Mount Wise opposite Cremyll, three larger buildings, Mount Wise House, Admiralty House, and Government House. Here, too, is a memorial to Robert Falcon Scott, the Antarctic explorer. There are wonderful views up St John's and Millbrook 'Lakes'.

In the present century the growing city has continued to swallow up formerly independent neighbours – though their independence would have ended anyway with the reorganization of local boundaries in 1974. Plympton is treated under its own gazetteer heading. Of the others, the oldest is King's Tamerton, going back to King Athelstan, with its neighbour Stoke, or Stoke Damerel. The latter's church is the mother-church of Plymouth: fifteenth-century, enlarged to keep pace with Stoke's growth in the eighteenth. Here, as in Stonehouse, the bombs have left a number of pleasing houses, some designed by the prolific Foulston. At the extreme west of Plymouth, by the hither end of the Saltash bridges, St Budeaux, otherwise an unimpressive suburb, has a hilltop church of 1563, in which Drake and his wife were married and she lies buried. Sir William Gorges, first Governor of Maine, USA, also has a memorial.

Plympton   Devon   4C5   (*pop.* 17,736)
There are really two Plymptons, St Maurice and St Mary, which grew up round castle and priory respectively. St Maurice is now just about swallowed up in Plymouth, but, like say Kensington or Hampstead long since engulfed in London, this former stannary town has retained a certain identity. Of the castle, an important post from pre-Norman times, only the mound and outer wall of the Norman shell-keep remain, but these are now carefully preserved. The church is in fact dedicated to St Thomas, but is commonly called St Maurice after a fourteenth-century chantry chapel so dedicated. Norman originally, the building underwent two medieval transformations. It is of less interest architecturally than for some of the articles in it. Other worthwhile buildings, all close to church and castle, are the Grammar School of 1630, the arcaded Guildhall of 1696 (rebuilt in the last century), and Plympton House, 1600, now a hospital. The Grammar School and Guildhall are

Saltram, S of the Plymptons : the W front

both associated with the artist Sir Joshua Reynolds, a native of Plympton; he was taught at the school, of which his father was master, and in the Council Chamber of the Guildhall (open to view when no function is being held) he presided as Mayor in 1773.

Plympton St Mary used to stand at the head of a creek, long since reclaimed and turned into pasture. The Augustinian priory, founded in 1121 to supersede an earlier community, later rivalled Tavistock in importance. The priory church of St Mary survives, in open ground that was once the priory land, but of the other buildings all that is left is a Norman door now incorporated in a private house. The church is a dignified building, in the Decorated and Perpendicular styles, and consisting of chancel, nave, two aisles, two chapels, and a tower. There is one very good fifteenth-century tomb, and among families recorded in wall tablets are the Parkers, whose home was BORINGDON (not open to the public), just beyond Plympton's northern fringe. Although only half the mansion remains, it is outstanding of its type: Elizabethan, with vestiges of a fourteenth-century predecessor, and some Stuart alterations. It

belonged to the Vincents until 1564 and then to the Parkers until the early eighteenth century, when they moved into Saltram; in 1784 John Parker was created Baron Boringdon, and in 1815 the second Lord Boringdon became the Earl of Morley. The mansion is visible from the road.

SALTRAM (NT) qualifies for any list of England's great houses. It stands south of the Plymptons, in a landscaped park with views down the Plym estuary to Plymouth Sound. In the grounds are an eighteenth-century orangery and summer-house. When John Parker acquired Saltram it was a Tudor house, which he and his wife Catherine set about Georgianizing and enlarging, hiring Robert Adam to create a new salon and dining-room. This Adam did in 1768, himself designing even the fittings and carpets: only the paintings for the dining-room were sub-contracted to his friend the Italian artist Zucchi. The pre-Adam rooms are adorned with much plaster work and carving. Every part of the house is fully furnished with exquisite period pieces and valuable china, and John Parker installed a notable collection of paintings, including fourteen portraits by his friend

Saltram: the Velvet Drawing Room

Reynolds. The NT acquired Saltram in 1961 from the Treasury, which had accepted it in lieu of death duties. It is open from late March to the end of October.

North-west of Plympton St Mary is OLD NEWNHAM, the Elizabethan seat of the Strode family until they abandoned it for Newnham Park, immediately north, in 1700. A fair amount of Old Newnham remains, including some remarkable chimneys, and the remainder has been admirably restored. It is now an opulent-looking farmhouse, easily seen from the road.

Polperro Cornwall 3G3
(*pop.* – inc. Lansallos – 1,491)
Polperro is a martyr to its own very real charm. Like Clovelly in Devon, from start to finish of the holiday season it is choked with carload after carload and coachload after coachload of tourists until it resembles an exhibition for which the authorities have declined to stop selling tickets. (Fortunately there is a summer ban on the entry of the vehicles themselves.) It is well worth seeing, but to see it in any tranquillity see it in winter.

The Logan Rock, near Porthcurno

The Minack Theatre, Porthcurno

Steep cliffs, well wooded, hem in a narrow mini-estuary, and the tiers of houses drop right down, in places, sheer into the water, producing, with their reflections, a strongly Mediterranean impression; the House on Props is a variation of this style. Artists, some phonier than others, abound, and so do piskies and 'Cornish' souvenirs, some of which must have been surprised when they found themselves in Cornwall. Where most of the buildings are cottages and most of the cottages mellowed by time, no particular structure predominates. Polperro is part of the parish of Lansallos, so has no parish church; the present church of St John the Baptist was built as a chapel of ease in 1838. Fishermen still fish from the small harbour when they are not taking tourists out to see the caves, but the souvenir and teashop bandwaggon has long taken over from smuggling, although smuggling was once so active that Polperro is believed to have been the location of the very first station of the Preventive Men.

The cliffs facing the open sea on either side of the Polperro creek are owned by the NT, which has converted part of them into allotments for the villagers. There are also some splendid terraced walks, from which you can look down and speculate on the submerged

forest that lies below the sea just opposite. Between Polperro and West Looe lies TALLAND, a little place with a medieval and Tudor church (restored, of course) in which are some exceptionally interesting Tudor bench-ends.

Porthcurno Cornwall 2A6
Forget the village, which has been ruined aesthetically by the buildings of Cable & Wireless and by a very large, very obtrusive car park. But Porthcurno Bay is interesting in several ways. It has rare shells in some areas; at one end is a LOGAN ROCK, differing from Cornwall's other logan rocks in that in 1824 it was pushed over by an exuberant naval lieutenant and his merry men, and had to be replaced at the lieutenant's personal expense because of the public outcry; and at the other, or western, end stands the unique MINACK THEATRE, an open-air theatre of the Ancient Greek type fashioned in 1932 out of a natural amphitheatre halfway down the cliffs. Here Shakespeare, Classical Greek dramas (in English), and modern plays are given throughout the summer. Nearby is an Iron Age headland fortress belonging to the NT, and the remnants of one of the earliest chapels or oratories in the county. This is not

inappropriate, for the name Porthcurno comes from Kirniu, which is also the source of the first syllable of 'Cornwall'.

The Logan Rock is also a NT possession, part of an area that includes TRERYN DINAS, another prehistoric fort on an almost islanded headland; and PENBERTH COVE, a minute and wholly unspoilt fishing hamlet at the mouth of a small valley in which in springtime you may see thousands of daffodils and violets being commercially grown in the gardens.

Porthleven Cornwall 2C5
(*pop.* – inc. Sithney – 3,024)

On the coast of Mount's Bay close to Helston. Once a small fishing village, Porthleven had a commercial harbour built for it, just after the Napoleonic wars, by a company intending to use it for exporting stone and copper. In 1824, six years after its completion, it was washed away in a south-westerly gale. It was at once re-built, but because it faced the bad weather it continued to fare ill. In 1855 another company bought it and built lock gates to the inner harbour, but it remained un-profitable, and today, although a number of fishermen live there, most of them keep their boats at Newlyn. However, Porthleven is far from commercially defunct; it has a fish-canning works, and a very active ship-building yard. As a resort, it is on the side of dignity and quiet, and among its patrons the Kiss-Me-Quick-Hat contingent is not conspicuous. The only old buildings of any note are the Harbour House and Harbour Hotel, both of the eighteenth century.

A km. or so south-east of the harbour, a neck of land called LOE BAR separates the sea from LOE POOL, Corn-wall's largest freshwater lake. This is the rival to Doz-mary Pool (qv) as the scene of the Excalibur episode in the Arthurian legend. In another legend the wicked squire Tregeagle, also associated with Dozmary, crops up again, being held responsible for creating Loe Bar by dropping a sack of sand he was carrying while pursued by his ever-attentive tormentor the Devil. Loe Pool is really the blocked-off estuary of the River Cober, and in the old days the Bar had to be cut whenever the waters built up too much after heavy rains; but today there are culverts. The Pool abounds in fish and wildfowl, and is girt with handsome woods. Most of them were until very recently inaccessible, being part of a private estate, PENROSE; but they have now been acquired by the NT and are open daily. Penrose, seat of the family of that name (who used to receive a token fee whenever the Bar was cut), is essentially a seventeenth-century building, with additions belonging to several later periods.

SITHNEY, which the census authorities lump together with Porthleven (they form part of the newly-created Kerrier District), is not a suburb but a village nearly 3km. north with a Norman and fifteenth-century church of above-average interest. In the churchyard is a monu-ment put up in 1741 by Dr William Oliver of Bath to

his parents, recording the fact that all the blessing he was enjoying in life he felt he owed to them. We ourselves owe one to him, for it was he who devised the Bath Oliver biscuit. In the parish is TRUTHALL, a fine example of the old manor-house-turned-farm so common in the South-West. Truthall has a medieval hall and a main part dat-ing from 1642. The manor possessed its own chapel, licensed *c.* 1500. On the western side of Sithney is BREAGE, or St Breage (*pop.* 2,380), with a church that was wholly fifteenth-century prior to the Victorian restoration, fortunately a good deal better here than most. It was the restorers who discovered, under the Puritan whitewash on the walls, the medieval frescoes that make the church of outstanding interest. It also possessed at one time Cornwall's mightiest bell, made in 1776 from a set of four bells. In 1928 the huge bell was again melted down, and the present carillon of eight bells made from it. The giant clapper was saved and now rests by the tower arch. Breage was one of the places reached by that extraordinary band of bellicose Irish saints (and some non-saints) who irrupted into north Cornwall during the sixth century. It is named after St Breaca, a lady saint. Some of the heather-covered cliffs nearest to Breage (itself inland), including RINSEY HEAD and TREWAVAS HEAD, belong to the NT. On the former stands, even gaunter than most of its kind, the engine-house of the old Wheal Prosper tin and copper mine, closed down more than a century ago. The NT has enterprisingly made the ruin safe for public entry, as a memorial to its numerous kind.

Port Isaac Cornwall 3E1
(*pop.* – parish of St Endellion – 1,028)

A very attractive fishing village that would be even more so if motorists were provided with a car park on the cliff-top and prohibited from driving in the narrow, winding, and very steep streets. This is a reasonably prosperous lobster-fishing port, formerly devoted to the ubiquitous pilchards. The stone pier was built in about 1300, the rest of the harbour – a very inadequate one in a northerly gale – in the nineteenth century. The charm of the place lies in its tiers of old cottages, the stream that tumbles under a series of footbridges beside one of the main streets, and the several good inns. Two km. south is TRESUNGERS, an unusually fine sixteenth-century farm-house with mullioned windows and an impressive entrance-tower added in 1660: not open to the public, but excellently observed from the B3314; there is even a well-placed lay-by.

One km. west of Port Isaac lie the massed buildings of ROSCARROCK, a farm group of partly monastic origin, and in truth large enough to have been run as a self-contained community. Its features include a fair amount

OPPOSITE: *C15 painting of St Christopher on the N wall of St Breaca's church, Breage*

of medieval work, a ruined chapel, a holy well, a pond, a monks' walk, a beggars' window, and a typical vast monastic kitchen. The Roscarrocks lived in the secular part of the complex from before 1200 to when the family died out in 1673. One of the later members, Nicholas, who died about 1634, wrote a hymn about the life of St Endellienta, the devout Celtic damsel to whom the church of St Endellion is dedicated. Roscarrock is now a guest-house, but the exterior can be seen in some detail from the public footpath between Port Isaac and PORT QUIN, an almost non-existent fishing-port 2½km. west of Port Isaac. At the close of the last century Port Quin was threatened with real non-existence, after all its small male population had been drowned when their only fishing-vessel was wrecked. But today most of the derelict cottages – there are only a handful – have been restored and reoccupied. Even here there is a former 'pilchard palace', the only large building in the little port. Various cliff areas around both Port Quin and Port Isaac belong to the NT.

Portreath   Cornwall   *see* **Godrevy Point**

Postbridge   Devon   4C3
In the very heart of Dartmoor, this historic centre has always been a settlement rather than a village. Its status as a centre dates from Stone Age times, for so many hut-circles and other evidences are grouped round it that it has been called a Neolithic metropolis. Twice later Postbridge was the tin-mining centre for south-west Dartmoor: during the Middle Ages and in the nineteenth century. But whereas the Stone Age folk have left plenty of traces of their presence, the later miners have left none, apart from the mines themselves. By and large, the mines ceased working at about the turn of the century, though the very last two (operated by the same company), both near Warren House Inn (*see below*), struggled on until 1939. 'Amenities' at Postbridge include a Victorian chapel of ease, a Wesleyan chapel, an early-medieval clapper-bridge, restored in 1880, over the East Dart River, an eighteenth-century bridge, and an inn where there used to be a coaching-house. But the pub the miners patronized is WARREN HOUSE INN, 2km. north-east on the road to Moretonhampstead; and opposite here there *is* a hint of their presence, for one can still see the traces of the four allotments they cut in which to grow their food, each in the shape of a different ace in a card pack. The inn, pleasant enough, is not old; until well into the last century it had a predecessor on the opposite side of the road. One km. further up the trail is BENNET'S CROSS, an ancient boundary stone.

Prehistoric sites round Postbridge include BROADUN POUND, 2km. north-west, the largest enclosure on Dartmoor, containing over 1,700 hut circles; ASSYCOMBE HILL, 2km. north-west of Warren House Inn, Bronze Age hut circles and a double row of eighty-four standing stones; 4½km. north of Postbridge, near Sittaford Tor, the GREY WETHERS, two Bronze Age stone circles; and many more.

Poughill   Cornwall   *see* **Stratton and Bude**

Poughill   Devon   *see* **Cheriton Fitzpaine**

Princetown   Devon   4C3
Popularly called the 'capital' of Dartmoor, the only justification for this being that it houses the Duchy of Cornwall's administrative headquarters for her extensive share of the Moor. The site of the town was in fact given by the Duke of Cornwall, or Prince of Wales; hence the name. Originally it was intended to be an agricultural settlement, the idea of Thomas Tyrwhitt, the Prince's secretary and Lord Warden of the Stannaries. This was in 1785, but the dream took no account of the untameability of the Moor. By 1803 the settlement had failed. Then Tyrwhitt thought of a new prison for some of the many prisoners-of-war who were already overcrowding the existing facilities. Work was begun in 1805, but, thanks to labour troubles in the bitter Dartmoor winters, not completed until 1809. All ranks were accepted, but commissioned officers could live out, on parole, in neighbouring towns (*see* Moretonhampstead). In 1813 the French were transferred to hulks at Plymouth and 250 Americans sent to Princetown. Their sojourn there was brief but nightmarish.

The war over, Tyrwhitt proposed to the Government that his building be used as a criminal prison. Mindful of his original agricultural project and the convict labour likely to be available to prepare the land, he was also anxious to build a tramway link with Plymouth. The project for the prison was turned down, but the tramway plan succeeded; in 1823 the line was opened, and ten years later, when Tyrwhitt died, it was briskly trundling granite to Plymouth. But ten years later again the granite industry collapsed, and after unsuccessful experiments to use the gaol as a factory it was decided, after all, to make it a convict prison: a decision helped by the ending in 1846, as a result of protests from Australia, of the transportation of criminals there. The first convicts entered the gaol in 1850. More than a century and a quarter later they are still there (well, others are), and the buildings have become vastly extended. Tourists agog in their coaches outside are sometimes rewarded by the glimpse of a grey uniform. Some, even luckier, can train their field-glasses on a working-party.

Princetown parish church (1810–15), originally built by the French and American prisoners, was considerably altered in 1908, after a fire that gutted the interior had already occasioned a restoration in 1875. The east window was given by American women as a memorial to American prisoners who died, but of their compatriots' own handiwork little is left for modern visitors to see. As for Tyrwhitt's tramway, quite a lot of its course can still be traced. In the high moors north of Princetown is CROCKERN TOR. Here, from 1305, met the 'Stannary Parliament', twenty-four delegates from each of the four Devon stannary towns, to discuss such common problems as uncooperative landowners or the careless silting of rivers by tin-streamers. The 'Parliament' was ruthless in disciplining its members; in fact it went considerably beyond that, at one point (in the reign of Henry VIII) seizing Sir Richard Strode of Plympton (qv) for introducing a bill that displeased it into the national Parliament and putting him in Lydford Castle (*see* Lydford Gorge). The Deputy-Warden of the Stannaries, a fellow-knight, had to bail him out. The last session on or near Crockern Tor was held in 1749 – or rather it opened there and was adjourned to Tavistock, like its recent predecessors; some historians doubt whether the meetings ever took place actually *on* the damp and windy hilltop, and suggest a nearby building known to have existed. This would be the building called 'Tinners' Hall' in S. Baring-Gould's book *Guavas the Tinner*. North-west of Princetown, at no distance at all, is NORTH HESSORY TOR, its 517m. height raised several m. more by the BBC's television aerial on the summit. West of this, across the timbered valley of the River Walkham, VIXEN TOR is crowned by the tallest rock on Dartmoor, 28m. on the deeper side. Very spectacular. North-west of the town, at 2km., is Two BRIDGES, scarcely more than the two items of its name and a solitary hotel, but one of the best-known spots on Dartmoor because it lies at the intersection of the only two roads to span the Moor. Both bridges cross the West Dart, the older 1780, the newer, carrying both modern roads where they merge for a short distance, 1928. But the point has known human activity since long before 1780, almost certainly in prehistoric times and quite certainly in Roman, when a market was held here. An interesting variant on the hut circles, barrows, standing stones, and whatnot that are to be found in the same profusion round here as all over south Dartmoor is WISTMAN'S WOOD, 2km. north up the West Dart Valley: a strange, and in some conditions creepy, assembly of ancient oak-trees, wide in span but of less than half the proper height as though grown by a community of dwarfs. The trees are mentioned in the Domesday Book.

Probus Cornwall 2D4 (*pop.* 1,429)

A village well set on the high ground between the rivers Tresillian and Fal, but miserably riven in two by the busy A390 linking Truro with St Austell. Probus's chief claim to fame is its sixteenth-century church tower, at 38m. the highest in the county. Late Perpendicular in style, it is very ornately decorated all over the surface, like St Mary Magdalene at Launceston (qv). It is also reminiscent of the lofty church towers of Somerset rather than those of Cornwall. The tower escaped the restoration undergone by the rest of the building, in which the best things are the east window and a monu-

ment to Thomas Hawkins who died in 1766. There is nothing left of the religious foundation once established here, probably by King Athelstan in the tenth century.

Two and a half km. east, at the curiously-named hamlet of GOLDEN, is a farm incorporating all that is left of the mansion of the Tregian family, once noted Roman Catholics. In the early years of Elizabeth I's reign Francis Tregian hid a Jesuit missionary from Douai, Cuthbert Mayne, at Golden, for which he was imprisoned for nearly twenty years. Mayne was executed at Launceston in 1577, and later beatified by Leo XIII as the first martyr under Elizabeth's 'persecution' of Catholics. The Tregian homestead must have been fairly new at the time, for the earliest surviving fragments date from the 1530s. The best survival, however, is a medieval barn of two storeys, with a stone spiral stair, the original roof timbers, a small round-arched window, and a round-arched door. It is not open to the public, but the building abuts on to the lane to Golden Mill. Were it not for the division into two storeys one would say it was almost certainly a former chapel. Nearby is a large prehistoric earth fort.

Between Probus and Golden stands TREWITHEN, a genuine 'stately' home built between 1715 and about 1760, and owned by the Johnstone family since 1723. The south front is of ashlar, the east front of Pentewan stone. Inside, the best room is the dining-room, with columns on either side and stucco wall decoration. The gardens are renowned beyond our own shores for their shrubs of the rhododendron family and other rare plants. They are open on weekday afternoons from the beginning of March to the end of September; the house is open on Thursday afternoons only, between May and September inclusive.

Rattery Devon 4D4 (*pop.* 344)

A pleasant village just over 1km. outside the southeastern rim of Dartmoor National Park, and, more fortunately, the same distance away from two main roads. On high ground, it has in one direction views of the Moor, rising fairly close at hand to the 311m. summit of Brent Tor, and in the other the gentler hills towards Torbay. The church is partly thirteenth-century, the walls covered inside by the Victorian restorers with not unattractive decorated plaster. The Victorians must also have been responsible for the attractive oil lamps, now discreetly converted to electricity. There is a well-carved screen. But undoubtedly the most edifying feature of this modestly attractive building is a framed notice inside the door that runs as follows:

Hints to those who worship God in this church
  1. Be in time.
  2. Go straight into Church.
  3. Kneel down on your Knees.
  4. Do not look round every time the door opens.
  5. Join in all the Prayers and Singing and Amens.
  6. Stand up directly the Hymns are given out.

7. Do not whisper to your neighbour.
8. Keep your thoughts fixed.
9. Bow your head at the Most Holy Name of Jesus.
10. If you bring Children see that they kneel too.
11. Make Almsgiving a regular part of your Worship.
12. Pray for those who Minister.
When the CHOIR and CLERGY enter or leave the CHURCH then stand up in a body. When they have passed by, kneel down in Prayer for them and for yourselves.

In the village the Church House Inn, the former priest's house, claims to date from the eleventh century; if it does, it is among the half-dozen oldest in the land. Certainly it is among the most charming. One km. south-west, a mere breath from the A36 sub-motorway, is Georgian Marley House, now renamed SYON ABBEY since being taken over by a community of Bridgettine nuns, who renamed it after their order's original foundation on the fringe of London. Emphatically not open, and best seen from the A385, to the south. Three km. farther west from Rattery, on the northern fringe of South Brent, is LYDIA BRIDGE over the River Avon, a typical ancient packhorse bridge over a stream broken up into tinkling waterfalls, and with one or two pretty cots looking on. It is all a bit like one of those nineteenth-century copperplate engravings.

Redruth Cornwall *see* **Camborne and Redruth**

St Agnes Cornwall 2C3 *(pop.* 4,747)
Nowadays just another holiday resort, this was once the centre of as close a concentration of tin mines as even Cornwall can show: their tall chimneys and roofless engine-houses dot the landscape on all sides. The church has been restored out of all semblance, and the only ancient parts of the town still surviving are the sixteenth-century cottages near the church, belonging to the NT, some other old cottages in a lane known as Stippy Stappy, and a few venerable shops in the church area. St Agnes did produce one nationally famous man, John Opie (1761–1807), the figure and portrait painter, who was born in Harmony Cottage near Trevellas Cove. But apart from the mines, it is the scenery that makes the area worth the traveller's while, especially if he or she can avoid the main holiday months. Foremost comes ST AGNES BEACON, also a NT property: heath-covered, rising to 191m., with views right and left along more than 40km. of coast from beyond St Ives to Trevose Head nearly at Padstow. On the opposite side of Cornwall you can see the Fal estuary and St Michael's Mount, and if the sun is right the eastward view extends to Brown Willy on Bodmin Moor.

Geologically the Beacon is interesting too, for it consists partly of granite, partly of the slaty rocks locally called 'killas', and partly of china clay. During the nineteenth century this last was used to fix the miners' candles to their helmets and to the walls of the mine, as

The Wheal Coates engine-house, near St Agnes

well as for pipes and pottery. At the nearest point on the coast – all of it rocky and beautiful – is the small port of TREVAUNANCE. Or perhaps would-be port is more accurate, for at Trevaunance no fewer than five successive harbours were built between 1632 and 1794, all by one family, the Tonkins. But every harbour was destroyed by the sea, and the Tonkins lost all their wealth – despite the fact that the last harbour survived until the 1920s, doing a good trade meanwhile. It even served Truro, whose merchants could communicate with Bristol and South Wales without having to send ships round Land's End, a venture not much less dangerous in the days of sail than sending them round Cape Horn. At present the chief animation at Trevaunance Cove comes from the presence of the Cornish Seal Sanctuary, though even this is shortly to move. TREVELLAS PORTH, on the other hand, just round the next small headland, is the height of sophisticated animation, having a flourishing restaurant and 'night spot' on its shores and the Cornish Gliding Club at its back. South of St Agnes Beacon the NT owns CHAPEL COOMBE and CHAPEL PORTH, the latter a small bathing resort, the former a wild, heath-clad valley containing the engine-houses of several disused mines.

Lanhydrock: the picture-gallery

Berry Pomeroy Castle, NE of Totnes. View looking into the courtyard

Holy Trinity church, St Austell, showing the Perpendicular tower of yellow Pentewan stone

St Austell Cornwall 3E3
(*pop.* – inc. Charlestown – 18,350)
The china-clay 'capital' of Cornwall and consequently of England. Like so many Cornish towns and villages, St Austell has had two phases of prosperity, the difference being that for the others it is a history of either fishing or tin-mining being replaced by tourism, but for St Austell it is tin-mining replaced by clay-mining. Not that the holiday-maker is absent from its streets, but it is

the seaside suburbs – Charlestown, Carlyon Bay, Porthpean, and so on – that are the resorts. Though St Austell had a market very early on in the Middle Ages, and was always associated with the handling of tin, it remained little more than a village until less than 200 years ago, and its very magnificent church, fully worthy of a large town, was actually a village church when it was built in the fifteenth century. Its outstanding feature is the beautiful Perpendicular tower, embellished all round with little statues in niches, its summit adorned with graceful ornamentation and the slender corner pinnacles familiar throughout the West Country. It was erected before 1487. The interior of the building has been restored, but a number of original bits and pieces are to be found by those diligent enough to seek them. Apart from the church and some rows of quiet cottages, old buildings are few, the most notable being the older parts of the White Hart Hotel, a former eighteenth-century coaching-inn, and the Quaker Meeting House of 1829. In contrast there are some good modern buildings, and a well-designed shopping precinct. Another feature that takes the traveller's eye is the palm-trees, some strikingly tall, dotted about all over the place.

But nothing in the town takes his eye like the bizarre scenery outside: the great white pyramids of clay waste (five tonnes of waste to every tonne of usable clay or kaolin) – resembling a close-up photograph of another planet televised back by a space rocket – that stretch away northward and westward into the distance. Roads honeycomb the area, which rises to a climax in the 312m. of HENSBARROW BEACON; and on a map the uncountable man-made lakes make the terrain look like Finland. Hard-paste porcelain, for which china clay is used, is like silk – the Chinese discovered how to make it, and kept their secret for many centuries. It was independently re-discovered, so to speak, by experiment at Dresden in 1708, after an Englishman, John Dwight, had come within an ace of success nearly forty years earlier. But the first true English success was the work of William Cookworthy (*see* Godolphin House), the Quaker of Kingsbridge, Devon, and the first genuine English porcelain – as opposed to the soft-paste kind – was made in his factory at Plymouth in 1768. St Austell's china-clay industry therefore dates from soon after this time, and because China is the only other place where the same quality clay is found, exports are nearly worldwide. In addition to porcelain-making, kaolin is used in a wide number of other manufactures, from floor-covering to face-cream. It is possible to visit some of the St Austell-area pits; arrangements should be made at the company offices in the town.

The port for St Austell (but *see also* Fowey) is CHARLESTOWN, originally called Porthmeor, but re-named after Charles Rashleigh who built its harbour in 1791 and twice enlarged it. In some ways it is a surprising little place, contriving to retain much of its eighteenth-century look while carrying on briskly as a commercial

China-clay workings, Carclaze Downs, near St Austell

port, yachting harbour, and diving centre, all at the same time. On the northern edge of St Austell, in woods beside the A391, is the Holy Well of MENACUDDLE, and near it a single-piece granite chair, reputedly hacked out in Druidical times.

St Buryan (*pron.* Berry-an)   Cornwall   2A5
(*pop.* 971)
Named after St Beriana, daughter of an Irish chieftain, a damsel whose saintliness was equalled by her beauty, which must have been rather frustrating. In common with nearly all the Irish saints in Cornwall, she established her own oratory, of which nothing is now left but which probably stood where the church now stands. During the tenth century King Athelstan returned from conquering the Isles of Scilly to establish a collegiate

foundation at the spot from which he had first sighted the islands, namely St Buryan. A church was built, but was replaced in the thirteenth century; in 1473 a commission recommended that this replacement should in turn be pulled down and rebuilt. (The Victorians had their precedents.) The fine fourteenth-century tower was left, and a new church was put up in the Perpendicular style of the day. Later this underwent not one restoration but several, much to the detriment of such vulnerable features as bench-ends, of which a few made into a desk are all that remain. The superbly carved and painted rood-screen, running the whole width of the building, fared slightly better, for although it was inexcusably broken up in 1814, the pieces, or some of them, were left stacked up, and a whole century later they were reassembled. Many missing parts of the jigsaw had

St Buryan church : the reassembled rood-screen

to be replaced, but nevertheless the scene today is one of the ecclesiastical showpieces of west Cornwall.

St Buryan is at the heart of yet another of the county's many concentrations of the legacies of prehistory. One of the most striking is the NINE MAIDENS (a constantly recurrent Cornish name) at BOSCAWEN-NOON, or BOS-CAWEN-UN, 2km. north. Old Welsh documents give this as one of three places in England where there were poetic contests on what today we should call the eistedfodd pattern; and for this reason the first revival of the Gorsedd was held here in 1928 (*see* Introduction, p. 46). The name shows imperfect counting, for there are nineteen of the Maidens, plus one in the middle: all turned to stone for dancing on Sunday. Nearby are two Bronze Age barrows, a single standing stone called the BLIND FIDDLER, another standing stone, and traces of a village.

One km. west yet another group includes a multiple-chambered round cairn-tomb of the Bronze Age at BRANE, a hill-fort (Iron Age) at CAER BRAN, and a settlement, also Iron Age, at CARN EUNY, that seems to have lasted from a period of round timber-and-turf huts to one of round stone huts; in one of these last pottery of the first century BC was found. Associated with the settlement is a fogou, or semi-underground refuge or granary (*see* Pendeen and Mawgan-in-Meneage for further explanation of a fogou). Three km. south-east of St Buryan are the MERRY MAIDENS, also nineteen in number; what was the significance of this figure? Neighbouring them to the north are two standing stones, THE PIPERS, and a fogou. We are now at the head of the LAMORNA VALLEY, a wooded ravine at whose sea-ward end is LAMORNA COVE, once a small – very small –

port for shipping granite, now teetering near the tawdry as a resort of all-too-real tourists and questionably real artists. Lamorna, says the legend, was a lovely girl who was captured by a witch resident in the fogou mentioned above, and turned into a hare. One day the master of TREWOOF, a largely seventeenth-century manor-house (now a farmhouse) near the head of the Valley, was out hunting and caught the hare, which thereupon turned back into the girl.

St Cleer Cornwall 3G2 *(pop.* 1,802)
A village on the southern fringe of Bodmin Moor, roughly midway between Liskeard (qv) and The Cheesewring (qv). St Cleer is a corruption of St Clarus, who for once was not a sixth-century Irishman but a high-ranking Briton who entered a monastery and was

murdered by a woman annoyed at his rejection of her love. Like many another Cornish saint, St Clarus had a well with a chapel over it that has survived. It nearly did not, for in spite of a reputation for having power to cure insanity it was allowed to fall into serious disrepair, from which it was rescued in the nick of time by a sensitive and intelligent restoration. The chapel is one of the most pleasing of its kind in the county: mainly of the fifteenth century, with round arches and a pointed Gothic vault, and little niches in one of the walls to take the non-wettable possessions of those about to immerse themselves. The church of St Clarus is close to the well, and rejoices in a very fine fifteenth-century tower; otherwise, restoration has left some old roofing, one Norman door with dog-tooth decoration, and some original stonework between the nave and aisles, but what seems to have

The Blind Fiddler, St Buryan

King Doniert's Stone, NW of St Cleer

been a beautifully carved rood-screen was replaced in 1904.

St Cleer enjoyed its greatest prosperity during the heyday of mining and quarrying in the area. Today the deserted quarries and engine-houses are as dead as the prehistoric monuments that share the moorland landscape with them, and the railway along which the trucks of ore and stone once rattled is becoming part of the natural scene. Among the archaeological relics some are noticed in the article on The Cheesewring, but of the remainder two are very noteworthy. One, in a green field on the edge of the village, TRETHEVY (or less accurately Trevethy) QUOIT, 'The Place of the Stone', a Neolithic tomb, probably for a number of dead, consisting originally of seven enormous upright outer stones surmounted by a capstone nearly 3½m. long and raised

3m. from the ground. Inside, a further upright, a vast granite block with a little doorway in one corner, divides the space into one small and one large chamber. One outer upright is missing and one has fallen in, but the collapse of this astonishing monument is unlikely; after all, it has stood for probably 4,000 years.

The other monument, KING DONIERT'S STONE, is a good deal less ancient. Situated some 1½km. north-west of the village, it consists of two stones, one the shaft of a sculptured cross, the other a smaller complete cross similarly sculptured and bearing a Latin inscription that in translation reads either 'Doniert prayed for his soul' or 'Doniert ordered [this cross to be erected] for [the good of] his soul', according to how one interprets the word *rogavit*. Doniert, or Dungerth or Durngarth, was a Cornish king who perished by drowning in 875. I prefer the latter translation: to erect a cross for your soul's good was a common medieval practice; to erect one in celebration of having prayed suggests that he who prayed did not do so very often.

Finally, in complete contrast to so much aridity, less than 2km. west of King Doniert's Stone, near the head of the wooded valley of the River Fowey, is to be seen something not too common among Cornwall's many beauties – an exquisite waterfall, the GOLETHA FALLS (also spelt Golitha and Golytha).

St Clether   Cornwall   *see* **Altarnun**

St Columb Major   Cornwall   2D2   (*pop.* 3,953)
Despite the traffic one of the pleasantest inland towns of the county, standing on a hill in the midst of a bleak area of country. The name derives not from Columbus but from Columba, martyr and virgin. So large a church was built in her honour that it was seriously considered for Cornwall's new cathedral before the decision was taken to build a new one at Truro. The tall tower replaces one destroyed by lightning, and was itself struck during the present century. The body of the church was restored by the noted G. E. Street, but retains some Perpendicular windows and other Decorated and Perpendicular features. In 1903 the then rector gave a rood-screen and handsome new chancel roof. With its aisles, transepts, and chapels the interior does have a cathedral-like majesty. The south aisle of the chancel is filled with monuments and brasses (one or two very fine) to the Arundells of Lanherne (*see* St Mawgan-in-Pydar), whose family burial-place it is. In 1332 Sir John de Arundel was granted a royal charter (later confirmed by Elizabeth I) for a weekly market at St Columb.

In the town many of the houses are slate-hung, including Glebe Cottage, 1638, near the churchyard. Several of the best individual buildings are the work of William White in the second half of the nineteenth century, especially his Venetian-style Bank House, as it used to be, in stone and marble of various colours, now an administrative office. Another distinguished nineteenth-

The impressive Norman W doorway of St Germans church

century building, rather earlier, is the Red Lion Hotel. St Columb is condemned the year round to the turmoil of through traffic (it is bisected by the A39 trunk road), but every Shrove Tuesday and the next Saturday but one it experiences turmoil of another sort, when the traditional game of hurling takes over, a sort of hockey played by unlimited numbers of town youths versus parish youths. The goals are a mile apart, and traditionally a silver ball is used; a much-prized volume, the St Columb Green Book, records the payment of ten shillings for such a ball in 1593.

On the town's northern outskirts stands TREWAN, a large former manor-house, originally of 1633 but with nineteenth-century Gothic windows and other additions.

This is $\frac{1}{2}$km. west of the A39. Alongside that highway, 4km. farther north, stands one of the many Cornish groups of stones called the NINE MAIDENS. This time there really are nine, and they are unique in being in a row, not a circle, extending more than 100m. Between here and St Mawgan-in-Pydar, 6km. south-west, there are several dozen tumuli. Three km. south-east of St Columb stands CASTLE-AN-DINAS, also with a namesake near Penzance (*see* Gulval). With four rings of ramparts (the outermost, however, ill-defined), this is the best round hill-fort in Cornwall. There are remains of ancient tin-working nearby, which it was probably built to defend. Much later, according to tradition, King Arthur hunted in the forests then surrounding the Castle.

St Germans Cornwall 3H3 *(pop.* 1,884)
The cathedral city (in rivalry, to some extent, with
Bodmin) of the old and short-lived Bishopric of Cornwall, created during the reign of Edward the Elder (900–
25) and merged with the see of Devon in 1040. But its
religious associations go back a long way farther than
that, to the foundation of its church during the visit to
Cornwall in about 430 of St Germanus, Bishop of
Auxerre in central France, to combat the heresy of the
Celtic theologian Pelagius, who denied Original Sin and
proclaimed the complete freedom of the will. During the
twelfth century a foundation of Augustinian canons was
established, so that the former cathedral became a
priory church. Underneath its Victorian restoration
much of the present building is Norman work of that
period. Not surprisingly in view of its history, the church
is large and most impressive, especially inside where a
south aisle as wide as the nave is divided from it by
massive Norman pillars and arches. The chancel is very
late Tudor, the thirteenth-century one having suddenly
fallen down one Friday in 1592. The cathedral impression is further maintained by two west towers, both
of the twelfth century, with a gabled doorway between
them; and perhaps by the fact that there is today a
Bishop of St Germans once more, though his office,
revived in 1905 under a sanction granted by Henry VIII
but hitherto left in abeyance, is only that of suffragan.

At the Dissolution John Champernowne, of Devon,
acquired the priory, but his heir 'swapped' it for Court-
land, near Exmouth, with John Eliot, a Plymouth
merchant, in a lengthy transaction lasting from 1565 to
1574; and the Eliots – who later became the Earls of
St Germans – have been the 'great family' there ever
since. In 1803 a north transept was specially added to the
church to hold their pew. The priory site, on which the
mansion stands, is now called PORT ELIOT, and lies
between the village and the estuary of the Tiddy, a
tributary of the River Lynher, or St Germans, which in
turn is a tributary of the lower Tamar. The present
house was largely designed by Sir John Soane (who
built the Dulwich Art Gallery in London) in the first
decade of the nineteenth century, but incorporates an
undercroft belonging to the priory and also its refectory.
The grounds, which make the most of the excellent
views, were laid out by Humphrey Repton in the 1790s.
The village of St Germans remains uniformly good to
look at, but especially noteworthy is the row of gabled
and balconied seventeenth-century almshouses west of
the church.

St Ives Cornwall 2B4
(pop. – inc. Leland and Carbis Bay – 9,939)
In Cornish Porth Ia, after St Ia or Hia, one of the feminine
members of the great cohort of Irish saints who burst
into Cornwall in the sixth century, St Ives is that rare
phenomenon, a place that has become a major holiday
resort without losing its aesthetic appeal. It is also that

even rarer thing, a resort of unquestionably genuine
artists. Whistler worked here, Walter Sickert, Frank
Brangwyn, Stanhope Forbes, Bernard Leach the potter,
and many others, not least – indeed, very far from least –
Dame Barbara Hepworth, internationally renowned (if
highly controversial) sculptor, who died tragically in a
fire at her cottage here in 1975. The novelist Virginia
Woolf spent much of her childhood at St Ives (the
Stephens had a summer house there) and always retained a fond memory of the place. The Penwith
Society of Arts has a pleasant gallery in Back Road
West; the St Ives Society of Artists holds continuous
exhibitions at the Old Mariners' church (or Norway
Chapel) in Norway Square; contemporary artists also
exhibit in the Wills Gallery, Wills Lane; and in her will
Dame Barbara Hepworth left her home and studio to be
used for public display purposes: even the garden is
included, to accommodate some of her larger works.
There are also the town museum in the public-library
building, and the Barnes Museum of Cinematography,
the first of its kind in Britain.

The main part of St Ives is in keeping with the artistic
patronage, and the authorities have had the enlightened
sense to do all in their power to see it remains so. Little
corkscrew streets, nearly all steep and many cobbled,
tiny alleys and courtyards, cottages of plain granite or
colour-washed, often slate-hung, chapels all over the
place – Wesley came here twenty-seven times – com-
bine to produce an impression that is sometimes
Mediterranean rather than English or Cornish (compare, in its different way, Polperro), but is always
genuine and never precious.

St Ia built herself the usual cell, round which a village
grew up, but St Ives remained small, overshadowed by
Lelant *(see below)* until the fourteenth century, when
their relative importance began to be reversed. During
this period St Ives did not have even a chapel. When one
was sanctioned in 1408 the St Ives people took care to
build a large and grand one; but it did not become a
separate parish church until 1826. Built of buff-coloured
granite and completed in 1426, it has a lofty tower
(25m.), chancel, nave with north and south aisles, and
an outer south aisle (added *c.* 1500), called the Lady
Chapel. Inside there are a number of good things, not
least a rather endearing lack of perpendicularity in
some of the walls and columns. A similar homely touch
is provided by the carving of a blacksmith, his wife, and
the tools of his trade on the choir-stall panels – a motif
explicable by the fact that it was a blacksmith who did
the work. There are some good bench-ends, fascinating
carvings (with the paintwork restored) on the old barrel
roofs, and by contrast a screen carved in 1915. In still
further contrast, and very striking, is the enormous
Madonna and Child carved by Barbara Hepworth for
the Lady Chapel. A baptistery was added to the church
by local craftsmen in 1956. There were formerly a fine
early organ and an apparently exquisite rood-screen of

the same date as the fabric, but both these were removed by the Puritans. There was no 'victory' destruction, however, for St Ives had from the outset been on the side of Parliament. Exactly a century and a half earlier, in 1497, the pretender Perkin Warbeck, having landed nearby, was proclaimed King Richard IV here. In 1685 another pretender, the Duke of Monmouth, also landed, but afterwards sailed on to Lyme Regis.

St Ives became a harbour of no small importance: fishing, the tin trade, and passenger-ferries to Ireland kept it busy. Smeaton, who built the third Eddystone Lighthouse, gave it a pier in 1770, and there was much extension in the 1890s. In addition to the pilchard cellars (*de rigueur* in almost any Cornish fishing port) there were by this time kilns for kipper-smoking, fish-net factories, and derricks for shipping stone. The railway had come, and with it the first tourists; the artists were already established. Today, except for a little fishing, it is the preserve of the tourists and artists. Nevertheless, such fishing-craft as there are, together with the yachts, make the harbour still the town's focal point. St Ia's church is near it, and near it, too, is the little Chapel of St Leonard, medieval but drastically restored in 1911. Here a friar used to be posted to bless the fishermen when they put out. Perhaps his function should have continued longer, for a memorial on the chapel wall to people drowned between 1833 and 1940 includes a great many names. In contrast with too many Cornish reputations (many of them quite unjustified), St Ives has an inspiring record of helpfulness and charity towards shipwrecked persons and others in distress: a record carried on by its lifeboat on this wicked coast. Just how *did* St Ia make the passage from Ireland on a floating leaf?

At the back of the town Tregenna Castle, now a hotel, is a 'stately home' of the 1770s, much mauled. A still more romantic hotel is Pedn-Olva, on the site of the engine-house of a disused mine and containing a rock stairway cut for the mine itself. Also behind the town is Knill's Monument of 1782. Here on 25 July every five years since 1801 (i.e. on every date ending in 1 or 6) ten girls ten years old, and two widows, all dance round the monument to music played by 'the town fiddler' and must then sing the Hundredth Psalm. Immediately south of St Ives is the modern resort of Carbis Bay, and then 2km. beyond that – right opposite Hayle (qv), in fact – is St Ives's ecclesiastical parent, LELANT. Its chief distinction today is that it is the home of the West Cornwall Golf Club, whose links extend over the now grass-covered sand that was responsible (together with the rise of St Ives) for killing Lelant as a seaport. The tidal sands on the estuary side of the village are a bird sanctuary. One tradition says that the palace of King Tewdrig, the Cornish ruler who received (not always too hospitably) all those saints from Ireland, stood here and not on the Hayle side of the estuary: certainly when the sand was dug into for the construction of the branch railway to St Ives many old skeletons were found. The

church, dedicated to St Ia's brother St Uny, is over-restored and not of much interest, and Lelant today consists largely of twentieth-century villas of the well-to-do. The country behind St Ives and Lelant abounds in Celtic crosses, disused mine-workings, and prehistoric remains. The most important of the last-named is TRENCROM HILL, an isolated 158m. eminence 2km. south-west of Lelant with a well-preserved, stone-walled Iron Age fortress on top containing hut circles. The hill, from which the views embrace long stretches of both Cornish coasts (here only 6km. apart), was given to the NT in 1964 as a memorial to the Cornish fallen in both World Wars – an appropriate dedication, for during the 1939–45 war much commando traning went on near here. The NT also owns the enormous BOWL ROCK nearby.

St John (St John-in-Cornwall)   *see* **Antony House**

St Just-in-Penwith   Cornwall   2A5
(*pop.* – inc. Pendeen and Botallack – 3,576)
One of the two centres – Pendeen (qv) being the other – of Cornwall's westernmost mining area. Though a shadow of its riproaring self in the mining heyday (copper as well as tin), the little town is among the beneficiaries from the modest tin-mining revival. For once it is not the church but the Methodist chapel (the larger of two chapels, the smaller being now disused) that dominates the scene: 1833, Doric-fronted, with a second storey added in 1860. The most interesting feature of the large church – of the fifteenth century, but grossly over-restored – is two wall-paintings of about 1500, also restored, but of great power, especially the one of Christ sprinkling his heart's blood over a collection of trade-tools. This is variously interpreted as a blessing on the trades or a warning to those practising them on the Sabbath. In the town square is a round stone-and-earth enclosure called Plane-an-Gwarry, or Plan-an-Guare, in which miracle plays once took place, and later wrestling. The layout and granite houses of St Just are not unappealing.

Halfway between here and Pendeen is CARN KENID-JACK, or Kenidzhek, 'the Hooting Cairn', where there are tumuli and several stone circles. This is not the same as KENIDJACK CASTLE, a promontory surmounted by a ruined castle north-west of the town and just north of CAPE CORNWALL, the only promontory bearing the name 'cape' on the entire English and Welsh coast. On the Cape is the medieval St Helen's Chapel, now a farm building, and out to sea, 1km. south-west, are the formidable Brisons rocks, the largest 150m. long. South of Cape Cornwall is PRIEST'S COVE, St Just's somewhat rudimentary little fishing harbour. Rudimentary or not, it still holds a water-sports festival every July. All along this stretch of coast the old mine chimneys point sinister fingers skyward as though in warning of impending doom.

St Just-in-Roseland Cornwall 2D4 *(pop.* 1,329)
immed. W of St Just Lane

Unfortunately for the sentimental, 'Roseland' does not mean an area devoted to the sight and perfume of roses, which in fact do not grow particularly well here, but comes from 'Rosinis' or 'Rhos-inis', meaning moorland isle; the neck of the peninsula is less than 3km. wide, so it is not far from being an island. But if disassociated from roses, the area is very beautiful, to its financial gain but, at least in some degree, aesthetic cost, for in the summer it becomes choked to suffocation with holiday-makers and their cars. St Just is situated on its own little wooded creek, St Just Pool, off Carrick Roads, and its church is close to the water of an even smaller sub-creek. This church was dedicated in 1261, and the chancel and north transept are of this time; the nave and south aisles are Perpendicular, the roof, floors, and pews Victorian. But it is the churchyard that impresses the traveller,

rising steeply up the coombeside to the lychgate at the top, level with the summit of the tower. Flowering shrubs of many lands shade the granite tombstones, and it is all very idyllic.

Three km. south, the larger ST MAWES occupies the end of the western prong of the two prongs into which Roseland is divided by the 'River' Percuil – in reality just a long, twisting creek. St Mawes thus stands on a level with Falmouth, to which it is linked by a 4km.-long ferry route across the mouth of Carrick Roads. The great clover-leaf-shaped castle, part of Henry VIII's precautions against French invasion, is the 'opposite number' to Pendennis (*see* Falmouth), and, like Pendennis, can be visited. In practice the first attack it experienced was by Englishmen, namely the Parliamentary troops under Fairfax, who took it without a shot fired from a Royalist defender with the good Cornish name of Hannibal Bonython, in 1646. St Mawes was

The Methodist chapel, St Just-in-Penwith: the interior from the E end of the centre aisle

probably founded by Mauditus, variously described as Welsh, Irish, and Breton, and grew up around his cell and Holy Well. The Well is still to be seen, close to the Victory Inn, and a stone chair referred to as the Saint's by Henry VIII's antiquary John Leland is now in a private house. A harbour-pier was built in 1536, the present harbour in 1874 after an earlier attempt had been washed away. There are some old cottages, but modern St Mawes, apart from its tremendous castle, is a rather odd amalgam of boatyards, expensive villas in large gardens belonging to the wealthy retired, and holidaymakers, particularly yachtsmen.

Opposite, beside a little inlet of the Percuil estuary and on the eastern prong of Roseland, is ST ANTHONY-IN-ROSELAND, a small settlement with two interesting buildings. One is Place (meaning 'a palace' – cf. Fowey), now Place Manor Hotel but formerly a mansion of the 1840s built by Admiral Spry on the site of an earlier house that before the Dissolution had been a small priory belonging to Plympton Priory in Devon. The present house is neo-Gothic in style. The other building, immediately adjoining, is the church, which is cruciform with a spire rising from the central point, like a miniature cathedral, and very unusual in Cornwall. Little is left of the original twelfth- and thirteenth-century fabric (the tower arches, a Norman door), but the rebuilding carried out in early Victorian times by the Revd Clement Carlyon at the behest of the Sprys was so lovingly and sensitively done that one feels it to be in complete harmony.

North, south, and east of the village most of the peninsula is NT land. At the southern tip are ST ANTHONY HEAD, where the NT has removed many deserted military buildings (a task the Army should undertake itself, but seldom does) and there is a lighthouse of 1825: and ZONE POINT, the most southerly tip of England east of the Lizard.

St Mawgan-in-Pydar Cornwall 2D2 (*pop.* 1,478)
Despite the double presence of an RAF airfield immediately north and a civil airfield immediately south, St Mawgan (or just Mawgan) and the VALE OF LANHERNE in which it is situated are unquestionably beautiful. The valley has a small river, the Menalhyl, running through it amid many trees, which extend close to church and village. The church, politely referred to in an earlier guide as the subject of a 'restoration conducted without enthusiasm' in 1861, nevertheless retains a good deal of thirteenth- and fifteenth-century material, including a handsome pinnacled tower, a font of 1100, a well-carved pulpit (1530), fifteenth-century bench-ends, and a graceful, very tall rood-screen. There are many monuments to the Arundell family – one of the premier Roman Catholic families in England, whose great house, Lanherne, was given in 1794 by the Lord Arundell of the time to a party of Carmelite nuns fleeing from the French Revolution, and has remained a Carmelite

convent ever since. The front of the house is late-Tudor, much of the rest is of the seventeenth and eighteenth centuries. Since the Carmelites are a closed order the house cannot be visited, but the chapel can, with its paintings by Van Dyck and Rubens; indeed, one may attend public services there. Near the entrance is an unusually elaborate Cornish cross.

Less than 1km. south of St Mawgan is another large mansion mainly of the eighteenth century, CARNANTON, standing in a spacious park amid woods that link up with those lining the valley. The Menalhyl reaches the sea at MAWGAN PORTH alongside the village of Trenance, which need detain no one except its own residents. Deep, exciting caves pit the cliffs hereabouts, reaching a climax 1½km. from the Porth with the BEDRUTHAN STEPS, a jumble of tremendous rocks honeycombed with caverns. They are safe to explore, but the explorer needs to keep a sharp eye on the tides, which race in across the sands and cut off some of the caves in next to no time at all. PENDARVES POINT, a 90m.-high headland overlooking the Steps, is a NT property. South of Mawgan Porth the cliffs are equally exciting along the wide WATERGATE BAY. One rock, Porth, is joined to the mainland by a thrilling bridge; one cave, the Banqueting Hall, is so large that concerts have been held in it.

St Michael's Mount Cornwall 2B5 (*pop.* 43) (NT)
One of the most attractive sights in the county, which is saying not a little. Situated in Mount's Bay and rising 70m. from the sea, the isle can be reached at low tide by a causeway from Marazion, and at high tide by a ferry (summer only). The church and certain other features, but not the whole of the Mount, can be visited, in conducted parties only, on certain days during every week of the year. The resemblance in both name and appearance to Mont St Michel in Normandy is not coincidental, for in the eleventh century the Celtic shrine or monastery on the Mount (the exact nature of what was there is uncertain) was granted by Edward the Confessor to the Benedictines of Mont St Michel, who after a delay of some decades established a priory here. In Richard I's reign a military fortress was added, which for a time was held against Richard by the partisans of the future King John. During the Wars of the Roses the Lancastrian Earl of Oxford and a party of his followers obtained entry in the guise of pilgrims and held the castle until they won a free pardon from the by then victorious Yorkists. Two years after the death of Henry VIII a member of the uncompromisingly Catholic Arundells (*see* St Mawgan-in-Pydar) staged a revolt against the Protestant régime. The Civil War saw the Mount defended for the King by its new owners (they had only just bought it), the Bassets. After Sir Arthur

OPPOSITE: *St Michael's Mount: the house from the E*

A detail from the plaster frieze in the Chevy Chase Room, St Michael's Mount

Basset had surrendered, the property was given to the St Aubyns, of whom the head in 1887 was created Baron St Levan, and who remained the owners until the third Lord St Levan gave it to the NT in 1954.

Some of the old monastic buildings survive, notably the refectory, now known as the Chevy Chase Room (or Hall) because of the plaster frieze added in 1641 showing that event made famous in ballad and a number of other hunting scenes. The chapel is mainly a fourteenth-century building, or was before heavy-handed Victorian restoration by – inevitably, since he was one of the owning family – J. P. St Aubyn. On top of the tower is an old stone beacon or lantern popularly called St Michael's Chair, though the 'real' chair is a seat-like depression in the granite on the west side of the isle. In the mid eighteenth century a St Aubyn with better taste than his descendant remodelled the Lady Chapel into a pair of charming drawing-rooms, which he equipped with Chippendale furniture. During the 1870s J. P. St Aubyn added a new wing to the residential buildings, and for once had the good sense to site it down the slope in order not to spoil the island's famous outline. For the rest, the pier replaced an earlier one in 1824, the tropical garden was planted barely a century ago, and the north-west wing dates from the 1920s.

St Michael's Mount is a stimulating sight, especially against the setting sun; but the best view of all is the hardest for most travellers to come by, for it is the view from the seaward side by night, when the island's lights are twinkling. Then indeed this is a scene from fairyland.

St Neot Cornwall 3F2 *(pop. 824)*
On the southern fringe of Bodmin Moor. To the north, heath-covered downs, interspersed with marshes and devoid of human settlements (more people lived there in the Iron Age than today), rising to the isolated 339m. summit of BROWN GELLY: barrows, tumuli, and hut circles everywhere. To the south, a series of small wooded valleys running into the master-valley of the Fowey: unvisited, unspoilt, and extremely beautiful, St Neot possesses a remarkable church, especially noteworthy for a feature not too prominent in Cornish churches – its stained glass. Quite a bit of the glass was very cleverly replaced in about 1830 by the artist who performed a similar service for King's College Chapel at Cambridge, but at last half of it, distributed over fifteen windows, is fifteenth- and sixteenth-century. All the windows were the gift of the villagers themselves, and two, known as the Young Women's Window and the Wives' Window, were the particular gifts of those members of the community. The very dignified church has a Decorated tower and is otherwise nearly all Perpendicular.

Among the many legends that have attached themselves to St Neot like barnacles to a hull is one that he lived off two fish in his well, which in spite of being regularly dined off were never any the worse for it. An offshoot of the Bible story of the loaves and fishes? This holy well, in common with so many of its kind in Cornwall, still exists, ½km. west of the church, but without any historic chapel – just a Victorian canopy. The village is pretty, but lacks buildings that merit individual comment. Two and a half km. west, in the next valley, the road crosses the River Warleggan by a splendid fifteenth-century granite bridge at PANTERBRIDGE. St Neot's own bridge, over the St Neot River, is an eighteenth-century structure, and 3km. south TREVERBYN OLD BRIDGE over the Fowey is again of the fifteenth, or even fourteenth, century. The manor of Treverbyn Vean, nearby, must

by ancient custom provide the Duke of Cornwall with a grey cloak whenever he visits the county. Mellow old manor-houses, nearly all farmhouses now, are plentiful in the area.

St Winnow Cornwall *see* **Lostwithiel**

Salcombe Devon 4D6 (*pop.* 2,496)
With the British holidaymaker's passion for visiting everything that claims to be Farthest South, East, West, or whatever, Salcombe would have become popular as Devon's southernmost resort regardless of its merits, but in fact it is most beautifully sited near the mouth of the many-branched Kingsbridge Estuary. The creeks are bordered by a gentle countryside of small green fields, green-hedged and terminating at the waterside in mainly wooded banks steep enough to afford shelter from the worst of the winds. Salcombe itself ranges up a much-wooded slope, and is sufficiently snug to enjoy extremely mild winters and grow all manner of sub-tropical plants. Naturally it is a place held in high regard by yachtsmen, especially of the wealthier sort, and also by people interested in wildfowl and by fishermen, professional and otherwise. The professionals, indeed, were responsible for its existence in the first place, though the well-to-do began to build houses here in the mid eighteenth century. Among the earliest were the two (The Mount and Woodcote) in which the nineteenth-century historian James Anthony Froude, a Devon man himself, later lived for much of his life. Among his visitors was Lord Alfred Tennyson, who is said by some to have composed *Crossing the Bar* after a difficult passage past the bar that blocks much of the estuary-mouth, though other authorities attribute the inspiration for this well-known

poem to a voyage between the Hampshire mainland and Tennyson's home in the Isle of Wight.

Surprisingly, in view of its present non-commercial appearance, Salcombe during the nineteenth century was a thriving port, notable for West Indian and American imports, and had four busy shipyards. All this activity, except for some yawl- and yacht-building, died with the coming of steam. But despite the Bar several hundred yachts from various countries use the harbour every summer, and hundreds more are berthed there. Many never leave the long reaches of 'inland' waterway, enjoying conditions rather like a warmer version of the Norfolk Broads; others that put to sea – for example, for the popular shark-fishing – and the visitors, see a splendid coastline on either side of the estuary, from Devon's southernmost cape, PRAWLE POINT, in the east, to BOLT HEAD, in the west, and beyond to BOLT TAIL, the eastern tip of Bigbury Bay. For non-sailors there are in Salcombe itself a charming, winding waterside walk (no cars!) bordered by fishermen's cottages; the ruins of a Henry VIII castle, Fort Charles, also by the water, which withstood a four months' siege for the Royalists during 1646, the garrison of sixty-six men and two laundry-women eventually leaving with drums and banners; and a first-rate 8km. walk along the cliffs to Bolt Tail, via Bolt Head, the entire length of it through NT territory. The cliffs near Bolt Head are grotesque, having crumbled and fallen into all manner of shapes.

Two km. from the start of this walk are the NT's SHARPITOR GARDENS, not very large (2½ha., or 6 acres), but filled with rare and delicate plants and offering glorious views. There is also a small museum, the Overbecks, in part of Sharpitor House, showing items of local interest and open every day except Saturday from the

OPPOSITE: *St Neot: the Harys Window: St John, St Gregory the Great, St Leonard, St Andrew; below, the Harys family*

ABOVE: *The Saltash bridges spanning the Tamar, seen from the Devon side. Brunel's is the only suspension bridge carrying heavy railway traffic that now survives anywhere in the world*

end of March to the end of October. The gardens are open daily throughout the year.

Saltash Cornwall 3H2 *(pop. 9,926)*
For some reason Saltash is the point on the long Cornwall–Devon border that is always chosen for the popular jests about Cornwall being one side of the divide and England on the other. Perhaps it is the width of the Tamar here that inspires the quips, or Brunel's wonderful railway bridge, the Royal Albert of 1859, now accompanied by the road bridge opened a century later (1961). Saltash was probably first established in the time of the Romans, or even earlier, as the terminal point of a ferry crossing. It received a charter under King John, was incorporated in the reign of Henry III, and became a busy harbour for the export of tin and pilgrims. But gradually it lost all its advantages. The Earls of Cornwall appropriated its ferry rights; the pilgrim trade and eventually the tin trade died away; the railway, which brought tourists and their money in the nick of time to so many Cornish parts, ended the constant influx of ferry passengers without the compensation of depositing

tourists; after the popularization of the motor-car had partly redressed matters, the road bridge put paid to that too; the port lost its right to one shilling for every ship anchoring in its very wide area of nautical jurisdiction; and it sold its oyster rights to the Navy.

Yet today the original part of the town, climbing steeply up the hillside, is full of old cottages worth the traveller's attention, including the birthplace of Lady Francis Drake. The church, though only a chapel of ease until 1881, retains a Norman tower and such thirteenth- to fifteenth-century features as the Victorian restorers graciously allowed to remain. And there is an eighteenth-century Guildhall on granite pillars. But the outskirts of Saltash are another matter: acres of council houses and 'dormitory' homes of Plymouth commuters, mostly in sad stylistic contrast to the late-Victorian houses of the area called Port View, where the commuters of that time established themselves after the coming of the railway.

The mother-church of Saltash is at ST STEPHENS-BY-SALTASH, a hilltop suburb to the south, and is not of great interest. There are a late-Georgian rectory and a few

TOP: *Trematon Castle, Saltash: the C13 gatehouse*
BOTTOM: *Trematon Castle: the sally port in the bailey wall*

old cottages, but the best things in the parish are the two great castles, TREMATON and INCE. Trematon, south-west of St Stephens, is one of the largest and oldest castles in Cornwall, already flourishing when the Domesday Book was compiled. Edward III gave it to the Dukes of Cornwall in perpetuity. It was sacked during the Catholic insurrection of 1549 but defended during the Civil War, though largely in ruins. Today the keep and inner-bailey walls remain, and there is a splendid thirteenth-century gatehouse (intact); in 1807 the Surveyor-General of the Duchy used some of the stones to build himself a house in the prevailing style. Trematon is not open to the public, but its romantic external appearance and the views over the network of waterways on this side of Plymouth Sound are available to all.

Ince Castle, farther south overlooking the estuary of the Lynher, is something of a rarity in Cornwall, a house of brick. Four-square, with a slate-hung tower at each corner, it is probably an early-seventeenth-century building, on the site of a predecessor. It belonged successively to the Inces, Earls of Devon, and Killigrews. Not open to the public, though its gardens occasionally are, it looks to best advantage from across the water.

Sandford Devon *see* **Crediton**

The Isles of Scilly Cornwall 2A1 (*pop.* 2,430)
'A small sweet world of wave-encompassed wonder', Swinburne called Scilly, and though the visitor can hardly fail to agree – after, perhaps, some initial dismay at the absence of cliffs or (except on Tresco) woods – less flattering comments must have occurred to many thousands of sea voyagers wrecked or all but wrecked on one of the 150 or so islands, islets, and rocks that make up the archipelago. It is a fascinating thought that despite the hazards of navigation and the distance from the mainland (40km. from Land's End to St Mary's), more people possibly lived here in prehistoric times than do today – certainly they occupied more islands than the five at present inhabited. Out of 250 Bronze Age chamber-tombs throughout England and Wales, fifty are in Scilly, three times as many as in the whole of the rest of Cornwall. There have been persistent – and continuing – attempts to equate the Isles of Scilly with the Cassiterides or Tin Islands visited by the Phoenicians, but this is most unlikely, since very little tin exists, and although geologists accept that the isles are the summits of hills in a landscape now submerged, the submergence took place long before Man could have appeared and extracted the metal from what is now the sea bed. The legend of Lyonesse may indeed have some substance, but it implies an impossible postdating of the real happenings that would have turned it into a 'lost land'.

The Romans made only a token conquest of the Isles, though they did find them useful as a place of banishment. Athelstan visited them, probably *c.* 936, and founded Tresco Abbey (*see below*), to which in 993 King

Olaf of Norway was brought after being wounded during a pillaging expedition. As the price of being nursed he agreed to be baptised. Henry I granted Tresco and the north-eastern islands to Tavistock Abbey, which retained them until the Dissolution. During the remainder of the sixteenth century ownership was chaotic until possession was granted to the Godolphin family (*see* Godolphin House) in 1571. Scilly was so Royalist that it held out for King Charles for two years after the war on the mainland had ended. The Godolphins were then expelled under the Commonwealth, but returned with Charles II, who doubtless recalled that St Mary's had been his last place of refuge before he left for France.

The Godolphins ended their control in 1830, after which came a period of great economic stringency for the Scillonians. Smuggling, one of their main sources of livelihood, had been virtually extinguished, in farming they could not compete with the mainland, fishing had for some reason never caught on with them, and the export of kelp – various seaweeds used in the production of iodine and soda – had suddenly slumped. An attempt at shipbuilding failed with the advent of the iron steamship. In 1835 Augustus Smith became 'uncrowned king' of the islands, and there was some improvement, for he was an able 'ruler', introducing compulsory education years before the mainland obtained it. But it was Smith's nephew and successor Lieutenant Dorrien-Smith who in about 1880 suggested experimenting with the export of early flowers to the London market. From then on improvement was assured, and the early-flower trade is still one of the two staples of the Scilly economy, the other, of course, being tourism, especially since the rather testing sea voyage from Penzance has been supplemented by regular air services from several mainland centres. In 1920 Dorrien-Smith II ceded all the islands except Tresco (which the family still owns) to the Duchy of Cornwall.

ST MARY'S (*pop.* 1,958). The largest island and possessor of the only town, HUGH TOWN, to whose harbour comes the ship from Penzance, and from which the smaller vessels set forth to the Off-Shore Islands, as the four other inhabited isles are called. The town is excitingly situated, on an isthmus, so that it has a beach on either side. The eighteenth- and nineteenth-century granite buildings, if uninspiring, are simple, appropriate, and diversified by fewer eyesores than confront the traveller in so many mainland towns. Hugh Town is dominated by Star Castle, now a hotel, built on the orders of Queen Elizabeth I in 1593; on the other (east) side of the town a structure called Harry's Walls is all that remains of a square enclosure dating from Henry VIII's time. The church dates from 1834, replacing one at the former chief settlement, Old Town, dating from the thirteenth century. Only a small part of the older church survives, restored. Even scantier are the remnants of what was once the chief residence on St Mary's, Ennor Castle, also built in the thirteenth century. The

only older evidences of man are a number of prehistoric graves and a cliff fort, Giant's Castle. Of the numerous memorials of shipwrecks in the two churches, one of the most interesting is a painted wooden lion from the *Association*, the chief of three vessels under Admiral Sir Cloudesley Shovel that were wrecked off St Mary's in 1707, with the loss of 2,000 lives, including Shovel's. Renewed interest in this event was roused in 1967 with the underwater discovery of the *Association*'s hulk and the subsequent salvaging of some of her effects. The Isles of Scilly Museum in Hugh Town contains many wreck relics as well as ship models and numerous exhibits to do with the Islands' very rich and varied fauna and flora.

Of the Off-Shore Islands TRESCO (*pop.* 246) is the largest, the most beautiful, and has the fullest history. The present 'Abbey', the large house of the Smith-Dorriens, was built from 1831 onwards by Augustus Smith to his own design. Of Athelstan's foundation nothing remains, but some Norman fragments, including part of a fort, have been built into a wall of the garden, and in one wall of the house an inscribed stone of the sixth century suggests Celtic occupation before the Saxons, unless it was brought from elsewhere. But Tresco's pride is the Abbey Gardens, open to visitors on weekdays, in which grow plants gathered from every quarter of the globe, and including such tropicana as bananas, lemon trees, cinnamon, and prickly pears, all enclosed by tall yew hedges. Here, too, are many fine trees, almost the only ones in Scilly. On the fringe of the Gardens is Valhalla 'folly' containing a collection of repainted figureheads from wrecked ships. Most of the islanders live in two hamlets, Old and New Grimsby, to the north; and farther north are two castles, King Charles's, consisting of Civil War additions to a Tudor building, and Cromwell's, put up during the Commonwealth. Farther north still are a few prehistoric burial chambers and a superb cavern, Piper's Hole, 165m. long.

Just west of Tresco is BRYHER (*pop.* 57), where although much of it is less than a km. wide – it is 4km. long – the climate and scenery on the sheltered east coast are in complete contrast with the exposed west. On Bryher is the oldest still-functioning Off-Island church, 1742 with 1822 additions. The isle must have been of importance in prehistoric times, for its northern end is peppered with barrows, and there is a chambered tomb in the south. Farther west and most isolated of the inhabited isles is ST AGNES (*pop.* 63). Here there is a likeable plain church of 1845, and a splendid retired lighthouse of 1680, almost the oldest in the kingdom. There are tumuli near the east coast, and two groups of burial chambers and a standing stone, mysterious and fascinating in their remoteness, on GUGH, a tidally-detached lesser island to the east. Near the west coast of St Agnes is the dried-up Well of St Warna, yet another of Cornwall's invading Irish saints. Off this coast the 1½km.-long island of ANNET is a bird sanctuary.

TOP: *Isles of Scilly: the Abbey Gardens, Tresco*

BOTTOM: *Isles of Scilly: looking over Hugh Town on St Mary's; Tresco is in the background*

Isles of Scilly : part of the coast of St Martin's

East of Tresco and north of St Mary's lies ST MARTIN'S (*pop.* 106), the third-largest island. Its most conspicuous man-made feature is a conical tower or 'daymark', a kind of blind lighthouse to guide shipping in daylight only, erected in 1683. Older than the church (1867) is a galleried chapel of 1845 with a most pleasing interior. St Martin's is almost the only accessible part of Scilly where there are, on the north-east side, abrupt cliffs, Cornish style, backed by downland. Of the now un-inhabited islands, GREAT GANILLY, ARTHUR, TEAN, WHITE ISLAND, and SAMSON all have prehistoric burial chambers. ST HELEN'S has the remnants of a sixth-century monastery dedicated to (or founded by) Teilo – a name that became corrupted into Elid and then Helen – and the ruins of the oldest Scilly church. Samson and Tean were both occupied in Victorian times. On an islet off Great Ganilly archaeologists found, during the 1960s, an Iron Age pottery workshop, with evidence of Romano-British costume-jewellery works above it!

Remotest and farthest west of all the Isles of Scilly is BISHOP ROCK, with its famous lighthouse, 49m. high, the successor to one that was washed away before its completion. It is not open to visitors, but pleasure launches circle close round it.

Seaton Devon 5G2 (*pop.* 4,139)
A modern resort with little history and less artistic merit, Seaton is redeemed (leaving aside its holiday festivities) only by the scenery, coastal and inland, and places of interest surrounding it. The most original of its ameni-ties is the use of the disused railway as a track for open-topped trams – real trams – which travel beside the River Axe for the 2½km. to Colyford (*see* Colyton). The Axe, now largely silted at its mouth, once had a wide estuary, as it still does behind the coastal bar, and when it was wide AXMOUTH (*pop.* 454), on the left bank op-posite Seaton, was once a port of some note; though the silting killed it before the end of the Middle Ages, Telford surveyed it as recently as 1825 with a view to constructing a canal between here and Bristol. Today it is a most agreeable village, well back from the sea, possessing a largely Norman church, many thatched cottages, and a splendid thatched inn of great antiquity. Seaward of the village the concrete bridge of 1877 that carries the road over the shrunken river-mouth is ugly but historic, being among the earliest concrete bridges in the world.

On the west side of Seaton is BEER (*pop.* 1,534), smaller but with more personality, and with a history going back to the Romans, who operated the famous quarries. Fishing and smuggling have been other prominent interests, and so has lace-making. This is a pretty village at the mouth of an attractive combe ending in a pleasantly curved bay. Fishing is still a leading pursuit, and some of the craft take part in the annual regatta, one of the best on this coast. The quarries, too, remain in action. Part of Exeter Cathedral is built of Beer stone.

Between the mouth of the Axe and the Dorset border is an exceptionally fascinating piece of coast. The geological situation is that porous chalk and greensand of the Cretaceous Period lie on top of non-porous, older rocks of the Jurassic Period. The rain seeps through the upper layers, forms a watery film on top of the Jurassic rocks, and the Cretaceous chalk and greensand slip into the sea, sometimes in huge quantities at a time. The process has been going on for thousands of years and is continuing today, but the most spectacular recorded fall took place in the winter of 1839–40, and involved the DOWLAND CLIFFS between 3km. and 5km. east of Seaton. First the villagers who farmed the area on top of the cliffs noticed cracks appearing in the land; but they had seen cracks before, and were not alarmed. As the year passed, however, the cracks grew. There were noises like breaking roots. Plaster began to fall, doors to stick. Fields suddenly developed cavities or threw up mounds. On Christmas Eve a man who had been to a party found his garden path about 30cm. lower than it had been when he went out. In the morning he had to climb a 2m. bank to get help. With some difficulty his family and goods were evacuated, but at first no further subsidence occurred.

On Christmas night two coastguards noticed the sea being violently agitated, while beneath their feet the beach began to heave like the deck of a boat. There were noises as strange as they were loud. Suddenly there was a tremendous roar, and through the darkness they could see an enormous black object in the water. Daylight revealed it as an island more than 1km. long and 14m. high, lying 170m. out to sea. Landward, fields ended abruptly in a sheer cliff of immense height; isolated pinnacles of rock still carried pastureland on top. An orchard and two cottages had been brought down to sea level.

Today the island, being of soft material, has long been washed away, but the Dowlands Landslip, its harsh appearance mellowed by luxuriant vegetation, still lies there as a fascinating collection of hills and ravines that are a paradise for botanists, bird-lovers, entomologists, and simply those who love tough walking in a unique environment.

Shaugh Prior Devon 4C4 (*pop.* 799)
A delightful if declining (population drop of 160 since the previous census despite new villas – or maybe because of them) village on the south-west fringe of Dartmoor, high enough to have long views down to Plymouth

Sound and across the Tamar to Cornwall. The fifteenth-century church, unusually dedicated, for Devon, to King Edward the Martyr, is granite, with a conspicuous tower. Inside the church is a font with a remarkable fifteenth-century carved wooden cover rescued after some oaf of a 'restorer' had thrown it into a fodder-shed. The country on every side is of exceptional fascination, whether due to Nature or to Man. North-west of the village, close to the venerable Shaugh Bridge, the rivers Meavy and Plym unite, to flow presently through beautiful BICKLEIGH VALE (marred in parts by certain Army activities), past the extensive PLYM FOREST, some of which is NT property, including bathing and picnicing places very popular with Plymothians. The NT area also includes the thirteenth-century Plym Bridge, and two formidable seventeenth-century granite gate-pillars that marked the western entrance to the estate of Boringdon (*see* Plympton).

North of Shaugh Prior, and just above the junction of the rivers, is the DEWERSTONE ROCK, an awesome formation of granite. Beside the upper Plym lie more hut circles, enclosures, cairn-tombs, standing stones, and stone rows than in any other area of Dartmoor, culminating in the almost unbelievable concentration at TROWLESWORTHY WARREN. (A warren is not necessarily an area infested with rabbits, but one set aside for game. Trowlesworthy was made a 'warren' in the thirteenth century.) LEE MOOR at one end of the time-scale possesses the only Iron Age chambered hut yet found on Dartmoor, and at the other a china-clay works, founded in the 1840s and still very much in being, with the usual accompaniment of bizarre white spoil tips, St Austell style, streams apparently flowing with milk, and, in this case, the remains of the original railway-track along which horse-drawn waggons used to carry the clay to Plymouth. A number of medieval stone crosses are to be seen in the Shaugh neighbourhood.

Sidmouth Devon 5G2 (*pop.* 8,502)
It might have been just another featureless seaside resort, but in fact it is elegant, with a long history even as a watering-place, and as redolent of the Regency as the Regency squares of Brighton. It is old enough to have sent ships and men to the siege of Calais in 1347, which it would not have been called upon to do if it were not already a venerable fishing-port. Royalty made its appearance in 1819 with the arrival of the (penniless) Duke and Duchess of Kent and their baby daughter Victoria, after which Indian rajahs, English noblemen, and Continental pillars of the Almanach de Gotha graced the scene in an unbroken procession. Today half the redundant administrators of our vanished Empire seem to have retired here, making Sidmouth the unchallenged capital of the Devon Geriatric Coast, which includes Budleigh Salterton (qv) and Exmouth.

Its position could hardly be bettered, at the mouth of a deep valley (the raised estuary of the River Sid) from which pink cliffs curve away westward. Nevertheless, to give permanence to the situation a price had to be paid, for the rock is very insecure; huge cliff falls have occurred, including a most spectacular one in 1893, and before that the tendency to encroachment meant that until the building of the sea-wall in 1835 it was not rare for an extra high tide, combined with an on-shore gale, to sweep away a house or two. One effect of the erosion has been to leave spurs of rock, grass-capped, as islands, which over the years gradually get washed away, to be replaced by others. Because the gap between the cliffs is narrow, it was filled with buildings in a very short time, resulting in an unusual homogeneity of architecture – nearly all of it 1820–30 – in the most enchanting villa style of the period; and fortunately for us none of it has had to make way for 'modern' intrusions, whether of the nineteenth century or the twentieth. Even Woolbrook Cottage, the castle-like house in which the Kents and the future Queen Victoria lodged before any of the seafront houses existed, survives as the Royal Glen Hotel.

Back from the sea a few older buildings are still to be found, including part of the church, the rest of which was rebuilt in 1860. It contains a memorial window to the Duke of Kent (who died in Woolbrook Cottage a few months after arriving there) given by Queen Victoria. Other windows contain some medieval glass. The back of the town is less pleasing, but things perk up a little with SIDFORD (*pop.* 2,735), where there are some pleasant cottages and the sixteenth-century Porch House, said to have sheltered Charles II after his narrow escape from Cromwell's men at Charmouth. Another 1½km. up the same Sid Valley road (the A375

Church of St Peter, Salcombe Regis

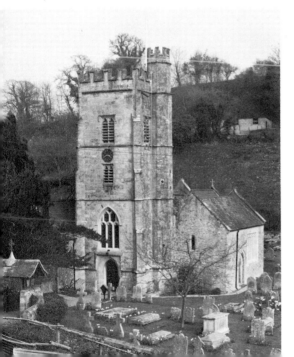

to Honiton) is SIDBURY (*pop.* 958), an unravished village noted for the large prehistoric fort, Sidbury Castle, on the adjacent height, and for the annual fair during which hot pennies are thrown to children from the windows of the inns. The church is restored, but preserves some Norman and later medieval work above a Saxon crypt, and an eighteenth-century gallery. There are many old cottages, dating from the seventeenth century onwards, and, on the grander level, the sixteenth- and eighteenth-century Court House. One and a half km. further toward Honiton, SAND BARTON was the late-Tudor mansion of the Huish family, and is now a farm. It lies off the main road, but can be seen at short range from the lane to Lower Mincombe.

Probably even older than Sidmouth is SALCOMBE REGIS (*pop.* 881), 2½km. east and slightly inland, which was a manor of King Alfred – hence the suffix. Athelstan gave it to the monks of Exeter, who worked the salt-pans formerly at the mouth of the combe ('salt-combe'). The church, originally of 1150, now displays mainly fifteenth-century features. After salt, smuggling was the village's principal occupation. There are some magnificent farms in the vicinity, and some magnificent (and dangerous) coast at DUNSCOMBE CLIFFS, from which spring petrifying streams.

South Hams   Devon
Traditionally the southernmost part of the county, bounded by the estuary of the Erme, the southern edge of Dartmoor, and the estuary of the Dart. But the newly-created administrative South Hams District includes more. *See* **Kingsbridge, Holbeton** and **Salcombe**.

Spiceland   Devon   7H4   2km. W of Culmstock
A negligible hamlet except that it contains the best Quaker Meeting House in Devon, comparable with that at Come-to-Good in Cornwall (*see* Trelissick). The Spiceland Meeting House was founded in 1650, one of the first in the country, and rebuilt in 1815. Inside, the bleached pine benches and gallery exactly resemble those of Come-to-Good – the normal Quaker style, very simple yet aesthetically very satisfying. In the Cornish building the roof extends over a stable for the Friends' horses; here there is no stable, but instead the original seventeenth-century open shed, usually called a linny or linhay, for storing the animals' provender grown by the meeting-house warden in an adjacent field. Another feature not duplicated at Come-to-Good is the little graveyard, as unpretentious as the rest, with small head-stones bearing just the names and dates of the departed. At Spiceland the Warden's House forms one end of the Meeting House block; it is occupied, though not by the Warden.

Less than 1km. north-west, in the hamlet of PRESCOTT, a Baptist chapel forms a companion-piece to the Spiceland Meeting House, for it, too, retains its eighteenth-century gallery and original simple furniture. Built in

1715 and rebuilt in 1785, it was renovated in 1892, but, probably because the Baptists could not afford an eminent architect, was spared the ruination that befell so many 'restored' Anglican churches.

Sticklepath Devon 4C2
(*pop.* – South Tawton and Sticklepath – 1,333)
A tiny place, but a triple focus of pilgrimage for Quakers, Americans, and industrial archaeologists. Furthermore, all Old Uncle Tom Cobley's six friends named in the famous Widecombe Fair song – they were real people, not fictional inventions – hailed from Sticklepath. The hamlet lies beside the River Taw on the northern rim of Dartmoor, where the National Park is bounded by the A30. It was a centre of Friends almost from the foundation of the Society (1646); by Charles II's reign there were 200 here, and Friends from Sticklepath formed a strong contingent in the party that sailed with William Penn in 1682 to found what eventually became Pennsylvania. In the following century it was the Quakers who first received Charles Wesley at Sticklepath, but Dissent of various kinds had already found a stronghold here, and when he preached (as he was often to do on later visits) the great crowd who had gathered to hear him remained unstirring despite 'a storm of hail and rain'.

The Quakers are commemorated today by their burial-ground, now interdenominational and managed by trustees; but a stone in the boundary hedge records their connexion, which lasted in strength until the early nineteenth century. Wesley is remembered in the Methodist church, which is surmounted by a wayside cross on the gable. The industrial-archaeological element is embodied in Finch's Foundry, a cutting-tool factory from 1814 to 1960, which has been preserved *in toto* and transferred into the Finch Foundry and Museum of Rural Industry (open all the year). The Foundry's three water-wheels and other equipment are seen working. With woods on the slope behind the church and the land behind that rising to the 550m. summit of Cawsand Beacon, Sticklepath might be in Norway. There is a holy well called Lady Well – more properly a spring, which never dries up – and near it an old water-mill.

Stoke Devon *see* Hartland

Stowford Devon *see* Lewtrenchard

Stratton and Bude Cornwall 6B4 (*pop.* 5,643)
Stratton is the historic town, Bude the relatively modern resort. 'Development' of the latter is steadily closing the short gap between them. Bude's huge stretch of sands – nearly 2km. from shore to sea at low water – and absence of formidable cliffs (though they are formidable enough a few km. away on either side) make it an untypical Cornish seaside town. It stands at the mouth of a small river, the Neet or Strat, and was once a modest

seaport until the river-mouth silted up. Alongside the river is the BUDE CANAL (qv), built 1819–26, which once connected with the Tamar.

Stratton, inland, dates from Roman times, and in the Middle Ages, as a change from tin, copper, or china clay, it was a centre of the salt trade. The delightfully unspoilt old town, with its narrow streets and old houses, climbs steeply from the Neet to the church, formerly Bude's parish church as well. Mainly of the fifteenth century, with a sixteenth-century tower, the building retains its carved barrel roofs and was not too aggressively restored. There is an impressive black-marble Tudor monument to one of the Arundells. In the churchyard is buried Anthony Payne, $1\frac{1}{4}$m. (7ft. 4in.)-tall, 242kg. (38 stone) servant of the Sir Bevil Grenville. He was born in what is now the Tree Inn, once a manor-house of the Grenvilles (*see also* Coombe Valley), where there is a life-sized portrait of him. To lower his body for burial the floor-beams of his room had to be cut away, as may still be seen. In 1643 Sir Bevil, together with Sir Ralph Hopton, commanded the Cornish army that defeated the Parliamentary forces under the Earl of Stamford in what is known (rather ironically, in the circumstances) as the Battle of Stamford Hill, fought just outside Stratton. A cairn now marks the battle site. Also nearby is POUGHILL (*pron.* Poffil), a pretty thatched village whose church has an exceptionally interesting interior. Built between the fourteenth and sixteenth centuries, it has two large medieval murals, repainted in the 1890s (rather harshly, although the artist was an R.A.), beautifully carved and painted original barrel roofs, nearly eighty carved bench-ends, a lock on the south door well over $\frac{1}{2}$m. long, a Charles II coat of arms dated five years before his accession (the Royalist Cornish had not forgotten Stamford Hill), and a tablet to Sir Goldsworthy Gurney (1793–1875), who lived in the battlemented 'folly' by the river-mouth at Bude, and invented an early steam coach, a steam blow-pipe, and the 'Bude Light' (an oxyhydrogen burner) for lighthouses. The tablet says 'his inventions and discoveries in steam and electricity made communication by land and sea so rapid that it became necessary for all England to keep uniform clock time'.

Just over 1km. south-east of Stratton is LAUNCELLS (*pop.* 372), a village with one of the few completely unrestored churches in Cornwall. Snugly set in a wooded valley, with St Swithin's Holy Well opposite the south door, it has a granite north arcade and a polyphant south arcade, splendid bench-ends comparable with Kilkhampton's (*see* Coombe Valley), a Royal Arms by Michael Chuke of Kilkhampton, and fifteenth-century Barnstaple-ware encaustic tiles in the chancel. It is easily Cornwall's most pleasing unrestored church.

Tavistock Devon 4B3 (*pop.* 7,620)
On the River Tavy between Dartmoor and the Tamar. Two things bestride the town: the tremendous railway

viaduct and the influence of the Dukes of Bedford. Of the great Abbey that made Tavistock such a power in the Middle Ages no more is left than of the fabulously prosperous but ephemeral mining industry of a later day. Tavistock began with the prehistoric settlement still to be traced on a hill near Kelly College. Almost the only record of Roman occupation is some Romano-British inscribed stones in the garden of the parish vicarage, but the Saxons had already been long established when work on building the Abbey was begun in 974. It received its charter from Ethelred II in 981, only to be burnt down by Danish pirates in 997. However, it was promptly rebuilt, and both Harold and William I were crowned here. Henry I authorized a market in about 1105: the wool trade flourished, monopoly in making a certain cloth being granted in 1467; and development was given a further boost by the discovery of tin in the neighbouring hills, following which Tavistock became one of the four Devon stannary towns in 1281. In 1525 the Abbey installed the first printing-press in the South-West. At the Dissolution the property was assigned to Lord Russell, whose family became the Dukes of Bedford: it was this Lord Russell who crushed the Catholic rising of 1549. In 1626 plague carried off 460 citizens in six months. Around twenty years later, during that other plague the Civil War, the survivors endured no fewer than six changes of occupation by the contesting armies.

As a stannary town Tavistock had the duty of assaying and stamping the local tin product, but the real tin and copper boom came in the first half of the nineteenth century: the Devon Great Consols Mine was the richest source of copper in Europe (it also produced, before it closed down, enough arsenic to poison every living creature on earth). The Duke of Bedford's royalties would have gratified a Caliph of Baghdad (or his successor, a modern oil sheikh), and it is to the credit of the seventh Duke, in particular, that they were used to rebuild the entire town, or town centre as it now is. In consequence Tavistock's architecture is more uniformly early- and mid-nineteenth-century in style than might seem possible in a town of its size; and the aesthetic effect of this homogeneity is enhanced by the prevalence of a unique building material, a rare local form of greenstone known as Hurdwick stone. Of the few older buildings the most interesting is the Abbey, or rather the sadly few remnants of the Abbey, which, because of its great extent, are scattered about so that to find them involves a form of hide-and-seek.

The majority are near Bedford Square, the pivot about which the town revolves. The most impressive is the Court Gate, an archway linking Bedford and Guildhall Squares. Through this the great courtyard of the Abbey was entered. The arch is large enough to house an antique shop and even a small library, the Duke's Library, founded in 1799. In the vicarage garden, already referred to, stands another gatehouse, ruined this time, known as Betsy Grimbal's Tower because a

monk or a soldier is supposed to have murdered Betsy there. Across the road the churchyard contains a tiled pavement and other foundation work of the Abbey church, as well as part of the cloister wall. From the cloisters the monks would pass through a splendidly vaulted and pinnacled porch (used for a time as a dairy by the adjacent Bedford Hotel) into what was probably the abbot's dining-hall and is now a Nonconformist chapel. Remains in other parts of the town include fragments in the police station, and down by the river a section of the outer wall and the Still Tower, used not for distilling spirits but for dispensing medicines. Straddling the river itself is what is called the Abbey Weir, very dramatic when floodlit on autumn evenings. Finally, it is worth remembering that stones taken from the Abbey have been incorporated in the walls of houses all over the town!

The parish church, consisting of chancel, nave, north aisle, and *two* south aisles, was founded in the thirteenth century but rebuilt (except for the tower) in the fifteenth by the makers of the exclusive cloth referred to above. The Clothworkers' Aisle was paid for in 1445 by the widow of John Wyse, a master-clothworker, as a chapel for the Clothworkers' Guild. It has a magnificent carved roof. There are a few old bench-ends (and some good new copies), William Morris windows in the north aisle, and one or two elaborate tombs. An inscribed floor-stone marks where the bones of a very tall man were reinterred after their discovery in an old stone coffin. They may be those of Ordulf, Earl of Devon, who founded the Saxon abbey and is on record as having been a very large individual.

Bedford Square, containing the Town Hall and Guildhall, is a worthy tribute to the seventh Duke of Bedford. In addition to public buildings he erected 250 cottages in Tavistock and surrounding areas, most of them still standing. They cost £22 each. The Bedford Hotel is a slightly earlier ducal creation, 1829: a remodelling of an eighteenth-century house, the ballroom of which is now the hotel dining-room. In Plymouth Road is a statue of Tavistock's – and Devon's – most famous son, Sir Francis Drake, commissioned by the ninth Duke in 1883. Edgar Boehm was the sculptor, and the well-known statue on Plymouth Hoe is a replica, without the bas-reliefs of scenes from Drake's life that adorn the pedestal of the Tavistock prototype. Drake's actual birthplace was almost certainly CROWNDALE, 1km. south-west of the town, but there is no vestige of the building in the present Crowndale Farm.

Tavistock's great volume of copper was mostly exported down the Tamar from MORWELLHAM QUAY (open daily throughout the year), in its heyday a thriving port that could accommodate eight ocean-going ships at once. It fell into disuse with the failure of the mines, and in particular the Devon Great Consols group, about the turn of the century, and was lapsing into complete decay when in 1970 the Dartington

The Town Hall, Tavistock

Amenity Research Trust set about restoring it as a working museum and educational centre. It had started its existence eight or nine centuries before its boom years, when ships unloaded lime here for the acid soil of the Abbey gardens and orchards and took away cloth and wool. At the Dissolution the port passed – almost needless to say – to the Russells, who retained it until the 1950s, when most of it was sold to the Earl of Bradford, who immediately became concerned with its conservation. Besides the quay, with its copper chutes, arsenic warehouses (the arsenic was used to kill the boll weevil in the American cotton plantations), inclined railways, and workshops, the present complex includes a museum, a waterwheel, a hydro-electric power station, the mouth of the Tavistock Canal, a water-powered thresher and other farm equipment, and an inn. There are regular audio-visual programmes to explain how it all functioned.

The place is pronounced 'Morwell-*ham*', with the stress on the last syllable. High above the harbour is MORWELL BARTON, a country retreat built by the Tavistock abbots, which remains a perfect example of a fifteenth-century small quadrangular stone house. A public footpath passes it. Also near Tavistock, in the direction of Sydenham Damerel, is the late-fifteenth-century COLLACOMBE MANOR (or Barton), with additions of 1547: for long the seat of the Tremaynes. The great hall has a magnificent window containing more than 3,275 panes. The house is best seen from the public footpath between Woodley and the Gulworthy–Longcross road.

Four and a half km. south-east of Morwellham Quay and 5½km. from the centre of Tavistock is BUCKLAND MONACHORUM, notable for the abbey that gave it its name. This was a Cistercian house founded in 1278, but its interest for the traveller begins with the Dissolution, when the buildings were sold to the Grenvilles of Bideford and in due course passed to Sir Richard Grenville of Stowe, north Cornwall, who was to earn fame aboard the *Revenge*. By that time the family had converted the abbey church into a slightly bizarre mansion, which Sir Richard improved. He then sold it and the estate to two purchasers who in 1581 resold them to Sir Francis Drake. From then on until his death overseas Buckland

ABOVE: *Buckland Abbey, near Tavistock: the secular conversion shows a strong compromise with the original form of the church: note the survival of the transept roof-line, for example*

BELOW: *Buckland Abbey: the tithe barn*

Abbey was Drake's home, and it remained in his family until acquired by the NT in 1948. Leased by the NT to Plymouth Corporation, it has been turned into a museum displaying Drake relics, items of naval interest, and a reconstructed Dartmoor farmhouse. Open in summer daily except Sundays, in winter on Wednesdays, Saturdays, and Sundays only. There are beautiful gardens, an avenue of yews that is among those claiming to be the oldest in England, and a very long tithe barn.

Tawstock Devon *see* **Barnstaple**

Teignmouth Devon 5E3
(*pop.* – without Shaldon – 11,040)
There is a covered-in stream, the Tame, in the centre of Teignmouth, which when it flowed openly formed a boundary between two distinct towns, East and West Teignmouth. East Teignmouth was part of the royal manor of Doflise, or Dawlish; West Teignmouth, the less important, formed part of Taintona, or Bishopsteignton. Long before their importance as fishing centres – itself dating probably from Saxon times – they were notable producers of salt, a commodity vital in the preservation of meat and fish. There is some evidence of salt pans being worked even in the Bronze Age, and the Domesday Book mentions twenty-four salt works. The two Teignmouths were united in the mid thirteenth century, when the Crown granted them markets. In 1302 Teignmouth had to furnish one ship and a crew to Edward I for his Scottish war, and in 1347 seven ships and 120 men for the siege of Calais. How many Teignmouth men sailed against the Armada is not recorded, but there was undoubtedly a contingent. Meanwhile the fishing industry, like the port, was growing fast, until by 1770 there were forty-three ships in the Newfoundland trade alone.

All this took place despite the fact that Teignmouth has always been a prime target for raiders. The Danes sacked the Saxon village in 770 and 1001, the French 'burnt up' the town in 1340 and, under Admiral de Tourville, destroyed half of it in 1690, and German air-raiders wrecked many houses in the west of the town during the Second World War. But the town seems to have an above-average resilience. In the commercial field, for instance, the salt trade has long vanished, the fishing industry, if vigorous, is a fraction of its former size, but a new port activity has arisen to take their place. This is the export of ball (potters') clay, originally just to Staffordshire, now to many parts of Europe. The clay comes from quarries opened in 1743 at Kingsteignton, half a dozen km. up the Teign, and was originally cut into blocks called balls. Although consisting, like china clay, of broken-down granite, its properties are wholly different, and it is used not only for earthenware, tiles, and insulators, but in paint and certain rubber products. The quays were improved in the 1820s and 1930s. There used also to be an export of Dartmoor granite for

such purposes as the building of the new London Bridge (the 1831 one), and an old-established shipbuilding industry continues to build high-grade yachts. Teignmouth came early on the scene as a resort, being already fashionable in the late eighteenth century; Fanny Burney and John Keats were among its early visitors. Few buildings date from before that time, but of late-eighteenth- and early-nineteenth-century work a good deal remains, especially round the large open space called the Den (where there is also an aquarium) and in the streets near it. The Assembly Rooms – now a cinema but not yet a bingo hall – were designed in 1826 by Andrew Patey, an Exeter architect; in Georgian Northumberland Place Keats stayed at No. 20 long enough in 1818 to finish composing *Endymion*. Teignbridge District Council offices occupy Bicton House, a large Regency mansion now accessible through public pleasure-gardens. From earliest times there were two churches, one for East and one for West Teignmouth, but today both are nineteenth-century buildings. The more interesting of a not very exciting pair is St James, which retains a Norman tower but is otherwise of 1820, octagonal, with a lantern roof-light and the roof itself supported on cast-iron pillars. The Roman Catholic church (1878) was designed by Joseph Hansom, a noted architect in his day, though known to most people nowadays only for his invention of the hansom cab forty-five years earlier. Not all the distinguished visitors, even when they admitted to liking Teignmouth, did so without reservations. William Praed (1802–39), the poet, wrote:

> The buildings in strange order lay,
> As if the streets had lost their way . . .
> But still about that humble place
> There was a look of rustic grace.

Across the estuary lies SHALDON (*pop.* 1,535) a ward of Teignmouth nearly a century before they both became (in 1974) part of Teignbridge District. There was a ferry across the estuary before the thirteenth century, when the rights were held by the Earl of Cornwall, who owned part of West Teignmouth; later Queen Elizabeth I granted the rights to the Cecil family. In spite of two bridges there is still a ferry service, the modern rights belonging to the council. The first bridge was a wooden one of twenty-four arches, erected in 1827, but it has now been virtually rebuilt in iron in order to carry the ever-weightier traffic on the Exeter–Torquay road. Away from the waterside Shaldon is a pretty, very Georgian place; so is its counterpart RINGMORE, adjoining it on the upstream side. Shaldon Ness, where the Teign reaches the sea, supports a recently-enlarged zoo.

Tintagel Cornwall 6A6 (*pop.* 2,372)
Alas for romance! Except for the coast, the castle, and the Old Post Office (of which only the last-named is in or visible from the village – even the church is ½km. away), Tintagel is a sad let-down, a tawdry, formless,

Tintagel Castle : the entrance

The C14 Post Office, Tintagel

characterless collection of buildings straggled along a single dull street. Pursuing your way down this, however, and pausing only to inspect the Old Post Office, a craggy, lumpy-roofed, and fascinating small fourteenth-century stone manor-house restored by the NT, you come to a different world of precipitous dark cliffs and grim-looking rocks, and on a high crag that is barely joined to the mainland by a narrow isthmus and is in fact called The Island, King Arthur's Castle, as romantic a sight as the most ardent Arthurophile could desire, and likely to make even the most sceptical draw breath. In face of this, one feels guilty of near-blasphemy in stating that there is no firm evidence of Arthur's presence here at all, let alone of his birth here as alleged in the twelfth century by Geoffrey of Monmouth. But the legend was strongly established long before Tennyson, and somehow it all *looks* so right, even though the present castle was not begun until the twelfth century and was much added to in the thirteenth, that surely none but the most leaden-witted could avoid suspending disbelief while moving amid the famous walls. The ruins are admirably maintained by the Dept of the Environment, which issues a

first-class guide-book. In the village a modern building named King Arthur's Hall, and made out of fifty different kinds of Cornish stone, contains stained-glass windows depicting Arthurian scenes and a small library of relevant books and manuscripts.

Also on The Island are the remains of a Celtic monastery of the sixth century or earlier, apparently abandoned before the Norman Conquest. Little of the stonework is now much above grass level, but what is left provides perhaps the most complete ground-plan of such an early foundation in all England. It is a pity the overshadowing interest of the Castle denies it more attention. Tintagel church is most oddly situated, out on the bare windy cliff top, far from any other building, looking just as if its village had been swept away by an encroaching sea and it was waiting to be engulfed in its turn. Nor is the impression of desertion lessened by the appearance of its churchyard, enormous out of all proportion and as unkempt as it is huge. Most of the church is Norman, some of it Saxon; the tower is more recent. Inside, the most interesting thing is probably the bench-ends, which have been made into a reredos.

Beyond the church, southward, lies Penhallic Point, where the cliffs take a sharp turn east to form the northern side of the km.-wide bay that includes TREBARWITH STRAND and PORT WILLIAM. All the cliff from opposite The Island to Port William is under the NT. The back of the three-sided bay, known as TRECKNOW CLIFF, is comparatively straight, but very beautiful, with many caves. To see it at its best, stand at Penhallic Point when the sun is low in the west, shining full on the cliffs and on Gull Rock off the bay's southern tip. Access to the Strand is from Port William, a tiny place bordering a single steeply-inclined road, with a pleasant row of old white-washed cottages above the seaward end.

Immediately north-east of Tintagel is BOSSINEY, once the larger village of the two, built around an ancient castle represented today merely by a mound. In the days when (like Tintagel) it returned its own member of Parliament, it was represented at one time by Sir Francis Drake. Bossiney village, however, is eclipsed in interest by the local scenery, both coastal and inland. BOSSINEY HAVEN may have sands excellent for bathing, but it is surrounded by cliffs of great majesty and savageness, reaching a climax in the terrifying chasm called Bossiney Hole. East of the Haven is the mouth of ROCKY VALLEY, really the gorge of a small stream. In its upper reaches the gorge is lushly wooded and leads up amidst great beauty to ST NECTAN'S KIEVE, where the saint had his oratory near a spectacular 12m. waterfall. A tablet proclaims that the oratory has been rebuilt, but it is difficult to discern it in the modern shack-café on the site. Legends, Arthurian and otherwise, are many concerning the Kieve. Even in modern times Wilkie Collins, the father of the detective novel, wrote of his own walk up there and unexpected meeting with two strange ladies who lived there as recluses. Less than 1km. east of the Kieve is TREWITTEN, a thirteenth-century farmhouse that is among the oldest houses in the county: not open to the public, but clearly seen from the public footpath (partly incorporated in its own approach-lane) that links the Trevalga–Davidstow and Tintagel–Davidstow roads, also passing the neighbouring farmhouse of Trewinnick.

Tiverton Devon 7G4 *(pop.* 15,556)
The principal town (after Exeter) of east Devon, and growing to the tune of more than 3,000 additional inhabitants between the 1961 and 1971 censuses. If perhaps a little short on architectural beauty, it is a pleasant town, adroitly concealing its large amount of industry from the visitor; and it is certainly not short on waterways, having within its bounds the rivers Exe and Lowman and one end of the Grand Western Canal. This last, opened in 1814, used to join up with the Bridgwater and Taunton Canal in Somerset, but now terminates at Greenham on the county border. The Devon stretch, however, has been fully restored throughout its 17km. by its owners, Devon County Council, and there are

trips to be had by horse-drawn barge from Tiverton on weekdays during July, August, and September. Surprisingly, the Tiverton Canal Basin is situated high above the town on a hillside.

The first settlement in the area was at CRANMERE CASTLE, an oval earthwork on neighbouring Exeter Hill; here, in 1549, the local Catholic troops in the Cornish and Devon uprising of that year were defeated. The town proper – the name means 'two fords' – dates from at least the time of Alfred the Great. The castle later belonged to King Harold's mother Gytha, who crops up so often in this guide; but the building, of which fragments (though mostly fourteenth-century additions) survive today, was begun in 1105 by the first Earl of Devon, and when the earldom passed to the Courtenays it remained in their hands until the family fell from grace in 1539. It was a quadrangular building, with corner towers, and in Elizabethan times the southern side was turned into a mansion by the Giffards. The Castle was severely damaged during a fierce siege (eventually successful) by Fairfax during the Civil War, and was afterwards 'slighted', or partly dismantled. Today only the south-east and south-west towers remain, together with remnants of the Great Hall and much of the Tudorized fourteenth-century gatehouse.

Most of the rest of Tiverton's history is commercial. A grant for a market and a three-day fair was obtained in 1245, soon extended to three fairs a year (today two). The woollen trade probably got under way about the same time; and just as Tavistock (qv) had its own 'patent' cloth, Tiverton achieved great success with 'Tiverton Kersey', a fine woollen cloth exported in large quantities by sea from Exeter. The town became a borough in 1515, and its prosperity was commented on by several writers in the seventeenth and eighteenth centuries, including Daniel Defoe. Among its Members of Parliament was the great nineteenth-century statesman Lord Palmerston, who represented it for thirty years.

An unusual asset in earlier times was the town's clean drinking-water supply, obtained from a stream that rises on an outlying common and still bubbles up at Coggan's Well in Fore Street. Its course has been (and still is, though there are other supplies today) the local administration's responsibility to protect from what we now call 'pollution' ever since 1250. The best part of the parish church (St Peter) is the outside, the southern face, porch, and Greenway Chapel being covered with fine carvings, including a very unusual frieze depicting ships of Henry VIII's time. This part of the church was added by John Greenway in 1517 to a building consecrated in 1073 and much altered during the fifteenth century. Unfortunately many less felicitous alterations have taken place since: despoilation after the Reformation, damage during the Civil War, and too zealous Victorian restoration, which among other achievements removed the screen. This, luckily, was handed over to become the chancel screen in the church of Holcombe

C15 St Peter's church, Tiverton, showing the early-C16 Greenway Chapel

Rogus (qv), a village near the Somerset border. St Peter's has a 30m. tower dating from 1400.

The Baptist church in Newport Street, founded in 1607, was one of the first five of its kind in England. The Congregational (now United Reformed) church in St Peter Street, founded 1660, was the scene of the first Sunday School in Devon and perhaps in England, established in 1774 – six years before Robert Raikes's Sunday School at Gloucester. Both the original churches have been replaced. Of secular buildings the most illustrious is Blundell's School on the eastern outskirts.

The Old School (now a NT property) was built in 1604, five years after the school's foundation by Peter Blundell, a wool merchant. On the triangular lawn here John Ridd, the hero of *Lorna Doone*, had his fight with Robin Snell. Later the school was moved about 1½km. further east. There are three sets of Tudor almshouses: Greenway's and Slee's, both in the centre, and Waldron's in the Westexe district. Here, too, is Tiverton's largest factory, now a general textile works, but founded in 1816 as a lace factory by John Heathcoat, inventor of the bobbinet lace machine, after Luddite opposition had

Old Blundell's School, Tiverton

driven him from his former premises at Loughborough. For the remainder, the town centre contains a number of unobtrusive mid- and late-Georgian houses, but little from earlier periods because of a vast fire in 1731. There is a comprehensive museum, founded in 1960, which advertises its presence in dramatic style with an inter-war-period GWR tank locomotive parked outside close to the main road. It is open all the year on weekdays.

The countryside about Tiverton, particularly to the north and west, is the most exciting in Devon after the two coasts and Dartmoor, and much less known. Very

large, smoothly rounded hills, covered with green-hedged fields of grass or red soil (much brighter than the Torbay red), plentifully sprinkled with woods, dip into narrow, dramatic valleys. Huge views open out every-where, and the narrow, steep, twisting, and high-banked lanes fortunately discourage all but the most deter-mined visiting motorists, so that the villages tend to be little spoilt. There are also a number of fine mansions such as CHEVITHORNE BARTON, 4km. north-east. There was a house here even in Saxon times, but the present one dates from Elizabeth's last years and has seen a fair

ABOVE: *Dutch-style houses on the Strand, Topsham*

amount of alteration. Nevertheless, it remains a gracious sight at the end of its beech-lined approach. A public right-of-way from the Chevithorne–East Mere road leads right past it and its gardens. KNIGHTSHAYES COURT, 2km. north on a hillside above the Exe, is a NT property open to the public in the afternoon, Sunday to Thursday, from April to October inclusive. For once this is a relatively new mansion, built in 1870 by William Burges, an architect who deserves to be better known, for the Heathcoat-Amory family. It is notable for its picture collection and for the elegant terraced gardens and rare-tree woodlands surrounding it. Seven and a half km. west of Tiverton CRUWYS MORCHARD HOUSE in the village of that name – not open but in full view, next to the church – was built largely in the late seventeenth century, with a west side rebuilt in 1732 and some good Elizabethan timberwork retained from the previous house. The Cruwyses have lived there for nearly 800 years. The church, too, is interesting: a fourteenth- and sixteenth-century building, with the interior remodelled in the eighteenth and given two almost disproportionately grand Classical pillared screens, plain box pews bearing the names of the farms to whose occupants they were allocated, and other Georgian features. Outside is a revolving lychgate.

BICKLEIGH, 5km. south of Tiverton, is famous for its thatched cottages, fishermen's inn, old postbridge, and Norman castle, rebuilt by the Courtenays and later the Carews, who presided over Bickleigh 1510–1922.

Topsham   Devon   5E2, 7G6   (*pop.* 4,829)

Though Exeter has now spread down the A377 to meet it, Topsham remains a town with its own identity, and a very pleasant one. It began under the Romans, whose ships could probably get no further up the Exe, and who therefore built a harbour here and a road into their westernmost city. As time passed, however, other designs of ship were able to reach the city, including those of the Danes who several times between 876 and 1003 sailed in and sacked it. Under the Normans it became a much more important port than Topsham, until in 1290 Isabel, Countess of Devon, who held the manor of Topsham, piqued by something the citizenry had done, built a weir across the Exe above the smaller port, effectively sealing Exeter off. There was an immediate enquiry, on the grounds that the Countess had wantonly obstructed Exeter's navigation, and further enquiries were held over the next 250 years – it is not only modern litigation that is slow – but the weir stayed in place until an Act of Parliament at last authorized its demolition in 1539, by which time the river above it had become unsuitable for navigation. This was overcome in 1563 by the construction of the Exeter Canal (*see* Exeter), but meanwhile Topsham had profited enormously by the weir, which stood opposite the suburb now named Countess Weir, or Wear. Nor did the cutting of the canal affect this prosperity much: by now there was trade

enough to activate both ports. It was the railway that killed them.

In 1316 the Earl of Devon built a quay at Topsham, which remained in use until 1861. The wool trade used the port a lot. Shipyards were built (Topsham-built ships sailed against the Spanish Armada), and this industry, too, lasted until the 1860s. A great deal of the trade was with Holland, which accounts for the charming Dutch-style houses, most of them built in the eighteenth century and all now safeguarded by preservation orders, that line the Strand. Even the bricks of some of them are Dutch, brought back as ballast by ships that had carried exports. Topsham's last major flourish as a port was during the great nineteenth-century mining boom; today rail, and increasingly road, have taken over, though there is still a little trade left, one of the imports, curiously, being Danish lager. There is also some (professional) salmon-fishing, and a factory to prepare sprats for canning abroad and consumption, in smoked form, at home.

But primarily Topsham is now a high-level commuter area – Exeter's version of London's stockbroker belt – and after a disastrous decline during the latter part of the last century and the first part of this its prosperity had revived. One effect of this is the number of old, attractive, and flourishing waterside inns; and from the waterside, too, the views right down the estuary are superb, especially during a good autumn sunset. The most famous view (though challenged by some) is from the graveyard of the church, a building with a 'landmark' tower and one notable monument, but not otherwise of great interest. There is a small museum in Lower Shapter Street, and the town contains several antique shops.

Down-river from Topsham, and on the other side of the water, stands POWDERHAM CASTLE, the seat of the Earls of Devon since Sir Philip Courtenay built it in 1390-odd. Unhappily for the traveller, what with repairs after extensive Civil War damage and considerable rebuilding in both the eighteenth and nineteenth centuries, it is today something of a pastiche. Nevertheless, it is not without interest, especially the Music Room designed by James Wyatt. Ground-floor rooms open to the public on Monday to Thursday afternoons from mid May to mid September: certain of the private rooms additionally open on Thursdays only. The Castle is surrounded by a deer park, in which falconry demonstrations are given twice a week. One km. south-west is KENTON (*pop.* 1,782), a village with a remarkable church. Built either just before or just after 1400, and not subsequently added to, it gives the impression of being untouched, so delicate was the nineteenth-century restoration by Herbert Read and others. The outside is decorated like a wedding-cake with pinnacles, 'battlements', and other conceits, there is a red sandstone tower 36m. high, and the south porch lacks only statues in its niches to be worthy of a cathedral in miniature. Inside, the

Powderham Castle: the present house is largely 1760–1860 with a medieval core

magnificent fifteenth-century painted wooden pulpit was cleverly restored from dismembered fragments found in a schoolroom cupboard by the Revd Sabine Baring-Gould in 1866, after it had been destroyed by a previous 'restorer'. (It is a wonder Gould did not carry them off to Lewtrenchard, qv.) The pulpit is, however, surpassed by the rood screen and loft, which are outstanding even for Devon. The screen, probably part-Flemish, spans the church and dates from 1478–86; beautifully carved, it also displays a fascinating series of painted panels. The original loft was destroyed by order of Elizabeth I in 1559 but replaced (using surviving pieces) by Read. Other carving in the church includes a door made from bench-ends, a reredos by Kempe, and – in stone – fine capitals to the white Beerstone columns. Three km. west, OXTON HOUSE was built in 1789 by a clergyman, the Revd John Swete, on the site of several earlier houses; he also designed the beautiful grounds, with lake. The house is now a girls' school, but house and grounds are both visible.

Back on the Topsham side, at the mouth of the estuary sprawls EXMOUTH (*pop.* – without holidaymakers – 25,827). In two adjacent houses in a Georgian row called the Beacon, Lady Byron and Lady Nelson spent their grass-widowhoods.

Torbryan Devon *see* **Newton Abbot**

Torquay Devon 5E4 (*pop.* 56,000 approx.)
Devon's pride and joy among seaside resorts, and indeed one of the most distinguished larger resorts on the British coast. Claiming to be built on seven hills, which seem to the panting explorer more like seventy, the town began as the Quay and fishing-base for Torre Abbey, a Premonstratensian foundation (the name is not that of a heretical sect, but of an order of white canons established at Premontré, near Laon in north-east France) started by William de Brewer, Lord of Torre Manor, in 1196 (*see* Newton Abbot). Four years later King John awarded the monks the fishing rights for the whole of what we now call Torbay. John Leland, doing his survey for Henry VIII shortly before the Dissolution, wrote of Torre 'Prior's' pier and harbour. The pier was improved during Elizabeth's reign by fishermen from Sidmouth, in quest of a better refuge than their own. Kingsley, at his most flamboyant, wrote of the 'glow passing through our hearts as we remember the terrible and glorious July days of 1588, when the Spanish Armada ventured slowly past Berry Head, with Elizabeth's gallant pack of Devon captains following fast in its wake and dashing into the midst of the vast line, undismayed by size and numbers, while their kin and friends stood watching and praying on the cliffs, spectators of Britain's Salamis'. That the gallant captains' dash was to good effect we all know, but it has a special relevance for Torquay, because after the capture of the Spanish flagship its crew were imprisoned in the former Abbey's tithe barn, which still survives and to this day is called the Spanish Barn.

But it was the 'kin and friends' of a later British fleet, involved in another war, who made the first glimmerings of a resort out of what in 1800 was still 'nothing more than a few cottages with their little herb gardens', and below them the fishermen's cots near the 'rude pier'. During the Napoleonic wars the Navy looked kindly on Torbay as an anchorage, and the families of the officers began to look kindly on Torquay – which was being made into a supply base – as a convenient site for their temporary homes.

To assist in their achievement of this aim there came into the picture the Palk family, owners of Tor Quay village, possessors of immense wealth acquired in India, and already, in the person of Sir Laurence Palk, responsible for building the 67m.-long South Pier and Inner Harbour, completed in 1806. Like many owners of a fortune, the Palks saw their chance to use it to make another, and the result was the core of the Torquay we see today. Progress was rapid. Napoleon himself, captive aboard the *Bellerophon* anchored in the Bay, praised the developing Elysium in lavish terms, comparing it with Elba. By the time the Navy had moved on – not that it has ever forsaken Torbay entirely – the Palks had seen to it that Torquay's reputation as a place for seaside relaxation was securely established. Alongside the development as a resort went increasing importance as a commercial port and even, hard though it is to imagine, a ship-building centre. Lord Haldon, who owned the harbour, organized the building of the Haldon Pier and Outer Harbour, completed in 1870, which earned itself

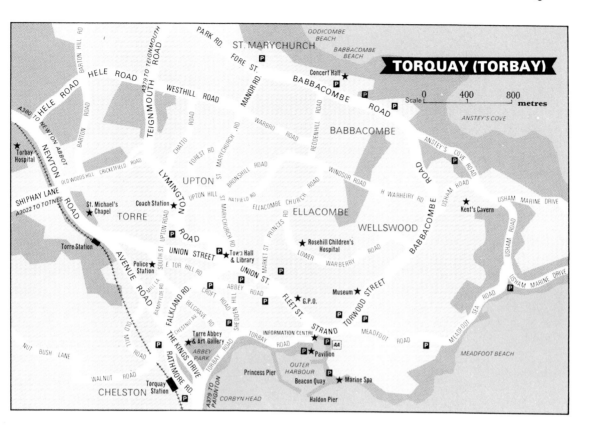

the name of the best purely artificial harbour in south-west England. In 1887 the Corporation bought it.

But the taint of trade did not prevent the steady in-crease of visitors, including those of the highest calibre. The international 'social set' loved it. British noblemen built their permanent homes there. The literary set – Kingsley, Elizabeth Barrett Browning, Philip Gosse, Lord Lytton – favoured it. Perhaps depressed by the sight of so much idle luxury, the commercial ventures faded away; and with the sounding of the death-knell of their epoch in 1914 the internationals and the aristo-cratic *flâneurs* faded away too, leaving modern Torquay a still rather stylish holiday centre for those whose time off had been earned by a year's work.

Architecturally there is not a great deal to single out; some of the older streets continue to evidence the homogeneity that comes of being planned as whole units, and units for the well-to-do at that; but in the main it is the setting of the houses on the steep hillsides, with their semi-tropical gardens giving on to roads of which the majority curve in a manner wholly delightful, except when you wish to find your way in a hurry, that give Torquay its charm. After the remains of Torre Abbey – the Spanish Barn already mentioned, a fourteenth-century gatehouse, parts of the church, the Norman gateway to the chapter-house, and various

vestiges of the domestic buildings – the oldest building is the 'mother' church, St Saviour's, Tormohun. Restored at an early stage of the town's expansion, it nevertheless still carries the stamp of its fifteenth-century origin, and contains some interesting Tudor monu-ments as well as its original decorated font.

On the subject of churches, Torquay offers the chance to see original designs by two of the Victorian architects more widely known for their restorations: St John's, Montpellier Terrace, by G. E. Street (glass by William Morris and Edward Burne-Jones); and All Saints, Babbacombe, by William Butterfield.

The only secular building of any antiquity is the mansion of the Carys (a well-known Devon family that played a part second only to that of the Palks in Tor-quay's development), built into part of Torre Abbey ruins in the eighteenth century. Now owned by the local authority, this is today a permanent art gallery open daily from Easter to October. The rest of the Abbey is open all the year, but not at weekends in the winter. Other museums are the Natural History in Babbacombe Road, open all the year on weekdays; and a well-stocked aquarium, called Aqualand, on Beacon Quay, open daily from April to September inclusive, and at weekends for the rest of the year.

Also often listed as a museum is KENT'S CAVERN at

Wellswood, the most remarkable feature of the very fine stretch of coast immediately north of Torbay. The Cavern consists of a pair of parallel caves, over 60m. above the sea, interconnected and divided into chambers. Beginning in 1825, a series of surveys revealed the remains of mammoth, sabre-toothed tiger, woolly rhinoceros, great Irish elk, cave bear, and pottery and tools indicating occupation at two separate epochs by early man. Many of the discoveries are in the Natural History Museum just mentioned, others are in the British Museum. The Cavern itself, which possesses natural ventilation and a constant temperature and humidity, now has its stalactites and stalagmites discreetly floodlit, and is open daily throughout the year. Perhaps its most arresting feature, however, is relatively modern and fortuitous; under each floodlight there has grown a clump of fern. Nearby and north-west of ANSTEY's COVE, a much admired beauty spot, is another reminder of somewhat less early man in the shape of a field system on the cliffs that end in LONG QUARRY POINT; south-east of the Cove, past Black Head, is the easternmost tip of the peninsula separating Babbacombe Bay from Torbay, HOPE's NOSE, a great bird-haunt; and south again, but out to sea, are the three rocks familiar to every Torquay visitor, FLAT ROCK, or the LEAD STONE, ORE STONE, a full km. off-shore, and THATCHER ROCK. Next comes the DADDY HOLE, an enormous cleft in the

cliff, and finally, within ½km. of the harbour, the natural arch puzzlingly known as LONDON BRIDGE.

Administratively reckoned as part of Torquay long before everything in sight was herded into the County Borough (now District) of Torbay, is the thatched village of COCKINGTON, so exactly like the innumerable postcards of it that one gets the impression it was copied from them. Wholly owned by the Torquay Corporation and its successors since 1935, it could have been allowed to become as unreal as a film set, but in fact is very natural and charming. It has a water-mill, the famous forge, a church, a manor-house, and a number of cottages, to live in one of which must be rather like living in a NT village, say Laycock. The original church was acquired by Torre Abbey in 1236, and the Abbey masons probably built the present tower. The rest of the fabric has a fifteenth-century origin, but has been extensively modernized. Cockington Court, the former manor-house, was the seat of the Carys until 1654 and is basically Elizabethan, though updated a little in the eighteenth century. The village pub, the Drum, looks to the casual eye as old as the rest, but was designed in 1934 by Sir Edwin Lutyens.

Three km. north-west of Cockington, and not yet engulfed in the Torbay conurbation, is the NT's COMPTON CASTLE, ancestral home of the Gilberts whose most famous scion, Sir Humphrey, was commissioned by

Torquay: Torre Abbey: the tithe barn (C13?) and house (C17–C18)

Torquay: Thatcher Rock. Berry Head is in the distant background

Elizabeth I to seek out new lands for her and sought out Newfoundland, thus establishing England's first colony. The 'castle' is more accurately a fortified manor-house, and as such one of the most notable in England. Built originally in 1320, it was greatly added to in 1440 and 1520; to the last period belongs the massive machicolated front, presumably intended, like Henry VIII's castles along the coast, to guard against French invasion. When the Gilberts sold Compton in 1800 it was already falling into decay, which continued until in the twentieth century Commander Walter Raleigh Gilbert (Raleigh was Sir Humphrey's half-brother) bought back the ruins and spent many years completely restoring them. The NT acquired the property in 1951, but the Gilberts still live

there. It is open on Mondays, Wednesdays, and Thursdays, April to October inclusive.

Totnes Devon 4D4 *(pop.* 5,772)
Its very position gives it away as an ancient port – at the top of a navigable estuary and the lowest fordable point of a river, to whit the Dart; and a port it still is, in a modest way, in spite of being more than 16km. from the open sea. No one knows quite when its history began. If you believe the medieval historian Geoffrey of Monmouth's account of the Brutus Stone embedded in the pavement near the East Gate, it marks the spot where Brutus, grandson of the Trojan Aeneas, landed in Britain as a refugee after the Greek capture of Troy and

founded the British race, which is accordingly named after him. Less nebulous is the fact that by Anglo-Saxon times Totnes was already an important market centre, minting its own coins. In the Domesday survey its importance is confirmed and only Exeter, of Devon boroughs, is said to have a larger population. A charter was granted in 1205.

Today there is plenty of old Totnes to be seen. At the top of the town are the ruins of the castle built by Judhael, William I's principal commander in the South-West, and extensively rebuilt in the fifteenth century, probably by the Seymours of Berry Pomeroy (*see below*) who at one time owned it. Rather unusually, there appears to be no clear evidence on when or by whom the fortress was destroyed; today only the ruined shell-keep on its mound, or motte, survives, with the surrounding bailey, both carefully tended by the Dept of the Environment, which opens it on weekdays throughout the year and on Sundays as well in the summer. One can still ascend to the battlements, the view from which is worth the climb. But the real nucleus of the town for centuries past has been Fore Street, leading from the bridge up to the photogenic Eastgate and High Street on beyond. Fore Street is a close jumble of houses that (above the modern shop fronts of most) date from the sixteenth century onwards and in many instances belonged to wool-weavers. They include a fine Georgian building that replaced the original home of the King Edward VI Grammar School; and the 'Elizabethan House', now the Totnes Museum, housing a comprehensive local collection (open on weekdays April–September inclusive). The Eastgate itself, arched across the road, was set up in the fifteenth century, but has been considerably restored. It has a cupola, an oriel window, and a clock. There is also a much simpler North Gate, both being features in the still traceable walls built round the original Saxon town area. In the High Street the highlights are the parish church, the slate-hung Poultry-walk and Butterwalk – both with pillared arcades in which the wares indicated by the names used to be sold (cf. Dartmouth) – and the Civic Centre.

The church, once obscured from the street by houses, is a Gilbert Scott restoration of a fifteenth-century building that replaced a thirteenth-century predecessor on the site of a Saxon original. There is a mighty red sandstone tower with statues in niches; inside the church are several interesting monuments (one with an epitaph in Russian), and an outstanding fifteenth-century gilded and painted stone screen that would stand out even more if Scott had not removed the rood-loft from above it. The Civic Centre, opened in 1960, consists of a shopping precinct and the Civic Hall, the latter carefully designed to harmonize with the Butterwalk opposite and similarly slate-hung. Totnes also has a Guildhall, built in the thirteenth century but given a 'new' pillared frontage in 1611. Here the Town Council met before Totnes became merged in South Hams District, and here too was

Totnes: No. 16 High Street, dated 1585: a much altered example of the Dutch house of Elizabethan date

the old town lock-up. Inside the Guildhall is a tablet to a Totnes native, W. J. Wills, who in 1860–1, with R. O'H. Burke, made the first successful south-to-north crossing of Australia but, like Burke, died during the return. A pioneer of a different sort, also born at Totnes, was Charles Babbage, who in 1823 began work on a calculating machine. He never finished it, but his principles were adopted a century later. His plans and the incomplete prototype of this forerunner of the computer are in the museum.

Dartington (NW of Totnes): the Great Hall

A second, privately owned, museum is to be found near the bridge. This is the Totnes Motor Museum, open daily from Easter to October, comprising a large collection of cars spanning half a century, most of them currently used and raced.

Four km. north-east of Totnes brings the traveller to BERRY POMEROY CASTLE, which offers everything the most romantic castle-lover could ask, except solitude, for it has recently been 'opened up' with refreshments and souvenirs on sale. There is even a celebrated ghost. Built high on a craggy bluff and girt by thick woods, its origin is attributed to Ralph de Pomeroy, one of the Conqueror's inner circle. More than a century later Henry de Pomeroy added to the fortifications, as he did to those of St Michael's Mount (qv), on behalf of Prince John in his revolt against Richard I. When this ended in failure he is supposed to have fled, but legend says he remained at Berry and died in a leap on horseback from the walls. The oldest part of the present-day ruins are thirteenth-century – a double gateway between hexagonal towers. In addition there are walls, staircases, dungeons, and much of the keep, within which stand the remnants of the uncompleted Tudor mansion built by one of the Seymours in the early seventeenth century. The Seymours had acquired the Castle after the last Pomeroy owner had been implicated in the Catholic rising of 1549, and they have remained the owners since, last occupying it in 1688. It is open daily all the year. In Berry Pomeroy village, 2km. nearer Totnes, the church has one of those magnificent carved and painted rood-screens for which Devon is famous.

Two km. north-west of Totnes stands DARTINGTON HALL (*pop.* – Dartington parish – 1,560) focal point of the famous experiment in running a self-supporting community that should offer a degree of 'uplift' to the surrounding world. The initiative came from two Americans, Leonard Elmhirst and his wife Dorothy, in 1925, and six years later they handed over control to a trust. After half a century the venture may be considered a major success, progressive coeducational school and all. 'All' includes an Adult Educational Centre, a College of Art, and an Arts Centre that, with its North Devon offshoot the Beaford Centre, organizes exhibitions, plays, and concerts. Commercial enterprises include dairy farming, woollen cloth mills, timber cultivation and processing (together with a forestry training course), building and electrical enterprises, and the famous Dartington Glass Works, now removed to Great Torrington (qv).

Despite the eccentricity of some of its features, the Dartington venture, highly suspect at first, is now an indispensable amenity both for the employment it provides and the tourist trade it stimulates; for apart from what can be seen merely by walking round the place, the gardens of Dartington Hall and the Textile Mill are both open to the public daily throughout the year. When the Elmhirsts took over the Hall – fourteenth-century and later, a former seat of the Dukes of Exeter – it was in ruins. Painstakingly they restored it, first the Great Hall, then the buildings on the other sides of the quadrangle. Adjoining is a medieval tiltyard; this and the Great Hall are included with the gardens shown to the public. Near at hand, contrasting but not clashing, are the new houses, designed by the leading architects of the day, put up by the Elmhirsts to accommodate their staff. On the eastern edge of Dartington, where long ago people visiting the ducal seat from that direction had to ford the Dart, stands the Old Manor of LITTLEHEMPSTON, some distance from its village. It is a delightful fourteenth-century house, built round a quadrangle like Dartington Hall but much smaller. Its interesting interior is not on view, but the exterior is clearly to be seen from several viewpoints.

Tregonning Hill   Cornwall   *see* **Godolphin House**

Trelissick   Cornwall   2D4
1½km. NE of Feock   (NT)
The name of a large Greek-style mansion of the 1820s standing in very beautiful gardens that are open to the public from March to October. The gardens are rich in hardwood trees, azaleas, rhododendrons, and many sub-tropical shrubs and plants, but not a little of their charm derives from their situation at the head of a small creek opening into the KING HARRY'S PASSAGE reach of the River Fal just before it widens out into Carrick

Trelissick

Roads. In consequence the views, especially when glimpsed through the trees, are a perfect backdrop to the grounds. Close to their north-east corner is the well-known KING HARRY'S FERRY, large enough to take cars, that forms part of the shortest route between Truro and Roseland. The ferry is an intriguing contraption that hauls itself across the water by means of chains.

South of Trelissick modern villadom has taken over many of the places on the north side of RESTRONGUET CREEK; but 1km. north of Penpol, and the same distance south of Playing Place (so named because in the Middle Ages miracle plays were staged here, as elsewhere in Cornwall, for the education of the illiterate), is the strangely-named COME-TO-GOOD, which owes its title to the perfectly-preserved Quaker Meeting House of 1709, the oldest in England. (Others, founded earlier, were later rebuilt.) Thatched, whitewashed outside and in, it still contains the original unstained wood benches, gallery, and elders' pews. The roof also covers a stable for the Friends' horses. The meeting house is not open, but the interior is easily visible through the low windows.

Trelowarren Cornwall *see* **Mawgan-in-Meneage**

Trerice Cornwall *see* **Newquay**

Truro Cornwall 2D4 (*pop.* 14,849)
Although the title of County Town is still proudly retained by Bodmin, many people (and all Truronians) look on Truro as the Cornish capital: understandably, since it is the county's only city, graced by the only cathedral, and houses the administrative offices. There may have been a castle here before the Conquest, but Truro's history virtually begins with the establishment of a manor by the Conqueror, who bestowed it on one Robert, creating him first Earl of Truro for the occasion. Less than a century later the manor passed to Chief Justice of England Richard de Lucy, who previously, perhaps with an eye to this pleasant contingency, had granted the town a charter. Later Reginald Fitzroy, Earl of Cornwall, confirmed it with a second charter. At that time the name was spelt 'Triueru', meaning 'the town where three roads meet', and it was probably this accessibility that prompted King John to grant the local authorities jurisdiction over the Fal estuary, a right formerly held by Falmouth. John also made Truro a stannary town, where Cornish-mined tin was 'coigned', or tested and stamped, by officials from London. Stannary courts lasted until 1837.

After being looted by the French in 1377 and again in 1404, and having acquired sundry new privileges under Elizabeth I, Truro sided with the Royalists during the Civil War, when it twice became the headquarters of Sir Ralph Hopton. The second time (1646) the great Fairfax laid siege, and Hopton was forced to surrender. By the end of the seventeenth century, despite steady shipments of tin and copper, Truro had

begun to lose out to its rival Falmouth, which in 1709 regained control of the estuary. Nevertheless, Truro continued to flourish as a commercial and cultural centre, and the Georgian era saw the building of many good houses and public buildings, a high proportion of which, happily, are still there (*see below*). By the latter half of the nineteenth century the town was an obvious choice as the site of the new cathedral. The coming of this was unquestionably the greatest single event in Truro's history. For eight centuries the old Bishopric of Cornwall, founded in 909, had been merged in that of Devon, and during its independent existence it had been centred on St Germans and Bodmin. Now, in response to thirty years of agitation, an Order in Council of 1876 established a Bishopric of Truro; a year later the town was promoted to a city, and J. L. Pearson was appointed to design a cathedral. Construction lasted from 1880 until 1910.

Truro began on the tongue of land between the Kenwyn and Allen rivers, and it was decided to build the cathedral in the heart of the oldest part, on the very site of the parish church of St Mary, most of which was accordingly demolished, only the south aisle being incorporated in the new edifice. Thanks to this piece of imaginative placing, the cathedral looks as if it has always presided over the city centre. All the materials used were Cornish: granite, china stone, polyphant, serpentine, copper. The style is Early English with Normandy Gothic spires, the whole being an outstanding example of the Victorian Gothic Revival. But if one examines the building, especially from St Mary's Street, it is the old south aisle (now called St Mary's Aisle), ornate in the manner of St Mary's, Launceston, or the tower of Probus church, that catches the attention; and inside it is the same. St Mary's Aisle, rich and colourful beneath its elegant waggon-roof, was completed in 1518. Features of note include a fifteenth- or sixteenth-century Breton stone figure of St Nicholas, several good early tombs, including that of Owen Phippen (d. 1636) bearing a long account of his adventures with the Turks and the King of Spain, an unusual organ by Byfield, and a magnificent eighteenth-century marqueterie pulpit by Henry Bone. Other monuments from the former parish church have been given places in the new building, and are likely to remain the most interesting objects in it until the passage of a few centuries has allowed the cathedral to acquire some of the personality it at present completely lacks.

Truro's secular centre is Boscawen Street, short and wide, the width being due to the removal of a row of houses that once ran down the middle. Here and in Lemon Street, leading off Boscawen St, are the best Georgian houses, including the Royal Hotel; other streets worth exploring for gracious survivals are Prince's Street (for Prince's House and the Mansion House), Malpas Road (the Parade), Kenwyn Road (Trehaverne House), Strangways Terrace, and Walsingham

TRURO

Place. Casualties include the Red Lion Hotel – once the home of the Foote family – in Boscawen Street, recently pulled down, and the Assembly Rooms in High Cross, of which only the façade remains from the 1772 original. This being Cornwall, Methodist chapels are prominent, most of them late-eighteenth-century buildings heavily restored in the late nineteenth. To date, the best twentieth-century buildings are the County Hall group completed in 1966, outside the city to the south-west. Also outside the city, north-west on the B3284, the suburb of KENWYN (named after St Keyne, an impeccable virgin of the early Church) deserves a visit to see the church lychgate with a room over it, the Bishop's Palace (Georgian: it was Kenwyn vicarage before it was a palace, and is now a school), and the extensive views over Truro's roofs and spires, the lush agricultural countryside, and the mighty granite railway viaduct built in 1904.

Two notable city amenities, one for wet days and one for dry, are the Museum and Art Gallery in River Street, and Boscawen Park, a repository of many semi-tropical plants alongside the wide tidal Truro River below the confluence of the Kenwyn and Allen. This is the port area of Truro, too, from which commercial and excursion vessels sail down into the Fal estuary proper and thence through beautiful wooded scenery to Carrick Roads and Falmouth. The other inlet at the head of the Fal estuary is the broad lower reach of the River Tresillian, and on the tongue of land between this and the Truro is MALPAS, the city's port for small pleasure craft when low tide prevents them from proceeding further. Despite some fairly picturesque yacht bases, Malpas's distinction lies less in itself than in the views it affords along the various wooded reaches. It also supplies a ferry service across all three rivers.

Less than 2km. up the Tresillian, and only 1km. from Truro by the direct lane, the waterside trees are briefly interrupted by the church and colour-washed cottages of ST CLEMENT. Near the church porch a stone pillar with a cross carved at the top bears an incised Latin inscription dating from a century or so after the Romans had left Britain. This is interesting for the light it sheds on the westward extent of Roman penetration, and on the persistence of the Roman tongue in isolation, even in a region that never became Romanized. For a long time the pillar was used as a gatepost! Up-river again, at the head of the tidal section, TRESILLIAN BRIDGE, carrying the Truro–St Austell road, is the spot at which Hopton signed the Royalist surrender; where his army lay is still called Campfields.

OPPOSITE: *Truro Cathedral, seen from a lane to the E*
RIGHT: *Truro Cathedral: detail from the Robartes Monument, c. 1620. Death is a good piece of carving (as is Father Time, on the left entablature), far superior to the main figures*

A number of 'period' mansions, some now used as farm houses, adorn the environs of Truro. None is open to the public, but often their exteriors are visible from the nearest lane or highway to reward the more observant traveller.

Veryan Bay Cornwall 3E4
A wide bay (8km. across) between St Austell and Falmouth, misleadingly named after an inland village, VERYAN (*pop.* 876), that is actually closer to the next bay, Gerrans. 'Veryan' was originally St Symphorian, which then became Severian – without the 'St' – then St Veryan. The village is beautifully placed amid woods, but is interesting mainly for its five circular thatched cottages, dating from the early nineteenth century, and each surmounted by a cross. By eliminating corners, the shape was supposed to make it difficult for the Devil to lurk. (In Southern Italy there is an entire village of such round houses, with the same object.) The whole long coastline of Veryan Bay is magnificent – lonely and unspoilt; much of it at either end is owned by the NT. There are no towns, and only three small fishing villages, timeless and unaltered, of which the largest is PORTLOE, looking exactly as such a place should and all too rarely does. Even the caravan colonies at Boswinger and Tregenna are discreetly sited so as not to spoil the scene.

One large estate extends to the Bay's edge, that of CAERHAYES by PORTHLUNEY COVE. Within a lovely park famous for its rhododendrons Caerhayes Castle looks across a lake to the open sea. The present battlemented mansion was designed by the celebrated John Nash, and completed in 1808, replacing the older castle that for centuries had been the home of the Trevanion family. The house is not open to visitors, but a public road crosses the neck of land between the lake and the Cove, giving a fine sight of the exterior. The sword supposedly wielded by one of the Trevanions at the Battle of Bosworth (1485) is one of many souvenirs and memorials of the family in the church of ST MICHAEL CAERHAYES, on the hill west of the park.

Werrington Cornwall 6C6 (*pop.* 386)
1km. E of Yeolmbridge
Until 1966 this parish, together with its western neighbour North Petherwin, was in Devon, and many maps, including several in supposedly current tourist brochures, continue to show the old boundary. Local legend has it that the original boundary commissioners, being somewhat inebriated when they worked their way up the Cornish bank of the Tamar, on coming to its tributary the Ottery unwittingly followed this instead, discovering their error so late that they decided to return to the Tamar round the opposite side of the two parishes. A more likely explanation of this curious intrusion of Devon into east Cornwall is that the Abbots of Tavistock, having been given the manor of Werrington by King Harold's mother Gytha about the time of the Norman

conquest, had no mind to see it incorporated in Cornwall and perhaps lost to them. Even earlier than that, place-names indicate that when the Saxons first colonized north-east Cornwall, the Ottery formed a frontier between their land and that of the Celts.

At the Dissolution Werrington passed to Lord Russell, who however sold it in 1651 to Sir William Morice, later Charles II's Secretary of State. The Morices continued in residence, and built the present Werrington Park house toward the middle of the eighteenth century. Instances of an estate-owner causing a village to be removed because it spoiled the view from his mansion are not uncommon, but now the Morices found Werrington church just where they wished to instal a new tennis-court, so they caused the building to be demolished and a new church to be built higher up the slope. Confronted with this sacrilege, and perhaps fearing they might otherwise be identified with it, the villagers pronounced a collective curse on the Morices, whose fortunes began forthwith to decline. In 1775 they sold the estate to the Duke of Northumberland, and subsequently it was acquired by the Williams family who have now owned it for three generations. The Morices and the Duke between them made a beautiful thing of the interior decor, but unfortunately much of it was destroyed by a fire in the oldest part of the house in 1974. At least until rehabilitation is complete the house will not be open to the public, though the superb gardens on both sides of the Ottery are opened on special occasions, usually for charity. The outside of the house can be seen from the road to Ham Mill. The countryside all around is typical of the middle Tamar region, hilly, lush, and crowd-free.

The church, though built only in 1712 and presumably built soundly, did not satisfy the Victorians, who 'restored' it in their harshest manner in 1891, when the chancel was added at the expense of the first Mrs Williams. The outside is much more agreeable than the inside, with statues in niches all round the walls and a memorial tablet to an African boy ill-treated by one of the Morices and rescued by Lady Morice. Part of it reads: 'Deposited here are the remains of PHILIP SCIPIO . . . AN AFRICAN Whose Qualitys Might have done Honour to any Nation or Climate And give us to see that Virtue is confined to no Countrey or Complexion'.

West Down Devon *see* **East Down**

Westward Ho! Devon *see* **Appledore**

Widecombe-in-the-Moor Devon 4D3 (*pop.* 523)
It is interesting to conjecture how many of the coaches that solemnly trundle their tourists to Widecombe would do so if it were not for Uncle Tom Cobley and his friends; for though it is not without its attractions, these are fewer than those of some other Moor villages that

barely gather in a tenth of the tourists. If one must go to Widecombe, let it be in spring or autumn, for in winter the chances are weighted too heavily in favour of freezing cold, snow, or blinding mist, and in high summer (including September when *the* Fair is held) the sightseers are out-numbered only by the flies. The sobriquet 'Cathedral of the Moor' sometimes applied to the church is a brochure-compiler's exaggeration, but the building is certainly large, even majestic, like many other Devon churches, and it has a pinnacled tower 36m. high as if determined not to be dwarfed by the surrounding tors. Originally fourteenth-century, the tower was partly rebuilt in the seventeenth after being struck by lightning in 1638 during a service. Four people were killed. Inside the building little deserves particular comment, except the spaciousness; what was probably a fine screen has been cut down to wainscot height, and the paintings on the surviving part are in poor condition. In the churchyard are the graves of many whose coffins were borne on foot across the Moor from isolated places, often being rested *en route* upon the Coffin Stone (*see* Dartmeet).

Near at hand is the colonnaded fifteenth-century Old Church House, long used as a school, now part cottage, part village hall, and belonging to the NT. Also fronting the village square is Glebe House, built in Henry VIII's day, now a gift shop. Otherwise the best feature of Widecombe is its magnificent environment – the very essence of Dartmoor, whether in terms of downs, tors,

or prehistoric remains. To the east are HAYTOR ROCKS, popular with the not-too-nimble or people with children because of their ease of access; Haytor Vale, alongside, was originally a quarriers' village, and part of the old tramway for ferrying the stone still exists north of the old quarries. Even better views than from Hay Tor are to be had (on a clear day!) from HOUND TOR, north-west of Haytor; north-west again rises HAMILDON TOR, at 529m. the greatest height near Widecombe. On its slopes is GRIMSPOUND, one of the most striking of the Moor's Bronze Age villages: twenty-four hut circles within a stone outer wall, some with the jambs and lintels of their doorways yet in place, some with remains of fireplaces, and outside the pound clear traces of the walls once enclosing the villagers' fields. There are two LOGAN STONES – boulders so balanced that they rock at a touch – within reach of Widecombe: one on RIPPON TOR, south-east, the other also south-east but much closer to the village; this is the RUGGLESTONE, estimated to weigh nearly 110 tonnes.

Woody Bay   Devon   *see* Introduction, pp. 15–16

Zennor   Cornwall   2A4
(*pop.* 202 – a drop of 44 since the previous census)
Named after St Senner, or Senar, a damsel whose only established claim to saintliness would appear to be that she preserved her virginity to the end. Certainly she was very different from the 'Mermaid of Zennor', whom you

Grimspound, near Widecombe-in-the-Moor

can see combing her hair before a mirror, like a strayed Lorelei, on an antique bench-end that, with another similarly old, helps to form a miniature pew in the children's chapel of Zennor church; this sea-nymph haunted the coast for generations, luring the youths of Zennor to their doom, until one Sunday the exquisite singing of the Squire's son prompted her to leave the water, don a long dress, and attend service (walking, presumably, on her tail). After she had done this for a number of Sundays the pair eloped and were never seen again.

Zennor is also the place where, they say, the cow ate the bellrope (or some say – others say it was at Morvah). The pasturage in this stony wasteland between St Just and St Ives is so scanty that, if the bellrope were made of straw as many were, the story could be true. Less likely to be true is the tale that the men of Zennor once tried to wall up a cuckoo to keep the summer with them; but this story is told only by the St Ives folk, and the Zennor people retort with a story that the St Ives fishermen once tried to keep the hake from molesting the mackerel shoals by catching a large hake and spanking it as an example to its brothers.

The village stands in a hollow, as well it might in view of the gales that blow on this Atlantic-facing coast. There is little to comment on in the granite houses or the restored church, but the great cliffs with their succession of headlands are magnificent, particularly on a rough day. High on the flank of the valley that leads from church and inn down to Pendour Cove is a superbly-sited modern house. Below ZENNOR HEAD (a NT preserve) is a thrilling blow-hole. Inland, we are at once in the territory of quoits and hill-forts and hut circles that make West Penwith seem as though in the Stone and Iron Ages it must have been as populous as a modern city suburb. ZENNOR QUOIT, 1km. south-east, has had a stormy history, and not from the weather. First a farmer removed some of the uprights to build a byre; then another farmer blew up what was left. Restoration has been only partial, for one end of the mighty capstone still rests on the ground; but the quoit is nevertheless highly impressive. Between the quoit and the village is a very good logan stone.

About 300m. east is SPERRIS QUOIT, but this is in so completely ruined a state, one wonders whether it were not this quoit that was blown up. The most peninsula-like of the coastal headlands also has its reminder of pre-history: GURNARD'S HEAD, 2km. west of Zennor, was turned into a fortress – by name another TRERYN DINAS – with five lines of fortifications across the neck, which remain clearly visible. These are only a few of the archaeological relics within two or three km. of Zennor. Interest of quite another kind centres on TREGERTHEN, a lonely hamlet 1½km. north-east; for here during the First World War D. H. Lawrence and his German wife Frieda spent a miserable time, with everyone convinced they were spies. Tregerthen Cliff is also NT property, largely on account of the fine cliff flora, though these are not limited to the area.

One further feature of Zennor deserves notice – the first-rate Wayside Museum in the Old Millhouse, open from Easter to October, the exhibits covering every local activity past or present that one can think of, even to a working model of the surface-gear of a typical tin mine of the sort that has left so many ruined engine-houses about the landscape.

View from Zennor Head

Further Reading

General
Baldwin, W. G. V. *Cornwall* (1954).
Berry, C. *Portrait of Cornwall* (1971).
Chope, R. P. (ed.) *Early Tours in Devon and Cornwall* (1967).
Fox, A. *South West England* (1974).
Gill, C. (ed.) *Dartmoor: a New Study* (1977),
    The Isles of Scilly (1975).
Hoskins, W. G. *Devon* (revised ed. 1972).
Hoskins, W. G. and Finberg, R. P. H. *Devonshire Studies* (1952).
Jenkin, A. K. H. *Cornwall and Its People* (1970).
Langham, A. and M. *Lundy* (1970).
Mumford, C. *Portrait of the Isles of Scilly* (3rd edit. 1970).
Peel, J. H. B. *Portrait of Exmoor* (1970).
Rowse, A. L. *A Cornish Childhood* (1975).
St Leger-Gordon, D. *Portrait of Devon* (3rd edit. 1970).
Shorter, A. H., Ravenhill, W. L. D., and Gregory, K. J. *South West England* (1969).
Stevens, G. A. (ed.) *Do You Know Cornwall?* (n.d.).
Trewin, J. C. *Portrait of Plymouth* (1971).
Worth, R. H. (ed.), Spooner, G. M., and Russell, F. S. *Worth's Dartmoor* (1971).

Geology and Scenery
Axford, E. C. *Bodmin Moor* (1975).
Barton, R. M. *An Introduction to the Geology of Cornwall* (1964).
Boyle, V. C. and Payne, D. *Devon Harbours* (1952).
Chitty, Susan. *Charles Kingsley's Landscape* (1976).
Crossing, W. *Amid Devonia's Alps* (ed. Le Messurier, B.) (1974),
    Guide to Dartmoor (1912).
Dewey, H. *British Regional Geology: South West England* (3rd edit. – revised Edmonds, E. A.
  et al. – 1969).
Perkins, J. W. *Geology Explained: Dartmoor and the Tamar Valley* (1974),
    Geology Explained: in South and East Devon (1971).

Flora and Fauna
Borlase, W. *The Natural History of Cornwall* (1758).
Burrows, R. *A Naturalist in Devon and Cornwall* (1971).
Lousley, J. E. *Flora of the Isles of Scilly* (1973).
Moore, R. *Birds of Devon* (1969).
Paton, J. A. *Flowers of the Cornish Coast* (n.d.),
    Wild Flowers in Cornwall and the Isles of Scilly (1968).

Archaeology and History
Andriette, E. A. *Devon and Exeter in the Civil War* (1973).
Ashbee, P. *Ancient Scilly* (1974).

Bordaz, J. *Tools of the Old and New Stone Age* (1971).

Borlase, W. *Observations on the Antiquities, Monumental and Historical, of the County of Cornwall* (1754).

Branigan, K. and Fowler, P. J. *The Roman West Country: Classical Culture and Celtic Society* (1976).

Chadwick, N. K. *Celt and Saxon: Studies in the Early English Border* (1962),
    Celtic Britain (1963),
        (ed.) *Studies in the Early British Church* (1958).

Cornell-Smith, G. *Forerunners of Drake* (1954).

Crossing, W. *A Hundred Years on Dartmoor* (ed. Le Messurier, B.) (1968).

Dilke, O. A. W. *The Ancient Romans: How They Lived and Worked* (1976).

Elliott-Binns, L. E. *Medieval Cornwall* (1955).

Fox, A. *South West England, 3500 BC – AD 600* (1964).

Gill, C. *Plymouth: a New History* (1966).

Grinsell, L. V. *The Archaeology of Exmoor* (1970).

Halliday, F. E. *A History of Cornwall* (1959).

Hencken, H. O'M. *The Archaeology of Cornwall and Scilly* (1932).

Henderson, C. *et al.* (ed.) *The Cornish Church Guide and Parochial History of Cornwall* (1964).

Hoskins, W. G. *Two Thousand Years in Exeter* (1960).

Jenkins, A. *History of Exeter* (1806).

Lester, G. A. *The Anglo-Saxons: How They Lived and Worked* (1976).

Lloyd, C. *Sir Francis Drake* (1957).

MacDermot, E. T. *History of the Forest of Exmoor* (1973).

Marsh, H. *Dark Age Britain: Some Sources of History* (1973).

Pettit, P. *Prehistoric Dartmoor* (1974).

Phillipson, D. *Smuggling: A History* (1973).

Polwhele, R. *The History of Cornwall* (1803).

Rose-Troup, F. *The Western Rebellion of 1549* (1913).

Rowse, A. L. *Tudor Cornwall* (1969).

Stephan, J. *The Ancient Religious Houses of Devon* (1935).

Stone, J. F. S. *Wessex Before the Celts* (1958).

Thomas, A. P. *Britain and Ireland in Early Christian Times* (1971).

Walling, R. A. J. *The Story of Plymouth* (1950).

Wesley, J. *Journals, 1735–90*.

Woolf, C. *An Introduction to the Archaeology of Cornwall* (1970).

Industry and Communications

Barton, D. B. *A Historical Survey of the Mines and Mineral Railways of East Cornwall and West Devon* (1964).

Behenna, J. *West Country Shipwrecks: a Pictorial Record 1876–1973* (1974).

Booker, F. *Industrial Archaeology of the Tamar Valley* (1974).

Bouquet, M. *West Country Sail: Merchant Shipping 1840–1960* (1971).

Carter, C. *et al. Cornish Shipwrecks* (3 vols) (1973).

Crossing, W. *The Dartmoor Worker* (1966).

Endicott, D. L. *Steam In the West* (1974).

Hadfield, C. *Canals of South West England* (1967).

Harris, H. *Industrial Archaeology of Dartmoor* (1972).

Harris, H. and Ellis, M. *The Bude Canal* (1975).

Jenkin, A. K. H. *The Cornish Miner* (1971),
> *Mines in Devon* (Vol. 1: South Devon) (1974).

Larn, R. *Devon Shipwrecks* (1974).

Lewis, G. R. *The Stannaries: a Study of the English Tin Miner* (1965).

Margary, I. D. *Roman Roads In Britain* (1973).

Marriott, M. *The Shell Book of the South-West Peninsula Path* (1970).

Marshall, W. *The Rural Economy of the West of England* (1976).

Minchinton, W. *Devon At Work: Past and Present* (1974).

Prideaux, J. C. A. *The Lynton & Barnstaple Railway* (1971).

Pyatt, E. C. *Coastal Paths of the South West* (1971).

Thomas, D. St J. *Great Way West: the History and Romance of the Great Western Railway Route to the West* (1975),
> *Regional History of the Railways of Great Britain* (Vol. 1: the West Country) (1973).

Todd, A. C. and Laws, P. *Industrial Archaeology of Cornwall* (1972).

Architecture

Brown, H. M. *What to Look For In Cornish Churches* (1975).

Delderfield, E. R. *West Country Historic Houses and Their Families* (Vol. 1: Cornwall, Devon &c.) (1968).

Langdon, A. G. *Old Cornish Crosses* (1896).

Pevsner, N. 'Buildings of England' series:
> *Cornwall* (2nd edit. – revised Radcliffe, E. – 1970),
> *North Devon* (1952),
> *South Devon* (1952).

Smith, J. C. D. *A Guide to Church Woodcarvings* (1973).

Slader, J. M. *Churches of Devon* (1973).

Stubb, J. *Some Old Devon Churches* (3 vols) (1908–16).

Language, Customs, Folklore

Baring-Gould, S., with additional matter by Hancock, G. *Folk Songs of the West Country* (1974).

Dexter, T. F. C. *Cornish Names: an Attempt to Explain Over 1,600 Cornish Names* (1968).

Grinsell, L. V. *Folklore of Prehistoric Sites In Britain* (1976).

Jenner, H. *A Handbook of the Cornish Language* (1954).

Lothian, E. *Devonshire Flavour: a Treasury of Recipes and Personal Notes* (1976).

Palmer, K. *Oral Folk Tales of Wessex* (1973).

Phillips, K. C. *West Country Words and Ways* (1976).

St Leger-Gordon, R. E. *The Witchcraft and Folklore of Dartmoor* (1965).

Smith, A. S. D. *The Story of the Cornish Language: Its Extinction and Revival* (1969).

Conversion Tables for Weights and Measures

The figures in bold type can be used to represent either measure for the purposes of conversion, eg 1in. = 2·540cm., 1cm. = 0·394in.

kilometres		miles
1·609	**1**	0·621
3·219	**2**	1·243
4·828	**3**	1·864
6·437	**4**	2·485
8·047	**5**	3·107
9·656	**6**	3·728
11·265	**7**	4·350
12·875	**8**	4·971
14·484	**9**	5·592
16·093	**10**	6·214
32·187	**20**	12·427
48·280	**30**	18·641
64·374	**40**	24·855
80·467	**50**	31·069
96·561	**60**	37·282
112·654	**70**	43·496
128·748	**80**	49·710
144·841	**90**	55·923
160·934	**100**	62·137

centimetres		inches
2·540	**1**	0·394
5·080	**2**	0·787
7·620	**3**	1·181
10·160	**4**	1·575
12·700	**5**	1·969
15·240	**6**	2·362
17·780	**7**	2·756
20·320	**8**	3·150
22·860	**9**	3·543
25·400	**10**	3·937
50·800	**20**	7·874
76·200	**30**	11·811
101·600	**40**	15·748
127·000	**50**	19·685
152·400	**60**	23·622
177·800	**70**	27·559
203·200	**80**	31·496
228·600	**90**	35·433
254·000	**100**	39·370

hectares		acres
0·405	**1**	2·471
0·809	**2**	4·942
1·214	**3**	7·413
1·619	**4**	9·884
2·023	**5**	12·355
2·428	**6**	14·826
2·833	**7**	17·297
3·237	**8**	19·769
3·642	**9**	22·240
4·047	**10**	24·711
8·094	**20**	49·421
12·140	**30**	74·132
16·187	**40**	98·842
20·234	**50**	123·553
24·281	**60**	148·263
28·328	**70**	172·974
32·375	**80**	197·684
36·422	**90**	222·395
40·469	**100**	247·105

metres		yards
0·914	**1**	1·094
1·829	**2**	2·187
2·743	**3**	3·281
3·658	**4**	4·374
4·572	**5**	5·468
5·486	**6**	6·562
6·401	**7**	7·655
7·315	**8**	8·749
8·230	**9**	9·843
9·144	**10**	10·936
18·288	**20**	21·872
27·432	**30**	32·808
36·576	**40**	43·745
45·720	**50**	54·681
54·864	**60**	65·617
64·008	**70**	76·553
73·152	**80**	87·489
82·296	**90**	98·425
91·440	**100**	109·361

kilograms		av. pounds
0·454	**1**	2·205
0·907	**2**	4·409
1·361	**3**	6·614
1·814	**4**	8·819
2·268	**5**	11·023
2·722	**6**	13·228
3·175	**7**	15·432
3·629	**8**	17·637
4·082	**9**	19·842
4·536	**10**	22·046
9·072	**20**	44·092
13·608	**30**	66·139
18·144	**40**	88·185
22·680	**50**	110·231
27·216	**60**	132·277
31·752	**70**	154·324
36·287	**80**	176·370
40·823	**90**	198·416
45·350	**100**	220·462

Appendix I

A selection of Cornish place-names based on saints' names, showing, where applicable, the corruption from the prototype:

St Austell – St Austol
St Blazey – St Blaise (Bishop Blaise, martyred)
St Breage – St Breaca (sister of St Euny)
St Breoke – St Brioc
St Breward – St Bruered
St Buryan – St Beriana (beautiful daughter of an Irish chieftain)
St Cleer – St Clarus (one of the Children of Brychan)
St Clether – St Clederus (also a Child of Brychan)
St Columb – St Columba
St Constantine (son of Cador and King of Cornwall, converted in old age by St Petroc)
St Dennis – St Dionisius
St Dominick – St Dominica
St Endellion – St Endelienta or St Teilo
St Erme – St Hermes (he went from Cornwall to Brittany)
St Erney – St Terninus
St Erth – St Ercus (a royal page at Tara, converted by St Patrick and later made a bishop)
St Ervan – St Hermes
St Euny – *see* St Uny
St Eval – St Uvelus
St Ewe – St Ewa
St Gennys – St Genesius (beheaded, but continued, like St Nectan and Ann Boleyn, to walk about with his head tucked underneath his arm)
St Germans – St Germanus (Bishop of Auxerre in central France – where there are ruins of an Abbaye de St Germain – who came to Cornwall as early as AD 430 and tarried long)
St Gerrans, or plain Gerrans – Geraint (a Cornish King about whose end there are conflicting accounts)
St Gluvias – St Gluviacus (known to the Welsh as Glywys or Gluvias the Cornishman)
St Gwinear – St Winierus (murdered by King Tewdrig: *see* St Ives below)
St Gwithian (also murdered by Tewdrig)
St Helen – St Teilo
St Issey – St Ida
St Ive – St Ivo
St Ives – St Ia or Hia (converted by St Patrick, reached The Island at St Ives traditionally on a leaf or at best in a coracle, and did much good work before being murdered, apparently, by King Tewdrig, or Tendar, of Riviere, near Hayle)
St Juliot – St Julitta
St Kea – St Kea or Kenan (converted by St Patrick, floated to Cornwall, they do say, on a granite boulder)

St Keverne – either St Askeveranus or Achebrann, a Welsh saint, or St Kieran, Irish

St Levan – either St Levan from Ireland or a corruption of (St) Silvanus (in either case, a seaside hermit who lived on fish, in connexion with which there are several legends: brother of St Euny and St Breaca)

St Mabyn – St Mabena the Virgin (probably a daughter of Brychan; tradition asserts that in 1500 a hymn was composed and sung in her honour)

St Mawes – either Irish St Mauditus or Breton St Maclovius

St Mawgan – St Meugan or Maughan (from Ireland via Wales: a bard and tutor of missionaries)

St Mellion – St Melenus (a Cornish prince; martyred)

St Merryn – St Merin (Welsh)

St Mewan – St Mewanus (pupil of St Samson and colleague of St Austol)

St Michael (the Archangel, protector of churches built on heights, as St Michael's Mount, against evil spirits in the air)

St Minver – St Menefreda or Minfre (another of the Children of Brychan)

St Morwenna (of Morwenstow: again a Child of Brychan, and sister of St Nectan)

St Nectan, brother of St Morwenna; see Hartland, in the gazetteer section, for the St Nectan's Day foxglove tradition

St Neot – St Anietus (traditionally an uncle or elder brother of King Alfred, with nearly as many fables about him as about the King)

St Newlyn – St Newlina or Noualen (martyred in Brittany)

St Petroc or Petrock. Instead of coming to Cornwall from Ireland via Wales, he came from Wales via Ireland, landing in the Camel estuary c. 560. See Bodmin and Padstow in the gazetteer section.

St Pinnock – St Pynnochus

St Piran, a follower of St Patrick

St Roche (he was disturbed by Tregeagle, for whom see Dozmary Pool in the gazetteer section)

St Ruan – St Rumon (a Breton, much honoured in his day in Brittany, who perhaps came to Cornwall to minister to Breton immigrants; buried at Ruan Lanihorne)

St Samson, a Welsh saint familiar in Wales, Cornwall, Scilly, Guernsey, and Brittany; precursor of St Petroc at Padstow

St Teath – St Tetha the Virgin (Irish)

St Tudy – St Tudius (Breton)

St Uny or Euny – St Euinus, or in Irish Eoghan and in Breton Uniac (of Irish royal lineage, held prisoner in Wales before coming to Cornwall with St Ia and St Ercus)

St Veep – St Wymp or Wennapa (Welsh)

St Wenn – St Wenna

St Winnow – St Winnow or Gwynno, the Welsh Gwynog ap Gildas (son of Gildas, the historian).

Appendix II

Cornish-language Elements in Place-names

Cornish	English	Cornish	English
Bal	Mine	Men (maen)	Stone
Bod, boj, bos	House	Nans	Valley
Carn	Cairn (usually over a grave)	Pen	Headland
		Pol	Pool
Chy	House	Porth	Bay, cove
Dinas	Hill-fort	Praze	Meadow
Du	Black	Ruan	River
Eglos	Church	Tol	Hole
Enys	Island		
Goon	Moor	Towan	Sandhill, dune
Hal	Moor	Tre	House, town
Kelly	Grove	Treryn	House on a headland
Lan	Monastery	Wheal	Mine
Loe	Lake	Zawn	Cave

Photograph and Map Credits

Abbreviations used:
BTA   *British Tourist Authority*
NMR   *National Monuments Record*

Colour Plates:

Facing p. 82   Dartmoor landscape: *A. F. Kersting*
Facing p. 83   Gardens at Cotehele: *A. F. Kersting*
Facing p. 106   Lanhydrock: *BTA*
Facing p. 107   Berry Pomeroy Castle: *A. F. Kersting*
                Jacket photograph: *A. F. Kersting*

Black-and-White Plates

Page

viii   Regional Map: *Allard Design Group Ltd*
52   Font, Altarnun: *NMR*
52   Antony House: *A. F. Kersting*
55   Atherington: rood-screen: *Maurice H. Ridgeway*
56   Barnstaple church: *A. F. Kersting*
57   Acland Barton: *NMR*
62   Landscape near Boscastle: *A. F. Kersting*
63   Pulpit, Bovey Tracey: *NMR*
65   Chancel screen, Brushford: *Maurice H. Ridgeway*
67   Hembury Castle: *A. F. Kersting*
68–9   Bench-ends, East Budleigh: *NMR*
70   Camborne tin mine: *NMR*
71   Gwennap Pit: *Janet & Colin Bord*
72   Crosses at Lanteglos: *NMR*
74   Bronze Age cup: *British Museum*
75   Clovelly: *Roy Nash*
76   Colyton church: *A. F. Kersting*
77   Monument to Sir John and Lady Elizabeth Pole: *A. F. Kersting*
78   Cotehele: King's Bedroom: *A. F. Kersting*
80   Cotehele: main entrance: *A. F. Kersting*
81   Crediton church: *A. F. Kersting*
82   Clapper bridge, Dartmeet: *Iris Hardwick*
83   Pulpit, Dartmouth: *Maurice H. Ridgeway*
84   Dartmouth Castle: *A. F. Kersting*
86   Castle Drogo: *Aerofilms Ltd*
87   Font, Luppit: *B. T. Batsford Ltd*
90   St Martin's church and Mol's Coffee House, Exeter: *A. F. Kersting*
94   Exeter Cathedral: the nave: *Maurice H. Ridgeway*
96   Exeter Cathedral: W front: *A. F. Kersting*
97   Exeter Cathedral: detail from W front: *Courtauld Institute*; misericords: *B. T. Batsford Ltd* (birds) and *NMR* (St George and the Dragon)
99   Place, Fowey: *NMR*
100   Landscape near Fowey: *A. F. Kersting*
104   Chysauster: *Janet & Colin Bord*
105   Hartland Quay: *Iris Hardwick*
109   Marwood House, Honiton: *A. F. Kersting*
111   Ilfracombe Harbour: *A. F. Kersting*
112   The Shambles, Kingsbridge: *A. F. Kersting*
115   Lanhydrock: *A. F. Kersting*
116   Launceston church: *B. T. Batsford Ltd*
117   Launceston from the N: *B. T. Batsford Ltd*
118   Lewtrenchard church: *NMR*
119   View of Liskeard by Rowlandson: *NMR*
121   Lostwithiel church: *A. F. Kersting*
123   Landscape near Lostwithiel: *A. F. Kersting*
126   Coastal scenery near Lynton: *A. F. Kersting*
127   Hound Tor: *A. F. Kersting*
129   Moretonhampstead almshouses: *A. F. Kersting*
130   Lanyon Quoit: *Janet & Colin Bord*
131   Chun Castle and Men-an-Tol: *both Janet & Colin Bord*
133   S porch, Morwenstow church: *A. F. Kersting*
134   Mullion church: *NMR*
136   Trerice ceiling: *A. F. Kersting*
137   Bradley Manor: *A. F. Kersting*
138   Okehampton Castle: *Janet & Colin Bord*
139   Dorset Aisle, Ottery St Mary: *A. F. Kersting*
140   Ottery St Mary church: *A. F. Kersting*
140   Cadhay: *Iris Hardwick*
146   Plymouth city centre: *A. F. Kersting*
148   Plymouth: part of the Hoe: *A. F. Kersting*
150   Saltram: W front: *A. F. Kersting*
151   Saltram: Velvet Drawing Room: *A. F. Kersting*
152   Logan Rock: *A. F. Kersting*
153   The Minack Theatre, Porthcurno: *BTA*
155   Wall-painting, Breage: *A. F. Kersting*
158   The Wheal Coates engine-house: *BTA*
159   St Austell church: *A. F. Kersting*
160   China-clay workings, Carclaze Downs: *Janet & Colin Bord*
161   Rood-screen, St Buryan: *A. F. Kersting*
162   The Blind Fiddler: *Janet & Colin Bord*
162–3 King Doniert's Stone: *Janet & Colin Bord*
164   Norman doorway, St Germans: *NMR*
167   Methodist chapel: *NMR*
169   St Michael's Mount: the house: *A. F. Kersting*
170–1 Plaster frieze, St Michael's Mount (a National Trust property): *Country Life*
172   The Harys Window, St Neot: *NMR*
173   The Saltash bridges: *A. F. Kersting*
174   Trematon Castle: gatehouse: *Country Life*
174   Trematon Castle: sally port: *Country Life*
176   Tresco: *A. F. Kersting*
176   Looking over Hugh Town, St Mary's: *A. F. Kersting*
177   St Martin's: *A. F. Kersting*
179   Salcombe Regis church: *A. F. Kersting*

PHOTOGRAPH AND MAP CREDITS

Index

INDEX

Map Section

GEOLOGY OF DEVON AND CORNWALL

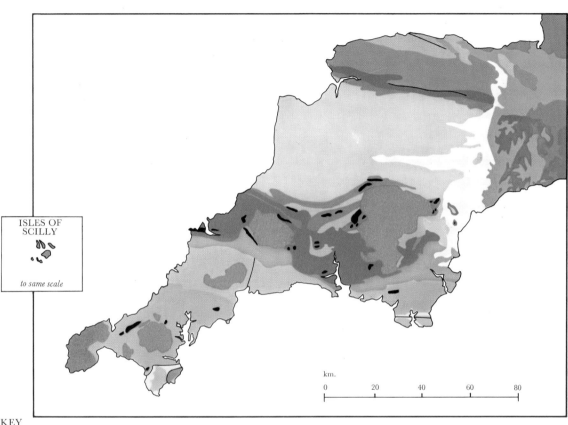

ISLES OF
SCILLY

to same scale

km.

0   20   40   60   80

KEY

Tertiary

   Sand, clay, and gravel

Cretaceous

   MIDDLE AND UPPER CHALK

   UPPER GREENSAND AND GAULT CLAY

Jurassic

   LIAS: *Marls, clays, limestones, and shales*

Triassic

   BUNTER SANDSTONE, KEUPER MARL, AND KEUPER SANDSTONE

Permian

   Marls, conglomerates, sandstones, and breccias

Carboniferous

   UPPER CARBONIFEROUS: *Shales, slates, and sandstones*

   LOWER CARBONIFEROUS: *Slates and volcanic extrusive rocks*

———— FAULTS

Devonian

   UPPER DEVONIAN: *Slates and sandstones*

   MIDDLE DEVONIAN: *Slates and limestones*

   LOWER DEVONIAN: *Sandstones and siltstones*

   Undifferentiated Devonian

Intrusive Igneous Rocks

   Granite

   Dolerite and Basalt

   Gabbro

   Serpentine

Metamorphic Rocks

   Gneiss and mica schist

   Schist

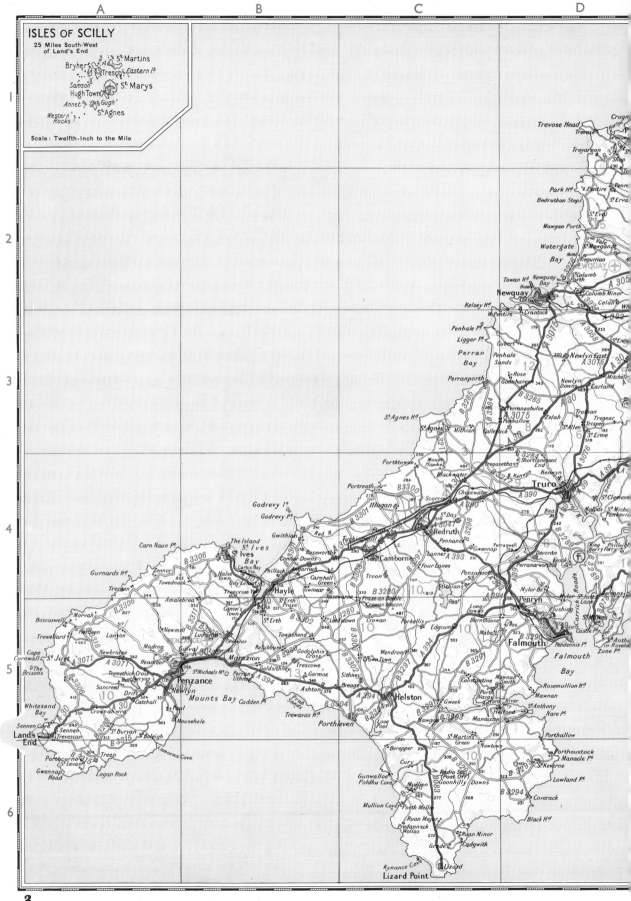

ISLES OF SCILLY
25 Miles South-West
of Land's End

St Martins
Bryher
Tresco   Eastern Is
Samson   St Marys
Hugh Town
Annet   Gugh
Western   St Agnes
Rocks

Scale : Twelfth-Inch to the Mile

Trevose Head
Trevose

Park Hd   Pentire
Bedruthan Steps   St Eval

Mawgan Porth
Watergate   St Mawgan
Bay   Trenarrian

Towan Hd   Newquay
Newquay   Porth   St Columb Minor
Kelsey Hd   Crantock

W. Pentire
Penhale Pt
Ligger Pt   Cubert
Penhale
Perran   Sands
Bay

Perranporth   Rose   Newlyn East   Newlyn
Goonhavern   Downs
Carland
Perranzabuloe
St Agnes Hd   Zelah   Truthan   Tregear
Penhallow   Trispen
St Agnes   Callestick   St Allen   St Erme
Mithian
Mount   Tregavethan   Kenwyn
Hawke   Shortlanesend
Porthtowan   Blackwater   Truro   St Clement
Scorrier   Chacewater   Moresk   St Michael
Portreath   St Day   Kea   Penkevil
Illogan   Pool   Redruth   King
Godrevy Is   Pennance   Gwennap   Harry Ferry
Godrevy Pt   Red R   Tuckingmill   Perranwell   Feock
Gwithian   Roseworthy   Camborne   Lanner   Sta   Devoran
Carn Naun Pt   Four Lanes   Perranarworthal
The Island   St Ives   Connor Downs   Troon   Ponsanooth   Mylor Br
Gurnards Hd   Bay   Carbis Bay   Phillack   Carnhell   Rest   Penryn   Flushing
Zennor   Halse-   Angarrach   Green   Long   St Just
Trereen   Towednack   town   Gwinear   Rosewarne   Downs   Mylor   in-Roseland
Amalebrea   Trencrom Hill   Hayle   Praze-an-Beeble   Burnthouse   Falmouth
Boscaswell   Morvah   Canon's   St Erth   Crowan Beacon   Mabe   Penjerrick   Castle Pt
Trewellard   Bosullow   Town   Praze   Leedstown   Mawnan   St Anthony-
Newmill   St Erth   Crowan   Wendron   Constantine   in-Meneage
Cape   Lanyon   Ludgvan   Towshend   Penpol   Zone Pt
Cornwall   St Just   Madron   Godolphin   Edgcumbe   Falmouth
The   Newbridge   Gulval   Relubbus   Cross   Mabe   Bay
Brisons   Tremethick Cross   Heamoor   Longrock   Nancegollan   Crowntown   Mawnan
Sancreed   Penzance   Marazion   Sithney   Constantine   Rosemullion Hd
Drift   St Michaels Mt   Perran   Goldsithney   Porth   Mawnan
Newlyn   Uthnoe   Germoe   Navas   Smith
Catchall   Trescowe   Ashton   Breage   Gweek   Helford River   St Anthony
Paul   Mounts Bay   Sithney   Halford   Nare Pt
Whitesand   Mousehole   Cudden Pt   Helston   Manaccan
Bay   Trewavas Hd   Gunwalloe   Mawgan   Porthallow
Sennen Cove   Porthleven   Loe   Pool   St Martin's   Newtown   Porthoustock
Land's   Sennen   Trevescan   Green   Manacle Pt
End   Berepper   St Keverne   Lowland Pt
Treen   Cury   Radio Stn   Goonhilly
Porthcurno   St Levan   (Post Off)   Downs   Coverack
Gwennap   Logan Rock   Gunwalloe   Mullion   Goonhilly   Black Hd
Head   Foldhu Cove
Camorna Cove   Mullion Cove   Porth Mellin   Ruan Major   Cadgwith
Predannack   Ruan Minor
Wollas   Grade
Kynance Cove   Lizard
Lizard Point

2

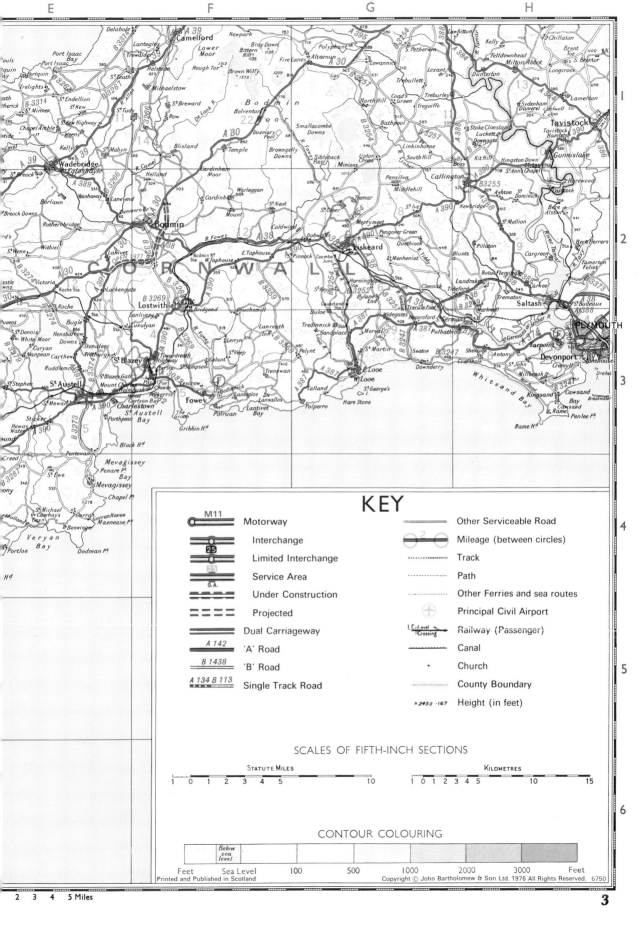

KEY

M11 ⊶⊶⊶	Motorway
⊖	Interchange
25	Limited Interchange
25 S.A.	Service Area
▬▬▬▬	Under Construction
▬ ▬ ▬ ▬	Projected
▬▬▬▬	Dual Carriageway
A 142	'A' Road
B 1438	'B' Road
A 134 B 113 ▪▪▪▪	Single Track Road
══════	Other Serviceable Road
⊖²⊙	Mileage (between circles)
▪▪▪▪▪▪	Track
··············	Path
··········	Other Ferries and sea routes
✈	Principal Civil Airport
Level Crossing ➤	Railway (Passenger)
————	Canal
+	Church
—·—·—·—	County Boundary
▲ 2450 ·167	Height (in feet)

SCALES OF FIFTH-INCH SECTIONS

STATUTE MILES
1 0 1 2 3 4 5 — 10

KILOMETRES
1 0 1 2 3 4 5 — 10 — 15

CONTOUR COLOURING

	Below sea level						
Feet	Sea Level	100	500	1000	2000	3000	Feet

Printed and Published in Scotland

Copyright © John Bartholomew & Son Ltd. 1976 All Rights Reserved. 6750

2   3   4   5 Miles

3

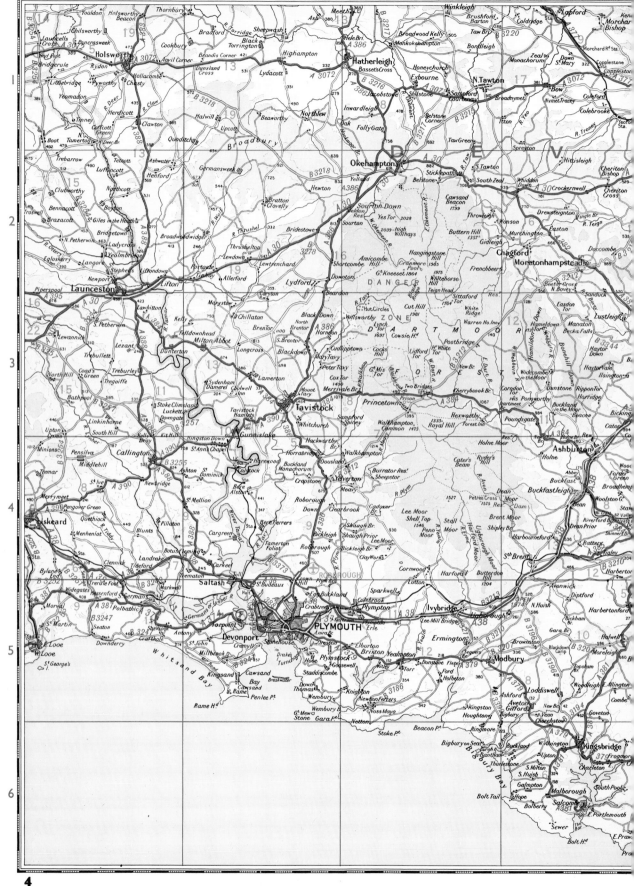

4

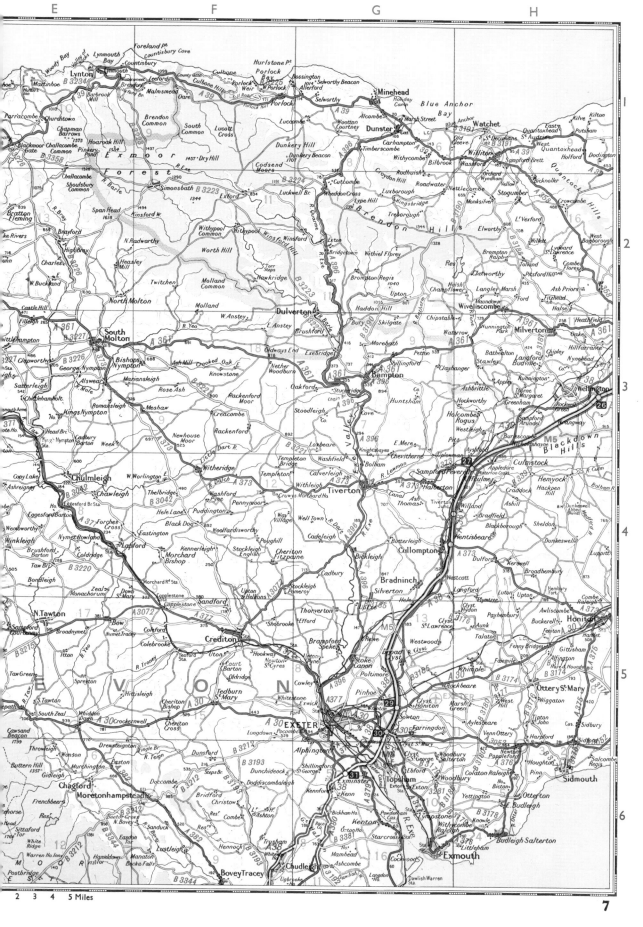

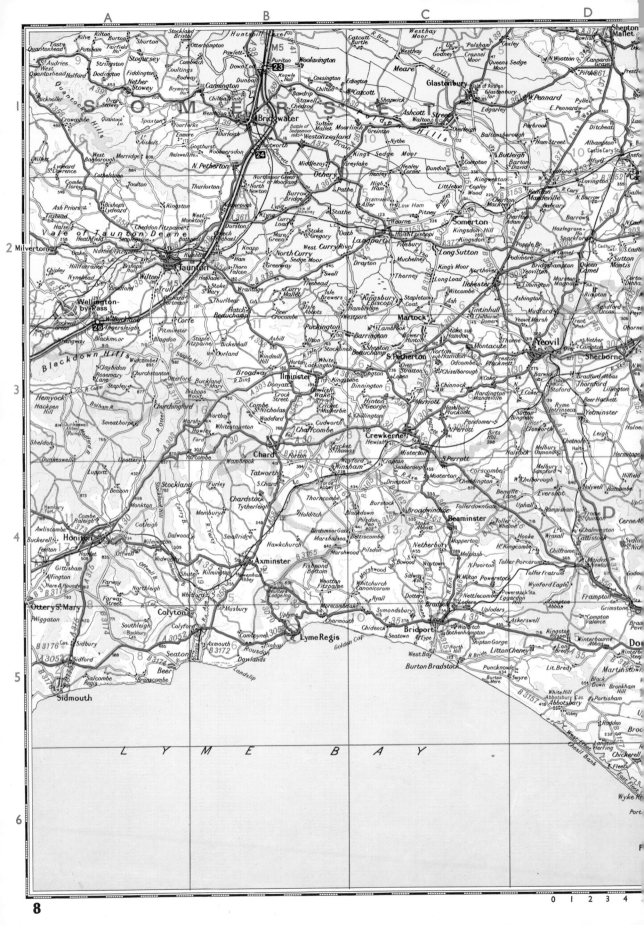